ELBERT S. MALONEY

Problems & Answers in Navigation & Piloting

NAVAL INSTITUTE PRESS
Annapolis, Maryland

Library of Congress Catalog Card Number: 78-58388
ISBN: 0-87021-529-9

Printed in the United States of America

Contents

Introduction

This book provides a wide range of problems, with answers, in the practice of dead reckoning, piloting, and celestial navigation. It was prepared for use with the 13th Edition of Dutton's Navigation and Piloting; however, it may be used with other standard navigation texts, or by itself. This book is suitable for both classroom use and self-study. It will also be of value to experienced navigators for review and refresher study.

Answers to all the problems are given at the end of the book. The answers are stated to a level of precision commensurate with the accuracy of the data and method of computation; a reasonable degree of tolerance should be applied to those solutions which have been worked out graphically.

This book contains all the necessary extracts from the N.O.S. Tide Tables and Tidal Current Tables, from the Nautical Almanac and Air Almanac, and from DMAHC Publications No. 229 and 249; but it is assumed that a copy of DMAHC Pub. No. 9 (Bowditch), Volume II (1975), is available for the tables included therein. (Older editions of Bowditch may be used but will not fully meet the requirements for tables.)

For the solutions to some problems, the user will need sheets from a Maneuvering Board pad, DMAHC No. 5090 or 5091; for working other problems, plotting sheets will be necessary. These may be from the DMAHC series, if available; or, small-area plotting sheets may be prepared following the instructions in Dutton's, Bowditch, or other texts. Worksheets are provided in this book and may be used to find the solutions to many navigational problems. The use of these sheets is optional; indeed, the student is cautioned against developing a dependence upon them which at some later time might handicap him if the sheets were not available. The worksheets included in this book are those used by the U.S. Navy and the U.S. Naval Academy, or are adaptations thereof; worksheets from other sources may, of course, be used.

Because of the increasing world usage of the metric system, a number of problems are included with heights, distances, etc., expressed in metric (SI) units.

Appreciation is extended to Mrs. Sharon Lannon for her usual fine work in typing the several drafts of this book. While the author of course retains the responsibility for the correctness of the problems and answers, acknowledgment and appreciation are extended to Commander John F. Hopper, U.S. Navy, for checking the solutions and offering valuable comments on the presentation of the problems and the book in general.

Problems

1. Convert 18.3 statute miles to nautical miles; convert 143.0 nautical miles to statute miles.

2. State the following times in the 24-hour clock system: 11:10 a.m.; 3:56 a.m.; 2:14 p.m.; 12:34 p.m.; 12:18 a.m.

3. Convert the following measurements in customary units to metric units: 2.7 n mi; 30 fathoms; 3 fathoms, 2 feet; 42.0 feet.

4. Convert the following measurements in metric units to conventional units: 22.9 km; 19 m (to feet); 6.7 m (to fathoms and feet).

5. What is the difference in latitude between: 46°19'N and 32°07'N? Between 20°19'N and 15°17'S?

6. What is the difference in longitude between: 146°18'E and 103°34'E? Between 152°27'W and 169°41'E? (State answer in degrees, minutes, and in total minutes.)

7. What is the mid- (mean) latitude between: 60°28'S and 49°26'S? Between 9°13'S and 6°27'N?

8. At latitude 41°N a difference in longitude is 7°53'. What is the departure?

9. What is the direction in the 360° system of a line 3° east of north? 92° east of north? 123° east of north? 42° west of north? 163° west of north?

10. State the reciprocal of 067°; 180°; 213°; 345°.

11. The difference in latitude between two points both at 39°W longitude is 3°13'; what is the distance in miles?

12. The scale of a chart is 1:80,000. What distance at sea does a distance of 3½ inches on the chart represent? What distance on the chart represents an actual distance of 14.3 miles?

13. In the sketch of a portion of a Mercator projection chart, shown on the next page, match each item in the list below with the appropriate letter designation in parentheses:

    (a) Bearing of B from A

    (b) Distance to B from A

    (c) Track from B to A

    (d) Difference of longitude between A and B

    (e) Mid-latitude between A and B

    (f) Distance between A and D

    (g) A rhumb line other than a parallel or a meridian

    (h) A segment of a great circle

    (i) A segment of a small circle

    (j) Difference in longitude from B to A

    (k) Direction of D from B

    (l) Track from A to D

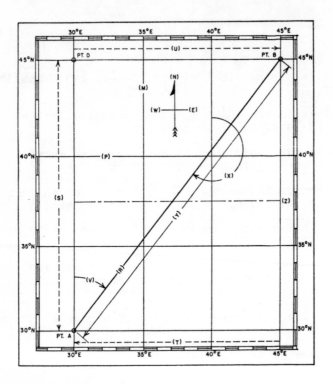

14. With respect to various chart projections, state whether the
    following statements are true or false.

    (a) On a Mercator chart rhumb lines are straight.

    (b) On an oblique gnomonic chart great circles are straight lines.

    (c) On a Mercator chart the scale is the same at all latitudes.

    (d) On a Mercator chart a great circle is a straight line.

    (e) On a Lambert conformal chart meridians are straight lines.

    (f) On a Mercator chart parallels of latitude are parallel
        straight lines.

    (g) On a Mercator chart meridians are straight lines which converge
        in the direction of the nearest pole.

15. Convert the following directions from compass points to degrees:
    NE, ESE, SSW, N by W.

16. Convert the following directions from degrees to compass points:
    135°, 157°30', 337.5°.

17. The true heading is 010° but the magnetic heading from the compass
    rose on the chart reads 012°; what is the variation?

18. The magnetic bearing of an object is known to be 138° but by compass
    it reads 135°; what is the deviation? If the compass bearing is
    146°, what is the deviation?

19. The variation is 14°W and the deviation is 2°W; what is the compass
    error? On another heading in the same vicinity, the deviation is
    5°E; what is then the compass error?

20. Fill in the blanks in the table below:

T	V	M	D	C	CE
114	6W		3W		
	7W		2E	045	
	6E	219	3E		
303		305		303	
002	4E		6W		
			5E	268	10E
234	3W				7E

21. The direction of a range is measured from a chart as 192.5°; the gyrocompass reads 194°. What is the gyro error?

22. The bearing of a distant object is known to be 008°T; the gyrocompass reads 005.5°. What is the gyro error?

23. If the gyro error is known to be 2.0°W, what will be the gyrocompass reading on a course of 315°T?

24. A ship is being steered on a heading of 069° by a gyrocompass with an error of 0.5°E. What is the true heading?

25. What is the distance to the horizon for a height of eye of 33 feet? For a height of eye of 16.2m?

26. Using the <u>Light List</u> extract on page 20, what is the visibility range of Matinicus Rock Light for an observer with a height of eye of 42 feet?

27. What is the visibility range of Monhegan Island Light for an observer with a height of eye of 9.5m?

28. Using the relationship of 2,000 yards to one nautical mile, what error is introduced for a distance of 3.4 miles?

29. Convert 75°F to °C; 14°C to °F; -10°F to °C; -6°C to °F; -22°C to °F (to nearest degree).

30. What is the interval between the following times: 0326 and 0731? 1054 and 1118? 2216 and 0509 the following day?

31. How far will a vessel traveling at 16.5 knots travel in 34 minutes? in 2h 24m?

32. How long will it take a ship traveling at 14 knots to go 0.8 miles? to go 69 miles?

33. What speed is a boat making that covers 1 mile in 7.8 minutes? 23.5 miles in 2h 14m?

For Problems 34-44, use the <u>Tide Tables</u> extracts starting on page 21.

34. Using Table 5, convert 4°25' to time units; 26°18' to time units.

35. What is the local time and height of the morning low water at Humboldt Bay, California, on 1 May 1977? On 18 June 1977? (In problems 35 through 54 Daylight Time is in effect.)

3

36. What is the local time and height of the afternoon high water at Humboldt Bay, California, on 4 June 1977? On 19 May 1977?

37. What is the local time and height of the morning high water at Trinidad Harbor, California, on 2 May 1977? What is the local time and height of the afternoon low water?

38. What is the local time and height of the morning low water at Kernville, Oregon, on 2 June 1977? What is the local time and height of the afternoon high water?

39. What is the height of tide at Humboldt Bay, California, at 1200 PDT on 3 June 1977?

40. What is the height of the tide in meters at Port Orford, Oregon, at 2300 PDT on 17 June 1977?

41. On the morning of 16 June 1977 at Humboldt Bay, California, when will the rising tide reach a depth of 3.5 feet?

42. A bridge over the Umpqua River near Gardiner, Oregon, has a charted vertical clearance of 65 feet. What is the predicted actual clearance in meters at 1100 PDT on 3 June 1977?

43. Using Table 4 of the Tide Tables, (a) what is the local mean time of sunrise at L38°N λ48°W on 7 March 1977? (b) what is the standard time of sunset at L40°N, λ 33°W on 9 April 1977?

44. Using information from the Tide Tables, (a) what is the phase of the moon on 8 June 1977? (b) what is the date and GMT of the full moon in November 1977? (c) what is the date and GMT of summer solstice in 1977?

45. At sea in the North Atlantic Ocean, the wind has been blowing for three days from the northeast at an average of 35 knots. What would be the approximate set and drift of the wind-driven current?

For problems 46-54, use the Tidal Current Tables extracts starting on page 27.

46. What is the local time of slack water before ebb begins at St. Johns River Entrance on the morning of 17 June 1977?

47. What is the local time and strength of the first maximum flooding current at St. Johns River Entrance on 1 June 1977?

48. What is the local time of slack water nearest noon on 2 June 1977 at St. Johns Bluff, Florida? What is the time, strength, and direction of the next following maximum current?

49. What is the strength and direction of the current at St. Johns River Entrance at 1200 EDT on 3 June 1977?

50. At what time after 1200 EDT on 1 June 1977 will the weakening ebb current at St. Johns River Entrance fall to 1.5 kn?

51. What is the strength and direction of the current at Red Bay Point in the St. Johns River at 2130 EDT on 16 May 1977? What is the time of the next slack water?

52. At what time after 1200 EDT on 1 May 1977 will a weakening ebbing current in the St. Johns River channel south of Drummond Point fall to 0.6 kn?

53. For the afternoon slack water at St. Johns River Entrance on 2 May 1977, how long will the current be 0.3 kn or less?

54. For the early afternoon slack water off Drummond Point, St. Johns River, on 16 June, how long will the current be 0.4 kn or less?

Prepare a small-area plotting sheet to be used for problems 55-58. The mid-latitude is 33°N; the central meridian is 79°W. (In this and subsequent problems, geographic coordinates are arbitrarily selected to enable the plotting of points; they do not represent any actual geographic location.) Plot the following points:

> Light A: L33°17'N, λ78°53'W
>
> Light B: L33°11'N, λ79°14'W
>
> Light C: L33°02'N, λ78°56'W

55. The DR position of your ship at 1500 is L33°30'N, λ78°35'W; the course is 196°, speed 16 knots. At 1610 the bearing of Light A is 289°; the bearing of Light C is 218°. What is the 1610 DR? What is the 1610 fix?

56. At 1625 the course is changed to 257° and the speed is slowed to 12 knots. At 1720, a round of bearings is taken as follows: A 039°, B 276°, C 157°. What is the 1720 fix?

57. At 1815 Light B is abeam to starboard, 3.4 miles distant by radar. What is the 1815 fix?

58. At 1830 another vessel at DR position L33°20'N, λ79°10'W obtains a fix by two radar-range measurements—11.0 miles to Light A and 12.6 miles to Light B. What is her 1830 position?

59. A ship is on a heading of 114°. A series of relative bearings are taken as follows: 030°, 178°, 285°. What are the respective true bearings?

60. Convert the following true bearings to relative bearings for a ship's heading of 302°: 009°, 158°, 328°.

61. The navigator of a ship on course 350°, speed 18 knots, identifies three prominent objects ashore on his port side as follows:

> D: L36°12.0'N, λ9°45.0'E
>
> E: L36°03.0'N, λ9°50.0'E
>
> F: L35°51.0'N, λ9°40.0'E

At 1430, he measures horizontal angles with a sextant as follows: DE 30°, EF 50°. Prepare a small-area plotting sheet and determine the 1430 position.

62. A ship is on course 062°, speed 15 knots; its 0900 DR position is L18°08.0'S, λ122°16.0'W. At 0920 a bearing of 300° is taken on Light G at L17°57.0'S, λ122°20.0'W; no other landmark is available at this time. At 1120 a bearing of 351° is taken on a tower at L17°39.0'S, λ121°44.0'W. Advance the 0920 LOP and determine the 1120 running fix.

63. A ship is on course 062°, speed 15 knots; its 1400 DR position is L18°08'S, λ122°16'W. At 1420 the distance to Light G is 9.5 miles; no accurate bearing can be taken. At 1620, the bearing of the tower at H is 351°. Advance the 1420 circle of position and determine the 1620 running fix.

64. A ship is on course 062°, speed 16 knots; its 0900 DR position is L18°08.0'S, λ10°44.0'E. At 0915 a bearing of 032° is taken on Light J at L17°46.0'S, λ11°00.0'E. At 1130 another bearing is taken on Light J, 291°. What is the 1130 running fix?

65. A ship is on course 062°, speed 18 knots; the 1600 DR position is L40°52.0'N, λ55°20.0'W. At 1610 Light K (L41°02.0'N, λ55°25.0'W) bears 333°. At 1700, course is changed to 084°, speed remains 18 knots. At 1745, lightship L (L40°55.0'N, λ54°52.0'W) bears 230°. What is the 1745 running fix?

66. A ship is on course 040°, speed 20 knots; its 1300 DR position is L34°40.0'N, λ19°30.0'E. At that time a bearing of 105° was taken on Light M (L34°35.0'N, λ19°40.0'E). At 1415 course was changed to 080°. At 1454 a course of 040° was resumed, but speed was reduced to 16 knots. At 1542, Light N (L35°20.0'N, λ20°10.0'E) bears 000°. What is the 1542 DR position and 1542 running fix?

67. A ship is on course 306°, speed 14 knots. Light P is observed at 1053 to bear 344°; at 1109 this light bears 008°. Using Bowditch Table 7, what is the distance to the light at 1109? What will be the distance when the light is abeam?

68. A ship is on course 083°, speed 17 knots. Light Q is observed to bear 313° when the log reads 128.3 miles from point of departure. When the log reads 132.2, the same light bears 291°. Using Bowditch Table 7, what is its distance at this time?

69. A ship is on course 185°, speed 16 knots. At 1708, Light Q has a relative bearing of 22.5°; by 1723 this relative bearing has increased to 45°. What is the distance to the light at the time of the second bearing? How close will the ship pass to this light?

70. A ship is on course 240°, speed 10 knots. At 0819, Light R bears 270°; at 0836, this light bears 300°. What is the distance to the light at the time of the second bearing? How close will the ship pass to the light?

71. A ship is on course 007°, speed 18 knots. At 1155, Tower S bears 338°; at 1208, the tower bears 316°. How far distant will the tower be when the ship is abeam?

72. A ship is at position L40°20.0'S, λ120°20.0'W. There is shoal water for a radius of 4 miles around Light T at L40°00.0'S, λ120°10.0'W. What is the danger bearing on Light U at L39°50'S, λ119°55.3'W?

73. A ship is on course 237°, speed 14 knots; its 0300 DR position is L28°40'S, λ5°20'E. At 0552 a single line of position is obtained. Light V (L29°10.0'S, λ5°00.0'E) bears 108°. What is the 0552 DR position and estimated position?

74. A ship is on course 104°, speed 18 knots; its 1500 DR position is L32°04.4'N, λ127°20.0'W. At 1545 landmark W (L32°07.0'N, λ126° 40.0'W) bears 078°; no other bearing can be taken. What is the 1545 DR position and estimated position?

75. In a given plotting situation, a horizontal danger angle of 43° has been established to keep a vessel offshore from a reef. Would a measured angle of 46° indicate that the vessel was on a safe course?

76. In a given piloting situation, a vertical danger angle of 2°35' has been established. Would a reading of 3°10' indicate that the vessel was nearer or farther from the object on which the angle is read?

77. A ship is on course 040°, speed 14.0 knots; the current has an estimated set of 190°, drift 2.0 knots. What is the anticipated track and speed of advance along this track?

78. In an estimated current of 2.8 knots setting 065°, it is desired to have a track of 120° and speed of advance of 13.5 knots. What is the necessary course and speed?

79. A navigator desires a track of 175° with a speed of advance of 12.0 knots; the current is estimated to set 200 degrees, drift 3.0 knots. What course and speed should be ordered?

80. In a current of set 160°, drift 2.5 knots, a ship is steaming on course 285° at a speed of 10.0 knots. What is the anticipated track and speed of advance?

81. The current is estimated to set 325°, drift 1.5 knots. A ship desires to make good a track of 280° while making a speed of 15.0 knots. What course should be steered and what speed of advance will result?

82. A navigator has a desired track of 040° through a current with a set of 330°, drift 2.0 knots. The speed is 15 knots. What course should be steered? What will be the speed of advance?

83. The 1200 DR position of a ship is L38°14'N, λ20°30'W. The 1200 fix was L38°10.1'N, λ20°16.4'W. The DR track has been run forward since a 0542 fix. What is the set and drift of the current?

84. A ship is on course 056°, speed 15.0 knots. The 1000 fix is at L34°40.0'N, λ20°30.0'W. The 1145 DR position is L34°54.7'N, λ20° 03.5'W, but a running fix at this time is at L34°57.0'N, λ20°08.0'W. A new DR track is started from this R Fix. The 1315 DR position is L35°09.6'N, λ19°45.2'W, but a 1315 fix places the ship at L35°12.0'N, λ19°39.0'W. What is the set and drift of the current?

85. A ship is on course 311°, speed 20 knots; the 1000 fix is at L22° 12.0'S, λ140°45.0'W. The current is estimated as setting 180°, drift 3.0 knots. At 1015 the bearing of Light X (L21°55.0'S, λ140° 42.0'W) was 026°. At 1115, the bearing of Light X was 101°. What is the 1115 R Fix with consideration given to the estimated current?

86. A ship is on course 112°, speed 18.0 knots. The 0800 DR position is L25°54.4'S, λ46°41.0'E; a current is estimated to set 230°, drift 2.0 knots. What is the 1000 DR and estimated position?

87. A ship is on course 284°, speed 15.0 knots. The 1200 fix is L22°03.4'N, λ171°46.7'W; a current is estimated to set 160°, drift 1.6 knots. At 1400, a bearing of 181° is taken on Light AA at L21°57.0'N, λ172°19.5'W. What is the 1400 EP with current?

88. A ship is proceeding up a channel on course 050°, speed 10 knots. At 1610, Light Z bears 356° at 550 yards distance. The next turn will be to course 350° directly toward Light ZZ which is 1500 yards 030° from Light Z. For a 60° turn, the advance is 950 yards, transfer is 350 yards. What is the turning bearing on Light Z?

89. A ship is making 20 knots approaching a harbor channel with a 10-knot speed limit. The ship requires 4.5 minutes to decelerate from 20 to 10 knots. How far from the entrance to the channel should action be taken to reduce speed?

90. It is desired to be making 20 knots when point Y is passed. The ship is now making 8 knots. The time to accelerate from 8 to 10 knots is 1.5 minutes, from 10 to 15 knots 2.0 minutes, and from 15 to 20 knots 2.5 minutes. How far from Point Y must the acceleration begin?

91. A ship is on course 010°, speed 10 knots. At 0835 Light A bears 060°, 1,630 yards distant. The assigned anchorage is 1,000 yards 350° from Light A, 800 yards 250° from Light B. A direct approach can be made toward Light B. Transfer and advance are 350 and 950 yards respectively. The distance from the hawsepipe to the bridge is 100 yards. (a) What is the turning bearing? (b) What is the approach track? (c) What is the letting-go bearing?

92. Your ship is on course 090°, speed 12.0 knots. At 0820, radar contact is made with another vessel on bearing 135°, range 16.0 miles. Successive times, bearings, and ranges are: 0830, 131.5°, 13.5 miles; 0840, 127°, 11.0; 0850, 119°, 8.6; 0900, 106°, 6.5; 0910, 083°, 5.0; 0920, 051°, 4.7; 0930, 024°, 5.8. Using a geographic plot, determine the course and speed of the other ship. What is the time and distance of the closest point of approach?

93. Your ship is on course 270°, speed 12.0 knots. At 1600, radar contact is made with another vessel on bearing 205°, range 9.4 miles. Successive times, bearings, and distances are: 1610, 202.5°, 7.5 miles; 1620, 198.5°, 5.6 miles; 1630, 191°, 3.8; 1640, 170°, 2.1; 1650, 108°, 1.5; 1700, 066°, 2.8. Using a geographic plot, what is the course and speed of the other vessel? What is the time and distance of the closest point of approach? What is the bearing of the other vessel at CPA?

94. Using the data of the previous problem, draw a relative motion plot and determine the direction and speed of relative motion.

95. Using the data of the previous problem, determine the other ship's course and speed from a speed triangle.

96. Your ship is on course 090°, speed 12.0 knots. A radar contact is made on another ship at 0320, bearing 104°, range 16.0 miles. Subsequent observations are 0330, 103°, 13.6 miles; 0340, 101.5°, 11.2; 0350, 099°, 8.8. It is determined that the distance at CPA is too close for safety; course will be altered to starboard to ensure a separation of 3 miles. What course should be taken by your ship, and at what time?

97. Your ship is on course 270°, speed 16 knots. At 2210 another ship is detected by radar, bearing 330°, range 16.4 miles. At 2220 the bearing is unchanged but range has decreased to 14.2 miles. At 2230 the bearing is still 330° and range is 12.0 miles. To avoid collision, your ship decides to stop rather than change course to starboard. (Assume that the stop is instantaneous, without further advance.) (a) What will be the bearing and distance of the other ship at 2240? (b) At 2250, your ship gets underway on its original course but at reduced speed; at 8 knots, what will be the distance to the other ship and her bearing when she crosses your bow?

98. Your ship is on course 160°, speed 15 knots. At 0810 another ship is detected on radar bearing 103°, range 18.0 miles. Subsequent radar bearings and ranges are: 0820, 103°, 14.4 miles; 0830, 095.5°, 11.2; 0840, 089.5°, 8.2; 0850, 077.5°, 5.3; 0900, 043.5°, 3.1; 0910, 345°, 3.4. (a) What is the other ship's course and speed? (b) What was the first maneuver of the other ship? (c) What was her second maneuver? (d) What was the distance and time of CPA and the bearing at that time?

99. Your ship is on course 080°, speed 9 knots. At 2220 another ship is detected by radar bearing 290°, range 10.0 miles. At 2230 the bearing is unchanged and the range is now 8.4 miles. Subsequent radar bearings and distances are: 2240, 290°, 6.8 miles; 2250, 284°, 5.1; 2300, 272°, 3.6; 2310, 245°, 2.4; 2320, 201°, 2.3. (a) What is the course and speed of the other ship when first detected? (b) What is her second course and speed? (c) What is the CPA distance and time?

100. At 1425, your ship is on course 090°, speed 14 knots. A distress call is heard from a ship 75 miles, 140° from your present position; she is on course 290°, speed 5 knots and will maintain course and speed. Your best speed is 18 knots. (a) What course do you take to reach the other ship? (b) How long will it take? (c) At what time should you be within visual range (estimated at 5 miles) of the other ship?

101. Your destroyer is in formation on course 320°, speed 18 knots; your relative position is 270°, 8 miles from the guide. You are ordered to take position 6 miles ahead of the guide. You decide to accomplish the maneuver at 24 knots. (a) What is the course? (b) How long will it take to reach the new station?

102. Your ship is on course 240°, speed 16 knots. The apparent wind is 6 knots from 300°. What is the true wind direction and force?

103. (a) An observer is in λ46°18'W. The Greenwich Hour Angle of the sun is 142°15'. What is the Local Hour Angle? the meridian angle (t)? (b) The same observer then uses the moon with a GHA of 31°03'. What are the LHA and t for this body?

104. (a) An observer is in λ123°45'E. The sun with GHA 270°19' is observed. What are the LHA and t? (b) The same observer next uses the moon with GHA 5°14'. What are its LHA and t?

105. A navigator observes a star whose SHA is 248°19.2'. The GHA of Aries for the time of observation is 91°31.8'. What is the GHA of the star at that time?

106. (a) An observer is in L16°18.0'S. What is the colatitude? (b) He observes the sun with a declination of 21°47.2'S at an altitude of 60°13.2'. What is the coaltitude? (c) What is the polar distance?

107. (a) An observer is in L41°41.3'S. What is the colatitude? (b) He observes a star with declination 28°14.9'N at an altitude of 29° 47.3'. What is the coaltitude? (c) What is the polar distance?

108. Convert the following azimuth angles (Z) to true azimuth (Zn): (a) N64°E; (b) N121°E; (c) S58°E; (d) S122°W; (e) N88°W.

109. (a) The observed altitude is 61°18.3'; the computed altitude is 61°03.4'. What is the intercept? (b) An observed altitude is 41°56.9'; the corresponding computed altitude is 42°00.8'. What is the intercept?

110. A navigator's DR position is L38°18.2'N, λ27°29.2'W. The GHA ♈ for the time of the beginning of morning civil twilight is 243°37.9'. What value of LHA ♈ should be used to set the template of a Star Finder?

111. A navigator wishes to plot Mars on the base of his Star Finder. If at a given time, the GHA ♈ is 46°19.1' and the GHA Mars is 23°43.1', to what value is the index mark of the red template set?

For problems 112-138, use the Nautical Almanac extracts starting on page 31 or the Pub. No. 229 extracts starting on page 54.

112. A navigator at DR position L44°54'N, λ128°15'W observes a star at 03-53-03 ZT on 3 June. The azimuth of the star is 083° and the corrected sextant altitude is 26°50'. Use Pub. No 229 to determine the approximate SHA and declination of the star and identify it from the Nautical Almanac.

113. A sextant is checked against a natural horizon for index error. The reading is 0°00.8'. What is the index correction?

114. A sextant is checked using a star. The micrometer drum reads 58.3' and the index mark on the arc is to the right of the 0° mark. What is the index correction?

115. The navigator's height of eye is 25 feet; there is no instrument correction, the index correction is +1.3'. The sextant altitude of a star is 39°16.2'. What is the apparent altitude?

116. On 13 May 1977, a navigator observes the lower limb of the sun from a height of eye of 9.6 meters; the sextant reading is 42°53.8'. The instrument correction is +0.2'; the index error is 2.3' "off the arc." What is the observed altitude?

117. On 4 November 1977, a navigator observes the star Capella from a height of eye of 22½ feet; the sextant reading is 23°11.8'. There is no instrument correction, and the index correction is +0.8'. What is the observed altitude?

118. The planet Saturn is observed on 10 December from a height of eye of 12.8 feet; the sextant altitude is 64°19.3'. There is no instrument error; the index error is 1.1' "on the arc." What is the observed altitude?

119. The planet Mars is observed on 23 October 1977 from a height of 7.1 meters; the sextant reading is 47°09.3'. The instrument correction is +0.3'; the index correction is -1.1'. What is the observed altitude?

120. A navigator observes the upper limb of the moon from a height of eye of 22.0 feet; the sextant reading is 21°51.1'. There is no instrument error and the index correction is -1.8'. The applicable horizontal parallax is 61.2'. What is the observed altitude?

121. At a time when the temperature is 23°F and the barometric pressure is 30.58 inches, a sextant observation is made which yields an apparent altitude of 9°08.2'. What is the additional correction for refraction using the Nautical Almanac?

122. What is the equation of time for noon on 4 June 1977?

123. (a) Convert 4 minutes 18 seconds of time to arc. (b) Convert 6°42.5' of arc to units of time.

124. (a) What is the difference in local time between Point A, L26°18.1'N, λ123°17.8'W and Point B, L18°15.7'N, λ67°43.1'W? (b) between Point B and Point C, L3°05.1'S, λ7°14.0'E?

125. It is 02-30-15 local time at Point B of the preceding problem. (a) What time is it at Point A? (b) What is the time at Point C?

126. (a) What is the zone description for zone time at λ125°46'W? (b) For λ73°11'E?

127. Convert the following local zone times and dates to GMT and date for the longitude given:

    (a) 11-22-33   9 February   λ67°32'W

    (b) 01-23-34   16 March   λ121°38'E

    (c) 03-04-05   19 July   λ43°19'E

    (d) 20-30-40   31 October   λ148°39'W

128. Convert the following local mean times to zone time for the longitudes given:

    (a)   0541   λ13°42'W

    (b)   0602   λ122°06'E

    (c)   11-58-41   λ28°06'E

    (d)   1922   λ92°54'E

129. On board a ship in λ32°14.2'E a chronometer is checked against an 0900 UTC time check. At the time of the tick, it read 08-51-08. What is the chronometer error on GMT?

130. On board a ship in λ140°17'E a chronometer is to be compared with an 0300 UTC time check using a comparing watch. At the time of the tick the watch, set approximately to ZT(-9), read 12-02-31. Later the watch read 12-11-19 when the chronometer read 03-10-00. What is the watch error, and the chronometer error?

131. On 30 June a chronometer in zone (+7) read 07-19-31 at the tick of a 1900 UTC time signal. On 10 July, it read 07-18-57 at the tick of the same time signal. What is the chronometer rate?

132. For the chronometer of the preceding problem, no time signal has been received since 10 July; what will be the chronometer error at 1715 zone time on 13 July (DR λ is 103°42'W)?

133. The GHA of the sun is 33°19.2'. (a) What is the LHA of the sun for an observer in λ65°22.3'E; (b) for an observer in λ95°28.1'W?

134. A navigator keeping ZT(+10) observes the sun at 09-52-16 on 3 June 1977. What is the GHA, declination, and semidiameter?

135. A navigator keeping ZT(-7) observes the moon at ZT 16-16-12 on 4 June 1977. What is the GHA and declination? What is the semidiameter and horizontal parallax?

136. A navigator keeping ZT(+3) observes Venus at ZT 04-53-29 on 5 June 1977. What is the GHA and declination?

137. A navigator keeping ZT(-3) observes Saturn at ZT 19-24-41 on 5 June 1977. What is the GHA and declination?

138. A navigator keeping ZT(-10) observes Alpheratz at ZT 19-25-16 on 3 June 1977. What is the GHA and declination?

For problems 139-142, use the Air Almanac extracts starting on page 43.

139. A navigator keeping ZT(+4) observes the moon at ZT 16-02-07 on 5 June 1977. What is the GHA, declination, semidiameter, and horizontal parallax?

140. A navigator keeping ZT(+12) observes the sun at ZT 15-25-53 on 4 June 1977. What is the GHA, declination, and semidiameter?

141. A navigator keeping ZT(-10) observes Venus at ZT 06-02-14 on 6 June 1977. What is the GHA and declination?

142. A navigator keeping ZT(+2) observes Sirius at ZT 20-17-22 on 5 June 1977. What is the GHA and declination?

For problems 143-146, use the Pub. No. 229, Volume 3, extracts starting on page 54.

143. A navigator observes the moon with a declination of 14°17.2'S; the local hour angle is 346°; the assumed latitude is 34°S. What is the calculated altitude and azimuth?

144. A navigator observes a star with a declination of 24°37.8'N; the local hour angle is 46°; the assumed latitude is 39°S. What is the calculated altitude and azimuth?

145. A navigator observes Venus with a declination of 4°26.6'S; the local hour angle is 294°; the assumed latitude is 44°N. What is the calculated altitude and azimuth?

146. A navigator observes a body with a declination of 25°18.1'S; the local hour angle is 346°; the assumed latitude is 32°S. What is the calculated altitude and azimuth?

For problems 147 and 148, use the Pub. No. 249, Volume I, extracts starting on page 67.

147. A navigator is in latitude 42°N and his LHA ♈ is 322°. What are the listed stars? Underline the names of those indicated for a three-body fix.

148. A navigator from latitude 42°N observes Vega with an assumed longitude yielding an LHA ♈ of 216°. What is the calculated altitude and azimuth?

For problems 149 and 150, use the Pub. No. 249, Volume III, extracts starting on page 69.

149. A navigator using assumed latitude of 41°S observes the moon with a declination of 12°43'S. The local hour angle is 284°. What is the calculated altitude and azimuth?

150. A navigator observes a star with a declination of 2°08'S. The local hour angle is 72° and the assumed latitude is 41°N. What is the calculated altitude and azimuth?

151. A navigator observes the sun with a declination of 13°28.7'N. His DR latitude is L33°10.1'N. The LHA is 333°44.2'. Using the Ageton Method (Table 35 in Pub. No. 9, Volume II), what is the calculated altitude and azimuth?

152. An observer in L4°48.2'S, λ26°19.2'W observes the sun from an Ho of 87°58.2'. The GP of the sun is determined to be L6°46.5'S, λ26°38.5'W. What is the radius of the circular LOP?

153. The computed altitude of a star is 38°49.7'. (a) What is the intercept if the corrected observed altitude is 38°31.6'? (b) If Ho is 39°02.3'?

154. A ship is on course 094°, speed 15.0 knots. The 1800 DR position is L34°24.9'N, λ156°45.7'E. Three stars are observed and the following data derived.

Body	Arcturus	Sirius	Capella
Time	1833	1837	1842
a	17.7A	24.6A	16.8T
Zn	081.2°	221.9°	304.1°
aL	34°00.0'N	34°00.0'N	34°00.0'N
aλ	157°20.5'E	156°43.2'E	157°02.3'E

What is the 1842 fix?

155. A ship is on course 170°, speed 20.0 knots; at 1900 the DR position is L28°52.3'S, λ94°17.8'E. At 1910 an observation is made of Mars. At 1922, course is changed to 120°. At 1928 an observation is made on Canopus. The observations are reduced as follows:

Body	Mars	Canopus
Time	1910	1928
a	9.0A	2.8T
Zn	245°	316°
aL	29°00.0'S	29°00.0'S
aλ	94°05.6'E	94°27.5'E

What is the 1928 fix?

156. A ship is on course 085°, speed 15 knots. The 1200 DR position is L33°54.8'S, λ122°02.1'W. Two high altitude observations were taken with results as follows:

Body	Sun	Sun
Time	1156	1204
Ho	88°33.1'	88°08.4'
L GP	32°33.6'S	32°33.6'S
λ GP	121°28.0'W	123°28.0'W

What is the 1204 fix?

157. A ship is on course 112°, speed 16 knots. The 1000 DR position is
L41°07.0'N, λ167°37.1'E. Two sun observations are made with
results as follows:

Body	Sun	Sun
Time	1006	1200
a	13.7A	5.5T
Zn	145.6°	178.2°
aL	41°00.0'N	41°00.0'N
aλ	167°53.5'E	168°25.1'E

What is the 1200 RFix?

158. A ship is on course 228°, speed 17 knots. The 0900 DR position is
L28°19.5'N, λ41°35.6'W. The sun is observed at 0918. Course is
changed at 1045 to 260°. The sun is observed again at 1200. The
observations yield the following data:

Body	Sun	Sun
Time	0918	1200
a	10.8A	6.6T
Zn	125.1	181.8°
aL	28°00.0'N	28°00.0'N
aλ	41°35.0'W	42°17.2'W

What is the 1200 RFix?

For problems 159-167, use the Nautical Almanac and Pub. No. 229 extracts
starting on pages 31 and 54.

159. A ship is on course 102°, speed 12 knots. The DR position at 0500
(ZT-9) on 4 June 1977 is L43°52.4'S, λ133°39.5'E. The navigator
takes a sight on Antares at 05-17-08; the watch error is 12 seconds
fast. The sextant reading is 22°47.1'; there is no instrument
error; the index correction is +1.7; the height of eye is 10.5
meters. What is the 0517 DR position? What is the assumed position?
What is the intercept and azimuth?

160. The ship in the preceding problem continues on and the navigator
takes a sight on Altair at 05-24-15. The sextant reading is
28°46.2'. (Other data are unchanged). What is the 0524 DR position?
What is the assumed position? What is the intercept and azimuth?

161. Plot the LOPs of the two preceding problems. What is the 0524 fix?

162. The ship of the preceding problems continues on. The 0853 DR
position is L44°05.9'S, λ134°42.9'E. The navigator makes a morning
sun (lower limb) observation at 08-54-10; watch error is 11 seconds
fast. The sextant reading is 11°06.6'. What is the assumed
position, intercept, and azimuth?

163. A ship is on course 094° speed 16.0 knots. On 3 June 1977, its
1926 DR position is L34°42.2'S, λ48°41.2'E. An observation is made
on Spica at watch time 19-25-37; the watch is 4 seconds slow; The
sextant altitude is 63°13.5'; the index correction is +1.2; the
height of eye is 8.1 meters. What is the assumed position, intercept,
and azimuth?

164. A ship is on course 254°, speed 17.5 knots. On 5 June 1977, its 0617 DR position is L39°02.3'N, λ159°46.4'E. An observation of the moon's lower limb is made at 06-17-23 ZT. The sextant reading is 19°19.8'; the index correction is -2.2'; the height of eye is 27 feet. What is the assumed position, intercept, and azimuth?

165. A ship is on course 065°, speed 16 knots. On 4 June 1977, the 0800 DR position is L38°04.7'S, λ159°08.1'W. At ZT 08-02-19 (watch error 4 seconds slow) the upper limb of the moon is observed; the sextant reading is 14°36.8'. The index error is -4.3'; the height of eye is 17 feet. What is the assumed position, intercept, and azimuth?

166. A ship is on course 288°, speed 18 knots. The 4 June 1977 2000 DR position is L38°17.2'S, λ131°44.3'W. An observation of Saturn is made at 20-17-33; sextant reading is 6°48.9'. Watch error is zero; instrument correction is +0.2; index correction is +3.7'; height of eye is 9.5 meters. (Altitude correction is -7.6'.) What is the assumed position, intercept, and azimuth?

167. A ship is on course 264°, speed 14 knots. The 5 June 1977 0900 DR position is L35°08.0'N, λ59°48.1'W. At 09-52-18 a daytime observation is made of Venus; sextant reading is 61°14.7'. Watch error is zero; index correction is -2.1'; height of eye is 11.5 feet. (For daylight phase correction, use value of additional correction from Table A2 on page 31.) What is the assumed position, intercept, and azimuth?

For problems 168-172, use the <u>Air Almanac</u> and Pub. No. 249 extracts starting on pages 43 and 67.

168. A ship is on course 333°, speed 9 knots. On 5 June 1977, the 2000 DR position is L41°48'N, λ18°42'W. An observation is made of Vega at 20-35-16; the sextant reading is 31°42.8'. There is no watch error; the index correction is -3.7'; the height of eye is 28 feet. Using Volume I, what is the assumed position, intercept, and azimuth? What is the P & N correction?

169. A ship is on course 226°, speed 8.0 knots. On 5 June 1977, the 2000 DR position is L42°02'N, λ34°47'W. A quick round of sights is taken at the following watch times: Vega, 20-00-23, 25°10.1'; Spica, 20-01-07, 36°05.2'; Pollux, 20-01-51, 29°53.8'. The watch error is 9 seconds fast; the index error is 0'; the height of eye is 23 feet. What is the 2002 fix?

170. A ship is on course 034°, speed 15 knots. On 6 June 1977, the 0600 DR position is L41°07'S, λ160°46'E. An observation is made on Mars at 06-42-29 (watch error is 11 seconds slow); the sextant reading is 28°18.6'. The index correction is +2.3'; the height of eye is 33 feet. What is the assumed position, intercept, and azimuth?

171. A ship's course is 242°, speed 12 knots. The 0900 DR on 5 June 1977 is L41°02'S, λ36°48'W. An observation is taken of the moon's lower limb at 09-29-38, using a watch that is 6 seconds slow; the sextant reading is 13°22.8'. The index correction is +4.1'; the height of eye is 6.8 meters. What is the assumed position, intercept, and azimuth?

172. On 5 June 1977, a ship is on course 234°, speed 13 knots. The 1500 DR position is L41°10'N, λ152°16'E. An observation of the sun's lower limb is taken at 15-08-21; there is no watch error. The sextant reading is 44°28.3'; the index correction is -1.9'; the height of eye is 29 feet. What is the assumed position, intercept, and azimuth?

173. A ship is on course 105°, speed 11 knots. On 3 June 1977, the 0900 DR position is L37°56.2'N, λ10°09.4'E. At 09-52-09 (no watch error) an observation is made on the sun (lower limb); the sextant reading is 55°19.7'. The height of eye is 3.3 meters; the index correction is -3.8'. Using the <u>Nautical Almanac</u> and the Ageton Method (DMAHC Pub. No. 9, Volume II, Table 35), what is the intercept and azimuth?

174. A ship is on course 262°, speed 18 knots. The predicted 1200 DR position on 3 June 1977 is L23°14.2'S, λ108°15.9'W. What is the ZT of local apparent noon?

175. A ship's course is 098°, speed 15 knots. On 4 June 1977, the predicted 1200 DR position is L32°51.8'N, λ32°11.4'E. What is the time of local apparent noon?

176. For the ship in the preceding problem, find the ZT of LAN (to nearest minute) using the time of meridian passage of the sun as given in the <u>Nautical Almanac</u>.

177. A navigator in north latitude observes the sun at meridian passage. The sun's declination is 22°19.3'N; the corrected sextant altitude is 70°18.9'. What is the latitude?

178. A navigator observes the sun at meridian passage to the south of his position. The sun's declination is 17°03.2'S; the corrected sextant altitude is 32°49.1'. What is the latitude?

179. A navigator observes the sun's meridian passage to the north of his position. The sun's declination is 22°18.8'N; the corrected sextant altitude is 76°34.5'. What is the latitude?

180. The sun is obscured by a cloud at the time of meridian passage, but an observation is made 7 minutes 38 seconds later. The DR latitude is 37°02.2'N; the sun's declination is 14°02.1'N; the corrected sextant altitude is 66°51.9'. Using Tables 29 and 30 in DMAHC Pub. No. 9, Volume II, what is the latitude?

181. A navigator at DR position L39°16.2'N, λ3°14.2'E observes Polaris on 3 June 1977 at 03-53-19 on a watch that is 14 seconds fast. The sextant reading is 39°29.5'; the index correction is +5.1'; the height of eye is 11.3 m. Using the <u>Nautical Almanac</u>, what is the latitude?

182. A navigator is at DR position L19°07.7'N, λ65°18.3'W. At 19-25-48 ZT on 5 June 1977, he observes Polaris with a sextant reading of 18°39.0'; the index correction is +3.8'; the height of eye is 24 feet. Using the <u>Air Almanac</u>, what is the latitude?

For problems 183-189, use the <u>Nautical Almanac</u> extracts starting on page 31.

183. (a) What is the local time of sunrise on 3 June 1977 at L20°S, λ45°W? (b) What is the local time of sunset on 3 June 1977 at L35°N, λ165°E?

184. (a) What is the zone time of sunrise on 4 June 1977 at L28°N, λ126°W? (b) What is the time of sunset on 4 June 1977 at L51°S, λ48°E?

185. (a) What is the zone time of the beginning of morning civil twilight on 5 June 1977 at L33°26'N, λ123°19'W? (b) What is the time of the end of evening civil twilight on 5 June 1977 at L33°02'S, λ39°32'W?

186.   (a) What is the zone time of moonrise on 4 June 1977 at L31°17'N, λ158°46'E?   (b) What is the zone time of moonset on 5 June 1977 at L22°31'S, λ40°47'W?

187.   A ship is on course 082°, speed 18 knots.   On 3 June 1977, the 0400 DR position is L28°19.2'S, λ4°06.2'E.   What is the zone time of sunrise?

188.   A ship is on course 279°, speed 22 knots.   On 4 June 1977, the 1600 DR position is 42°23.4'S, 96°15.8'W.   What is the zone time of sunset?

189.   A ship is on course 110°, speed 20 knots.   On 4 June 1977, the 0600 DR position is L41°38.9'N, λ162°08.0'E.   What is the zone time of moonset?

For problems 190-192, use the <u>Air Almanac</u> extracts starting on page 43.

190.   (a) What is the zone time of sunrise on 4 June 1977 at L36°42'N, λ168°11'E?   (b) What is the zone time of sunset on 5 June 1977 at L33°18'S, λ21°47'W?

191.   (a) What is the zone time of morning twilight on 4 June 1977 at L27°18'S, λ8°16'E?   (b) What is the zone time of evening twilight on 3 June 1977 at L16°54'N, λ24°57'W?

192.   What is the zone time of moonrise on 5 June 1977 at L32°54'N, λ133°31'W?

193.   At 07-53-56 ZT on 3 June 1977, a navigator observes the sun to obtain an azimuth.   The 0800 DR position was L38°19.2'S, λ91°31.2'W. Course is 286°; speed is 17.5 knots.   The gyrocompass bearing of the sun is 056°. What is the gyro error?

194.   On 4 June 1977, the DR position of a ship is L20°15.4'N, λ171°40.0'E when the navigator observes the sun centered on the visible horizon at 04-52-20 bearing 067° by gyro repeater.   What is the gyro error?

195.   A ship is on course 063°, speed 14.5 knots.   The 4 June 1977 0500 DR position is L18°19.7'N, λ164°44.0'E.   At 04-53-20 ZT the navigator, using a gyro repeater, observes Polaris to bear 001.5°. What is the gyro error?

196.   A vessel departs from L37°03.2'S, λ12°18.4'W at 0800 GMT on 3 June 1977 on course 218°, speed 17.5 knots.   Using mid-latitude sailing, what is her DR position at 0600 GMT on 5 June 1977?

197.   Using mid-latitude sailing, what is the course and distance from L35°32'N, λ139°48'E to 28°12'N, λ177°24'W?

198.   Using Mercator sailing, what is the course and distance from L11°44'N, λ43°14'E to L32°02'S, λ115°44'E?

199.   Using great-circle sailing from L51°59'N, λ177°30'E to L24°17'N, λ153°58'E, find: (a) distance; (b) initial great-circle course.

200.   Using great-circle sailing, from L8°57'N, λ79°34'W to L33°52'S, λ151°12'E, find: (a) distance; (b) initial great-circle course; (c) latitude and longitude of vertex; (d) latitude and longitude of points along the track at distance intervals of 20° to eastward of the vertex (5 points).

201. Using a great-circle sailing, from L34°53.0'S, λ56°10.0'W to L33°54.0'S, λ18°26.0'E find: (a) distance; (b) initial great-circle course; (c) latitude and longitude of the vertex; (d) latitude and longitude of points along the track at distance intervals of 10° in both directions from the vertex.

202. Using the tables of DMAHC Pub. No. 229 for great-circle sailing, from L38°48'N, λ122°30'W to L35°40'N, λ139°44'E, find: (a) distance; (b) initial great-circle course.

203. Convert: (a) 3,820 kHz to MHz; (b) 4.21 MHz to kHz; (c) 9,350 MHz to GHz.

204. (a) What is the wavelength of a 156.8 MHz signal; of a 9.38 GHz signal? (b) What is the frequency of a signal of 5.32 cm wavelength?

205. A ship at L40°23'N, λ26°47'W takes a radio bearing on another vessel at L35°17'N, λ37°02'W; the bearing is 241°. Using Table 1 in DMAHC Pub. No. 9, Volume II, what bearing should be plotted on a Mercator chart?

206. A lifeboat departs from L46°10'N, λ5°20'W on course 040°. Using simplified traverse tables (Tables A and B, page 73), what is its position after it has traveled 90 miles?

207. The approximate altitude of the sun is measured in a lifeboat using a shadow pin 11.5 cm high; the length of the shadow is 9.3 cm. Using Table C, page 73, what is the approximate altitude of the sun?

208. Using a graphic solution, what is the declination of the sun on 27 July?

209. Using the simplified traverse table (Table A, page 73), what is the declination of the sun on 18 July?

210. A lifeboat navigator has available Pub. No. 9, Volume II. Using the long-term almanac in Appendix H, determine: (a) the GHA and declination of the sun at 14-25-18 GMT on 12 December 1978; (b) the GHA ♈ for 05-16-51 on 17 November 1978; (c) the SHA and declination of Canopus on 22 October 1978.

211. (a) From a lifeboat, an observer with a height of eye of 9 feet above the water observes the top of a mountain known to be 2,650 feet high just appearing over the horizon. What is the estimated distance to the mountain? (b) An observer with a height of eye of 2.6 meters observes a lighthouse (height 103 m) just appearing above the horizon. What is the estimated distance to the mountain?

212. An observer in a lifeboat holds a ruler 26 inches from his right eye; two points on shore known to be 0.9 miles apart subtend a length of 3 3/4 inches on the ruler. What is the approximate distance to the island?

213. (a) At L82°N λ67°W convert 141°T to grid direction. (b) At L79°S, λ143°W, convert 049°T to grid direction. (c) At L83°S, λ143°E convert 259°T to grid direction. (d) At L84°N, λ156°E, convert 92°G to true direction. (e) At L86°S, λ41°E, convert 323°G to true direction.

For problems 214-216, use the <u>Air Almanac</u> diagrams starting on page 43.

214. An observer is at L76°30'N, λ49°12'E. What is the LMT and GMT of sunrise and sunset on 24 February 1977?

215. For the observer of the preceding problem, what is the LMT and GMT of the beginning of morning twilight and the ending of evening twilight?

216. For an observer at L76°N, λ62°35'W, what is the LMT and GMT of moonrise on 26 January 1977? When will the moon set? What is the phase of the moon?

Extracts

(1) No.	(2) Name Characteristic	(3) Location Lat. N. Long. W.	(4) Nominal Range	(5) Ht. above water	(6) Structure Ht. above ground Daymark	(7) Remarks Year
	(Chart 13260)					
	(For Gulf of Maine, see No. 199)					
1 227 J148	**MOUNT DESERT LIGHT** .... Fl. W., 15ˢ	On Mount Desert Rock, 20 miles south of Mount Desert Island 43 58.1 68 07.7	24	75	Conical gray granite tower 58	RBN: 314 kHz (▪ • • •)I. Antenna at light tower. HORN: 2 blasts ev 30ˢ (2 ˢbl-2ˢsi-2ˢbl-24ˢsi). 1830
2 239 J116	**MATINICUS ROCK LIGHT** .... Gp. Fl. W. (1 + 2), 15ˢ 0.2ˢfl., 5.8ˢec. 0.2ˢfl., 2.8ˢec. 0.2ˢfl., 5.8ˢec. 3 flashes.	On south part of rock. 43 47.0 68 51.3	23	90	Cylindrical gray granite tower and dwelling. 48	RBN: 314 kHz (• ▪ ▪ •)II. Antenna 105 feet 053° from light tower. HORN: 1 blast ev 15ˢ (2ˢbl). 1827–1857
3 282 J128	**MONHEGAN ISLAND LIGHT** ..... Fl. W., 30ˢ (2.8ˢfl)	Near center of island. 43 45.9 69 19.0	21	178	Gray conical tower covered way to dwelling. 47	Within 3 miles of island the light is obscured between west and southwest. 1824–1850
4 283 J130	Manana Island Fog Signal Station.	On west side of island, close to Monhegan Island. 43 45.8 69 19.7	....	....	Brown brick house	RBN: 314 kHz (▪▪▪ •)III. Antenna 2,880 feet 259° from Monhegan Island light tower. HORN: 2 blasts ev 60ˢ (3ˢbl-3ˢsi-3ˢbl-51ˢsi). 1855–1870
5 297 J146	**SEGUIN LIGHT** .... F. W.	On island, 2 miles south of mouth of Kennebec River. 43 42.5 69 45.5	19	180	White cylindrical granite tower connected to dwelling. 53	HORN: 2 blasts ev 20ˢ (2ˢbl-2ˢsi-2ˢbl-14ˢsi). 1795–1857
6 320 J176	**HALFWAY ROCK LIGHT** .... Fl. R., 5ˢ	On rock, midway between Cape Small Point and Cape Elizabeth. 43 39.4 70 02.2	19	76	White granite tower attached to dwelling. 77	RBN: 314 kHz (• • • • ▪▪ •)IV. Antenna on light tower. HORN: 2 blasts ev 30ˢ (2 ˢbl-2 ˢsi-2 ˢbl-24 ˢsi). 1871
	(Chart 13286)					
7.10 334.10	**Portland Lighted Horn Buoy P** .... Fl. W., 2ˢ	In 150 feet 43 31.6 70 05.5	14	....	Red	RBN: 314 kHz (• ▪▪ • • • • •)VI. HORN: 1 blast ev 30ˢ (3ˢ bl) . RACON: M (▪▪).
	(For Portland Harbor, see No. 334.10)					
8 338 J208	**CAPE ELIZABETH LIGHT** .... Gp. Fl. W., 30ˢ 0.2ˢfl., 2.3ˢec. 0.2ˢfl., 2.3ˢec. 0.2ˢfl., 2.3ˢec. 0.2ˢfl., 2.3ˢec. 0.2ˢfl., 2.3ˢec. 0.2ˢfl., 17.3ˢec. 6 flashes.	South of entrance to Portland Harbor. 43 34.0 70 12.0	27	129	White conical tower 67	HORN: 2 blasts ev 60ˢ (3ˢbl-3ˢsi-3ˢbl-51ˢsi). Located 266 yards 146° from light tower. 1829–1874
	Taylor Reef Buoy 1TR	In 75 feet, off southeast side of reef.	....	....	Black can	Ra ref. White reflector.
	Alden Rock Buoy 2AR	In 36 feet, 0.3 mile southwest of rock.	....	....	Red nun	Ra ref. Red reflector.
	East Hue and Cry Rock Buoy 1...	In 60 feet, eastsoutheast of ledge.	....	....	Black can	White reflector.
	Old Anthony Rock Buoy OA	In 48 feet, southeast rock.	....	....	Black and red horizontal bands; can.	White reflector.

TIMES AND HEIGHTS OF HIGH AND LOW WATERS

APRIL

DAY	TIME h.m.	HT. ft.	DAY	TIME h.m.	HT. ft.
1 F	0348	1.6	16 SA	0453	0.5
	0945	5.8		1102	5.3
	1612	0.5		1652	1.1
	2226	5.9		2302	6.1
2 SA	0434	0.9	17 SU	0531	0.2
	1036	6.0		1148	5.2
	1651	0.5		1726	1.4
	2301	6.3		2331	6.2
3 SU	0520	0.3	18 M	0607	0.0
	1126	6.0		1230	5.2
	1730	0.7		1800	1.7
	2334	6.6			
4 M	0606	-0.2	19 TU	0000	6.2
	1216	6.0		0645	-0.1
	1810	1.0		1308	5.0
				1834	2.0
5 TU	0012	6.9	20 W	0027	6.1
	0652	-0.6		0721	-0.2
	1308	5.8		1348	4.9
	1851	1.3		1905	2.2
6 W	0052	7.0	21 TH	0057	6.1
	0741	-0.8		0759	-0.2
	1401	5.6		1428	4.7
	1936	1.6		1944	2.5
7 TH	0134	7.0	22 F	0129	5.9
	0833	-0.9		0838	-0.1
	1459	5.3		1513	4.6
	2025	2.0		2021	2.7
8 F	0223	6.8	23 SA	0205	5.7
	0929	-0.7		0921	0.1
	1603	5.1		1603	4.5
	2120	2.3		2110	2.9
9 SA	0316	6.5	24 SU	0248	5.5
	1031	-0.5		1009	0.3
	1714	4.9		1658	4.4
	2229	2.6		2207	3.0
10 SU	0418	6.1	25 M	0339	5.2
	1135	-0.2		1103	0.4
	1828	4.9		1757	4.5
	2346	2.6		2316	2.9
11 M	0533	5.7	26 TU	0441	5.0
	1240	0.1		1159	0.6
	1935	5.1		1853	4.7
12 TU	0104	2.4	27 W	0031	2.7
	0654	5.4		0554	4.8
	1343	0.3		1253	0.6
	2031	5.4		1941	5.0
13 W	0216	2.0	28 TH	0137	2.2
	0810	5.3		0710	4.8
	1439	0.4		1346	0.7
	2116	5.7		2023	5.4
14 TH	0317	1.4	29 F	0236	1.5
	0915	5.3		0823	4.9
	1527	0.6		1438	0.8
	2156	5.9		2100	5.8
15 F	0407	1.0	30 SA	0327	0.8
	1013	5.3		0926	5.1
	1612	0.9		1523	0.9
	2230	6.0		2138	6.3

MAY

DAY	TIME h.m.	HT. ft.	DAY	TIME h.m.	HT. ft.
1 SU	0417	0.0	16 M	0513	-0.3
	1023	5.3		1141	4.7
	1609	1.1		1651	2.0
	2217	6.7		2252	6.3
2 M	0502	-0.7	17 TU	0551	-0.5
	1120	5.4		1223	4.7
	1654	1.3		1729	2.3
	2256	7.0		2322	6.3
3 TU	0550	-1.3	18 W	0627	-0.6
	1213	5.5		1306	4.7
	1740	1.5		1805	2.4
	2338	7.2		2351	6.2
4 W	0637	-1.6	19 TH	0702	-0.7
	1306	5.5		1343	4.7
	1828	1.8		1840	2.6
5 TH	0021	7.3	20 F	0023	6.1
	0727	-1.7		0737	-0.6
	1401	5.4		1422	4.7
	1917	2.0		1915	2.7
6 F	0109	7.1	21 SA	0057	6.0
	0818	-1.6		0814	-0.5
	1457	5.3		1502	4.7
	2009	2.2		2001	2.9
7 SA	0201	6.7	22 SU	0134	5.8
	0910	-1.3		0853	-0.4
	1556	5.2		1544	4.7
	2112	2.4		2049	2.9
8 SU	0257	6.2	23 M	0216	5.5
	1005	-0.9		0934	-0.2
	1658	5.2		1629	4.8
	2222	2.4		2144	2.9
9 M	0359	5.7	24 TU	0304	5.2
	1104	-0.4		1019	0.1
	1801	5.3		1715	4.9
	2339	2.3		2253	2.7
10 TU	0512	5.1	25 W	0405	4.8
	1202	0.1		1107	0.3
	1900	5.5		1757	5.2
11 W	0055	2.0	26 TH	0004	2.4
	0634	4.7		0515	4.5
	1300	0.5		1157	0.6
	1950	5.7		1845	5.5
12 TH	0204	1.5	27 F	0110	1.8
	0754	4.5		0638	4.3
	1356	0.9		1253	0.9
	2034	5.9		1928	5.9
13 F	0303	0.9	28 SA	0210	1.0
	0906	4.5		0758	4.3
	1444	1.2		1348	1.2
	2114	6.1		2013	6.3
14 SA	0352	0.4	29 SU	0306	0.2
	1005	4.6		0912	4.5
	1530	1.5		1439	1.5
	2148	6.2		2056	6.7
15 SU	0436	0.0	30 M	0358	-0.6
	1058	4.6		1017	4.7
	1612	1.8		1533	1.7
	2221	6.2		2142	7.1
			31 TU	0446	-1.3
				1115	5.0
				1625	1.9
				2228	7.4

JUNE

DAY	TIME h.m.	HT. ft.	DAY	TIME h.m.	HT. ft.
1 W	0536	-1.8	16 TH	0607	-0.8
	1212	5.2		1254	4.6
	1715	2.0		1739	2.7
	2314	7.5		2327	6.4
2 TH	0625	-2.0	17 F	0642	-0.8
	1303	5.3		1329	4.7
	1806	2.1		1818	2.8
				2359	6.3
3 F	0002	7.4	18 SA	0717	-0.8
	0713	-2.0		1401	4.8
	1353	5.4		1858	2.8
	1902	2.2			
4 SA	0050	7.1	19 SU	0035	6.2
	0801	-1.8		0750	-0.7
	1445	5.4		1436	4.9
	1959	2.3		1940	2.8
5 SU	0142	6.7	20 M	0113	5.9
	0849	-1.4		0826	-0.5
	1537	5.5		1512	5.0
	2102	2.3		2028	2.8
6 M	0238	6.1	21 TU	0155	5.6
	0938	-0.9		0902	-0.3
	1629	5.6		1550	5.2
	2208	2.2		2122	2.6
7 TU	0337	5.4	22 W	0244	5.3
	1029	-0.3		0940	0.0
	1722	5.7		1629	5.4
	2322	2.0		2226	2.4
8 W	0447	4.8	23 TH	0340	4.8
	1122	0.3		1023	0.4
	1814	5.8		1711	5.7
				2333	2.0
9 TH	0033	1.7	24 F	0453	4.4
	0605	4.3		1112	0.9
	1215	0.9		1756	6.0
	1903	5.9			
10 F	0142	1.3	25 SA	0042	1.4
	0731	4.0		0615	4.1
	1306	1.4		1207	1.3
	1948	6.1		1845	6.3
11 SA	0239	0.8	26 SU	0145	0.6
	0848	4.0		0741	4.1
	1357	1.8		1306	1.7
	2029	6.2		1934	6.7
12 SU	0330	0.3	27 M	0247	-0.1
	0952	4.1		0903	4.2
	1447	2.1		1405	2.0
	2108	6.3		2025	7.1
13 M	0415	-0.1	28 TU	0341	-0.8
	1048	4.3		1012	4.5
	1533	2.3		1504	2.2
	2143	6.4		2116	7.4
14 TU	0454	-0.4	29 W	0432	-1.4
	1135	4.4		1107	4.8
	1618	2.5		1603	2.2
	2220	6.4		2207	7.5
15 W	0531	-0.6	30 TH	0523	-1.8
	1215	4.5		1200	5.1
	1657	2.6		1658	2.2
	2252	6.4		2257	7.6

TIME MERIDIAN 120° W. 0000 IS MIDNIGHT. 1200 IS NOON.
HEIGHTS ARE RECKONED FROM THE DATUM OF SOUNDINGS ON CHARTS OF THE LOCALITY WHICH IS MEAN LOWER LOW WATER.

TABLE 2.—TIDAL DIFFERENCES AND OTHER CONSTANTS

No.	PLACE	POSITION		DIFFERENCES				RANGES		Mean Tide Level
				Time		Height				
		Lat.	Long.	High water	Low water	High water	Low water	Mean	Di- urnal	
		° ′ N.	° ′ W.	h. m.	h. m.	feet	feet	feet	feet	feet
	CALIFORNIA, Outer Coast—Continued *Time meridian, 120°W.*			on HUMBOLDT BAY, p.76						
719	Trinidad Harbor	41 03	124 09	−0 37	−0 40	+0.1	0.0	4.6	6.4	3.5
721	Crescent City	41 45	124 12	−0 32	−0 29	+0.6	0.0	5.1	6.9	3.7
	OREGON									
723	Brookings, Chetco Cove	42 03	124 17	−0 30	−0 26	+0.6	0.0	5.1	6.9	3.7
725	Wedderburn, Rogue River	42 26	124 25	−0 22	−0 14	+0.3	−0.1	4.9	6.7	3.6
727	Port Orford	42 44	124 30	−0 24	−0 21	+0.9	+0.1	5.3	7.3	3.9
729	Bandon, Coquille River	43 07	124 25	−0 08	−0 02	+0.6	−0.1	5.2	7.0	3.7
	Coos Bay									
731	Entrance	43 21	124 19	+0 02	+0 07	+0.7	0.0	5.2	7.0	3.8
733	Empire	43 24	124 17	+0 41	+0 50	+0.3	−0.1	4.9	6.7	3.5
735	Coos Bay	43 23	124 13	+1 30	+1 28	+1.0	−0.1	5.6	7.3	3.9
	Umpqua River									
737	Entrance	43 41	124 12	+0 09	+0 03	+0.6	0.0	5.1	6.9	3.7
739	Gardiner	43 44	124 07	+1 00	+1 09	+0.4	−0.2	5.1	6.7	3.5
741	Reedsport	43 42	124 06	+1 15	+1 24	+0.4	−0.2	5.1	6.7	3.6
	Siuslaw River									
743	Entrance	44 01	124 08	+0 10	+0 15	+0.6	−0.1	5.2	6.9	3.7
745	Florence	43 58	124 06	+0 48	+0 58	+0.3	−0.2	5.0	6.6	3.5
747	Waldport, Alsea Bay	44 26	124 04	+0 25	+0 31	+1.3	0.0	5.8	7.7	4.1
	Yaquina Bay and River									
749	Bar at entrance	44 37	124 05	+0 03	+0 09	+1.5	+0.1	5.9	7.9	4.2
751	Newport	44 38	124 03	+0 13	+0 12	+1.6	+0.1	6.0	8.0	4.3
752	Southbeach	44 38	124 03	+0 02	+0 03	+1.8	+0.1	6.2	8.2	4.4
753	Yaquina	44 36	124 01	+0 24	+0 25	+1.8	+0.1	6.2	8.2	4.4
755	Winant	44 35	124 00	+0 32	+0 46	+1.8	0.0	6.3	8.2	4.3
757	Toledo	44 37	123 56	+0 58	+1 09	+1.7	−0.1	6.3	8.1	4.2
759	Taft, Siletz Bay	44 56	124 01	+0 17	+0 43	+0.2	−0.3	5.0	6.6	3.4
761	Kernville, Siletz River	44 54	124 00	+0 53	+1 23	*0.95	*0.67	4.6	6.1	3.1
763	Nestucca Bay entrance	45 10	123 58	+0 24	+0 42	+1.2	−0.1	5.8	7.6	4.0
	Tillamook Bay									
765	Barview	45 34	123 57	+0 11	+0 26	+1.1	−0.1	5.7	7.5	3.9
767	Miami Cove	45 33	123 54	+0 44	+0 56	+1.0	−0.1	5.6	7.4	3.9
769	Bay City	45 31	123 54	+1 02	+1 30	+0.7	+0.2	5.4	7.1	3.7
771	Tillamook, Hoquarten Slough	45 28	123 51	+1 21	+2 45	*1.03	*0.58	5.2	6.6	3.3
	Nehalem River									
773	Brighton	45 40	123 56	+0 20	+0 24	+1.4	0.0	5.9	7.8	4.1
775	Nehalem	45 43	123 53	+0 46	+1 26	+0.8	−0.3	5.6	7.2	3.7
	OREGON and WASHINGTON Columbia River†			on ASTORIA, p.80						
777	Columbia River entrance (N. Jetty)	46 16	124 04	−0 46	−1 10	−0.7	+0.1	5.6	7.5	4.0
779	Ilwaco, Baker Bay, Wash	46 18	124 02	−0 15	−0 09	−0.5	−0.1	6.0	7.6	4.0
781	Chinook, Baker Bay, Wash	46 16	123 57	−0 15	−0 44	−0.2	0.0	6.2	7.9	4.2
783	Hungry Harbor, Wash	46 16	123 51	+0 02	−0 19	+0.1	+0.1	6.4	8.2	4.4
785	Point Adams, Oreg	46 12	123 57	−0 27	−0 48	+0.1	+0.1	6.4	8.3	4.4
787	Warrenton, Skipanon River, Oreg	46 10	123 55	−0 15	−0 29	+0.2	+0.1	6.5	8.3	4.4
789	Astoria (Youngs Bay), Oreg	46 10	123 50	−0 15	−0 24	+0.4	+0.1	6.7	8.6	4.5
791	Astoria (Port Docks), Oreg	46 11	123 52	−0 10	−0 13	−0.2	0.0	6.2	8.0	4.2
793	ASTORIA (Tongue Point), Oreg	46 13	123 46	Daily predictions				6.5	8.2	4.3
795	Settlers Point, Oreg	46 10	123 41	+0 20	+0 43	−0.2	−0.1	6.3	8.0	4.1
797	Harrington Point, Wash	46 16	123 39	+0 19	+0 42	−0.5	−0.2	6.1	7.7	3.9
799	Skamokawa, Steamboat Slough, Wash	46 16	123 27	+0 54	+1 35	------	------	5.6	6.9	----
801	Cathlamet, Wash	46 12	123 23	+1 13	+2 05	------	------	5.2	6.4	----
803	Wauna, Oreg	46 10	123 24	+1 15	+2 09	------	------	5.2	6.3	----
805	Eagle Cliff, Wash	46 10	123 14	+1 41	+2 51	------	------	4.5	5.5	----

*Ratio.
†The Columbia River is subject to annual freshets. Short range predictions are available at local river forecast centers. The data for stations above Harrington Point apply only during low river stages.

TABLE 3.—HEIGHT OF TIDE AT ANY TIME

Time from the nearest high water or low water

Duration of rise or fall, see footnote	h. m.	h. m.	h. m.	h. m.	h. m.	h. m.	h. m.	h. m.	h. m.	h. m.	h. m.	h. m.	h. m.	h. m.	h. m.
4 00	0 08	0 16	0 24	0 32	0 40	0 48	0 56	1 04	1 12	1 20	1 28	1 36	1 44	1 52	2 00
4 20	0 09	0 17	0 26	0 35	0 43	0 52	1 01	1 09	1 18	1 27	1 35	1 44	1 53	2 01	2 10
4 40	0 09	0 19	0 28	0 37	0 47	0 56	1 05	1 15	1 24	1 33	1 43	1 52	2 01	2 11	2 20
5 00	0 10	0 20	0 30	0 40	0 50	1 00	1 10	1 20	1 30	1 40	1 50	2 00	2 10	2 20	2 30
5 20	0 11	0 21	0 32	0 43	0 53	1 04	1 15	1 25	1 36	1 47	1 57	2 08	2 19	2 29	2 40
5 40	0 11	0 23	0 34	0 45	0 57	1 08	1 19	1 31	1 42	1 53	2 05	2 16	2 27	2 39	2 50
6 00	0 12	0 24	0 36	0 48	1 00	1 12	1 24	1 36	1 48	2 00	2 12	2 24	2 36	2 48	3 00
6 20	0 13	0 25	0 38	0 51	1 03	1 16	1 29	1 41	1 54	2 07	2 19	2 32	2 45	2 57	3 10
6 40	0 13	0 27	0 40	0 53	1 07	1 20	1 33	1 47	2 00	2 13	2 27	2 40	2 53	3 07	3 20
7 00	0 14	0 28	0 42	0 56	1 10	1 24	1 38	1 52	2 06	2 20	2 34	2 48	3 02	3 16	3 30
7 20	0 15	0 29	0 44	0 59	1 13	1 28	1 43	1 57	2 12	2 27	2 41	2 56	3 11	3 25	3 40
7 40	0 15	0 31	0 46	1 01	1 17	1 32	1 47	2 03	2 18	2 33	2 49	3 04	3 19	3 35	3 50
8 00	0 16	0 32	0 48	1 04	1 20	1 36	1 52	2 08	2 24	2 40	2 56	3 12	3 28	3 44	4 00
8 20	0 17	0 33	0 50	1 07	1 23	1 40	1 57	2 13	2 30	2 47	3 03	3 20	3 37	3 53	4 10
8 40	0 17	0 35	0 52	1 09	1 27	1 44	2 01	2 19	2 36	2 53	3 11	3 28	3 45	4 03	4 20
9 00	0 18	0 36	0 54	1 12	1 30	1 48	2 06	2 24	2 42	3 00	3 18	3 36	3 54	4 12	4 30
9 20	0 19	0 37	0 56	1 15	1 33	1 52	2 11	2 29	2 48	3 07	3 25	3 44	4 03	4 21	4 40
9 40	0 19	0 39	0 58	1 17	1 37	1 56	2 15	2 35	2 54	3 13	3 33	3 52	4 11	4 31	4 50
10 00	0 20	0 40	1 00	1 20	1 40	2 00	2 20	2 40	3 00	3 20	3 40	4 00	4 20	4 40	5 00
10 20	0 21	0 41	1 02	1 23	1 43	2 04	2 25	2 45	3 06	3 27	3 47	4 08	4 29	4 49	5 10
10 40	0 21	0 43	1 04	1 25	1 47	2 08	2 29	2 51	3 12	3 33	3 55	4 16	4 37	4 59	5 20

Correction to height

Range of tide, see footnote	Ft.	Ft.	Ft.	Ft.	Ft.	Ft.	Ft.	Ft.	Ft.	Ft.	Ft.	Ft.	Ft.	Ft.	Ft.
0.5	0.0	0.0	0.0	0.0	0.0	0.0	0.1	0.1	0.1	0.1	0.1	0.2	0.2	0.2	0.2
1.0	0.0	0.0	0.0	0.0	0.1	0.1	0.1	0.2	0.2	0.2	0.3	0.3	0.4	0.4	0.5
1.5	0.0	0.0	0.0	0.1	0.1	0.1	0.2	0.2	0.3	0.4	0.4	0.5	0.6	0.7	0.8
2.0	0.0	0.0	0.0	0.1	0.1	0.2	0.3	0.3	0.4	0.5	0.6	0.7	0.8	0.9	1.0
2.5	0.0	0.0	0.1	0.1	0.2	0.2	0.3	0.4	0.5	0.6	0.7	0.9	1.0	1.1	1.2
3.0	0.0	0.0	0.1	0.1	0.2	0.3	0.4	0.5	0.6	0.8	0.9	1.0	1.2	1.3	1.5
3.5	0.0	0.0	0.1	0.2	0.2	0.3	0.4	0.6	0.7	0.9	1.0	1.2	1.4	1.6	1.8
4.0	0.0	0.0	0.1	0.2	0.3	0.4	0.5	0.7	0.8	1.0	1.2	1.4	1.6	1.8	2.0
4.5	0.0	0.0	0.1	0.2	0.3	0.4	0.6	0.7	0.9	1.1	1.3	1.6	1.8	2.0	2.2
5.0	0.0	0.1	0.1	0.2	0.3	0.5	0.6	0.8	1.0	1.2	1.5	1.7	2.0	2.2	2.5
5.5	0.0	0.1	0.1	0.2	0.4	0.5	0.7	0.9	1.1	1.4	1.6	1.9	2.2	2.5	2.8
6.0	0.0	0.1	0.1	0.3	0.4	0.6	0.8	1.0	1.2	1.5	1.8	2.1	2.4	2.7	3.0
6.5	0.0	0.1	0.2	0.3	0.4	0.6	0.8	1.1	1.3	1.6	1.9	2.2	2.6	2.9	3.2
7.0	0.0	0.1	0.2	0.3	0.5	0.7	0.9	1.2	1.4	1.8	2.1	2.4	2.8	3.1	3.5
7.5	0.0	0.1	0.2	0.3	0.5	0.7	1.0	1.2	1.5	1.9	2.2	2.6	3.0	3.4	3.8
8.0	0.0	0.1	0.2	0.3	0.5	0.8	1.0	1.3	1.6	2.0	2.4	2.8	3.2	3.6	4.0
8.5	0.0	0.1	0.2	0.4	0.6	0.8	1.1	1.4	1.8	2.1	2.5	2.9	3.4	3.8	4.2
9.0	0.0	0.1	0.2	0.4	0.6	0.9	1.2	1.5	1.9	2.2	2.7	3.1	3.6	4.0	4.5
9.5	0.0	0.1	0.2	0.4	0.6	0.9	1.2	1.6	2.0	2.4	2.8	3.3	3.8	4.3	4.8
10.0	0.0	0.1	0.2	0.4	0.7	1.0	1.3	1.7	2.1	2.5	3.0	3.5	4.0	4.5	5.0
10.5	0.0	0.1	0.3	0.5	0.7	1.0	1.3	1.7	2.2	2.6	3.1	3.6	4.2	4.7	5.2
11.0	0.0	0.1	0.3	0.5	0.7	1.1	1.4	1.8	2.3	2.8	3.3	3.8	4.4	4.9	5.5
11.5	0.0	0.1	0.3	0.5	0.8	1.1	1.5	1.9	2.4	2.9	3.4	4.0	4.6	5.1	5.8
12.0	0.0	0.1	0.3	0.5	0.8	1.1	1.5	2.0	2.5	3.0	3.6	4.1	4.8	5.4	6.0
12.5	0.0	0.1	0.3	0.5	0.8	1.2	1.6	2.1	2.6	3.1	3.7	4.3	5.0	5.6	6.2
13.0	0.0	0.1	0.3	0.6	0.9	1.2	1.7	2.2	2.7	3.2	3.9	4.5	5.1	5.8	6.5
13.5	0.0	0.1	0.3	0.6	0.9	1.3	1.7	2.2	2.8	3.4	4.0	4.7	5.3	6.0	6.8
14.0	0.0	0.2	0.3	0.6	0.9	1.3	1.8	2.3	2.9	3.5	4.2	4.8	5.5	6.3	7.0
14.5	0.0	0.2	0.4	0.6	1.0	1.4	1.9	2.4	3.0	3.6	4.3	5.0	5.7	6.5	7.2
15.0	0.0	0.2	0.4	0.6	1.0	1.4	1.9	2.5	3.1	3.8	4.4	5.2	5.9	6.7	7.5
15.5	0.0	0.2	0.4	0.7	1.0	1.5	2.0	2.6	3.2	3.9	4.6	5.4	6.1	6.9	7.8
16.0	0.0	0.2	0.4	0.7	1.1	1.5	2.1	2.6	3.3	4.0	4.7	5.5	6.3	7.2	8.0
16.5	0.0	0.2	0.4	0.7	1.1	1.6	2.1	2.7	3.4	4.1	4.9	5.7	6.5	7.4	8.2
17.0	0.0	0.2	0.4	0.7	1.1	1.6	2.2	2.8	3.5	4.2	5.0	5.9	6.7	7.6	8.5
17.5	0.0	0.2	0.4	0.8	1.2	1.7	2.2	2.9	3.6	4.4	5.2	6.0	6.9	7.8	8.8
18.0	0.0	0.2	0.4	0.8	1.2	1.7	2.3	3.0	3.7	4.5	5.3	6.2	7.1	8.1	9.0
18.5	0.1	0.2	0.5	0.8	1.2	1.8	2.4	3.1	3.8	4.6	5.5	6.4	7.3	8.3	9.2
19.0	0.1	0.2	0.5	0.8	1.3	1.8	2.4	3.1	3.9	4.8	5.6	6.6	7.5	8.5	9.5
19.5	0.1	0.2	0.5	0.8	1.3	1.9	2.5	3.2	4.0	4.9	5.8	6.7	7.7	8.7	9.8
20.0	0.1	0.2	0.5	0.9	1.3	1.9	2.6	3.3	4.1	5.0	5.9	6.9	7.9	9.0	10.0

TABLE 4.-SUNRISE AND SUNSET, 1977

Date	30° N. Rise	30° N. Set	32° N. Rise	32° N. Set	34° N. Rise	34° N. Set	36° N. Rise	36° N. Set	38° N. Rise	38° N. Set	40° N. Rise	40° N. Set
	h. m.	h. m.	h. m.	h. m.	h. m.	h. m.	h. m.	h. m.	h. m.	h. m.	h. m.	h. m.
Jan. 1	6 56	17 11	7 01	17 07	7 06	17 02	7 11	16 57	7 16	16 51	7 22	16 45
6	6 57	17 15	7 02	17 11	7 06	17 06	7 11	17 01	7 17	16 56	7 22	16 50
11	6 57	17 19	7 02	17 15	7 06	17 10	7 11	17 05	7 16	17 00	7 22	16 55
16	6 57	17 23	7 01	17 19	7 05	17 15	7 10	17 10	7 15	17 05	7 20	17 00
21	6 55	17 28	6 59	17 24	7 04	17 20	7 08	17 15	7 12	17 11	7 17	17 06
26	6 54	17 32	6 57	17 28	7 01	17 25	7 05	17 21	7 09	17 16	7 14	17 12
31	6 51	17 36	6 55	17 33	6 58	17 29	7 02	17 26	7 06	17 22	7 10	17 18
Feb. 5	6 48	17 41	6 51	17 37	6 54	17 34	6 58	17 31	7 01	17 27	7 05	17 24
10	6 44	17 45	6 47	17 42	6 50	17 39	6 53	17 36	6 56	17 33	6 59	17 30
15	6 40	17 49	6 43	17 46	6 45	17 44	6 48	17 41	6 50	17 39	6 53	17 36
20	6 36	17 53	6 38	17 50	6 40	17 48	6 42	17 46	6 44	17 44	6 47	17 41
25	6 31	17 56	6 32	17 55	6 34	17 53	6 36	17 51	6 38	17 49	6 40	17 47
Mar. 2	6 25	18 00	6 27	17 58	6 28	17 57	6 29	17 56	6 31	17 54	6 32	17 53
7	6 20	18 03	6 21	18 02	6 22	18 01	6 23	18 00	6 24	17 59	6 25	17 58
12	6 14	18 06	6 14	18 06	6 15	18 05	6 16	18 05	6 16	18 04	6 17	18 04
17	6 08	18 10	6 08	18 09	6 08	18 09	6 09	18 09	6 09	18 09	6 09	18 09
22	6 02	18 13	6 02	18 13	6 01	18 13	6 01	18 13	6 01	18 14	6 01	18 14
27	5 56	18 16	5 55	18 16	5 55	18 17	5 54	18 18	5 53	18 18	5 53	18 19
Apr. 1	5 50	18 19	5 49	18 20	5 48	18 21	5 47	18 22	5 46	18 23	5 45	18 24
6	5 44	18 22	5 43	18 23	5 41	18 24	5 40	18 26	5 38	18 27	5 37	18 29
11	5 38	18 25	5 36	18 26	5 35	18 28	5 33	18 30	5 31	18 32	5 29	18 34
16	5 33	18 28	5 30	18 30	5 28	18 32	5 26	18 34	5 24	18 37	5 21	18 39
21	5 27	18 31	5 25	18 33	5 22	18 36	5 20	18 39	5 17	18 41	5 14	18 44
26	5 22	18 34	5 19	18 37	5 17	18 40	5 13	18 43	5 10	18 46	5 07	18 49
May 1	5 17	18 37	5 14	18 40	5 11	18 43	5 08	18 47	5 04	18 51	5 00	18 54
6	5 13	18 40	5 10	18 44	5 06	18 47	5 03	18 51	4 59	18 55	4 54	18 59
11	5 09	18 44	5 06	18 47	5 02	18 51	4 58	18 55	4 54	19 00	4 49	19 04
16	5 06	18 47	5 02	18 51	4 58	18 55	4 54	18 59	4 49	19 04	4 44	19 09
21	5 03	18 50	4 59	18 54	4 55	18 59	4 50	19 03	4 45	19 08	4 40	19 14
26	5 01	18 53	4 57	18 57	4 52	19 02	4 47	19 07	4 42	19 12	4 36	19 18
31	5 00	18 56	4 55	19 00	4 50	19 05	4 45	19 11	4 40	19 16	4 34	19 22
June 5	4 59	18 58	4 54	19 03	4 49	19 08	4 43	19 14	4 38	19 19	4 32	19 25
10	4 58	19 01	4 53	19 05	4 48	19 11	4 43	19 16	4 37	19 22	4 31	19 28
15	4 58	19 02	4 53	19 07	4 48	19 13	4 43	19 18	4 37	19 24	4 30	19 30
20	4 59	19 04	4 54	19 09	4 49	19 14	4 43	19 20	4 37	19 26	4 31	19 32
25	5 00	19 05	4 55	19 10	4 50	19 15	4 44	19 21	4 38	19 26	4 32	19 33
30	5 02	19 05	4 57	19 10	4 52	19 15	4 46	19 21	4 40	19 27	4 34	19 33
July 5	5 04	19 05	4 59	19 10	4 54	19 15	4 49	19 20	4 43	19 26	4 37	19 32
10	5 06	19 04	5 02	19 09	4 57	19 14	4 51	19 19	4 46	19 25	4 40	19 30
15	5 09	19 03	5 04	19 07	5 00	19 12	4 54	19 17	4 49	19 22	4 43	19 28
20	5 12	19 01	5 07	19 05	5 03	19 10	4 58	19 14	4 53	19 19	4 47	19 25
25	5 15	18 58	5 10	19 02	5 06	19 06	5 02	19 11	4 57	19 16	4 52	19 21
30	5 18	18 55	5 14	18 59	5 10	19 03	5 05	19 07	5 01	19 11	4 56	19 16
Aug. 4	5 20	18 51	5 17	18 55	5 13	18 58	5 09	19 02	5 05	19 06	5 01	19 11
9	5 24	18 47	5 20	18 50	5 17	18 54	5 13	18 57	5 09	19 01	5 05	19 05
14	5 27	18 42	5 24	18 45	5 21	18 48	5 17	18 52	5 14	18 55	5 10	18 58
19	5 29	18 37	5 27	18 40	5 24	18 43	5 21	18 45	5 18	18 48	5 15	18 52
24	5 32	18 32	5 30	18 34	5 28	18 37	5 25	18 39	5 23	18 42	5 20	18 44
29	5 35	18 26	5 33	18 28	5 31	18 30	5 29	18 32	5 27	18 34	5 24	18 37
Sept. 3	5 38	18 21	5 36	18 22	5 35	18 24	5 33	18 25	5 31	18 27	5 29	18 29
8	5 41	18 14	5 39	18 16	5 38	18 17	5 37	18 18	5 35	18 19	5 34	18 21
13	5 43	18 08	5 42	18 09	5 42	18 10	5 41	18 11	5 40	18 12	5 39	18 13
18	5 46	18 02	5 46	18 02	5 45	18 03	5 45	18 03	5 44	18 04	5 43	18 04
23	5 49	17 56	5 49	17 56	5 49	17 56	5 48	17 56	5 48	17 56	5 48	17 56
28	5 51	17 50	5 52	17 49	5 52	17 49	5 52	17 49	5 53	17 48	5 53	17 48
Oct. 3	5 54	17 43	5 55	17 43	5 56	17 42	5 56	17 41	5 57	17 41	5 58	17 40
8	5 57	17 38	5 58	17 36	5 59	17 35	6 01	17 34	6 02	17 33	6 03	17 32
13	6 00	17 32	6 02	17 30	6 03	17 29	6 05	17 27	6 06	17 26	6 08	17 24
18	6 04	17 26	6 05	17 25	6 07	17 23	6 09	17 21	6 11	17 19	6 13	17 17
23	6 07	17 21	6 09	17 19	6 11	17 17	6 14	17 15	6 16	17 12	6 19	17 10
28	6 11	17 17	6 13	17 14	6 16	17 12	6 18	17 09	6 21	17 06	6 24	17 03
Nov. 2	6 14	17 12	6 17	17 10	6 20	17 07	6 23	17 04	6 26	17 00	6 30	16 57
7	6 18	17 09	6 22	17 06	6 25	17 02	6 28	16 59	6 32	16 55	6 36	16 51
12	6 22	17 06	6 26	17 02	6 29	16 59	6 33	16 55	6 37	16 51	6 41	16 47
17	6 27	17 03	6 30	16 59	6 34	16 56	6 38	16 51	6 43	16 47	6 47	16 42
22	6 31	17 01	6 35	16 57	6 39	16 53	6 43	16 49	6 48	16 44	6 53	16 39
27	6 35	17 00	6 39	16 56	6 44	16 52	6 48	16 47	6 53	16 42	6 58	16 37
Dec. 2	6 39	17 00	6 43	16 55	6 48	16 51	6 53	16 46	6 58	16 41	7 03	16 35
7	6 43	17 00	6 47	16 56	6 52	16 51	6 57	16 46	7 02	16 40	7 08	16 35
12	6 46	17 01	6 51	16 56	6 56	16 52	7 01	16 46	7 07	16 41	7 12	16 35
17	6 49	17 03	6 54	16 58	6 59	16 53	7 04	16 48	7 10	16 42	7 16	16 36
22	6 52	17 05	6 56	17 00	7 01	16 55	7 07	16 49	7 12	16 44	7 18	16 38
27	6 54	17 08	6 59	17 03	7 04	16 58	7 09	16 53	7 15	16 47	7 21	16 41
Jan. 1	6 56	17 11	7 01	17 07	7 06	17 02	7 11	16 57	7 16	16 51	7 22	16 45

Local mean time. To obtain standard time of rise or set, see table 5.

TABLE 5.—REDUCTION OF LOCAL MEAN TIME TO STANDARD TIME

Difference of longitude between local and standard meridian	Correction to local mean time to obtain standard time	Difference of longitude between local and standard meridian	Correction to local mean time to obtain standard time	Difference of longitude between local and standard meridian	Correction to local mean time to obtain standard time
° ′ ° ′	*Minutes*	° ′ ° ′	*Minutes*	°	*Hours*
0 00 to 0 07	0	7 23 to 7 37	30	15	1
0 08 to 0 22	1	7 38 to 7 52	31	30	2
0 23 to 0 37	2	7 53 to 8 07	32	45	3
0 38 to 0 52	3	8 08 to 8 22	33	60	4
0 53 to 1 07	4	8 23 to 8 37	34	75	5
1 08 to 1 22	5	8 38 to 8 52	35	90	6
1 23 to 1 37	6	8 53 to 9 07	36	105	7
1 38 to 1 52	7	9 08 to 9 22	37	120	8
1 53 to 2 07	8	9 23 to 9 37	38	135	9
2 08 to 2 22	9	9 38 to 9 52	39	150	10
2 23 to 2 37	10	9 53 to 10 07	40	165	11
2 38 to 2 52	11	10 08 to 10 22	41	180	12
2 53 to 3 07	12	10 23 to 10 37	42		
3 08 to 3 22	13	10 38 to 10 52	43		
3 23 to 3 37	14	10 53 to 11 07	44		
3 38 to 3 52	15	11 08 to 11 22	45		
3 53 to 4 07	16	11 23 to 11 37	46		
4 08 to 4 22	17	11 38 to 11 52	47		
4 23 to 4 37	18	11 53 to 12 07	48		
4 38 to 4 52	19	12 08 to 12 22	49		
4 53 to 5 07	20	12 23 to 12 37	50		
5 08 to 5 22	21	12 38 to 12 52	51		
5 23 to 5 37	22	12 53 to 13 07	52		
5 38 to 5 52	23	13 08 to 13 22	53		
5 53 to 6 07	24	13 23 to 13 37	54		
6 08 to 6 22	25	13 38 to 13 52	55		
6 23 to 6 37	26	13 53 to 14 07	56		
6 38 to 6 52	27	14 08 to 14 22	57		
6 53 to 7 07	28	14 23 to 14 37	58		
7 08 to 7 22	29	14 38 to 14 52	59		

If local meridian is east of standard meridian, subtract the correction from local time.

If local meridian is west of standard meridian, add the correction to local time.

For differences of longitude less than 15°, use the first part of the table. For greater differences use both parts thus: 47°23′ is equivalent to 45°+2°23′, the correction for 45° is 3 hours, the correction for 2°23′ is 10 minutes, therefore the total correction for the difference in longitude 47°23′ is 3 hours and 10 minutes.

ASTRONOMICAL DATA, 1977

Greenwich mean time of the Moon's phases, apogee, perigee, greatest north and south declination, Moon on the Equator, and the solar equinoxes and solstices.

January

	d.	h.	m.
N	3	17	..
O	5	12	10
E	10	17	..
◑	12	19	55
P	16	10	..
S	17	01	..
●	19	14	11
◑	23	15	..
◑	27	05	11
A	28	06	..
N	31	02	..

February

	d.	h.	m.
O	4	03	56
E	7	00	..
P	11	04	..
◑	11	04	07
S	13	09	..
●	18	03	37
E	20	01	..
A	25	03	..
◑	26	02	50
N	27	11	..

March

	d.	h.	m.
O	5	17	13
E	6	08	..
P	8	23	..
◑	12	11	35
S	12	15	..
E	19	09	..
●	19	18	33
☉₁	20	17	43
A	24	22	..
N	26	19	..
◑	27	22	27

April

	d.	h.	m.
E	2	18	..
O	4	04	09
P	5	21	..
S	8	21	..
◑	10	19	15
E	15	15	..
●	18	10	35
A	21	12	..
N	23	02	..
◑	26	14	42
E	30	05	..

May

	d.	h.	m.
O	3	13	03
P	4	05	..
S	6	06	..
◑	10	04	08
E	12	21	..
●	18	02	51
A	18	18	..
N	20	09	..
◑	26	03	20
E	27	14	..

June

	d.	h.	m.
P	1	15	..
O	1	20	31
S	2	17	..
◑	8	15	07
E	9	04	..
A	14	21	..
N	16	16	..
●	16	18	23
☉₂	21	12	14
E	23	22	..
◑	24	12	44
P	30	00	..
S	30	04	..

July

	d.	h.	m.
O	1	03	24
E	6	13	..
◑	8	04	39
A	12	08	..
N	14	00	..
●	16	08	37
E	21	05	..
◑	23	19	38
S	27	15	..
P	28	02	..
O	30	10	52

August

	d.	h.	m.
E	2	23	..
◑	6	20	40
A	9	00	..
N	10	08	..
●	14	21	31
E	17	11	..
◑	22	01	04
S	23	22	..
P	24	09	..
O	28	20	10
E	30	09	..

September

	d.	h.	m.
◑	5	14	33
A	5	18	..
N	6	17	..
●	13	09	23
E	13	19	..
P	18	09	..
S	20	04	..
◑	20	06	18
☉₃	23	03	30
E	26	17	..
O	27	08	17

October

	d.	h.	m.
A	3	14	..
N	4	01	..
◑	5	09	21
E	11	04	..
●	12	20	31
P	15	09	..
S	17	10	..
◑	19	12	46
E	24	00	..
O	26	23	35
A	31	08	..
N	31	08	..

November

	d.	h.	m.
◑	4	03	58
E	7	15	..
●	11	07	09
P	12	12	..
S	13	19	..
◑	17	21	52
E	20	06	..
O	25	17	31
N	27	16	..
A	27	21	..

December

	d.	h.	m.
◑	3	21	16
E	5	01	..
●	10	17	33
P	10	23	..
S	11	06	..
◑	17	10	37
E	17	13	..
☉₄	21	23	24
A	24	21	..
N	24	23	..
O	25	12	49

●, new Moon; ◐, first quarter; O, full Moon; ◑, last quarter; E, Moon on the Equator; N, S, Moon farthest north or south of the Equator; A, P, Moon in apogee or perigee; $\odot_1$, Sun at vernal equinox; $\odot_2$, Sun at summer solstice; $\odot_3$, Sun at autumnal equinox; $\odot_4$, Sun at winter solstice.

0^h is midnight. 12^h is noon. The times may be adapted to any other time meridian than Greenwich by adding the longitude in time when it is east and subtracting it when west. (15° of longitude equals 1 hour of time).

This table was compiled from the American Ephemeris and Nautical Almanac.

ST. JOHNS RIVER ENTRANCE, FLA., 1977

F-FLOOD, DIR. 275° TRUE   E-EBB, DIR. 100° TRUE

MAY

DAY	SLACK WATER TIME H.M.	MAXIMUM CURRENT TIME H.M.	VEL. KNOTS	DAY	SLACK WATER TIME H.M.	MAXIMUM CURRENT TIME H.M.	VEL. KNOTS
1 SU	0327	0544	2.1F	16 M		0032	2.1E
	0824	1116	2.7E		0424	0625	1.6F
	1528	1809	2.7F		0906	1211	2.1E
	2105	2356	2.8E		1623	1846	2.2F
					2146		
2 M	0416	0634	2.2F	17 TU		0057	2.1E
	0914	1205	2.9E		0508	0709	1.6F
	1613	1858	3.0F		0947	1240	2.1E
	2156				1702	1926	2.2F
					2226		
3 TU	0505	0049	3.0E	18 W		0125	2.2E
	1003	0723	2.3F		0551	0749	1.6F
	1659	1256	3.0E		1026	1313	2.2E
	2247	1948	3.1F		1740	2007	2.2F
					2306		
4 W	0556	0140	3.1E	19 TH		0154	2.2E
	1053	0813	2.4F		0633	0831	1.6F
	1749	1347	3.1E		1105	1350	2.2E
	2338	2037	3.1F		1817	2051	2.2F
					2345		
5 TH	0648	0231	3.0E	20 F		0229	2.2E
	1144	0904	2.3F		0716	0914	1.5F
	1842	1437	3.0E		1145	1431	2.2E
		2129	3.0F		1854	2134	2.1F
6 F	0029	0322	2.9E	21 SA	0025	0306	2.3E
	0742	0957	2.2F		0758	1001	1.5F
	1238	1528	2.8E		1226	1512	2.2E
	1939	2223	2.8F		1932	2219	2.0F
7 SA	0122	0414	2.8E	22 SU	0105	0346	2.3E
	0839	1052	2.1F		0842	1047	1.4F
	1334	1623	2.6E		1310	1555	2.2E
	2041	2316	2.6F		2015	2308	1.9F
8 SU	0216	0509	2.5E	23 M	0148	0431	2.2E
	0938	1147	2.0F		0927	1136	1.4F
	1432	1724	2.3E		1359	1646	2.1E
	2147				2106	2355	1.8F
9 M	0311	0013	2.3F	24 TU	0233	0518	2.2E
	1037	0609	2.3E		1013	1227	1.5F
	1534	1246	1.9F		1452	1737	2.1E
	2254	1829	2.1E		2207		
10 TU	0407	0111	2.0F	25 W		0047	1.7F
	1136	0715	2.2E		0322	0609	2.2E
	1637	1347	1.8F		1059	1318	1.6F
	2359	1946	1.9E		1551	1833	2.1E
					2312		
11 W	0503	0211	1.8F	26 TH	0413	0141	1.7F
	1231	0824	2.0E		1147	0702	2.3E
	1739	1446	1.8F		1652	1411	1.8F
		2107	1.9E			1932	2.1E
12 TH	0100	0311	1.7F	27 F	0015	0233	1.7F
	0558	0931	2.0E		0507	0758	2.4E
	1324	1544	1.9F		1234	1505	2.0F
	1837	2221	1.9E		1753	2033	2.2E
13 F	0157	0405	1.6F	28 SA	0115	0328	1.7F
	0650	1026	2.0E		0602	0853	2.5E
	1413	1635	2.0F		1322	1558	2.3F
	1930	2320	2.0E		1852	2137	2.4E
14 SA	0250	0457	1.6F	29 SU	0211	0424	1.9F
	0739	1107	2.0E		0658	0950	2.6E
	1459	1722	2.1F		1410	1651	2.6F
	2019	2359	2.0E		1950	2238	2.6E
15 SU	0338	0544	1.6F	30 M	0305	0517	2.0F
	0824	1143	2.0E		0752	1045	2.8E
	1542	1805	2.1F		1459	1743	2.9F
	2104				2044	2335	2.7E
				31 TU	0357	0610	2.1F
					0846	1140	2.9E
					1549	1834	3.0F
					2138		

JUNE

DAY	SLACK WATER TIME H.M.	MAXIMUM CURRENT TIME H.M.	VEL. KNOTS	DAY	SLACK WATER TIME H.M.	MAXIMUM CURRENT TIME H.M.	VEL. KNOTS
1 W		0032	2.9E	16 TH		0102	2.1E
	0448	0701	2.2F		0528	0723	1.5F
	0940	1234	3.0E		0958	1246	2.1E
	1640	1926	3.1F		1714	1943	2.2F
	2229				2242		
2 TH		0125	3.0E	17 F		0132	2.2E
	0540	0753	2.3F		0610	0806	1.5F
	1033	1329	3.0E		1040	1323	2.2E
	1733	2018	3.1F		1752	2026	2.2F
	2320				2321		
3 F		0217	3.0E	18 SA		0207	2.2E
	0631	0845	2.3F		0650	0850	1.5F
	1127	1422	2.9E		1121	1406	2.2E
	1827	2109	3.0F		1829	2109	2.2F
4 SA	0011	0308	2.9E	19 SU	0000	0242	2.3E
	0724	0938	2.2F		0730	0935	1.6F
	1222	1513	2.8E		1203	1447	2.3E
	1925	2201	2.8F		1907	2153	2.1F
5 SU	0102	0401	2.8E	20 M	0040	0323	2.4E
	0818	1030	2.2F		0809	1020	1.6F
	1317	1609	2.5E		1248	1533	2.3E
	2024	2255	2.5F		1948	2239	2.0F
6 M	0152	0452	2.6E	21 TU	0120	0404	2.4E
	0914	1124	2.1F		0848	1107	1.6F
	1414	1708	2.3E		1336	1622	2.3E
	2126	2350	2.2F		2036	2327	1.9F
7 TU	0244	0545	2.4E	22 W	0202	0451	2.4E
	1009	1222	2.0F		0929	1157	1.7F
	1513	1809	2.1E		1429	1713	2.2E
	2230				2133		
8 W		0045	1.9F	23 TH		0016	1.8F
	0335	0641	2.2E		0248	0539	2.5E
	1105	1318	1.9F		1013	1248	1.8F
	1612	1917	1.9E		1526	1806	2.2E
	2332				2238		
9 TH		0141	1.7F	24 F		0111	1.7F
	0428	0740	2.0E		0338	0632	2.5E
	1159	1414	1.9F		1102	1341	2.0F
	1711	2029	1.8E		1626	1905	2.2E
					2345		
10 F	0033	0237	1.5F	25 SA		0205	1.7F
	0520	0836	1.9E		0432	0725	2.5E
	1251	1511	1.9F		1155	1436	2.2F
	1807	2140	1.8E		1728	2007	2.2E
11 SA	0130	0331	1.4F	26 SU	0049	0300	1.7F
	0611	0927	1.9E		0529	0824	2.6E
	1341	1602	1.9F		1249	1530	2.4F
	1901	2241	1.8E		1829	2112	2.3E
12 SU	0224	0422	1.4F	27 M	0149	0357	1.7F
	0700	1016	1.9E		0628	0921	2.6E
	1428	1650	2.0F		1344	1626	2.6F
	1950	2329	1.8E		1928	2217	2.5E
13 M	0314	0511	1.4F	28 TU	0245	0451	1.9F
	0748	1056	1.9E		0727	1023	2.7E
	1513	1733	2.1F		1439	1722	2.8F
	2036	2358	1.9E		2025	2320	2.6E
14 TU	0401	0556	1.4F	29 W	0339	0546	2.0F
	0833	1133	2.0E		0825	1122	2.8E
	1555	1818	2.1F		1533	1815	3.0F
	2120				2119		
15 W		0033	2.0E	30 TH		0018	2.8E
	0445	0641	1.5F		0431	0641	2.1F
	0916	1207	2.0E		0921	1221	2.9E
	1636	1900	2.2F		1627	1907	3.0F
	2201				2211		

TIME MERIDIAN 75° W.   0000 IS MIDNIGHT.   1200 IS NOON.

TABLE 2.—CURRENT DIFFERENCES AND OTHER CONSTANTS

No.	PLACE	POSITION		TIME DIF-FERENCES		VELOCITY RATIOS		MAXIMUM CURRENTS			
								Flood		Ebb	
		Lat.	Long.	Slack water	Maximum current	Maximum flood	Maximum ebb	Direction (true)	Average velocity	Direction (true)	Average velocity
		° ′	° ′	h. m.	h. m.			deg.	knots	deg.	knots
	ST. JOHNS RIVER—Continued	N.	W.	on ST. JOHNS RIVER ENTRANCE, p.88							
	Time meridian, 75°W.										
5380	St. Johns Bluff------------------	30 23	81 30	+0 05	+0 50	0.8	1.0	245	1.6	060	2.2
5385	Drummond Point, channel south of------	30 25	81 36	+2 00	+2 30	0.7	0.7	230	1.3	060	1.6
5390	Phoenix Park----------------------	30 23	81 38	+2 40	+3 10	0.6	0.4	190	1.1	350	1.0
5395	Chaseville, channel near----------	30 23	81 37	+2 35	+3 20	0.6	0.7	150	1.1	335	1.6
5400	Quarantine Station, Long Branch-------	30 21	81 37	+2 30	+3 05	0.6	0.5	185	1.1	000	1.2
5405	Commodore Point, terminal channel-----	30 19	81 38	+2 35	+3 10	0.5	0.4	210	1.0	060	1.0
5410	Jacksonville, off Washington St-------	30 19	81 39	+2 20	+2 50	0.9	0.8	280	1.8	120	1.9
5415	Jacksonville, F. E. C. RR. bridge-----	30 19	81 40	+2 20	+3 00	0.8	0.7	240	1.6	060	1.7
5420	Winter Point---------------------	30 18	81 40	+2 55	+3 10	0.6	0.5	200	1.1	015	1.1
5425	Mandarin Point-------------------	30 09	81 41	+3 00	+3 20	0.3	0.3	180	0.6	015	0.7
5430	Red Bay Point, bridge draw--------	29 59	81 38	(1)	(1)	0.5	0.3	115	0.9	300	0.6
5435	Tocoi to Lake George-------------	-----	-----	*Current too weak and variable to be predicted.*							
	FLORIDA COAST			on MIAMI HARBOR ENTRANCE, p.94							
5440	Ft. Pierce Inlet-----------------	27 28	80 18	+0 50	+0 25	1.4	1.5	250	2.6	070	3.1
5445	Lake Worth Inlet (between jetties)----	26 46	80 02	-0 10	-0 15	1.3	1.7	275	2.4	095	3.6
5450	Fort Lauderdale, New River---------	26 07	80 07	-0 40	-0 40	0.4	0.2	005	0.8	130	0.5
	PORT EVERGLADES										
5455	Pier 2, 1.3 miles east of--------	26 06	80 06	-----	-----	----	----	(2)	0.2	(2)	0.4
5460	Entrance (between jetties)--------	26 06	80 06	-0 40	-0 55	0.3	0.3	275	0.6	095	0.7
5465	Entrance from southward (canal)-------	26 05	80 07	+0 20	-0 15	0.7	0.8	165	1.3	000	1.7
5470	Turning Basin--------------------	26 06	80 07	-1 15	-1 20	0.1	0.2	320	0.2	155	0.5
5475	Turning Basin, 300 yards north of-----	26 06	80 07	-0 40	-0 55	0.5	0.9	350	0.9	160	1.8
5480	17th Street Bridge---------------	26 06	80 07	-0 50	-1 05	1.0	0.9	350	1.9	170	1.9
	MIAMI HARBOR										
5485	Bakers Haulover Cut--------------	25 54	80 07	-0 10	-0 15	1.5	1.2	270	2.9	090	2.5
5490	North Jetty (east end)-----------	25 46	80 07	-0 40	-0 35	0.4	0.6	250	0.8	105	1.3
5495	Miami Outer Bay Cut entrance----------	25 46	80 06	See table 5.							
5500	MIAMI HARBOR ENT. (between jetties)---	25 46	80 08	Daily predictions				290	1.9	125	2.1
5503	Fowey Rocks Light, 1.5 miles SW. of---	25 35	80 07	*Current too weak and variable to be predicted.*							
	FLORIDA REEFS to MIDNIGHT PASS			on KEY WEST, p.100							
5505	Caesar Creek, Biscayne Bay--------	25 23	80 14	-0 05	-0 05	1.2	1.0	315	1.2	125	1.8
5510	Long Key, drawbridge east of------	24 50	80 46	+1 40	+1 30	1.1	0.7	000	1.1	200	1.2
5515	Long Key Viaduct-----------------	24 48	80 52	+1 50	+1 40	0.9	0.7	350	0.9	170	1.2
5520	Moser Channel, drawbridge---------	24 42	81 10	+1 30	+1 40	1.4	1.0	340	1.4	165	1.8
5525	Bahia Honda Harbor, bridge--------	24 39	81 17	+1 25	+0 50	1.4	1.2	005	1.4	180	2.1
5530	No Name Key, NE. of--------------	24 42	81 19	+1 10	+1 10	0.7	0.5	310	0.7	140	0.9
	Key West										
5535	Main Ship Channel entrance--------	24 28	81 48	-0 15	0 00	0.2	0.3	040	0.2	180	0.4
5540	Maine Ship Channel---------------	24 30	81 48	(3)	3+0 30	(3)	0.2	065	(3)	135	0.4
5545	KEY WEST, 0.3 mi. W. of Ft. Taylor---	24 33	81 49	Daily predictions				020	1.0	195	1.7
5550	0.6 mile N. of Ft. Taylor--------	24 34	81 49	+0 05	+0 15	0.6	0.7	040	0.6	200	1.2
5555	Turning Basin--------------------	24 34	81 48	+0 35	+0 55	0.8	0.6	050	0.8	215	1.1
5560	Northwest Channel----------------	24 35	81 51	-0 10	-0 05	1.2	0.8	355	1.2	160	1.4
5565	Northwest Channel----------------	24 37	81 53	-0 25	-0 20	0.6	0.4	345	0.6	170	0.6
5570	Boca Grande Channel--------------	24 34	82 04	-0 20	-0 25	1.1	0.7	355	1.1	195	1.2
5575	New Ground†----------------------	24 39	82 25	+1 30	+1 35	0.7	0.4	070	0.7	245	0.7

[1] Flood begins, +2h 35m; maximum flood, +3h 25m; ebb begins, +5h 00m; maximum ebb, +4h 00m.
[2] Flood usually occurs in a southerly direction and the ebb in a northeastwardly direction.
[3] Times of slack are indefinite. Flood is weak and variable. Time difference is for maximum ebb.
† Current tends to rotate clockwise. At times for slack flood begins there may be a weak current flowing northward while at times for slack ebb begins there may be a weak current flowing southeastward.

TABLE 3.—VELOCITY OF CURRENT AT ANY TIME

TABLE A

Interval between slack and maximum current

Interval between slack and desired time	h. m. 1 20	h. m. 1 40	h. m. 2 00	h. m. 2 20	h. m. 2 40	h. m. 3 00	h. m. 3 20	h. m. 3 40	h. m. 4 00	h. m. 4 20	h. m. 4 40	h. m. 5 00	h. m. 5 20	h. m. 5 40
h. m.	f.	f.	f.	f.	f.	f.	f.	f.	f.	f.	f.	f.	f.	f.
0 20	0.4	0.3	0.3	0.2	0.2	0.2	0.2	0.1	0.1	0.1	0.1	0.1	0.1	0.1
0 40	0.7	0.6	0.5	0.4	0.4	0.3	0.3	0.3	0.3	0.2	0.2	0.2	0.2	0.2
1 00	0.9	0.8	0.7	0.6	0.6	0.5	0.5	0.4	0.4	0.4	0.3	0.3	0.3	0.3
1 20	1.0	1.0	0.9	0.8	0.7	0.6	0.6	0.5	0.5	0.5	0.4	0.4	0.4	0.4
1 40	------	1.0	1.0	0.9	0.8	0.8	0.7	0.7	0.6	0.6	0.5	0.5	0.5	0.4
2 00	------	------	1.0	1.0	0.9	0.9	0.8	0.8	0.7	0.7	0.6	0.6	0.6	0.5
2 20	------	------	------	1.0	1.0	0.9	0.9	0.8	0.8	0.7	0.7	0.7	0.6	0.6
2 40	------	------	------	------	1.0	1.0	1.0	0.9	0.9	0.8	0.8	0.7	0.7	0.7
3 00	------	------	------	------	------	1.0	1.0	1.0	0.9	0.9	0.8	0.8	0.8	0.7
3 20	------	------	------	------	------	------	1.0	1.0	1.0	0.9	0.9	0.9	0.8	0.8
3 40	------	------	------	------	------	------	------	1.0	1.0	1.0	0.9	0.9	0.9	0.9
4 00	------	------	------	------	------	------	------	------	1.0	1.0	1.0	1.0	0.9	0.9
4 20	------	------	------	------	------	------	------	------	------	1.0	1.0	1.0	1.0	0.9
4 40	------	------	------	------	------	------	------	------	------	------	1.0	1.0	1.0	1.0
5 00	------	------	------	------	------	------	------	------	------	------	------	1.0	1.0	1.0
5 20	------	------	------	------	------	------	------	------	------	------	------	------	1.0	1.0
5 40	------	------	------	------	------	------	------	------	------	------	------	------	------	1.0

TABLE B

Interval between slack and maximum current

Interval between slack and desired time	h. m. 1 20	h. m. 1 40	h. m. 2 00	h. m. 2 20	h. m. 2 40	h. m. 3 00	h. m. 3 20	h. m. 3 40	h. m. 4 00	h. m. 4 20	h. m. 4 40	h. m. 5 00	h. m. 5 20	h. m. 5 40
h. m.	f.	f.	f.	f.	f.	f.	f.	f.	f.	f.	f.	f.	f.	f.
0 20	0.5	0.4	0.4	0.3	0.3	0.3	0.3	0.3	0.2	0.2	0.2	0.2	0.2	0.2
0 40	0.8	0.7	0.6	0.5	0.5	0.5	0.4	0.4	0.4	0.4	0.3	0.3	0.3	0.3
1 00	0.9	0.8	0.8	0.7	0.7	0.6	0.6	0.5	0.5	0.5	0.4	0.4	0.4	0.4
1 20	1.0	1.0	0.9	0.8	0.8	0.7	0.7	0.6	0.6	0.6	0.5	0.5	0.5	0.5
1 40	------	1.0	1.0	0.9	0.9	0.8	0.8	0.7	0.7	0.7	0.6	0.6	0.6	0.6
2 00	------	------	1.0	1.0	0.9	0.9	0.9	0.8	0.8	0.7	0.7	0.7	0.7	0.6
2 20	------	------	------	1.0	1.0	1.0	0.9	0.9	0.8	0.8	0.8	0.7	0.7	0.7
2 40	------	------	------	------	1.0	1.0	1.0	0.9	0.9	0.9	0.8	0.8	0.8	0.7
3 00	------	------	------	------	------	1.0	1.0	1.0	0.9	0.9	0.9	0.9	0.8	0.8
3 20	------	------	------	------	------	------	1.0	1.0	1.0	1.0	0.9	0.9	0.9	0.8
3 40	------	------	------	------	------	------	------	1.0	1.0	1.0	1.0	0.9	0.9	0.9
4 00	------	------	------	------	------	------	------	------	1.0	1.0	1.0	1.0	0.9	0.9
4 20	------	------	------	------	------	------	------	------	------	1.0	1.0	1.0	1.0	0.9
4 40	------	------	------	------	------	------	------	------	------	------	1.0	1.0	1.0	1.0
5 00	------	------	------	------	------	------	------	------	------	------	------	1.0	1.0	1.0
5 20	------	------	------	------	------	------	------	------	------	------	------	------	1.0	1.0
5 40	------	------	------	------	------	------	------	------	------	------	------	------	------	1.0

Use table A for all places except those listed below for table B.
Use table B for Cape Cod Canal, Hell Gate, Chesapeake and Delaware Canal and all stations in table 2 which are referred to them.

1. From predictions find the time of slack water and the time and velocity of maximum current (flood or ebb), one of which is immediately before and the other after the time for which the velocity is desired.
2. Find the interval of time between the above slack and maximum current, and enter the top of table A or B with the interval which most nearly agrees with this value.
3. Find the interval of time between the above slack and the time desired, and enter the side of table A or B with the interval which most nearly agrees with this value.
4. Find, in the table, the factor corresponding to the above two intervals, and multiply the maximum velocity by this factor. The result will be the approximate velocity at the time desired.

TABLE 4.—DURATION OF SLACK

The predicted times of slack water given in this publication indicate the instant of zero velocity, which is only momentary. There is a period each side of slack water, however, during which the current is so weak that for practical purposes it may be considered as negligible.

The following tables give, for various maximum currents, the approximate period of time during which weak currents not exceeding 0.1 to 0.5 knot will be encountered. This duration includes the last of the flood or ebb and the beginning of the following ebb or flood, that is, half of the duration will be before and half after the time of slack water.

Table A should be used for all places *except* those listed below for table B.

Table B should be used for **Cape Cod Canal, Hell Gate, Chesapeake and Delaware Canal,** and all stations in table 2 which are referred to them.

Duration of weak current near time of slack water

TABLE A

Maximum current	Period with a velocity not more than—				
	0.1 knot	0.2 knot	0.3 knot	0.4 knot	0.5 knot
Knots	*Minutes*	*Minutes*	*Minutes*	*Minutes*	*Minutes*
1.0	23	46	70	94	120
1.5	15	31	46	62	78
2.0	11	23	35	46	58
3.0	8	15	23	31	38
4.0	6	11	17	23	29
5.0	5	9	14	18	23
6.0	4	8	11	15	19
7.0	3	7	10	13	16
8.0	3	6	9	11	14
9.0	3	5	8	10	13
10.0	2	5	7	9	11

TABLE B

Maximum current	Period with a velocity not more than—				
	0.1 knot	0.2 knot	0.3 knot	0.4 knot	0.5 knot
Knots	*Minutes*	*Minutes*	*Minutes*	*Minutes*	*Minutes*
1.0	13	28	46	66	89
1.5	8	18	28	39	52
2.0	6	13	20	28	36
3.0	4	8	13	18	22
4.0	3	6	9	13	17
5.0	3	5	8	10	13

When there is a difference between the velocities of the maximum flood and ebb preceding and following the slack for which the duration is desired, it will be sufficiently accurate for practical purposes to find a separate duration for each maximum velocity and take the average of the two as the duration of the weak current.

ALTITUDE CORRECTION TABLES 10°–90°—SUN, STARS, PLANETS

OCT.—MAR. **SUN** APR.—SEPT.						STARS AND PLANETS		DIP					
App. Alt.	Lower Limb	Upper Limb	App. Alt.	Lower Limb	Upper Limb	App. Alt.	Corrⁿ	App. Alt.	Additional Corrⁿ	Ht. of Eye	Corrⁿ	Ht. of Eye	Ht. of Eye Corrⁿ

OCT.—MAR. SUN	APR.—SEPT. SUN	STARS AND PLANETS	STARS AND PLANETS additional	DIP (m)	DIP (ft)	DIP (m extra)
9 34 +10·8 −21·5	9 39 +10·6 −21·2	9 56 −5·3	**1977**	2·4 −2·8	8·0	1·0 − 1·8
9 45 +10·9 −21·4	9 51 +10·7 −21·1	10 08 −5·2	**VENUS**	2·6 −2·9	8·6	1·5 − 2·2
9 56 +11·0 −21·3	10 03 +10·8 −21·0	10 20 −5·1	Jan. 1–Jan. 29	2·8 −3·0	9·2	2·0 − 2·5
10 08 +11·1 −21·2	10 15 +10·9 −20·9	10 33 −5·0	47 + 0·2	3·0 −3·1	9·8	2·5 − 2·8
10 21 +11·2 −21·1	10 27 +11·0 −20·8	10 46 −4·9		3·2 −3·2	10·5	3·0 − 3·0
10 34 +11·3 −21·0	10 40 +11·1 −20·7	11 00 −4·8	Jan. 30–Feb. 26	3·4 −3·3	11·2	See table
10 47 +11·4 −20·9	10 54 +11·2 −20·6	11 14 −4·7	46 + 0·3	3·6 −3·4	11·9	←
11 01 +11·5 −20·8	11 08 +11·3 −20·5	11 29 −4·6		3·8 −3·5	12·6	
11 15 +11·6 −20·7	11 23 +11·4 −20·4	11 45 −4·5	Feb. 27–Mar. 14	4·0 −3·6	13·3	m
11 30 +11·7 −20·6	11 38 +11·5 −20·3	12 01 −4·4	11 + 0·4	4·3 −3·7	14·1	20 − 7·9
11 46 +11·8 −20·5	11 54 +11·6 −20·2	12 18 −4·3	41 + 0·5	4·5 −3·8	14·9	22 − 8·3
12 02 +11·9 −20·4	12 10 +11·7 −20·1	12 35 −4·2		4·7 −3·9	15·7	24 − 8·6
12 19 +12·0 −20·3	12 28 +11·8 −20·0	12 54 −4·1	Mar. 15–Mar. 23	5·0 −4·0	16·5	26 − 9·0
12 37 +12·1 −20·2	12 46 +11·9 −19·9	13 13 −4·0	6 + 0·5	5·2 −4·1	17·4	28 − 9·3
12 55 +12·2 −20·1	13 05 +12·0 −19·8	13 33 −3·9	20 + 0·6	5·5 −4·2	18·3	
13 14 +12·3 −20·0	13 24 +12·1 −19·7	13 54 −3·8	31 + 0·7	5·8 −4·3	19·1	30 − 9·6
13 35 +12·4 −19·9	13 45 +12·2 −19·6	14 16 −3·7		6·1 −4·4	20·1	32 −10·0
13 56 +12·5 −19·8	14 07 +12·3 −19·5	14 40 −3·6	Mar. 24–Apr. 19	6·3 −4·5	21·0	34 −10·3
14 18 +12·6 −19·7	14 30 +12·4 −19·4	15 04 −3·5	4 + 0·6	6·6 −4·6	22·0	36 −10·6
14 42 +12·7 −19·6	14 54 +12·5 −19·3	15 30 −3·4	12 + 0·7	6·9 −4·7	22·9	38 −10·8
15 06 +12·8 −19·5	15 19 +12·6 −19·2	15 57 −3·3	22 + 0·8	7·2 −4·8	23·9	
15 32 +12·9 −19·4	15 46 +12·7 −19·1	16 26 −3·2		7·5 −4·9	24·9	40 −11·1
15 59 +13·0 −19·3	16 14 +12·8 −19·0	16 56 −3·1	Apr. 20–Apr. 28	7·9 −5·0	26·0	42 −11·4
16 28 +13·1 −19·2	16 44 +12·9 −18·9	17 28 −3·0	6 + 0·5	8·2 −5·1	27·1	44 −11·7
16 59 +13·2 −19·1	17 15 +13·0 −18·8	18 02 −2·9	20 + 0·6	8·5 −5·2	28·1	46 −11·9
17 32 +13·3 −19·0	17 48 +13·1 −18·7	18 38 −2·8	31 + 0·7	8·8 −5·3	29·2	48 −12·2
18 06 +13·4 −18·9	18 24 +13·2 −18·6	19 17 −2·7		9·2 −5·4	30·4	ft.
18 42 +13·5 −18·8	19 01 +13·3 −18·5	19 58 −2·6	Apr. 29–May 13	9·5 −5·5	31·5	2 − 1·4
19 21 +13·6 −18·7	19 42 +13·4 −18·4	20 42 −2·5	11 + 0·4	9·9 −5·6	32·7	4 − 1·9
20 03 +13·7 −18·6	20 25 +13·5 −18·3	21 28 −2·4	41 + 0·5	10·3 −5·7	33·9	6 − 2·4
20 48 +13·8 −18·5	21 11 +13·6 −18·2	22 19 −2·3		10·6 −5·8	35·1	8 − 2·7
21 35 +13·9 −18·4	22 00 +13·7 −18·1	23 13 −2·2	May 14–June 8	11·0 −5·9	36·3	10 − 3·1
22 26 +14·0 −18·3	22 54 +13·8 −18·0	24 11 −2·1	46 + 0·3	11·4 −6·0	37·6	See table
23 22 +14·1 −18·2	23 51 +13·9 −17·9	25 14 −2·0		11·8 −6·1	38·9	←
24 21 +14·2 −18·1	24 53 +14·0 −17·8	26 22 −1·9	June 9–July 23	12·2 −6·2	40·1	ft.
25 26 +14·3 −18·0	26 00 +14·1 −17·7	27 36 −1·8	47 + 0·2	12·6 −6·3	41·5	70 − 8·1
26 36 +14·4 −17·9	27 13 +14·2 −17·6	28 56 −1·7		13·0 −6·4	42·8	75 − 8·4
27 52 +14·5 −17·8	28 33 +14·3 −17·5	30 24 −1·6	July 24–Dec. 31	13·4 −6·5	44·2	80 − 8·7
29 15 +14·6 −17·7	30 00 +14·4 −17·4	32 00 −1·5	42 + 0·1	13·8 −6·6	45·5	85 − 8·9
30 46 +14·7 −17·6	31 35 +14·5 −17·3	33 45 −1·4		14·2 −6·7	46·9	90 − 9·2
32 26 +14·8 −17·5	33 20 +14·6 −17·2	35 40 −1·3	**MARS**	14·7 −6·8	48·4	95 − 9·5
34 17 +14·9 −17·4	35 17 +14·7 −17·1	37 48 −1·2	Jan. 1–Nov. 12	15·1 −6·9	49·8	
36 20 +15·0 −17·3	37 26 +14·8 −17·0	40 08 −1·1	60 + 0·1	15·5 −7·0	51·3	100 − 9·7
38 36 +15·1 −17·2	39 50 +14·9 −16·9	42 44 −1·0		16·0 −7·1	52·8	105 − 9·9
41 08 +15·2 −17·1	42 31 +15·0 −16·8	45 36 −0·9	Nov. 13–Dec. 31	16·5 −7·2	54·3	110 −10·2
43 59 +15·3 −17·0	45 31 +15·1 −16·7	48 47 −0·8	41 + 0·2	16·9 −7·3	55·8	115 −10·4
47 10 +15·4 −16·9	48 55 +15·2 −16·6	52 18 −0·7	75 + 0·1	17·4 −7·4	57·4	120 −10·6
50 46 +15·5 −16·8	52 44 +15·3 −16·5	56 11 −0·6		17·9 −7·5	58·9	125 −10·8
54 49 +15·6 −16·7	57 02 +15·4 −16·4	60 28 −0·5		18·4 −7·6	60·5	
59 23 +15·7 −16·6	61 51 +15·5 −16·3	65 08 −0·4		18·8 −7·7	62·1	130 −11·1
64 30 +15·8 −16·5	67 17 +15·6 −16·2	70 11 −0·3		19·3 −7·8	63·8	135 −11·3
70 12 +15·9 −16·4	73 16 +15·7 −16·1	75 34 −0·2		19·8 −7·9	65·4	140 −11·5
76 26 +16·0 −16·3	79 43 +15·8 −16·0	81 13 −0·1		20·4 −8·0	67·1	145 −11·7
83 05 +16·1 −16·2	86 32 +15·9 −15·9	87 03 0·0		20·9 −8·1	68·8	150 −11·9
90 00	90 00	90 00		21·4	70·5	155 −12·1

App. Alt. = Apparent altitude = Sextant altitude corrected for index error and dip.
For daylight observations of Venus, see page 260.

Temperature

−20°F. −10° 0° +10° 20° 30° 40° 50° 60° 70° 80° 90° 100°F.

−30°C. −20° −10° 0° +10° 20° 30° 40°C.

Pressure in millibars: 1050, 1030, 1010, 990, 970

Pressure in inches: 31·0, 30·5, 30·0, 29·5, 29·0

Zone letters (left to right): A B C D E F G H J K L M N

App. Alt.	A	B	C	D	E	F	G	H	J	K	L	M	N	App. Alt.
0 00	−6·9	−5·7	−4·6	−3·4	−2·3	−1·1	0·0	+1·1	+2·3	+3·4	+4·6	+5·7	+6·9	0 00
0 30	5·2	4·4	3·5	2·6	1·7	0·9	0·0	0·9	1·7	2·6	3·5	4·4	5·2	0 30
1 00	4·3	3·5	2·8	2·1	1·4	0·7	0·0	0·7	1·4	2·1	2·8	3·5	4·3	1 00
1 30	3·5	2·9	2·4	1·8	1·2	0·6	0·0	0·6	1·2	1·8	2·4	2·9	3·5	1 30
2 00	3·0	2·5	2·0	1·5	1·0	0·5	0·0	0·5	1·0	1·5	2·0	2·5	3·0	2 00
2 30	−2·5	−2·1	−1·6	−1·2	−0·8	−0·4	0·0	+0·4	+0·8	+1·2	+1·6	+2·1	+2·5	2 30
3 00	2·2	1·8	1·5	1·1	0·7	0·4	0·0	0·4	0·7	1·1	1·5	1·8	2·2	3 00
3 30	2·0	1·6	1·3	1·0	0·7	0·3	0·0	0·3	0·7	1·0	1·3	1·6	2·0	3 30
4 00	1·8	1·5	1·2	0·9	0·6	0·3	0·0	0·3	0·6	0·9	1·2	1·5	1·8	4 00
4 30	1·6	1·4	1·1	0·8	0·5	0·3	0·0	0·3	0·5	0·8	1·1	1·4	1·6	4 30
5 00	−1·5	−1·3	−1·0	−0·8	−0·5	−0·2	0·0	+0·2	+0·5	+0·8	+1·0	+1·3	+1·5	5 00
6	1·3	1·1	0·9	0·6	0·4	0·2	0·0	0·2	0·4	0·6	0·9	1·1	1·3	6
7	1·1	0·9	0·7	0·6	0·4	0·2	0·0	0·2	0·4	0·6	0·7	0·9	1·1	7
8	1·0	0·8	0·7	0·5	0·3	0·2	0·0	0·2	0·3	0·5	0·7	0·8	1·0	8
9	0·9	0·7	0·6	0·4	0·3	0·1	0·0	0·1	0·3	0·4	0·6	0·7	0·9	9
10 00	−0·8	−0·7	−0·5	−0·4	−0·3	−0·1	0·0	+0·1	+0·3	+0·4	+0·5	+0·7	+0·8	10 00
12	0·7	0·6	0·5	0·3	0·2	0·1	0·0	0·1	0·2	0·3	0·5	0·6	0·7	12
14	0·6	0·5	0·4	0·3	0·2	0·1	0·0	0·1	0·2	0·3	0·4	0·5	0·6	14
16	0·5	0·4	0·3	0·3	0·2	0·1	0·0	0·1	0·2	0·3	0·3	0·4	0·5	16
18	0·4	0·4	0·3	0·2	0·2	0·1	0·0	0·1	0·2	0·2	0·3	0·4	0·4	18
20 00	−0·4	−0·3	−0·3	−0·2	−0·1	−0·1	0·0	+0·1	+0·1	+0·2	+0·3	+0·3	+0·4	20 00
25	0·3	0·3	0·2	0·2	0·1	−0·1	0·0	+0·1	0·1	0·2	0·2	0·3	0·3	25
30	0·3	0·2	0·2	0·1	0·1	0·0	0·0	0·0	0·1	0·1	0·2	0·2	0·3	30
35	0·2	0·2	0·1	0·1	0·1	0·0	0·0	0·0	0·1	0·1	0·1	0·2	0·2	35
40	0·2	0·1	0·1	0·1	−0·1	0·0	0·0	0·0	+0·1	0·1	0·1	0·1	0·2	40
50 00	−0·1	−0·1	−0·1	−0·1	0·0	0·0	0·0	0·0	0·0	+0·1	+0·1	+0·1	+0·1	50 00

The graph is entered with arguments temperature and pressure to find a zone letter; using as arguments this zone letter and apparent altitude (sextant altitude corrected for dip), a correction is taken from the table. This correction is to be applied to the sextant altitude in addition to the corrections for standard conditions (for the Sun, stars and planets from page A2 and for the Moon from pages xxxiv and xxxv).

1977 JUNE 3, 4, 5 (FRI., SAT., SUN.)

G.M.T.	ARIES G.H.A.	VENUS −4.1 G.H.A.	Dec.	MARS +1.3 G.H.A.	Dec.	JUPITER −1.5 G.H.A.	Dec.	SATURN +0.6 G.H.A.	Dec.	STARS Name	S.H.A.	Dec.
3 00	251 20.1	225 19.6 N 8	27.0	225 15.5 N 9	38.9	179 21.4 N21	54.8	116 16.2 N18	02.6	Acamar	315 39.3	S40 23.7
01	266 22.6	240 20.0	27.6	240 16.2	39.6	194 23.2	54.9	131 18.4	02.5	Achernar	335 47.4	S57 20.9
02	281 25.1	255 20.4	28.3	255 16.9	40.3	209 25.0	55.0	146 20.7	02.5	Acrux	173 39.3	S62 58.8
03	296 27.5	270 20.8 ··	28.9	270 17.6 ··	41.0	224 26.9 ··	55.1	161 22.9 ··	02.4	Adhara	255 34.2	S28 56.7
04	311 30.0	285 21.2	29.5	285 18.3	41.6	239 28.7	55.1	176 25.2	02.3	Aldebaran	291 20.9	N16 27.7
05	326 32.4	300 21.6	30.1	300 19.0	42.3	254 30.6	55.2	191 27.4	02.3			
06	341 34.9	315 22.0 N 8	30.7	315 19.7 N 9	43.0	269 32.4 N21	55.3	206 29.7 N18	02.2	Alioth	166 44.3	N56 05.1
07	356 37.4	330 22.4	31.3	330 20.4	43.7	284 34.2	55.4	221 31.9	02.2	Alkaid	153 20.0	N49 25.7
08	11 39.8	345 22.8	31.9	345 21.1	44.4	299 36.1	55.4	236 34.2	02.1	Al Na'ir	28 17.7	S47 03.9
F 09	26 42.3	0 23.2 ··	32.5	0 21.8 ··	45.1	314 37.9 ··	55.5	251 36.4 ··	02.0	Alnilam	276 14.2	S 1 13.1
R 10	41 44.8	15 23.6	33.1	15 22.5	45.7	329 39.8	55.6	266 38.7	02.0	Alphard	218 22.9	S 8 33.8
I 11	56 47.2	30 24.0	33.7	30 23.2	46.4	344 41.6	55.7	281 40.9	01.9			
D 12	71 49.7	45 24.3 N 8	34.3	45 23.9 N 9	47.1	359 43.5 N21	55.7	296 43.2 N18	01.9	Alphecca	126 33.7	N26 47.5
A 13	86 52.2	60 24.7	34.9	60 24.6	47.8	14 45.3	55.8	311 45.4	01.8	Alpheratz	358 11.7	N28 57.8
Y 14	101 54.6	75 25.1	35.5	75 25.3	48.5	29 47.1	55.9	326 47.7	01.7	Altair	62 34.4	N 8 48.5
15	116 57.1	90 25.5 ··	36.1	90 26.0 ··	49.1	44 49.0 ··	56.0	341 49.9 ··	01.7	Ankaa	353 42.7	S42 25.5
16	131 59.6	105 25.9	36.7	105 26.7	49.8	59 50.8	56.0	356 52.2	01.6	Antares	112 59.2	S26 22.9
17	147 02.0	120 26.3	37.4	120 27.4	50.5	74 52.7	56.1	11 54.4	01.6			
18	162 04.5	135 26.6 N 8	38.0	135 28.1 N 9	51.2	89 54.5 N21	56.2	26 56.7 N18	01.5	Arcturus	146 20.2	N19 18.1
19	177 06.9	150 27.0	38.6	150 28.8	51.9	104 56.4	56.3	41 58.9	01.4	Atria	108 24.8	S68 59.2
20	192 09.4	165 27.4	39.2	165 29.5	52.5	119 58.2	56.3	57 01.2	01.4	Avior	234 29.5	S59 26.6
21	207 11.9	180 27.8 ··	39.8	180 30.2 ··	53.2	135 00.0 ··	56.4	72 03.4 ··	01.3	Bellatrix	279 01.5	N 6 19.6
22	222 14.3	195 28.1	40.4	195 30.9	53.9	150 01.9	56.5	87 05.7	01.3	Betelgeuse	271 31.0	N 7 24.1
23	237 16.8	210 28.5	41.0	210 31.6	54.6	165 03.7	56.5	102 07.9	01.2			
4 00	252 19.3	225 28.9 N 8	41.6	225 32.3 N 9	55.3	180 05.6 N21	56.6	117 10.2 N18	01.1	Canopus	264 08.7	S52 41.2
01	267 21.7	240 29.3	42.3	240 33.0	55.9	195 07.4	56.7	132 12.4	01.1	Capella	281 15.0	N45 58.4
02	282 24.2	255 29.6	42.9	255 33.7	56.6	210 09.3	56.8	147 14.7	01.0	Deneb	49 49.7	N45 11.9
03	297 26.7	270 30.0 ··	43.5	270 34.4 ··	57.3	225 11.1 ··	56.8	162 16.9 ··	01.0	Denebola	183 01.3	N14 41.9
04	312 29.1	285 30.4	44.1	285 35.1	58.0	240 12.9	56.9	177 19.2	00.9	Diphda	349 23.3	S18 06.6
05	327 31.6	300 30.8	44.7	300 35.8	58.6	255 14.8	57.0	192 21.4	00.8			
06	342 34.0	315 31.1 N 8	45.3	315 36.5 N 9	59.3	270 16.6 N21	57.1	207 23.7 N18	00.8	Dubhe	194 25.0	N61 52.6
07	357 36.5	330 31.5	45.9	330 37.2	10 00.0	285 18.5	57.1	222 25.9	00.7	Elnath	278 47.3	N28 35.2
S 08	12 39.0	345 31.9	46.6	345 37.9	00.7	300 20.3	57.2	237 28.2	00.7	Eltanin	90 58.2	N51 29.5
A 09	27 41.4	0 32.2 ··	47.2	0 38.6 ··	01.4	315 22.1 ··	57.3	252 30.4 ··	00.6	Enif	34 13.6	N 9 46.3
T 10	42 43.9	15 32.6	47.8	15 39.3	02.0	330 24.0	57.4	267 32.7	00.5	Fomalhaut	15 53.9	S29 44.3
U 11	57 46.4	30 32.9	48.4	30 39.9	02.7	345 25.8	57.4	282 34.9	00.5			
R 12	72 48.8	45 33.3 N 8	49.0	45 40.6 N10	03.4	0 27.7 N21	57.5	297 37.2 N18	00.4	Gacrux	172 30.9	S56 59.5
D 13	87 51.3	60 33.7	49.7	60 41.3	04.1	15 29.5	57.6	312 39.4	00.4	Gienah	176 20.1	S17 25.2
A 14	102 53.8	75 34.0	50.3	75 42.0	04.7	30 31.4	57.7	327 41.7	00.3	Hadar	149 25.9	S60 16.1
Y 15	117 56.2	90 34.4 ··	50.9	90 42.7 ··	05.4	45 33.2 ··	57.7	342 43.9 ··	00.2	Hamal	328 31.7	N23 21.2
16	132 58.7	105 34.7	51.5	105 43.4	06.1	60 35.0	57.8	357 46.1	00.2	Kaus Aust.	84 19.4	S34 23.6
17	148 01.2	120 35.1	52.1	120 44.1	06.8	75 36.9	57.9	12 48.4	00.1			
18	163 03.6	135 35.5 N 8	52.8	135 44.8 N10	07.4	90 38.7 N21	58.0	27 50.6 N18	00.0	Kochab	137 18.0	N74 15.1
19	178 06.1	150 35.8	53.4	150 45.5	08.1	105 40.6	58.0	42 52.9 18	00.0	Markab	14 05.4	N15 05.0
20	193 08.5	165 36.2	54.0	165 46.2	08.8	120 42.4	58.1	57 55.1 17	59.9	Menkar	314 43.7	N 4 00.0
21	208 11.0	180 36.5 ··	54.6	180 46.9 ··	09.5	135 44.3 ··	58.2	72 57.4 ··	59.9	Menkent	148 39.3	S36 15.7
22	223 13.5	195 36.9	55.3	195 47.6	10.1	150 46.1	58.2	87 59.6	59.8	Miaplacidus	221 45.7	S69 37.9
23	238 15.9	210 37.2	55.9	210 48.3	10.8	165 47.9	58.3	103 01.9	59.7			
5 00	253 18.4	225 37.6 N 8	56.5	225 49.0 N10	11.5	180 49.8 N21	58.4	118 04.1 N17	59.7	Mirfak	309 19.7	N49 46.7
01	268 20.9	240 37.9	57.1	240 49.7	12.2	195 51.6	58.5	133 06.4	59.6	Nunki	76 31.6	S26 19.4
02	283 23.3	255 38.3	57.8	255 50.4	12.8	210 53.5	58.5	148 08.6	59.6	Peacock	54 01.6	S56 48.2
03	298 25.8	270 38.6 ··	58.4	270 51.1 ··	13.5	225 55.3 ··	58.6	163 10.9 ··	59.5	Pollux	244 01.2	N28 04.8
04	313 28.3	285 39.0	59.0	285 51.8	14.2	240 57.1	58.7	178 13.1	59.4	Procyon	245 28.4	N 5 16.9
05	328 30.7	300 39.3 8	59.6	300 52.5	14.9	255 59.0	58.8	193 15.3	59.4			
06	343 33.2	315 39.6 N 9	00.3	315 53.2 N10	15.5	271 00.8 N21	58.8	208 17.6 N17	59.3	Rasalhague	96 31.3	N12 34.6
07	358 35.7	330 40.0	00.9	330 53.9	16.2	286 02.7	58.9	223 19.8	59.2	Regulus	208 12.5	N12 04.6
08	13 38.1	345 40.3	01.5	345 54.6	16.9	301 04.5	59.0	238 22.1	59.2	Rigel	281 38.5	S 8 13.8
S 09	28 40.6	0 40.7 ··	02.1	0 55.3 ··	17.5	316 06.4 ··	59.1	253 24.3 ··	59.1	Rigil Kent.	140 28.2	S60 44.6
U 10	43 43.0	15 41.0	02.8	15 56.0	18.2	331 08.2	59.1	268 26.6	59.1	Sabik	102 43.3	S15 41.8
N 11	58 45.5	30 41.4	03.4	30 56.7	18.9	346 10.0	59.2	283 28.8	59.0			
D 12	73 48.0	45 41.7 N 9	04.0	45 57.4 N10	19.6	1 11.9 N21	59.3	298 31.1 N17	58.9	Schedar	350 11.7	N56 24.6
A 13	88 50.4	60 42.0	04.7	60 58.1	20.2	16 13.7	59.3	313 33.3	58.9	Shaula	96 58.3	S37 05.2
Y 14	103 52.9	75 42.4	05.3	75 58.8	20.9	31 15.6	59.4	328 35.6	58.8	Sirius	258 58.0	S16 41.3
15	118 55.4	90 42.7 ··	05.9	90 59.5 ··	21.6	46 17.4 ··	59.5	343 37.8 ··	58.8	Spica	158 59.7	S11 02.7
16	133 57.8	105 43.0	06.6	106 00.2	22.2	61 19.2	59.6	358 40.0	58.7	Suhail	223 12.6	S43 20.8
17	149 00.3	120 43.4	07.2	121 00.9	22.9	76 21.1	59.6	13 42.3	58.6			
18	164 02.8	135 43.7 N 9	07.8	136 01.6 N10	23.6	91 22.9 N21	59.7	28 44.5 N17	58.6	Vega	80 56.9	N38 45.8
19	179 05.2	150 44.0	08.5	151 02.3	24.3	106 24.8	59.8	43 46.8	58.5	Zuben'ubi	137 35.2	S15 56.9
20	194 07.7	165 44.4	09.1	166 03.0	24.9	121 26.6	59.9	58 49.0	58.4		S.H.A.	Mer. Pass.
21	209 10.1	180 44.7 ··	09.7	181 03.7 ··	25.6	136 28.5 21	59.9	73 51.3 ··	58.4		° ′	h m
22	224 12.6	195 45.0	10.4	196 04.4	26.3	151 30.3 22	00.0	88 53.5	58.3	Venus	333 09.6	8 58
23	239 15.1	210 45.3	11.0	211 05.1	26.9	166 32.1	00.1	103 55.7	58.3	Mars	333 13.0	8 57
Mer. Pass.	7 09.5	v 0.4 d 0.6		v 0.7 d 0.7		v 1.8 d 0.1		v 2.2 d 0.1		Jupiter	287 46.3	11 58
										Saturn	224 50.9	16 09

SUN / MOON

G.M.T.	SUN G.H.A.	SUN Dec.	MOON G.H.A.	v	MOON Dec.	d	H.P.
3 00	180 30.4	N22 16.2	342 44.5	3.6	S18 46.2	1.2	61.1
01	195 30.3	16.5	357 07.1	3.6	18 45.0	1.2	61.1
02	210 30.2	16.8	11 29.7	3.7	18 43.8	1.4	61.1
03	225 30.1 ··	17.1	25 52.4	3.7	18 42.4	1.5	61.0
04	240 30.0	17.4	40 15.1	3.7	18 40.9	1.7	61.0
05	255 29.9	17.7	54 37.8	3.8	18 39.2	1.8	61.0
06	270 29.8	N22 18.1	69 00.6	3.8	S18 37.4	1.9	61.0
07	285 29.7	18.4	83 23.4	3.9	18 35.5	2.1	61.0
08	300 29.6	18.7	97 46.3	3.9	18 33.4	2.2	60.9
F 09	315 29.5 ··	19.0	112 09.2	3.9	18 31.2	2.3	60.9
R 10	330 29.4	19.3	126 32.1	4.1	18 28.9	2.5	60.9
I 11	345 29.3	19.6	140 55.2	4.0	18 26.4	2.6	60.9
D 12	0 29.2	N22 19.9	155 18.2	4.1	S18 23.8	2.7	60.8
A 13	15 29.1	20.2	169 41.3	4.2	18 21.1	2.9	60.8
Y 14	30 29.0	20.5	184 04.5	4.3	18 18.2	3.0	60.8
15	45 28.9 ··	20.8	198 27.7	4.3	18 15.2	3.1	60.8
16	60 28.8	21.1	212 51.0	4.4	18 12.1	3.3	60.7
17	75 28.7	21.4	227 14.4	4.4	18 08.8	3.4	60.7
18	90 28.6	N22 21.7	241 37.8	4.5	S18 05.4	3.5	60.7
19	105 28.5	22.0	256 01.3	4.5	18 01.9	3.7	60.7
20	120 28.4	22.3	270 24.8	4.6	17 58.2	3.7	60.6
21	135 28.3 ··	22.6	284 48.4	4.7	17 54.5	3.9	60.6
22	150 28.2	22.9	299 12.1	4.7	17 50.6	4.0	60.6
23	165 28.1	23.2	313 35.8	4.8	17 46.6	4.2	60.5
4 00	180 28.0	N22 23.5	327 59.6	4.9	S17 42.4	4.2	60.5
01	195 27.9	23.8	342 23.5	4.9	17 38.2	4.4	60.5
02	210 27.8	24.1	356 47.4	5.1	17 33.8	4.5	60.5
03	225 27.7 ··	24.4	11 11.5	5.1	17 29.3	4.6	60.4
04	240 27.6	24.7	25 35.6	5.1	17 24.7	4.8	60.4
05	255 27.5	25.0	39 59.7	5.3	17 19.9	4.8	60.4
06	270 27.4	N22 25.3	54 24.0	5.3	S17 15.1	5.0	60.3
07	285 27.3	25.6	68 48.3	5.4	17 10.1	5.0	60.3
S 08	300 27.1	25.9	83 12.7	5.4	17 05.1	5.2	60.3
A 09	315 27.0 ··	26.1	97 37.1	5.6	16 59.9	5.3	60.2
T 10	330 26.9	26.4	112 01.7	5.6	16 54.6	5.4	60.2
U 11	345 26.8	26.7	126 26.3	5.7	16 49.2	5.6	60.2
R 12	0 26.7	N22 27.0	140 51.0	5.8	S16 43.6	5.6	60.1
D 13	15 26.6	27.3	155 15.8	5.9	16 38.0	5.7	60.1
A 14	30 26.5	27.6	169 40.7	6.0	16 32.3	5.8	60.1
Y 15	45 26.4 ··	27.9	184 05.7	6.0	16 26.5	6.0	60.0
16	60 26.3	28.2	198 30.7	6.1	16 20.5	6.0	60.0
17	75 26.2	28.4	212 55.8	6.2	16 14.5	6.2	60.0
18	90 26.1	N22 28.7	227 21.0	6.3	S16 08.3	6.2	59.9
19	105 26.0	29.0	241 46.3	6.4	16 02.1	6.3	59.9
20	120 25.9	29.3	256 11.7	6.5	15 55.8	6.5	59.9
21	135 25.8 ··	29.6	270 37.2	6.5	15 49.3	6.5	59.8
22	150 25.7	29.9	285 02.7	6.7	15 42.8	6.6	59.8
23	165 25.5	30.1	299 28.4	6.7	15 36.2	6.8	59.7
5 00	180 25.4	N22 30.4	313 54.1	6.8	S15 29.4	6.8	59.7
01	195 25.3	30.7	328 19.9	6.9	15 22.6	6.9	59.7
02	210 25.2	31.0	342 45.8	7.0	15 15.7	7.0	59.6
03	225 25.1 ··	31.3	357 11.8	7.1	15 08.7	7.0	59.6
04	240 25.0	31.5	11 37.9	7.2	15 01.7	7.2	59.6
05	255 24.9	31.8	26 04.1	7.2	14 54.5	7.3	59.5
06	270 24.8	N22 32.1	40 30.3	7.4	S14 47.2	7.3	59.5
07	285 24.7	32.4	54 56.7	7.4	14 39.9	7.4	59.5
08	300 24.6	32.6	69 23.1	7.5	14 32.5	7.5	59.4
S 09	315 24.5 ··	32.9	83 49.6	7.6	14 25.0	7.6	59.4
U 10	330 24.4	33.2	98 16.2	7.7	14 17.4	7.6	59.3
N 11	345 24.2	33.5	112 42.9	7.8	14 09.8	7.8	59.3
D 12	0 24.1	N22 33.7	127 09.7	7.9	S14 02.0	7.8	59.3
A 13	15 24.0	34.0	141 36.6	8.0	13 54.2	7.9	59.2
Y 14	30 23.9	34.3	156 03.6	8.0	13 46.3	7.9	59.2
15	45 23.8 ··	34.5	170 30.6	8.2	13 38.4	8.0	59.1
16	60 23.7	34.8	184 57.8	8.2	13 30.4	8.2	59.1
17	75 23.6	35.1	199 25.0	8.3	13 22.2	8.1	59.1
18	90 23.5	N22 35.4	213 52.3	8.4	S13 14.1	8.3	59.0
19	105 23.4	35.6	228 19.7	8.5	13 05.8	8.3	59.0
20	120 23.3	35.9	242 47.2	8.6	12 57.5	8.3	58.9
21	135 23.1 ··	36.2	257 14.8	8.7	12 49.2	8.5	58.9
22	150 23.0	36.4	271 42.5	8.8	12 40.7	8.5	58.9
23	165 22.9	36.7	286 10.3	8.8	12 32.2	8.5	58.8
	S.D. 15.8 d 0.3		S.D. 16.6		16.4		16.1

Twilight / Sunrise / Moonrise

Lat.	Twilight Naut.	Civil	Sunrise	Moonrise 3	4	5	6
N 72	□	□	□	■	01 33	01 02	00 50
N 70	□	□	□	24 18	00 18	00 26	00 28
68	□	□	□	23 40	24 00	00 00	00 11
66	////	////	01 00	23 13	23 40	23 57	24 09
64	////	////	01 51	22 52	23 24	23 46	24 02
62	////	////	02 22	22 35	23 11	23 36	23 55
60	////	01 18	02 45	22 21	22 59	23 28	23 50
N 58	////	01 55	03 04	22 09	22 49	23 20	23 45
56	////	02 20	03 19	21 59	22 41	23 14	23 40
54	01 11	02 40	03 32	21 49	22 33	23 08	23 36
52	01 45	02 57	03 44	21 41	22 26	23 03	23 33
50	02 09	03 11	03 54	21 34	22 20	22 58	23 30
45	02 50	03 39	04 15	21 18	22 06	22 47	23 22
N 40	03 19	04 00	04 32	21 05	21 55	22 39	23 16
35	03 41	04 17	04 46	20 54	21 46	22 31	23 11
30	03 59	04 32	04 59	20 44	21 37	22 24	23 07
20	04 26	04 55	05 20	20 27	21 23	22 13	22 59
N 10	04 48	05 15	05 38	20 13	21 10	22 03	22 52
0	05 06	05 32	05 55	19 59	20 58	21 54	22 45
S 10	05 22	05 49	06 11	19 45	20 46	21 44	22 39
20	05 38	06 05	06 29	19 31	20 33	21 34	22 32
30	05 53	06 23	06 49	19 14	20 19	21 22	22 24
35	06 01	06 33	07 01	19 04	20 10	21 16	22 19
40	06 10	06 44	07 14	18 53	20 01	21 08	22 14
45	06 20	06 57	07 30	18 40	19 49	20 59	22 08
S 50	06 31	07 12	07 50	18 24	19 36	20 48	22 00
52	06 36	07 19	07 59	18 17	19 29	20 43	21 57
54	06 41	07 26	08 09	18 08	19 22	20 38	21 53
56	06 47	07 35	08 21	17 59	19 14	20 32	21 49
58	06 53	07 44	08 35	17 48	19 05	20 25	21 44
S 60	07 00	07 55	08 51	17 36	18 55	20 17	21 39

Sunset / Twilight / Moonset

Lat.	Sunset	Twilight Civil	Naut.	Moonset 3	4	5	6
N 72	□	□	□	■	03 02	05 35	07 40
N 70	□	□	□	02 35	04 17	06 10	08 00
68	□	□	□	03 26	04 54	06 35	08 16
66	23 01	////	////	03 58	05 21	06 54	08 29
64	22 07	////	////	04 22	05 41	07 09	08 39
62	21 36	////	////	04 41	05 58	07 22	08 48
60	21 12	22 41	////	04 56	06 11	07 33	08 56
N 58	20 54	22 03	////	05 09	06 23	07 42	09 03
56	20 38	21 37	////	05 21	06 33	07 50	09 08
54	20 25	21 17	22 48	05 31	06 42	07 58	09 14
52	20 13	21 00	22 13	05 40	06 50	08 04	09 18
50	20 03	20 46	21 48	05 47	06 57	08 10	09 23
45	19 42	20 18	21 07	06 04	07 12	08 22	09 32
N 40	19 25	19 57	20 38	06 18	07 25	08 33	09 40
35	19 10	19 40	20 16	06 30	07 36	08 42	09 46
30	18 58	19 25	19 58	06 40	07 45	08 49	09 52
20	18 37	19 01	19 30	06 57	08 01	09 03	10 02
N 10	18 19	18 42	19 08	07 13	08 15	09 14	10 11
0	18 02	18 24	18 50	07 27	08 28	09 25	10 19
S 10	17 45	18 08	18 34	07 41	08 40	09 36	10 27
20	17 27	17 51	18 19	07 56	08 54	09 47	10 35
30	17 07	17 33	18 03	08 13	09 10	10 00	10 45
35	16 55	17 23	17 55	08 23	09 19	10 07	10 50
40	16 42	17 12	17 46	08 35	09 29	10 16	10 57
45	16 26	16 59	17 36	08 48	09 41	10 26	11 04
S 50	16 07	16 44	17 20	09 04	09 56	10 38	11 12
52	15 57	16 37	17 20	09 12	10 02	10 43	11 16
54	15 47	16 30	17 15	09 21	10 10	10 49	11 21
56	15 35	16 21	17 10	09 30	10 18	10 56	11 26
58	15 21	16 12	17 03	09 41	10 28	11 03	11 31
S 60	15 05	16 01	16 56	09 53	10 38	11 12	11 37

SUN / MOON

Day	SUN Eqn. of Time 00h	12h	Mer. Pass.	MOON Mer. Pass. Upper	Lower	Age	Phase
	m s	m s	h m	h m	h m	d	
3	02 02	01 57	11 58	01 12	13 43	16	
4	01 52	01 47	11 58	02 13	14 43	17	◑
5	01 42	01 37	11 58	03 12	15 39	18	

POLARIS (POLE STAR) TABLES, 1977
FOR DETERMINING LATITUDE FROM SEXTANT ALTITUDE AND FOR AZIMUTH

L.H.A. ARIES	240°–249°	250°–259°	260°–269°	270°–279°	280°–289°	290°–299°	300°–309°	310°–319°	320°–329°	330°–339°	340°–349°	350°–359°
	a_0	a_0	a_0	a_0	a_0	a_0	a_0	a_0	a_0	a_0	a_0	a_0
°	° ′	° ′	° ′	° ′	° ′	° ′	° ′	° ′	° ′	° ′	° ′	° ′
0	1 43·5	1 38·9	1 33·1	1 26·2	1 18·5	1 10·2	1 01·5	0 52·7	0 44·1	0 36·0	0 28·5	0 22·0
1	43·1	38·4	32·4	25·5	17·7	09·3	1 00·6	51·9	43·3	35·2	27·8	21·4
2	42·7	37·8	31·8	24·7	16·9	08·4	0 59·7	51·0	42·5	34·4	27·1	20·8
3	42·3	37·3	31·1	24·0	16·0	07·6	58·9	50·1	41·6	33·6	26·4	20·2
4	41·8	36·7	30·4	23·2	15·2	06·7	58·0	49·3	40·8	32·9	25·8	19·6
5	1 41·4	1 36·1	1 29·7	1 22·4	1 14·4	1 05·9	0 57·1	0 48·4	0 40·0	0 32·1	0 25·1	0 19·1
6	40·9	35·5	29·0	21·6	13·5	05·0	56·2	47·5	39·2	31·4	24·4	18·6
7	40·4	34·9	28·3	20·9	12·7	04·1	55·3	46·7	38·4	30·7	23·8	18·0
8	39·9	34·3	27·6	20·1	11·9	03·2	54·5	45·8	37·6	29·9	23·2	17·5
9	39·4	33·7	26·9	19·3	11·0	02·4	53·6	45·0	36·8	29·2	22·6	17·0
10	1 38·9	1 33·1	1 26·2	1 18·5	1 10·2	1 01·5	0 52·7	0 44·1	0 36·0	0 28·5	0 22·0	0 16·5

Lat.	a_1	a_1	a_1	a_1	a_1	a_1	a_1	a_1	a_1	a_1	a_1	a_1
°	′	′	′	′	′	′	′	′	′	′	′	′
0	0·5	0·4	0·3	0·3	0·2	0·2	0·2	0·2	0·2	0·3	0·4	0·4
10	·5	·4	·4	·3	·3	·2	·2	·2	·3	·3	·4	·5
20	·5	·5	·4	·4	·3	·3	·3	·3	·3	·4	·4	·5
30	·5	·5	·5	·4	·4	·4	·4	·4	·4	·4	·5	·5
40	0·6	0·5	0·5	0·5	0·5	0·5	0·5	0·5	0·5	0·5	0·5	0·6
45	·6	·6	·6	·5	·5	·5	·5	·5	·5	·5	·6	·6
50	·6	·6	·6	·6	·6	·6	·6	·6	·6	·6	·6	·6
55	·6	·6	·7	·7	·7	·7	·7	·7	·7	·7	·6	·6
60	·7	·7	·7	·8	·8	·8	·8	·8	·8	·7	·7	·7
62	0·7	0·7	0·8	0·8	0·8	0·8	0·9	0·8	0·8	0·8	0·7	0·7
64	·7	·7	·8	·8	0·9	0·9	0·9	0·9	·9	·8	·8	·7
66	·7	·8	·8	0·9	1·0	1·0	1·0	1·0	0·9	·9	·8	·7
68	0·7	0·8	0·9	1·0	1·0	1·1	1·1	1·1	1·0	0·9	0·9	0·8

Month	a_2	a_2	a_2	a_2	a_2	a_2	a_2	a_2	a_2	a_2	a_2	a_2
	′	′	′	′	′	′	′	′	′	′	′	′
Jan.	0·4	0·5	0·5	0·5	0·5	0·5	0·6	0·6	0·6	0·7	0·7	0·7
Feb.	·4	·4	·4	·4	·4	·4	·4	·5	·5	·5	·6	·6
Mar.	·4	·3	·3	·3	·3	·3	·3	·3	·3	·4	·4	·5
Apr.	0·5	0·4	0·4	0·3	0·3	0·3	0·2	0·2	0·2	0·3	0·3	0·3
May	·6	·5	·5	·4	·4	·3	·3	·2	·2	·2	·2	·2
June	·8	·7	·6	·6	·5	·4	·4	·3	·3	·3	·2	·2
July	0·9	0·8	0·8	0·7	0·7	0·6	0·5	0·5	0·4	0·4	0·3	0·3
Aug.	·9	·9	·9	·8	·8	·8	·7	·7	·6	·5	·5	·4
Sept.	·9	·9	·9	·9	·9	·9	·9	·8	·8	·7	·7	·6
Oct.	0·8	0·8	0·9	0·9	0·9	0·9	0·9	0·9	0·9	0·9	0·8	0·8
Nov.	·6	·7	·8	·8	·9	·9	1·0	1·0	1·0	1·0	1·0	1·0
Dec.	0·5	0·6	0·6	0·7	0·8	0·8	0·9	1·0	1·0	1·0	1·0	1·0

Lat.	AZIMUTH											
°	°	°	°	°	°	°	°	°	°	°	°	°
0	0·4	0·6	0·7	0·7	0·8	0·8	0·8	0·8	0·8	0·7	0·6	0·5
20	0·5	0·6	0·7	0·8	0·8	0·9	0·9	0·9	0·8	0·8	0·7	0·5
40	0·6	0·7	0·9	1·0	1·0	1·1	1·1	1·1	1·0	0·9	0·8	0·7
50	0·7	0·9	1·0	1·1	1·2	1·3	1·3	1·3	1·2	1·1	1·0	0·8
55	0·8	1·0	1·1	1·3	1·4	1·4	1·5	1·4	1·4	1·2	1·1	0·9
60	0·9	1·1	1·3	1·5	1·6	1·7	1·7	1·6	1·6	1·4	1·3	1·0
65	1·0	1·3	1·5	1·7	1·9	2·0	2·0	2·0	1·9	1·7	1·5	1·2

Latitude = Apparent altitude (corrected for refraction) $-1° + a_0 + a_1 + a_2$

The table is entered with L.H.A. Aries to determine the column to be used; each column refers to a range of 10°. a_0 is taken, with mental interpolation, from the upper table with the units of L.H.A. Aries in degrees as argument; a_1, a_2 are taken, without interpolation, from the second and third tables with arguments latitude and month respectively. a_0, a_1, a_2 are always positive. The final table gives the azimuth of *Polaris*.

CONVERSION OF ARC TO TIME

0°–59°		60°–119°		120°–179°		180°–239°		240°–299°		300°–359°		′	0′·00	0′·25	0′·50	0′·75
°	h m	°	h m	°	h m	°	h m	°	h m	°	h m	′	m s	m s	m s	m s
0	0 00	60	4 00	120	8 00	180	12 00	240	16 00	300	20 00	0	0 00	0 01	0 02	0 03
1	0 04	61	4 04	121	8 04	181	12 04	241	16 04	301	20 04	1	0 04	0 05	0 06	0 07
2	0 08	62	4 08	122	8 08	182	12 08	242	16 08	302	20 08	2	0 08	0 09	0 10	0 11
3	0 12	63	4 12	123	8 12	183	12 12	243	16 12	303	20 12	3	0 12	0 13	0 14	0 15
4	0 16	64	4 16	124	8 16	184	12 16	244	16 16	304	20 16	4	0 16	0 17	0 18	0 19
5	0 20	65	4 20	125	8 20	185	12 20	245	16 20	305	20 20	5	0 20	0 21	0 22	0 23
6	0 24	66	4 24	126	8 24	186	12 24	246	16 24	306	20 24	6	0 24	0 25	0 26	0 27
7	0 28	67	4 28	127	8 28	187	12 28	247	16 28	307	20 28	7	0 28	0 29	0 30	0 31
8	0 32	68	4 32	128	8 32	188	12 32	248	16 32	308	20 32	8	0 32	0 33	0 34	0 35
9	0 36	69	4 36	129	8 36	189	12 36	249	16 36	309	20 36	9	0 36	0 37	0 38	0 39
10	0 40	70	4 40	130	8 40	190	12 40	250	16 40	310	20 40	10	0 40	0 41	0 42	0 43
11	0 44	71	4 44	131	8 44	191	12 44	251	16 44	311	20 44	11	0 44	0 45	0 46	0 47
12	0 48	72	4 48	132	8 48	192	12 48	252	16 48	312	20 48	12	0 48	0 49	0 50	0 51
13	0 52	73	4 52	133	8 52	193	12 52	253	16 52	313	20 52	13	0 52	0 53	0 54	0 55
14	0 56	74	4 56	134	8 56	194	12 56	254	16 56	314	20 56	14	0 56	0 57	0 58	0 59
15	1 00	75	5 00	135	9 00	195	13 00	255	17 00	315	21 00	15	1 00	1 01	1 02	1 03
16	1 04	76	5 04	136	9 04	196	13 04	256	17 04	316	21 04	16	1 04	1 05	1 06	1 07
17	1 08	77	5 08	137	9 08	197	13 08	257	17 08	317	21 08	17	1 08	1 09	1 10	1 11
18	1 12	78	5 12	138	9 12	198	13 12	258	17 12	318	21 12	18	1 12	1 13	1 14	1 15
19	1 16	79	5 16	139	9 16	199	13 16	259	17 16	319	21 16	19	1 16	1 17	1 18	1 19
20	1 20	80	5 20	140	9 20	200	13 20	260	17 20	320	21 20	20	1 20	1 21	1 22	1 23
21	1 24	81	5 24	141	9 24	201	13 24	261	17 24	321	21 24	21	1 24	1 25	1 26	1 27
22	1 28	82	5 28	142	9 28	202	13 28	262	17 28	322	21 28	22	1 28	1 29	1 30	1 31
23	1 32	83	5 32	143	9 32	203	13 32	263	17 32	323	21 32	23	1 32	1 33	1 34	1 35
24	1 36	84	5 36	144	9 36	204	13 36	264	17 36	324	21 36	24	1 36	1 37	1 38	1 39
25	1 40	85	5 40	145	9 40	205	13 40	265	17 40	325	21 40	25	1 40	1 41	1 42	1 43
26	1 44	86	5 44	146	9 44	206	13 44	266	17 44	326	21 44	26	1 44	1 45	1 46	1 47
27	1 48	87	5 48	147	9 48	207	13 48	267	17 48	327	21 48	27	1 48	1 49	1 50	1 51
28	1 52	88	5 52	148	9 52	208	13 52	268	17 52	328	21 52	28	1 52	1 53	1 54	1 55
29	1 56	89	5 56	149	9 56	209	13 56	269	17 56	329	21 56	29	1 56	1 57	1 58	1 59
30	2 00	90	6 00	150	10 00	210	14 00	270	18 00	330	22 00	30	2 00	2 01	2 02	2 03
31	2 04	91	6 04	151	10 04	211	14 04	271	18 04	331	22 04	31	2 04	2 05	2 06	2 07
32	2 08	92	6 08	152	10 08	212	14 08	272	18 08	332	22 08	32	2 08	2 09	2 10	2 11
33	2 12	93	6 12	153	10 12	213	14 12	273	18 12	333	22 12	33	2 12	2 13	2 14	2 15
34	2 16	94	6 16	154	10 16	214	14 16	274	18 16	334	22 16	34	2 16	2 17	2 18	2 19
35	2 20	95	6 20	155	10 20	215	14 20	275	18 20	335	22 20	35	2 20	2 21	2 22	2 23
36	2 24	96	6 24	156	10 24	216	14 24	276	18 24	336	22 24	36	2 24	2 25	2 26	2 27
37	2 28	97	6 28	157	10 28	217	14 28	277	18 28	337	22 28	37	2 28	2 29	2 30	2 31
38	2 32	98	6 32	158	10 32	218	14 32	278	18 32	338	22 32	38	2 32	2 33	2 34	2 35
39	2 36	99	6 36	159	10 36	219	14 36	279	18 36	339	22 36	39	2 36	2 37	2 38	2 39
40	2 40	100	6 40	160	10 40	220	14 40	280	18 40	340	22 40	40	2 40	2 41	2 42	2 43
41	2 44	101	6 44	161	10 44	221	14 44	281	18 44	341	22 44	41	2 44	2 45	2 46	2 47
42	2 48	102	6 48	162	10 48	222	14 48	282	18 48	342	22 48	42	2 48	2 49	2 50	2 51
43	2 52	103	6 52	163	10 52	223	14 52	283	18 52	343	22 52	43	2 52	2 53	2 54	2 55
44	2 56	104	6 56	164	10 56	224	14 56	284	18 56	344	22 56	44	2 56	2 57	2 58	2 59
45	3 00	105	7 00	165	11 00	225	15 00	285	19 00	345	23 00	45	3 00	3 01	3 02	3 03
46	3 04	106	7 04	166	11 04	226	15 04	286	19 04	346	23 04	46	3 04	3 05	3 06	3 07
47	3 08	107	7 08	167	11 08	227	15 08	287	19 08	347	23 08	47	3 08	3 09	3 10	3 11
48	3 12	108	7 12	168	11 12	228	15 12	288	19 12	348	23 12	48	3 12	3 13	3 14	3 15
49	3 16	109	7 16	169	11 16	229	15 16	289	19 16	349	23 16	49	3 16	3 17	3 18	3 19
50	3 20	110	7 20	170	11 20	230	15 20	290	19 20	350	23 20	50	3 20	3 21	3 22	3 23
51	3 24	111	7 24	171	11 24	231	15 24	291	19 24	351	23 24	51	3 24	3 25	3 26	3 27
52	3 28	112	7 28	172	11 28	232	15 28	292	19 28	352	23 28	52	3 28	3 29	3 30	3 31
53	3 32	113	7 32	173	11 32	233	15 32	293	19 32	353	23 32	53	3 32	3 33	3 34	3 35
54	3 36	114	7 36	174	11 36	234	15 36	294	19 36	354	23 36	54	3 36	3 37	3 38	3 39
55	3 40	115	7 40	175	11 40	235	15 40	295	19 40	355	23 40	55	3 40	3 41	3 42	3 43
56	3 44	116	7 44	176	11 44	236	15 44	296	19 44	356	23 44	56	3 44	3 45	3 46	3 47
57	3 48	117	7 48	177	11 48	237	15 48	297	19 48	357	23 48	57	3 48	3 49	3 50	3 51
58	3 52	118	7 52	178	11 52	238	15 52	298	19 52	358	23 52	58	3 52	3 53	3 54	3 55
59	3 56	119	7 56	179	11 56	239	15 56	299	19 56	359	23 56	59	3 56	3 57	3 58	3 59

The above table is for converting expressions in arc to their equivalent in time ; its main use in this Almanac is for the conversion of longitude for application to L.M.T. (*added* if *west*, *subtracted* if *east*) to give G.M.T. or vice versa, particularly in the case of sunrise, sunset, etc.

2	SUN PLANETS	ARIES	MOON	v or Corr^n d		v or Corr^n d		v or Corr^n d	
s	° ′	° ′	° ′	′	′	′	′	′	′
00	0 30.0	0 30.1	0 28.6	0.0	0.0	6.0	0.3	12.0	0.5
01	0 30.3	0 30.3	0 28.9	0.1	0.0	6.1	0.3	12.1	0.5
02	0 30.5	0 30.6	0 29.1	0.2	0.0	6.2	0.3	12.2	0.5
03	0 30.8	0 30.8	0 29.3	0.3	0.0	6.3	0.3	12.3	0.5
04	0 31.0	0 31.1	0 29.6	0.4	0.0	6.4	0.3	12.4	0.5
05	0 31.3	0 31.3	0 29.8	0.5	0.0	6.5	0.3	12.5	0.5
06	0 31.5	0 31.6	0 30.1	0.6	0.0	6.6	0.3	12.6	0.5
07	0 31.8	0 31.8	0 30.3	0.7	0.0	6.7	0.3	12.7	0.5
08	0 32.0	0 32.1	0 30.5	0.8	0.0	6.8	0.3	12.8	0.5
09	0 32.3	0 32.3	0 30.8	0.9	0.0	6.9	0.3	12.9	0.5
10	0 32.5	0 32.6	0 31.0	1.0	0.0	7.0	0.3	13.0	0.5
11	0 32.8	0 32.8	0 31.3	1.1	0.0	7.1	0.3	13.1	0.5
12	0 33.0	0 33.1	0 31.5	1.2	0.1	7.2	0.3	13.2	0.6
13	0 33.3	0 33.3	0 31.7	1.3	0.1	7.3	0.3	13.3	0.6
14	0 33.5	0 33.6	0 32.0	1.4	0.1	7.4	0.3	13.4	0.6
15	0 33.8	0 33.8	0 32.2	1.5	0.1	7.5	0.3	13.5	0.6
16	0 34.0	0 34.1	0 32.5	1.6	0.1	7.6	0.3	13.6	0.6
17	0 34.3	0 34.3	0 32.7	1.7	0.1	7.7	0.3	13.7	0.6
18	0 34.5	0 34.6	0 32.9	1.8	0.1	7.8	0.3	13.8	0.6
19	0 34.8	0 34.8	0 33.2	1.9	0.1	7.9	0.3	13.9	0.6
20	0 35.0	0 35.1	0 33.4	2.0	0.1	8.0	0.3	14.0	0.6
21	0 35.3	0 35.3	0 33.6	2.1	0.1	8.1	0.3	14.1	0.6
22	0 35.5	0 35.6	0 33.9	2.2	0.1	8.2	0.3	14.2	0.6
23	0 35.8	0 35.8	0 34.1	2.3	0.1	8.3	0.3	14.3	0.6
24	0 36.0	0 36.1	0 34.4	2.4	0.1	8.4	0.4	14.4	0.6
25	0 36.3	0 36.3	0 34.6	2.5	0.1	8.5	0.4	14.5	0.6
26	0 36.5	0 36.6	0 34.8	2.6	0.1	8.6	0.4	14.6	0.6
27	0 36.8	0 36.9	0 35.1	2.7	0.1	8.7	0.4	14.7	0.6
28	0 37.0	0 37.1	0 35.3	2.8	0.1	8.8	0.4	14.8	0.6
29	0 37.3	0 37.4	0 35.6	2.9	0.1	8.9	0.4	14.9	0.6
30	0 37.5	0 37.6	0 35.8	3.0	0.1	9.0	0.4	15.0	0.6
31	0 37.8	0 37.9	0 36.0	3.1	0.1	9.1	0.4	15.1	0.6
32	0 38.0	0 38.1	0 36.3	3.2	0.1	9.2	0.4	15.2	0.6
33	0 38.3	0 38.4	0 36.5	3.3	0.1	9.3	0.4	15.3	0.6
34	0 38.6	0 38.6	0 36.7	3.4	0.1	9.4	0.4	15.4	0.6
35	0 38.8	0 38.9	0 37.0	3.5	0.1	9.5	0.4	15.5	0.6
36	0 39.0	0 39.1	0 37.2	3.6	0.2	9.6	0.4	15.6	0.7
37	0 39.3	0 39.4	0 37.5	3.7	0.2	9.7	0.4	15.7	0.7
38	0 39.5	0 39.6	0 37.7	3.8	0.2	9.8	0.4	15.8	0.7
39	0 39.8	0 39.9	0 37.9	3.9	0.2	9.9	0.4	15.9	0.7
40	0 40.0	0 40.1	0 38.2	4.0	0.2	10.0	0.4	16.0	0.7
41	0 40.3	0 40.4	0 38.4	4.1	0.2	10.1	0.4	16.1	0.7
42	0 40.5	0 40.6	0 38.7	4.2	0.2	10.2	0.4	16.2	0.7
43	0 40.8	0 40.9	0 38.9	4.3	0.2	10.3	0.4	16.3	0.7
44	0 41.0	0 41.1	0 39.1	4.4	0.2	10.4	0.4	16.4	0.7
45	0 41.3	0 41.4	0 39.4	4.5	0.2	10.5	0.4	16.5	0.7
46	0 41.5	0 41.6	0 39.6	4.6	0.2	10.6	0.4	16.6	0.7
47	0 41.8	0 41.9	0 39.8	4.7	0.2	10.7	0.4	16.7	0.7
48	0 42.0	0 42.1	0 40.1	4.8	0.2	10.8	0.5	16.8	0.7
49	0 42.3	0 42.4	0 40.3	4.9	0.2	10.9	0.5	16.9	0.7
50	0 42.5	0 42.6	0 40.6	5.0	0.2	11.0	0.5	17.0	0.7
51	0 42.8	0 42.9	0 40.8	5.1	0.2	11.1	0.5	17.1	0.7
52	0 43.0	0 43.1	0 41.0	5.2	0.2	11.2	0.5	17.2	0.7
53	0 43.3	0 43.4	0 41.3	5.3	0.2	11.3	0.5	17.3	0.7
54	0 43.5	0 43.6	0 41.5	5.4	0.2	11.4	0.5	17.4	0.7
55	0 43.8	0 43.9	0 41.8	5.5	0.2	11.5	0.5	17.5	0.7
56	0 44.0	0 44.1	0 42.0	5.6	0.2	11.6	0.5	17.6	0.7
57	0 44.3	0 44.4	0 42.2	5.7	0.2	11.7	0.5	17.7	0.7
58	0 44.5	0 44.6	0 42.5	5.8	0.2	11.8	0.5	17.8	0.7
59	0 44.8	0 44.9	0 42.7	5.9	0.2	11.9	0.5	17.9	0.7
60	0 45.0	0 45.1	0 43.0	6.0	0.3	12.0	0.5	18.0	0.8

3	SUN PLANETS	ARIES	MOON	v or Corr^n d		v or Corr^n d		v or Corr^n d	
s	° ′	° ′	° ′	′	′	′	′	′	′
00	0 45.0	0 45.1	0 43.0	0.0	0.0	6.0	0.4	12.0	0.7
01	0 45.3	0 45.4	0 43.2	0.1	0.0	6.1	0.4	12.1	0.7
02	0 45.5	0 45.6	0 43.4	0.2	0.0	6.2	0.4	12.2	0.7
03	0 45.8	0 45.9	0 43.7	0.3	0.0	6.3	0.4	12.3	0.7
04	0 46.0	0 46.1	0 43.9	0.4	0.0	6.4	0.4	12.4	0.7
05	0 46.3	0 46.4	0 44.1	0.5	0.0	6.5	0.4	12.5	0.7
06	0 46.5	0 46.6	0 44.4	0.6	0.0	6.6	0.4	12.6	0.7
07	0 46.8	0 46.9	0 44.6	0.7	0.0	6.7	0.4	12.7	0.7
08	0 47.0	0 47.1	0 44.9	0.8	0.0	6.8	0.4	12.8	0.7
09	0 47.3	0 47.4	0 45.1	0.9	0.1	6.9	0.4	12.9	0.8
10	0 47.5	0 47.6	0 45.3	1.0	0.1	7.0	0.4	13.0	0.8
11	0 47.8	0 47.9	0 45.6	1.1	0.1	7.1	0.4	13.1	0.8
12	0 48.0	0 48.1	0 45.8	1.2	0.1	7.2	0.4	13.2	0.8
13	0 48.3	0 48.4	0 46.1	1.3	0.1	7.3	0.4	13.3	0.8
14	0 48.5	0 48.6	0 46.3	1.4	0.1	7.4	0.4	13.4	0.8
15	0 48.8	0 48.9	0 46.5	1.5	0.1	7.5	0.4	13.5	0.8
16	0 49.0	0 49.1	0 46.8	1.6	0.1	7.6	0.4	13.6	0.8
17	0 49.3	0 49.4	0 47.0	1.7	0.1	7.7	0.4	13.7	0.8
18	0 49.5	0 49.6	0 47.2	1.8	0.1	7.8	0.5	13.8	0.8
19	0 49.8	0 49.9	0 47.5	1.9	0.1	7.9	0.5	13.9	0.8
20	0 50.0	0 50.1	0 47.7	2.0	0.1	8.0	0.5	14.0	0.8
21	0 50.3	0 50.4	0 48.0	2.1	0.1	8.1	0.5	14.1	0.8
22	0 50.5	0 50.6	0 48.2	2.2	0.1	8.2	0.5	14.2	0.8
23	0 50.8	0 50.9	0 48.4	2.3	0.1	8.3	0.5	14.3	0.8
24	0 51.0	0 51.1	0 48.7	2.4	0.1	8.4	0.5	14.4	0.8
25	0 51.3	0 51.4	0 48.9	2.5	0.1	8.5	0.5	14.5	0.8
26	0 51.5	0 51.6	0 49.2	2.6	0.2	8.6	0.5	14.6	0.9
27	0 51.8	0 51.9	0 49.4	2.7	0.2	8.7	0.5	14.7	0.9
28	0 52.0	0 52.1	0 49.6	2.8	0.2	8.8	0.5	14.8	0.9
29	0 52.3	0 52.4	0 49.9	2.9	0.2	8.9	0.5	14.9	0.9
30	0 52.5	0 52.6	0 50.1	3.0	0.2	9.0	0.5	15.0	0.9
31	0 52.8	0 52.9	0 50.3	3.1	0.2	9.1	0.5	15.1	0.9
32	0 53.0	0 53.1	0 50.6	3.2	0.2	9.2	0.5	15.2	0.9
33	0 53.3	0 53.4	0 50.8	3.3	0.2	9.3	0.5	15.3	0.9
34	0 53.5	0 53.6	0 51.1	3.4	0.2	9.4	0.5	15.4	0.9
35	0 53.8	0 53.9	0 51.3	3.5	0.2	9.5	0.6	15.5	0.9
36	0 54.0	0 54.1	0 51.5	3.6	0.2	9.6	0.6	15.6	0.9
37	0 54.3	0 54.4	0 51.8	3.7	0.2	9.7	0.6	15.7	0.9
38	0 54.5	0 54.6	0 52.0	3.8	0.2	9.8	0.6	15.8	0.9
39	0 54.8	0 54.9	0 52.3	3.9	0.2	9.9	0.6	15.9	0.9
40	0 55.0	0 55.2	0 52.5	4.0	0.2	10.0	0.6	16.0	0.9
41	0 55.3	0 55.4	0 52.7	4.1	0.2	10.1	0.6	16.1	0.9
42	0 55.5	0 55.7	0 53.0	4.2	0.2	10.2	0.6	16.2	0.9
43	0 55.8	0 55.9	0 53.2	4.3	0.3	10.3	0.6	16.3	1.0
44	0 56.0	0 56.2	0 53.4	4.4	0.3	10.4	0.6	16.4	1.0
45	0 56.3	0 56.4	0 53.7	4.5	0.3	10.5	0.6	16.5	1.0
46	0 56.5	0 56.7	0 53.9	4.6	0.3	10.6	0.6	16.6	1.0
47	0 56.8	0 56.9	0 54.2	4.7	0.3	10.7	0.6	16.7	1.0
48	0 57.0	0 57.2	0 54.4	4.8	0.3	10.8	0.6	16.8	1.0
49	0 57.3	0 57.4	0 54.6	4.9	0.3	10.9	0.6	16.9	1.0
50	0 57.5	0 57.7	0 54.9	5.0	0.3	11.0	0.6	17.0	1.0
51	0 57.8	0 57.9	0 55.1	5.1	0.3	11.1	0.6	17.1	1.0
52	0 58.0	0 58.2	0 55.4	5.2	0.3	11.2	0.7	17.2	1.0
53	0 58.3	0 58.4	0 55.6	5.3	0.3	11.3	0.7	17.3	1.0
54	0 58.5	0 58.7	0 55.8	5.4	0.3	11.4	0.7	17.4	1.0
55	0 58.8	0 58.9	0 56.1	5.5	0.3	11.5	0.7	17.5	1.0
56	0 59.0	0 59.2	0 56.3	5.6	0.3	11.6	0.7	17.6	1.0
57	0 59.3	0 59.4	0 56.6	5.7	0.3	11.7	0.7	17.7	1.0
58	0 59.5	0 59.7	0 56.8	5.8	0.3	11.8	0.7	17.8	1.0
59	0 59.8	0 59.9	0 57.0	5.9	0.3	11.9	0.7	17.9	1.0
60	1 00.0	1 00.2	0 57.3	6.0	0.4	12.0	0.7	18.0	1.1

16ᵐ

16 (s)	SUN PLANETS	ARIES	MOON	v or Corrⁿ (d)	v or Corrⁿ (d)	v or Corrⁿ (d)
00	4 00.0	4 00.7	3 49.1	0.0 0.0	6.0 1.7	12.0 3.3
01	4 00.3	4 00.9	3 49.3	0.1 0.0	6.1 1.7	12.1 3.3
02	4 00.5	4 01.2	3 49.5	0.2 0.1	6.2 1.7	12.2 3.4
03	4 00.8	4 01.4	3 49.8	0.3 0.1	6.3 1.7	12.3 3.4
04	4 01.0	4 01.7	3 50.0	0.4 0.1	6.4 1.8	12.4 3.4
05	4 01.3	4 01.9	3 50.3	0.5 0.1	6.5 1.8	12.5 3.4
06	4 01.5	4 02.2	3 50.5	0.6 0.2	6.6 1.8	12.6 3.5
07	4 01.8	4 02.4	3 50.7	0.7 0.2	6.7 1.8	12.7 3.5
08	4 02.0	4 02.7	3 51.0	0.8 0.2	6.8 1.9	12.8 3.5
09	4 02.3	4 02.9	3 51.2	0.9 0.2	6.9 1.9	12.9 3.5
10	4 02.5	4 03.2	3 51.5	1.0 0.3	7.0 1.9	13.0 3.6
11	4 02.8	4 03.4	3 51.7	1.1 0.3	7.1 2.0	13.1 3.6
12	4 03.0	4 03.7	3 51.9	1.2 0.3	7.2 2.0	13.2 3.6
13	4 03.3	4 03.9	3 52.2	1.3 0.4	7.3 2.0	13.3 3.7
14	4 03.5	4 04.2	3 52.4	1.4 0.4	7.4 2.0	13.4 3.7
15	4 03.8	4 04.4	3 52.6	1.5 0.4	7.5 2.1	13.5 3.7
16	4 04.0	4 04.7	3 52.9	1.6 0.4	7.6 2.1	13.6 3.7
17	4 04.3	4 04.9	3 53.1	1.7 0.5	7.7 2.1	13.7 3.8
18	4 04.5	4 05.2	3 53.4	1.8 0.5	7.8 2.1	13.8 3.8
19	4 04.8	4 05.4	3 53.6	1.9 0.5	7.9 2.2	13.9 3.8
20	4 05.0	4 05.7	3 53.8	2.0 0.6	8.0 2.2	14.0 3.9
21	4 05.3	4 05.9	3 54.1	2.1 0.6	8.1 2.2	14.1 3.9
22	4 05.5	4 06.2	3 54.3	2.2 0.6	8.2 2.3	14.2 3.9
23	4 05.8	4 06.4	3 54.6	2.3 0.6	8.3 2.3	14.3 3.9
24	4 06.0	4 06.7	3 54.8	2.4 0.7	8.4 2.3	14.4 4.0
25	4 06.3	4 06.9	3 55.0	2.5 0.7	8.5 2.3	14.5 4.0
26	4 06.5	4 07.2	3 55.3	2.6 0.7	8.6 2.4	14.6 4.0
27	4 06.8	4 07.4	3 55.5	2.7 0.7	8.7 2.4	14.7 4.0
28	4 07.0	4 07.7	3 55.7	2.8 0.8	8.8 2.4	14.8 4.1
29	4 07.3	4 07.9	3 56.0	2.9 0.8	8.9 2.4	14.9 4.1
30	4 07.5	4 08.2	3 56.2	3.0 0.8	9.0 2.5	15.0 4.1
31	4 07.8	4 08.4	3 56.5	3.1 0.9	9.1 2.5	15.1 4.2
32	4 08.0	4 08.7	3 56.7	3.2 0.9	9.2 2.5	15.2 4.2
33	4 08.3	4 08.9	3 56.9	3.3 0.9	9.3 2.6	15.3 4.2
34	4 08.5	4 09.2	3 57.2	3.4 0.9	9.4 2.6	15.4 4.2
35	4 08.8	4 09.4	3 57.4	3.5 1.0	9.5 2.6	15.5 4.3
36	4 09.0	4 09.7	3 57.7	3.6 1.0	9.6 2.6	15.6 4.3
37	4 09.3	4 09.9	3 57.9	3.7 1.0	9.7 2.7	15.7 4.3
38	4 09.5	4 10.2	3 58.1	3.8 1.0	9.8 2.7	15.8 4.3
39	4 09.8	4 10.4	3 58.4	3.9 1.1	9.9 2.7	15.9 4.4
40	4 10.0	4 10.7	3 58.6	4.0 1.1	10.0 2.8	16.0 4.4
41	4 10.3	4 10.9	3 58.8	4.1 1.1	10.1 2.8	16.1 4.4
42	4 10.5	4 11.2	3 59.1	4.2 1.2	10.2 2.8	16.2 4.5
43	4 10.8	4 11.4	3 59.3	4.3 1.2	10.3 2.8	16.3 4.5
44	4 11.0	4 11.7	3 59.6	4.4 1.2	10.4 2.9	16.4 4.5
45	4 11.3	4 11.9	3 59.8	4.5 1.2	10.5 2.9	16.5 4.5
46	4 11.5	4 12.2	4 00.0	4.6 1.3	10.6 2.9	16.6 4.6
47	4 11.8	4 12.4	4 00.3	4.7 1.3	10.7 2.9	16.7 4.6
48	4 12.0	4 12.7	4 00.5	4.8 1.3	10.8 3.0	16.8 4.6
49	4 12.3	4 12.9	4 00.8	4.9 1.3	10.9 3.0	16.9 4.6
50	4 12.5	4 13.2	4 01.0	5.0 1.4	11.0 3.0	17.0 4.7
51	4 12.8	4 13.4	4 01.2	5.1 1.4	11.1 3.1	17.1 4.7
52	4 13.0	4 13.7	4 01.5	5.2 1.4	11.2 3.1	17.2 4.7
53	4 13.3	4 13.9	4 01.7	5.3 1.5	11.3 3.1	17.3 4.8
54	4 13.5	4 14.2	4 02.0	5.4 1.5	11.4 3.1	17.4 4.8
55	4 13.8	4 14.4	4 02.2	5.5 1.5	11.5 3.2	17.5 4.8
56	4 14.0	4 14.7	4 02.4	5.6 1.5	11.6 3.2	17.6 4.8
57	4 14.3	4 14.9	4 02.7	5.7 1.6	11.7 3.2	17.7 4.9
58	4 14.5	4 15.2	4 02.9	5.8 1.6	11.8 3.2	17.8 4.9
59	4 14.8	4 15.4	4 03.1	5.9 1.6	11.9 3.3	17.9 4.9
60	4 15.0	4 15.7	4 03.4	6.0 1.7	12.0 3.3	18.0 5.0

17ᵐ

17 (s)	SUN PLANETS	ARIES	MOON	v or Corrⁿ (d)	v or Corrⁿ (d)	v or Corrⁿ (d)
00	4 15.0	4 15.7	4 03.4	0.0 0.0	6.0 1.8	12.0 3.5
01	4 15.3	4 15.9	4 03.6	0.1 0.0	6.1 1.8	12.1 3.5
02	4 15.5	4 16.2	4 03.9	0.2 0.1	6.2 1.8	12.2 3.6
03	4 15.8	4 16.5	4 04.1	0.3 0.1	6.3 1.8	12.3 3.6
04	4 16.0	4 16.7	4 04.3	0.4 0.1	6.4 1.9	12.4 3.6
05	4 16.3	4 17.0	4 04.6	0.5 0.1	6.5 1.9	12.5 3.6
06	4 16.5	4 17.2	4 04.8	0.6 0.2	6.6 1.9	12.6 3.7
07	4 16.8	4 17.5	4 05.1	0.7 0.2	6.7 2.0	12.7 3.7
08	4 17.0	4 17.7	4 05.3	0.8 0.2	6.8 2.0	12.8 3.7
09	4 17.3	4 18.0	4 05.5	0.9 0.3	6.9 2.0	12.9 3.8
10	4 17.5	4 18.2	4 05.8	1.0 0.3	7.0 2.0	13.0 3.8
11	4 17.8	4 18.5	4 06.0	1.1 0.3	7.1 2.1	13.1 3.8
12	4 18.0	4 18.7	4 06.2	1.2 0.4	7.2 2.1	13.2 3.9
13	4 18.3	4 19.0	4 06.5	1.3 0.4	7.3 2.1	13.3 3.9
14	4 18.5	4 19.2	4 06.7	1.4 0.4	7.4 2.2	13.4 3.9
15	4 18.8	4 19.5	4 07.0	1.5 0.4	7.5 2.2	13.5 3.9
16	4 19.0	4 19.7	4 07.2	1.6 0.5	7.6 2.2	13.6 4.0
17	4 19.3	4 20.0	4 07.4	1.7 0.5	7.7 2.2	13.7 4.0
18	4 19.5	4 20.2	4 07.7	1.8 0.5	7.8 2.3	13.8 4.0
19	4 19.8	4 20.5	4 07.9	1.9 0.6	7.9 2.3	13.9 4.1
20	4 20.0	4 20.7	4 08.2	2.0 0.6	8.0 2.3	14.0 4.1
21	4 20.3	4 21.0	4 08.4	2.1 0.6	8.1 2.4	14.1 4.1
22	4 20.5	4 21.2	4 08.6	2.2 0.6	8.2 2.4	14.2 4.1
23	4 20.8	4 21.5	4 08.9	2.3 0.7	8.3 2.4	14.3 4.2
24	4 21.0	4 21.7	4 09.1	2.4 0.7	8.4 2.5	14.4 4.2
25	4 21.3	4 22.0	4 09.3	2.5 0.7	8.5 2.5	14.5 4.2
26	4 21.5	4 22.2	4 09.6	2.6 0.8	8.6 2.5	14.6 4.3
27	4 21.8	4 22.5	4 09.8	2.7 0.8	8.7 2.5	14.7 4.3
28	4 22.0	4 22.7	4 10.1	2.8 0.8	8.8 2.6	14.8 4.3
29	4 22.3	4 23.0	4 10.3	2.9 0.8	8.9 2.6	14.9 4.3
30	4 22.5	4 23.2	4 10.5	3.0 0.9	9.0 2.6	15.0 4.4
31	4 22.8	4 23.5	4 10.8	3.1 0.9	9.1 2.7	15.1 4.4
32	4 23.0	4 23.7	4 11.0	3.2 0.9	9.2 2.7	15.2 4.4
33	4 23.3	4 24.0	4 11.3	3.3 1.0	9.3 2.7	15.3 4.5
34	4 23.5	4 24.2	4 11.5	3.4 1.0	9.4 2.7	15.4 4.5
35	4 23.8	4 24.5	4 11.7	3.5 1.0	9.5 2.8	15.5 4.5
36	4 24.0	4 24.7	4 12.0	3.6 1.1	9.6 2.8	15.6 4.6
37	4 24.3	4 25.0	4 12.2	3.7 1.1	9.7 2.8	15.7 4.6
38	4 24.5	4 25.2	4 12.5	3.8 1.1	9.8 2.9	15.8 4.6
39	4 24.8	4 25.5	4 12.7	3.9 1.1	9.9 2.9	15.9 4.6
40	4 25.0	4 25.7	4 12.9	4.0 1.2	10.0 2.9	16.0 4.7
41	4 25.3	4 26.0	4 13.2	4.1 1.2	10.1 2.9	16.1 4.7
42	4 25.5	4 26.2	4 13.4	4.2 1.2	10.2 3.0	16.2 4.7
43	4 25.8	4 26.5	4 13.6	4.3 1.3	10.3 3.0	16.3 4.8
44	4 26.0	4 26.7	4 13.9	4.4 1.3	10.4 3.0	16.4 4.8
45	4 26.3	4 27.0	4 14.1	4.5 1.3	10.5 3.1	16.5 4.8
46	4 26.5	4 27.2	4 14.4	4.6 1.3	10.6 3.1	16.6 4.8
47	4 26.8	4 27.5	4 14.6	4.7 1.4	10.7 3.1	16.7 4.9
48	4 27.0	4 27.7	4 14.8	4.8 1.4	10.8 3.2	16.8 4.9
49	4 27.3	4 28.0	4 15.1	4.9 1.4	10.9 3.2	16.9 4.9
50	4 27.5	4 28.2	4 15.3	5.0 1.5	11.0 3.2	17.0 5.0
51	4 27.8	4 28.5	4 15.6	5.1 1.5	11.1 3.2	17.1 5.0
52	4 28.0	4 28.7	4 15.8	5.2 1.5	11.2 3.3	17.2 5.0
53	4 28.3	4 29.0	4 16.0	5.3 1.5	11.3 3.3	17.3 5.0
54	4 28.5	4 29.2	4 16.3	5.4 1.6	11.4 3.3	17.4 5.1
55	4 28.8	4 29.5	4 16.5	5.5 1.6	11.5 3.4	17.5 5.1
56	4 29.0	4 29.7	4 16.7	5.6 1.6	11.6 3.4	17.6 5.1
57	4 29.3	4 30.0	4 17.0	5.7 1.7	11.7 3.4	17.7 5.2
58	4 29.5	4 30.2	4 17.2	5.8 1.7	11.8 3.4	17.8 5.2
59	4 29.8	4 30.5	4 17.5	5.9 1.7	11.9 3.5	17.9 5.2
60	4 30.0	4 30.7	4 17.7	6.0 1.8	12.0 3.5	18.0 5.3

24ᵐ

24ᵐ	SUN PLANETS	ARIES	MOON	v or Corrⁿ d	v or Corrⁿ d	v or Corrⁿ d
s	° ′	° ′	° ′	′ ′	′ ′	′ ′
00	6 00.0	6 01.0	5 43.6	0.0 0.0	6.0 2.5	12.0 4.9
01	6 00.3	6 01.2	5 43.8	0.1 0.0	6.1 2.5	12.1 4.9
02	6 00.5	6 01.5	5 44.1	0.2 0.1	6.2 2.5	12.2 5.0
03	6 00.8	6 01.7	5 44.3	0.3 0.1	6.3 2.6	12.3 5.0
04	6 01.0	6 02.0	5 44.6	0.4 0.2	6.4 2.6	12.4 5.1
05	6 01.3	6 02.2	5 44.8	0.5 0.2	6.5 2.7	12.5 5.1
06	6 01.5	6 02.5	5 45.0	0.6 0.2	6.6 2.7	12.6 5.1
07	6 01.8	6 02.7	5 45.3	0.7 0.3	6.7 2.7	12.7 5.2
08	6 02.0	6 03.0	5 45.5	0.8 0.3	6.8 2.8	12.8 5.2
09	6 02.3	6 03.2	5 45.7	0.9 0.4	6.9 2.8	12.9 5.3
10	6 02.5	6 03.5	5 46.0	1.0 0.4	7.0 2.9	13.0 5.3
11	6 02.8	6 03.7	5 46.2	1.1 0.4	7.1 2.9	13.1 5.3
12	6 03.0	6 04.0	5 46.5	1.2 0.5	7.2 2.9	13.2 5.4
13	6 03.3	6 04.2	5 46.7	1.3 0.5	7.3 3.0	13.3 5.4
14	6 03.5	6 04.5	5 46.9	1.4 0.6	7.4 3.0	13.4 5.5
15	6 03.8	6 04.7	5 47.2	1.5 0.6	7.5 3.1	13.5 5.5
16	6 04.0	6 05.0	5 47.4	1.6 0.7	7.6 3.1	13.6 5.6
17	6 04.3	6 05.2	5 47.7	1.7 0.7	7.7 3.1	13.7 5.6
18	6 04.5	6 05.5	5 47.9	1.8 0.7	7.8 3.2	13.8 5.6
19	6 04.8	6 05.7	5 48.1	1.9 0.8	7.9 3.2	13.9 5.7
20	6 05.0	6 06.0	5 48.4	2.0 0.8	8.0 3.3	14.0 5.7
21	6 05.3	6 06.3	5 48.6	2.1 0.9	8.1 3.3	14.1 5.8
22	6 05.5	6 06.5	5 48.8	2.2 0.9	8.2 3.3	14.2 5.8
23	6 05.8	6 06.8	5 49.1	2.3 0.9	8.3 3.4	14.3 5.8
24	6 06.0	6 07.0	5 49.3	2.4 1.0	8.4 3.4	14.4 5.9
25	6 06.3	6 07.3	5 49.6	2.5 1.0	8.5 3.5	14.5 5.9
26	6 06.5	6 07.5	5 49.8	2.6 1.1	8.6 3.5	14.6 6.0
27	6 06.8	6 07.8	5 50.0	2.7 1.1	8.7 3.6	14.7 6.0
28	6 07.0	6 08.0	5 50.3	2.8 1.1	8.8 3.6	14.8 6.0
29	6 07.3	6 08.3	5 50.5	2.9 1.2	8.9 3.6	14.9 6.1
30	6 07.5	6 08.5	5 50.8	3.0 1.2	9.0 3.7	15.0 6.1
31	6 07.8	6 08.8	5 51.0	3.1 1.3	9.1 3.7	15.1 6.2
32	6 08.0	6 09.0	5 51.2	3.2 1.3	9.2 3.8	15.2 6.2
33	6 08.3	6 09.3	5 51.5	3.3 1.3	9.3 3.8	15.3 6.2
34	6 08.5	6 09.5	5 51.7	3.4 1.4	9.4 3.8	15.4 6.3
35	6 08.8	6 09.8	5 52.0	3.5 1.4	9.5 3.9	15.5 6.3
36	6 09.0	6 10.0	5 52.2	3.6 1.5	9.6 3.9	15.6 6.4
37	6 09.3	6 10.3	5 52.4	3.7 1.5	9.7 4.0	15.7 6.4
38	6 09.5	6 10.5	5 52.7	3.8 1.6	9.8 4.0	15.8 6.5
39	6 09.8	6 10.8	5 52.9	3.9 1.6	9.9 4.0	15.9 6.5
40	6 10.0	6 11.0	5 53.1	4.0 1.6	10.0 4.1	16.0 6.5
41	6 10.3	6 11.3	5 53.4	4.1 1.7	10.1 4.1	16.1 6.6
42	6 10.5	6 11.5	5 53.6	4.2 1.7	10.2 4.2	16.2 6.6
43	6 10.8	6 11.8	5 53.9	4.3 1.8	10.3 4.2	16.3 6.7
44	6 11.0	6 12.0	5 54.1	4.4 1.8	10.4 4.2	16.4 6.7
45	6 11.3	6 12.3	5 54.3	4.5 1.8	10.5 4.3	16.5 6.7
46	6 11.5	6 12.5	5 54.6	4.6 1.9	10.6 4.3	16.6 6.8
47	6 11.8	6 12.8	5 54.8	4.7 1.9	10.7 4.4	16.7 6.8
48	6 12.0	6 13.0	5 55.1	4.8 2.0	10.8 4.4	16.8 6.9
49	6 12.3	6 13.3	5 55.3	4.9 2.0	10.9 4.5	16.9 6.9
50	6 12.5	6 13.5	5 55.5	5.0 2.0	11.0 4.5	17.0 6.9
51	6 12.8	6 13.8	5 55.8	5.1 2.1	11.1 4.5	17.1 7.0
52	6 13.0	6 14.0	5 56.0	5.2 2.1	11.2 4.6	17.2 7.0
53	6 13.3	6 14.3	5 56.2	5.3 2.2	11.3 4.6	17.3 7.1
54	6 13.5	6 14.5	5 56.5	5.4 2.2	11.4 4.7	17.4 7.1
55	6 13.8	6 14.8	5 56.7	5.5 2.2	11.5 4.7	17.5 7.1
56	6 14.0	6 15.0	5 57.0	5.6 2.3	11.6 4.7	17.6 7.2
57	6 14.3	6 15.3	5 57.2	5.7 2.3	11.7 4.8	17.7 7.2
58	6 14.5	6 15.5	5 57.4	5.8 2.4	11.8 4.8	17.8 7.3
59	6 14.8	6 15.8	5 57.7	5.9 2.4	11.9 4.9	17.9 7.3
60	6 15.0	6 16.0	5 57.9	6.0 2.5	12.0 4.9	18.0 7.4

25ᵐ

25ᵐ	SUN PLANETS	ARIES	MOON	v or Corrⁿ d	v or Corrⁿ d	v or Corrⁿ d
s	° ′	° ′	° ′	′ ′	′ ′	′ ′
00	6 15.0	6 16.0	5 57.9	0.0 0.0	6.0 2.6	12.0 5.1
01	6 15.3	6 16.3	5 58.2	0.1 0.0	6.1 2.6	12.1 5.1
02	6 15.5	6 16.5	5 58.4	0.2 0.1	6.2 2.6	12.2 5.2
03	6 15.8	6 16.8	5 58.6	0.3 0.1	6.3 2.7	12.3 5.2
04	6 16.0	6 17.0	5 58.9	0.4 0.2	6.4 2.7	12.4 5.3
05	6 16.3	6 17.3	5 59.1	0.5 0.2	6.5 2.8	12.5 5.3
06	6 16.5	6 17.5	5 59.3	0.6 0.3	6.6 2.8	12.6 5.4
07	6 16.8	6 17.8	5 59.6	0.7 0.3	6.7 2.8	12.7 5.4
08	6 17.0	6 18.0	5 59.8	0.8 0.3	6.8 2.9	12.8 5.4
09	6 17.3	6 18.3	6 00.1	0.9 0.4	6.9 2.9	12.9 5.5
10	6 17.5	6 18.5	6 00.3	1.0 0.4	7.0 3.0	13.0 5.5
11	6 17.8	6 18.8	6 00.5	1.1 0.5	7.1 3.0	13.1 5.6
12	6 18.0	6 19.0	6 00.8	1.2 0.5	7.2 3.1	13.2 5.6
13	6 18.3	6 19.3	6 01.0	1.3 0.6	7.3 3.1	13.3 5.7
14	6 18.5	6 19.5	6 01.3	1.4 0.6	7.4 3.1	13.4 5.7
15	6 18.8	6 19.8	6 01.5	1.5 0.6	7.5 3.2	13.5 5.7
16	6 19.0	6 20.0	6 01.7	1.6 0.7	7.6 3.2	13.6 5.8
17	6 19.3	6 20.3	6 02.0	1.7 0.7	7.7 3.3	13.7 5.8
18	6 19.5	6 20.5	6 02.2	1.8 0.8	7.8 3.3	13.8 5.9
19	6 19.8	6 20.8	6 02.5	1.9 0.8	7.9 3.4	13.9 5.9
20	6 20.0	6 21.0	6 02.7	2.0 0.9	8.0 3.4	14.0 6.0
21	6 20.3	6 21.3	6 02.9	2.1 0.9	8.1 3.4	14.1 6.0
22	6 20.5	6 21.5	6 03.2	2.2 0.9	8.2 3.5	14.2 6.0
23	6 20.8	6 21.8	6 03.4	2.3 1.0	8.3 3.5	14.3 6.1
24	6 21.0	6 22.0	6 03.6	2.4 1.0	8.4 3.6	14.4 6.1
25	6 21.3	6 22.3	6 03.9	2.5 1.1	8.5 3.6	14.5 6.2
26	6 21.5	6 22.5	6 04.1	2.6 1.1	8.6 3.7	14.6 6.2
27	6 21.8	6 22.8	6 04.4	2.7 1.1	8.7 3.7	14.7 6.2
28	6 22.0	6 23.0	6 04.6	2.8 1.2	8.8 3.7	14.8 6.3
29	6 22.3	6 23.3	6 04.8	2.9 1.2	8.9 3.8	14.9 6.3
30	6 22.5	6 23.5	6 05.1	3.0 1.3	9.0 3.8	15.0 6.4
31	6 22.8	6 23.8	6 05.3	3.1 1.3	9.1 3.9	15.1 6.4
32	6 23.0	6 24.0	6 05.6	3.2 1.4	9.2 3.9	15.2 6.5
33	6 23.3	6 24.3	6 05.8	3.3 1.4	9.3 4.0	15.3 6.5
34	6 23.5	6 24.5	6 06.0	3.4 1.4	9.4 4.0	15.4 6.5
35	6 23.8	6 24.8	6 06.3	3.5 1.5	9.5 4.0	15.5 6.6
36	6 24.0	6 25.1	6 06.5	3.6 1.5	9.6 4.1	15.6 6.6
37	6 24.3	6 25.3	6 06.7	3.7 1.6	9.7 4.1	15.7 6.7
38	6 24.5	6 25.6	6 07.0	3.8 1.6	9.8 4.2	15.8 6.7
39	6 24.8	6 25.8	6 07.2	3.9 1.7	9.9 4.2	15.9 6.8
40	6 25.0	6 26.1	6 07.5	4.0 1.7	10.0 4.3	16.0 6.8
41	6 25.3	6 26.3	6 07.7	4.1 1.7	10.1 4.3	16.1 6.8
42	6 25.5	6 26.6	6 07.9	4.2 1.8	10.2 4.3	16.2 6.9
43	6 25.8	6 26.8	6 08.2	4.3 1.8	10.3 4.4	16.3 6.9
44	6 26.0	6 27.1	6 08.4	4.4 1.9	10.4 4.4	16.4 7.0
45	6 26.3	6 27.3	6 08.7	4.5 1.9	10.5 4.5	16.5 7.0
46	6 26.5	6 27.6	6 08.9	4.6 2.0	10.6 4.5	16.6 7.1
47	6 26.8	6 27.8	6 09.1	4.7 2.0	10.7 4.5	16.7 7.1
48	6 27.0	6 28.1	6 09.4	4.8 2.0	10.8 4.6	16.8 7.1
49	6 27.3	6 28.3	6 09.6	4.9 2.1	10.9 4.6	16.9 7.2
50	6 27.5	6 28.6	6 09.8	5.0 2.1	11.0 4.7	17.0 7.2
51	6 27.8	6 28.8	6 10.1	5.1 2.2	11.1 4.7	17.1 7.3
52	6 28.0	6 29.1	6 10.3	5.2 2.2	11.2 4.8	17.2 7.3
53	6 28.3	6 29.3	6 10.6	5.3 2.3	11.3 4.8	17.3 7.4
54	6 28.5	6 29.6	6 10.8	5.4 2.3	11.4 4.8	17.4 7.4
55	6 28.8	6 29.8	6 11.0	5.5 2.3	11.5 4.9	17.5 7.4
56	6 29.0	6 30.1	6 11.3	5.6 2.4	11.6 4.9	17.6 7.5
57	6 29.3	6 30.3	6 11.5	5.7 2.4	11.7 5.0	17.7 7.5
58	6 29.5	6 30.6	6 11.8	5.8 2.5	11.8 5.0	17.8 7.6
59	6 29.8	6 30.8	6 12.0	5.9 2.5	11.9 5.1	17.9 7.6
60	6 30.0	6 31.1	6 12.2	6.0 2.6	12.0 5.1	18.0 7.7

52ᵐ	SUN PLANETS	ARIES	MOON	v or Corrⁿ d	v or Corrⁿ d	v or Corrⁿ d
s	° ′	° ′	° ′	′ ′	′ ′	′ ′
00	13 00·0	13 02·1	12 24·5	0·0 0·0	6·0 5·3	12·0 10·5
01	13 00·3	13 02·4	12 24·7	0·1 0·1	6·1 5·3	12·1 10·6
02	13 00·5	13 02·6	12 24·9	0·2 0·2	6·2 5·4	12·2 10·7
03	13 00·8	13 02·9	12 25·2	0·3 0·3	6·3 5·5	12·3 10·8
04	13 01·0	13 03·1	12 25·4	0·4 0·4	6·4 5·6	12·4 10·9
05	13 01·3	13 03·4	12 25·7	0·5 0·4	6·5 5·7	12·5 10·9
06	13 01·5	13 03·6	12 25·9	0·6 0·5	6·6 5·8	12·6 11·0
07	13 01·8	13 03·9	12 26·1	0·7 0·6	6·7 5·9	12·7 11·1
08	13 02·0	13 04·1	12 26·4	0·8 0·7	6·8 6·0	12·8 11·2
09	13 02·3	13 04·4	12 26·6	0·9 0·8	6·9 6·0	12·9 11·3
10	13 02·5	13 04·6	12 26·9	1·0 0·9	7·0 6·1	13·0 11·4
11	13 02·8	13 04·9	12 27·1	1·1 1·0	7·1 6·2	13·1 11·5
12	13 03·0	13 05·1	12 27·3	1·2 1·1	7·2 6·3	13·2 11·6
13	13 03·3	13 05·4	12 27·6	1·3 1·1	7·3 6·4	13·3 11·6
14	13 03·5	13 05·6	12 27·8	1·4 1·2	7·4 6·5	13·4 11·7
15	13 03·8	13 05·9	12 28·0	1·5 1·3	7·5 6·6	13·5 11·8
16	13 04·0	13 06·1	12 28·3	1·6 1·4	7·6 6·7	13·6 11·9
17	13 04·3	13 06·4	12 28·5	1·7 1·5	7·7 6·7	13·7 12·0
18	13 04·5	13 06·6	12 28·8	1·8 1·6	7·8 6·8	13·8 12·1
19	13 04·8	13 06·9	12 29·0	1·9 1·7	7·9 6·9	13·9 12·2
20	13 05·0	13 07·1	12 29·2	2·0 1·8	8·0 7·0	14·0 12·3
21	13 05·3	13 07·4	12 29·5	2·1 1·8	8·1 7·1	14·1 12·3
22	13 05·5	13 07·7	12 29·7	2·2 1·9	8·2 7·2	14·2 12·4
23	13 05·8	13 07·9	12 30·0	2·3 2·0	8·3 7·3	14·3 12·5
24	13 06·0	13 08·2	12 30·2	2·4 2·1	8·4 7·4	14·4 12·6
25	13 06·3	13 08·4	12 30·4	2·5 2·2	8·5 7·4	14·5 12·7
26	13 06·5	13 08·7	12 30·7	2·6 2·3	8·6 7·5	14·6 12·8
27	13 06·8	13 08·9	12 30·9	2·7 2·4	8·7 7·6	14·7 12·9
28	13 07·0	13 09·2	12 31·1	2·8 2·5	8·8 7·7	14·8 13·0
29	13 07·3	13 09·4	12 31·4	2·9 2·5	8·9 7·8	14·9 13·0
30	13 07·5	13 09·7	12 31·6	3·0 2·6	9·0 7·9	15·0 13·1
31	13 07·8	13 09·9	12 31·9	3·1 2·7	9·1 8·0	15·1 13·2
32	13 08·0	13 10·2	12 32·1	3·2 2·8	9·2 8·1	15·2 13·3
33	13 08·3	13 10·4	12 32·3	3·3 2·9	9·3 8·1	15·3 13·4
34	13 08·5	13 10·7	12 32·6	3·4 3·0	9·4 8·2	15·4 13·5
35	13 08·8	13 10·9	12 32·8	3·5 3·1	9·5 8·3	15·5 13·6
36	13 09·0	13 11·2	12 33·1	3·6 3·2	9·6 8·4	15·6 13·7
37	13 09·3	13 11·4	12 33·3	3·7 3·2	9·7 8·5	15·7 13·7
38	13 09·5	13 11·7	12 33·5	3·8 3·3	9·8 8·6	15·8 13·8
39	13 09·8	13 11·9	12 33·8	3·9 3·4	9·9 8·7	15·9 13·9
40	13 10·0	13 12·2	12 34·0	4·0 3·5	10·0 8·8	16·0 14·0
41	13 10·3	13 12·4	12 34·2	4·1 3·6	10·1 8·8	16·1 14·1
42	13 10·5	13 12·7	12 34·5	4·2 3·7	10·2 8·9	16·2 14·2
43	13 10·8	13 12·9	12 34·7	4·3 3·8	10·3 9·0	16·3 14·3
44	13 11·0	13 13·2	12 35·0	4·4 3·9	10·4 9·1	16·4 14·4
45	13 11·3	13 13·4	12 35·2	4·5 3·9	10·5 9·2	16·5 14·4
46	13 11·5	13 13·7	12 35·4	4·6 4·0	10·6 9·3	16·6 14·5
47	13 11·8	13 13·9	12 35·7	4·7 4·1	10·7 9·4	16·7 14·6
48	13 12·0	13 14·2	12 35·9	4·8 4·2	10·8 9·5	16·8 14·7
49	13 12·3	13 14·4	12 36·2	4·9 4·3	10·9 9·5	16·9 14·8
50	13 12·5	13 14·7	12 36·4	5·0 4·4	11·0 9·6	17·0 14·9
51	13 12·8	13 14·9	12 36·6	5·1 4·5	11·1 9·7	17·1 15·0
52	13 13·0	13 15·2	12 36·9	5·2 4·6	11·2 9·8	17·2 15·1
53	13 13·3	13 15·4	12 37·1	5·3 4·6	11·3 9·9	17·3 15·1
54	13 13·5	13 15·7	12 37·4	5·4 4·7	11·4 10·0	17·4 15·2
55	13 13·8	13 15·9	12 37·6	5·5 4·8	11·5 10·1	17·5 15·3
56	13 14·0	13 16·2	12 37·8	5·6 4·9	11·6 10·2	17·6 15·4
57	13 14·3	13 16·4	12 38·1	5·7 5·0	11·7 10·2	17·7 15·5
58	13 14·5	13 16·7	12 38·3	5·8 5·1	11·8 10·3	17·8 15·6
59	13 14·8	13 16·9	12 38·5	5·9 5·2	11·9 10·4	17·9 15·7
60	13 15·0	13 17·2	12 38·8	6·0 5·3	12·0 10·5	18·0 15·8

53ᵐ	SUN PLANETS	ARIES	MOON	v or Corrⁿ d	v or Corrⁿ d	v or Corrⁿ d
s	° ′	° ′	° ′	′ ′	′ ′	′ ′
00	13 15·0	13 17·2	12 38·8	0·0 0·0	6·0 5·4	12·0 10·7
01	13 15·3	13 17·4	12 39·0	0·1 0·1	6·1 5·4	12·1 10·8
02	13 15·5	13 17·7	12 39·3	0·2 0·2	6·2 5·5	12·2 10·9
03	13 15·8	13 17·9	12 39·5	0·3 0·3	6·3 5·6	12·3 11·0
04	13 16·0	13 18·2	12 39·7	0·4 0·4	6·4 5·7	12·4 11·1
05	13 16·3	13 18·4	12 40·0	0·5 0·4	6·5 5·8	12·5 11·1
06	13 16·5	13 18·7	12 40·2	0·6 0·5	6·6 5·9	12·6 11·2
07	13 16·8	13 18·9	12 40·5	0·7 0·6	6·7 6·0	12·7 11·3
08	13 17·0	13 19·2	12 40·7	0·8 0·7	6·8 6·1	12·8 11·4
09	13 17·3	13 19·4	12 40·9	0·9 0·8	6·9 6·2	12·9 11·5
10	13 17·5	13 19·7	12 41·2	1·0 0·9	7·0 6·2	13·0 11·6
11	13 17·8	13 19·9	12 41·4	1·1 1·0	7·1 6·3	13·1 11·7
12	13 18·0	13 20·2	12 41·6	1·2 1·1	7·2 6·4	13·2 11·8
13	13 18·3	13 20·4	12 41·9	1·3 1·2	7·3 6·5	13·3 11·9
14	13 18·5	13 20·7	12 42·1	1·4 1·2	7·4 6·6	13·4 11·9
15	13 18·8	13 20·9	12 42·4	1·5 1·3	7·5 6·7	13·5 12·0
16	13 19·0	13 21·2	12 42·6	1·6 1·4	7·6 6·8	13·6 12·1
17	13 19·3	13 21·4	12 42·8	1·7 1·5	7·7 6·9	13·7 12·2
18	13 19·5	13 21·7	12 43·1	1·8 1·6	7·8 7·0	13·8 12·3
19	13 19·8	13 21·9	12 43·3	1·9 1·7	7·9 7·0	13·9 12·4
20	13 20·0	13 22·2	12 43·6	2·0 1·8	8·0 7·1	14·0 12·5
21	13 20·3	13 22·4	12 43·8	2·1 1·9	8·1 7·2	14·1 12·6
22	13 20·5	13 22·7	12 44·0	2·2 2·0	8·2 7·3	14·2 12·7
23	13 20·8	13 22·9	12 44·3	2·3 2·1	8·3 7·4	14·3 12·8
24	13 21·0	13 23·2	12 44·5	2·4 2·1	8·4 7·5	14·4 12·8
25	13 21·3	13 23·4	12 44·7	2·5 2·2	8·5 7·6	14·5 12·9
26	13 21·5	13 23·7	12 45·0	2·6 2·3	8·6 7·7	14·6 13·0
27	13 21·8	13 23·9	12 45·2	2·7 2·4	8·7 7·8	14·7 13·1
28	13 22·0	13 24·2	12 45·5	2·8 2·5	8·8 7·8	14·8 13·2
29	13 22·3	13 24·4	12 45·7	2·9 2·6	8·9 7·9	14·9 13·3
30	13 22·5	13 24·7	12 45·9	3·0 2·7	9·0 8·0	15·0 13·4
31	13 22·8	13 24·9	12 46·2	3·1 2·8	9·1 8·1	15·1 13·5
32	13 23·0	13 25·2	12 46·4	3·2 2·9	9·2 8·2	15·2 13·6
33	13 23·3	13 25·4	12 46·7	3·3 2·9	9·3 8·3	15·3 13·6
34	13 23·5	13 25·7	12 46·9	3·4 3·0	9·4 8·4	15·4 13·7
35	13 23·8	13 26·0	12 47·1	3·5 3·1	9·5 8·5	15·5 13·8
36	13 24·0	13 26·2	12 47·4	3·6 3·2	9·6 8·6	15·6 13·9
37	13 24·3	13 26·5	12 47·6	3·7 3·3	9·7 8·6	15·7 14·0
38	13 24·5	13 26·7	12 47·9	3·8 3·4	9·8 8·7	15·8 14·1
39	13 24·8	13 27·0	12 48·1	3·9 3·5	9·9 8·8	15·9 14·2
40	13 25·0	13 27·2	12 48·3	4·0 3·6	10·0 8·9	16·0 14·3
41	13 25·3	13 27·5	12 48·6	4·1 3·7	10·1 9·0	16·1 14·4
42	13 25·5	13 27·7	12 48·8	4·2 3·7	10·2 9·1	16·2 14·4
43	13 25·8	13 28·0	12 49·0	4·3 3·8	10·3 9·2	16·3 14·5
44	13 26·0	13 28·2	12 49·3	4·4 3·9	10·4 9·3	16·4 14·6
45	13 26·3	13 28·5	12 49·5	4·5 4·0	10·5 9·4	16·5 14·7
46	13 26·5	13 28·7	12 49·8	4·6 4·1	10·6 9·5	16·6 14·8
47	13 26·8	13 29·0	12 50·0	4·7 4·2	10·7 9·5	16·7 14·9
48	13 27·0	13 29·2	12 50·2	4·8 4·3	10·8 9·6	16·8 15·0
49	13 27·3	13 29·5	12 50·5	4·9 4·4	10·9 9·7	16·9 15·1
50	13 27·5	13 29·7	12 50·7	5·0 4·5	11·0 9·8	17·0 15·2
51	13 27·8	13 30·0	12 51·0	5·1 4·5	11·1 9·9	17·1 15·2
52	13 28·0	13 30·2	12 51·2	5·2 4·6	11·2 10·0	17·2 15·3
53	13 28·3	13 30·5	12 51·4	5·3 4·7	11·3 10·1	17·3 15·4
54	13 28·5	13 30·7	12 51·7	5·4 4·8	11·4 10·2	17·4 15·5
55	13 28·8	13 31·0	12 51·9	5·5 4·9	11·5 10·3	17·5 15·6
56	13 29·0	13 31·2	12 52·1	5·6 5·0	11·6 10·3	17·6 15·7
57	13 29·3	13 31·5	12 52·4	5·7 5·1	11·7 10·4	17·7 15·8
58	13 29·5	13 31·7	12 52·6	5·8 5·2	11·8 10·5	17·8 15·9
59	13 29·8	13 32·0	12 52·9	5·9 5·3	11·9 10·6	17·9 16·0
60	13 30·0	13 32·2	12 53·1	6·0 5·4	12·0 10·7	18·0 16·1

TABLES FOR INTERPOLATING SUNRISE, MOONRISE, ETC.

TABLE I—FOR LATITUDE

Tabular Interval			Difference between the times for consecutive latitudes																
10°	5°	2°	5m	10m	15m	20m	25m	30m	35m	40m	45m	50m	55m	60m	1h 05m	1h 10m	1h 15m	1h 20m
° ′	° ′	° ′	m	m	m	m	m	m	m	m	m	m	m	m	h m	h m	h m	h m
0 30	0 15	0 06	0	0	1	1	1	1	1	2	2	2	2	2	0 02	0 02	0 02	0 02
1 00	0 30	0 12	0	1	1	2	2	3	3	3	4	4	4	5	05	05	05	05
1 30	0 45	0 18	1	1	2	3	3	4	4	5	5	6	7	7	07	07	07	07
2 00	1 00	0 24	1	2	3	4	5	5	6	7	7	8	9	10	10	10	10	10
2 30	1 15	0 30	1	2	4	5	6	7	8	9	9	10	11	12	12	13	13	13
3 00	1 30	0 36	1	3	4	6	7	8	9	10	11	12	13	14	0 15	0 15	0 16	0 16
3 30	1 45	0 42	2	3	5	7	8	10	11	12	13	14	16	17	18	18	19	19
4 00	2 00	0 48	2	4	6	8	9	11	13	14	15	16	18	19	20	21	22	22
4 30	2 15	0 54	2	4	7	9	11	13	15	16	18	19	21	22	23	24	25	26
5 00	2 30	1 00	2	5	7	10	12	14	16	18	20	22	23	25	26	27	28	29
5 30	2 45	1 06	3	5	8	11	13	16	18	20	22	24	26	28	0 29	0 30	0 31	0 32
6 00	3 00	1 12	3	6	9	12	14	17	20	22	24	26	29	31	32	33	34	36
6 30	3 15	1 18	3	6	10	13	16	19	22	24	26	29	31	34	36	37	38	40
7 00	3 30	1 24	3	7	10	14	17	20	23	26	29	31	34	37	39	41	42	44
7 30	3 45	1 30	4	7	11	15	18	22	25	28	31	34	37	40	43	44	46	48
8 00	4 00	1 36	4	8	12	16	20	23	27	30	34	37	41	44	0 47	0 48	0 51	0 53
8 30	4 15	1 42	4	8	13	17	21	25	29	33	36	40	44	48	0 51	0 53	0 56	0 58
9 00	4 30	1 48	4	9	13	18	22	27	31	35	39	43	47	52	0 55	0 58	1 01	1 04
9 30	4 45	1 54	5	9	14	19	24	28	33	38	42	47	51	56	1 00	1 04	1 08	1 12
10 00	5 00	2 00	5	10	15	20	25	30	35	40	45	50	55	60	1 05	1 10	1 15	1 20

Table I is for interpolating the L.M.T. of sunrise, twilight, moonrise, etc., for latitude. It is to be entered, in the appropriate column on the left, with the difference between true latitude and the nearest tabular latitude which is *less* than the true latitude; and with the argument at the top which is the nearest value of the difference between the times for the tabular latitude and the next higher one; the correction so obtained is applied to the time for the tabular latitude; the sign of the correction can be seen by inspection. It is to be noted that the interpolation is not linear, so that when using this table it is essential to take out the tabular phenomenon for the latitude *less* than true latitude.

TABLE II—FOR LONGITUDE

Long. East or West	Difference between the times for given date and preceding date (for east longitude) or for given date and following date (for west longitude)																		
	10m	20m	30m	40m	50m	60m	1h+ 10m	20m	30m	1h+ 40m	50m	60m	2h 10m	2h 20m	2h 30m	2h 40m	2h 50m	3h 00m
°	m	m	m	m	m	m	m	m	m	m	m	m	h m	h m	h m	h m	h m	h m
0	0	0	0	0	0	0	0	0	0	0	0	0	0 00	0 00	0 00	0 00	0 00	0 00
10	0	1	1	1	1	2	2	2	2	3	3	3	04	04	04	04	05	05
20	1	1	2	2	3	3	4	4	5	6	6	7	07	08	08	09	09	10
30	1	2	2	3	4	5	6	7	7	8	9	10	11	12	12	13	14	15
40	1	2	3	4	6	7	8	9	10	11	12	13	14	16	17	18	19	20
50	1	3	4	6	7	8	10	11	12	14	15	17	0 18	0 19	0 21	0 22	0 24	0 25
60	2	3	5	7	8	10	12	13	15	17	18	20	22	23	25	27	28	30
70	2	4	6	8	10	12	14	16	17	19	21	23	25	27	29	31	33	35
80	2	4	7	9	11	13	16	18	20	22	24	27	29	31	33	36	38	40
90	2	5	7	10	12	15	17	20	22	25	27	30	32	35	37	40	42	45
100	3	6	8	11	14	17	19	22	25	28	31	33	0 36	0 39	0 42	0 44	0 47	0 50
110	3	6	9	12	15	18	21	24	27	31	34	37	40	43	46	49	0 52	0 55
120	3	7	10	13	17	20	23	27	30	33	37	40	43	47	50	53	0 57	1 00
130	4	7	11	14	18	22	25	29	32	36	40	43	47	51	54	0 58	1 01	1 05
140	4	8	12	16	19	23	27	31	35	39	43	47	51	54	0 58	1 02	1 06	1 10
150	4	8	13	17	21	25	29	33	38	42	46	50	0 54	0 58	1 03	1 07	1 11	1 15
160	4	9	13	18	22	27	31	36	40	44	49	53	0 58	1 02	1 07	1 11	1 16	1 20
170	5	9	14	19	24	28	33	38	42	47	52	57	1 01	1 06	1 11	1 16	1 20	1 25
180	5	10	15	20	25	30	35	40	45	50	55	60	1 05	1 10	1 15	1 20	1 25	1 30

Table II is for interpolating the L.M.T. of moonrise, moonset and the Moon's meridian passage for longitude. It is entered with longitude and with the difference between the times for the given date and for the preceding date (in east longitudes) or following date (in west longitudes). The correction is normally *added* for west longitudes and *subtracted* for east longitudes, but if, as occasionally happens, the times become earlier each day instead of later, the signs of the corrections must be reversed.

ALTITUDE CORRECTION TABLES 0°–35°—MOON

App. Alt.	0°–4° Corrn	5°–9° Corrn	10°–14° Corrn	15°–19° Corrn	20°–24° Corrn	25°–29° Corrn	30°–34° Corrn	App. Alt.
00	0 33·8	5 58·2	10 62·1	15 62·8	20 62·2	25 60·8	30 58·9	00
10	35·9	58·5	62·2	62·8	62·1	60·8	58·8	10
20	37·8	58·7	62·2	62·8	62·1	60·7	58·8	20
30	39·6	58·9	62·3	62·8	62·1	60·7	58·7	30
40	41·2	59·1	62·3	62·8	62·0	60·6	58·6	40
50	42·6	59·3	62·4	62·7	62·0	60·6	58·5	50
00	1 44·0	6 59·5	11 62·4	16 62·7	21 62·0	26 60·5	31 58·5	00
10	45·2	59·7	62·4	62·7	61·9	60·4	58·4	10
20	46·3	59·9	62·5	62·7	61·9	60·4	58·3	20
30	47·3	60·0	62·5	62·7	61·9	60·3	58·2	30
40	48·3	60·2	62·5	62·7	61·8	60·3	58·2	40
50	49·2	60·3	62·6	62·7	61·8	60·2	58·1	50
00	2 50·0	7 60·5	12 62·6	17 62·7	22 61·7	27 60·1	32 58·0	00
10	50·8	60·6	62·6	62·6	61·7	60·1	57·9	10
20	51·4	60·7	62·6	62·6	61·6	60·0	57·8	20
30	52·1	60·9	62·7	62·6	61·6	59·9	57·8	30
40	52·7	61·0	62·7	62·6	61·5	59·9	57·7	40
50	53·3	61·1	62·7	62·6	61·5	59·8	57·6	50
00	3 53·8	8 61·2	13 62·7	18 62·5	23 61·5	28 59·7	33 57·5	00
10	54·3	61·3	62·7	62·5	61·4	59·7	57·4	10
20	54·8	61·4	62·7	62·5	61·4	59·6	57·4	20
30	55·2	61·5	62·8	62·5	61·3	59·6	57·3	30
40	55·6	61·6	62·8	62·4	61·3	59·5	57·2	40
50	56·0	61·6	62·8	62·4	61·2	59·4	57·1	50
00	4 56·4	9 61·7	14 62·8	19 62·4	24 61·2	29 59·3	34 57·0	00
10	56·7	61·8	62·8	62·3	61·1	59·3	56·9	10
20	57·1	61·9	62·8	62·3	61·1	59·2	56·9	20
30	57·4	61·9	62·8	62·3	61·0	59·1	56·8	30
40	57·7	62·0	62·8	62·2	60·9	59·1	56·7	40
50	57·9	62·1	62·8	62·2	60·9	59·0	56·6	50

H.P.	L U	L U	L U	L U	L U	L U	L U	H.P.
54·0	0·3 0·9	0·3 0·9	0·4 1·0	0·5 1·1	0·6 1·2	0·7 1·3	0·9 1·5	54·0
54·3	0·7 1·1	0·7 1·1	0·7 1·2	0·8 1·3	0·9 1·4	1·1 1·5	1·2 1·7	54·3
54·6	1·1 1·4	1·1 1·4	1·1 1·4	1·2 1·5	1·3 1·6	1·4 1·7	1·5 1·8	54·6
54·9	1·4 1·6	1·5 1·6	1·5 1·6	1·6 1·7	1·6 1·8	1·8 1·9	1·9 2·0	54·9
55·2	1·8 1·8	1·8 1·8	1·9 1·9	1·9 1·9	2·0 2·0	2·1 2·1	2·2 2·2	55·2
55·5	2·2 2·0	2·2 2·0	2·3 2·1	2·3 2·1	2·4 2·2	2·4 2·3	2·5 2·4	55·5
55·8	2·6 2·2	2·6 2·2	2·6 2·3	2·7 2·3	2·7 2·4	2·8 2·4	2·9 2·5	55·8
56·1	3·0 2·4	3·0 2·5	3·0 2·5	3·0 2·5	3·1 2·6	3·1 2·6	3·2 2·7	56·1
56·4	3·4 2·7	3·4 2·7	3·4 2·7	3·4 2·7	3·4 2·8	3·5 2·8	3·5 2·9	56·4
56·7	3·7 2·9	3·7 2·9	3·8 2·9	3·8 2·9	3·8 3·0	3·8 3·0	3·9 3·0	56·7
57·0	4·1 3·1	4·1 3·1	4·1 3·1	4·1 3·1	4·2 3·1	4·2 3·2	4·2 3·2	57·0
57·3	4·5 3·3	4·5 3·3	4·5 3·3	4·5 3·3	4·5 3·4	4·6 3·4	4·6 3·4	57·3
57·6	4·9 3·5	4·9 3·5	4·9 3·5	4·9 3·5	4·9 3·5	4·9 3·5	4·9 3·6	57·6
57·9	5·3 3·8	5·3 3·8	5·2 3·8	5·2 3·7	5·2 3·7	5·2 3·7	5·2 3·7	57·9
58·2	5·6 4·0	5·6 4·0	5·6 4·0	5·6 4·0	5·6 3·9	5·6 3·9	5·6 3·9	58·2
58·5	6·0 4·2	6·0 4·2	6·0 4·2	6·0 4·2	6·0 4·1	5·9 4·1	5·9 4·1	58·5
58·8	6·4 4·4	6·4 4·4	6·4 4·4	6·3 4·4	6·3 4·3	6·3 4·3	6·2 4·2	58·8
59·1	6·8 4·6	6·8 4·6	6·7 4·6	6·7 4·6	6·7 4·5	6·6 4·5	6·6 4·4	59·1
59·4	7·2 4·8	7·1 4·8	7·1 4·8	7·1 4·8	7·0 4·7	7·0 4·7	6·9 4·6	59·4
59·7	7·5 5·1	7·5 5·0	7·5 5·0	7·5 5·0	7·4 4·9	7·3 4·8	7·2 4·7	59·7
60·0	7·9 5·3	7·9 5·3	7·9 5·2	7·8 5·2	7·8 5·1	7·7 5·0	7·6 4·9	60·0
60·3	8·3 5·5	8·3 5·5	8·2 5·4	8·2 5·4	8·1 5·3	8·0 5·2	7·9 5·1	60·3
60·6	8·7 5·7	8·7 5·7	8·6 5·7	8·6 5·6	8·5 5·5	8·4 5·4	8·2 5·3	60·6
60·9	9·1 5·9	9·0 5·9	9·0 5·9	8·9 5·8	8·8 5·7	8·7 5·6	8·6 5·4	60·9
61·2	9·5 6·2	9·4 6·1	9·4 6·1	9·3 6·0	9·2 5·9	9·1 5·8	8·9 5·6	61·2
61·5	9·8 6·4	9·8 6·3	9·7 6·3	9·7 6·2	9·5 6·1	9·4 5·9	9·2 5·8	61·5

DIP

Ht. of Eye (m)	Ht. of Eye (ft.)	Corrn	Ht. of Eye (m)	Ht. of Eye (ft.)	Corrn
2·4	8·0	−2·8	9·5	31·5	−5·5
2·6	8·6	−2·9	9·9	32·7	−5·6
2·8	9·2	−3·0	10·3	33·9	−5·7
3·0	9·8	−3·1	10·6	35·1	−5·8
3·2	10·5	−3·2	11·0	36·3	−5·9
3·4	11·2	−3·3	11·4	37·6	−6·0
3·6	11·9	−3·4	11·8	38·9	−6·1
3·8	12·6	−3·5	12·2	40·1	−6·2
4·0	13·3	−3·6	12·6	41·5	−6·3
4·3	14·1	−3·7	13·0	42·8	−6·4
4·5	14·9	−3·8	13·4	44·2	−6·5
4·7	15·7	−3·9	13·8	45·5	−6·6
5·0	16·5	−4·0	14·2	46·9	−6·7
5·2	17·4	−4·1	14·7	48·4	−6·8
5·5	18·3	−4·2	15·1	49·8	−6·9
5·8	19·1	−4·3	15·5	51·3	−7·0
6·1	20·1	−4·4	16·0	52·8	−7·1
6·3	21·0	−4·5	16·5	54·3	−7·2
6·6	22·0	−4·6	16·9	55·8	−7·3
6·9	22·9	−4·7	17·4	57·4	−7·4
7·2	23·9	−4·8	17·9	58·9	−7·5
7·5	24·9	−4·9	18·4	60·5	−7·6
7·9	26·0	−5·0	18·8	62·1	−7·7
8·2	27·1	−5·1	19·3	63·8	−7·8
8·5	28·1	−5·2	19·8	65·4	−7·9
8·8	29·2	−5·3	20·4	67·1	−8·0
9·2	30·4	−5·4	20·9	68·8	−8·1
9·5	31·5		21·4	70·5	

MOON CORRECTION TABLE

The correction is in two parts; the first correction is taken from the upper part of the table with argument apparent altitude, and the second from the lower part, with argument H.P., in the same column as that from which the first correction was taken. Separate corrections are given in the lower part for lower (L) and upper (U) limbs. All corrections are to be **added** to apparent altitude, *but 30′ is to be subtracted from the altitude of the upper limb.*

For corrections for pressure and temperature see page A4.

For bubble sextant observations ignore dip, take the mean of upper and lower limb corrections and subtract 15′ from the altitude.

App. Alt. = Apparent altitude = Sextant altitude corrected for index error and dip.

Increment to be added for intervals of G.M.T. to G.H.A. of: Sun, Aries ( ) and planets; Moon

No.	Name		Mag.	S.H.A. ° '	Dec. ° '
7*	Acamar		3·1	315 39	S. 40 24
5*	Achernar		0·6	335 47	S. 57 21
30*	Acrux		1·1	173 39	S. 62 59
19	Adhara	†	1·6	255 33	S. 28 57
10*	Aldebaran	†	1·1	291 20	N. 16 28
32*	Alioth		1·7	166 44	N. 56 05
34*	Alkaid		1·9	153 20	N. 49 25
55	Al Na'ir		2·2	28 17	S. 47 04
15	Alnilam	†	1·8	276 13	S. 1 13
25*	Alphard	†	2·2	218 22	S. 8 34
41*	Alphecca	†	2·3	126 33	N. 26 47
1*	Alpheratz	†	2·2	358 11	N. 28 58
51*	Altair	†	0·9	62 34	N. 8 49
2	Ankaa		2·4	353 42	S. 42 26
42*	Antares	†	1·2	112 59	S. 26 23
37*	Arcturus	†	0·2	146 20	N. 19 18
43	Atria		1·9	108 24	S. 68 59
22	Avior		1·7	234 29	S. 59 27
13	Bellatrix	†	1·7	279 01	N. 6 20
16*	Betelgeuse	†	0·1⁻	271 30	N. 7 24
17*	Canopus		—0·9	264 08	S. 52 41
12*	Capella		0·2	281 14	N. 45 59
53*	Deneb		1·3	49 50	N. 45 12
28*	Denebola	†	2·2	183 01	N. 14 42
4*	Diphda	†	2·2	349 23	S. 18 06
27*	Dubhe		2·0	194 24	N. 61 52
14	Elnath	†	1·8	278 46	N. 28 35
47	Eltanin		2·4	90 58	N. 51 29
54*	Enif	†	2·5	34 13	N. 9 46
56*	Fomalhaut	†	1·3	15 53	S. 29 44
31	Gacrux		1·6	172 30	S. 57 00
29*	Gienah	†	2·8	176 19	S. 17 25
35	Hadar		0·9	149 25	S. 60 16
6*	Hamal	†	2·2	328 31	N. 23 21
48	Kaus Aust.		2·0	84 19	S. 34 24
40*	Kochab		2·2	137 18	N. 74 15
57	Markab	†	2·6	14 05	N. 15 05
8*	Menkar	†	2·8	314 43	N. 4 00
36	Menkent		2·3	148 39	S. 36 16
24*	Miaplacidus		1·8	221 45	S. 69 38
9*	Mirfak		1·9	309 19	N. 49 47
50*	Nunki	†	2·1	76 31	S. 26 19
52*	Peacock		2·1	54 01	S. 56 48
21*	Pollux	†	1·2	244 00	N. 28 05
20*	Procyon	†	0·5	245 27	N. 5 17
46*	Rasalhague	†	2·1	96 31	N. 12 35
26*	Regulus	†	1·3	208 12	N. 12 04
11*	Rigel	†	0·3	281 38	S. 8 14
38*	Rigil Kent.		0·1	140 28	S. 60 45
44	Sabik	†	2·6	102 43	S. 15 42
3*	Schedar		2·5	350 11	N. 56 25
45*	Shaula		1·7	96 58	S. 37 05
18*	Sirius	†	—1·6	258 57	S. 16 41
32*	Spica	†	1·2	158 59	S. 11 03
23*	Suhail		2·2	223 12	S. 43 21
49*	Vega		0·1	80 57	N. 38 46
39	Zuben'ubi	†	2·9	137 35	S. 15 57

INTERPOLATION OF G.H.A.

Panel 1

SUN, etc. (m s)	° '	MOON (m s)
00 00	0 00	00 00
01	0 01	00 02
05	0 02	00 06
09	0 03	00 10
13	0 04	00 14
17	0 05	00 18
21	0 06	00 22
25	0 07	00 26
29	0 08	00 31
33	0 09	00 35
37	0 10	00 39
41	0 11	00 43
45	0 12	00 47
49	0 13	00 51
53	0 14	00 55
00 57	0 15	01 00
01 01	0 16	01 04
05	0 17	01 08
09	0 18	01 12
13	0 19	01 16
17	0 20	01 20
21	0 21	01 24
25	0 22	01 29
29	0 23	01 33
33	0 24	01 37
37	0 25	01 41
41	0 26	01 45
45	0 27	01 49
49	0 28	01 53
53	0 29	01 58
01 57	0 30	02 02
02 01	0 31	02 06
05	0 32	02 10
09	0 33	02 14
13	0 34	02 18
17	0 35	02 22
21	0 36	02 27
25	0 37	02 31
29	0 38	02 35
33	0 39	02 39
37	0 40	02 43
41	0 41	02 47
45	0 42	02 51
49	0 43	02 56
53	0 44	03 00
02 57	0 45	03 04
03 01	0 46	03 08
05	0 47	03 12
09	0 48	03 16
13	0 49	03 20
17	0 50	03 25
03 21		03 29

Panel 2

SUN, etc. (m s)	° '	MOON (m s)
03 17	0 50	03 25
21	0 51	03 29
25	0 52	03 33
29	0 53	03 37
33	0 54	03 41
37	0 55	03 45
41	0 56	03 49
45	0 57	03 54
49	0 58	03 58
53	0 59	04 02
03 57	1 00	04 06
04 01	1 01	04 10
05	1 02	04 14
09	1 03	04 19
13	1 04	04 23
17	1 05	04 27
21	1 06	04 31
25	1 07	04 35
29	1 08	04 39
33	1 09	04 43
37	1 10	04 48
41	1 11	04 52
45	1 12	04 56
49	1 13	05 00
53	1 14	05 04
04 57	1 15	05 08
05 01	1 16	05 12
05	1 17	05 17
09	1 18	05 21
13	1 19	05 25
17	1 20	05 29
21	1 21	05 33
25	1 22	05 37
29	1 23	05 41
33	1 24	05 46
37	1 25	05 50
41	1 26	05 54
45	1 27	05 58
49	1 28	06 02
53	1 29	06 06
05 57	1 30	06 10
06 01	1 31	06 15
05	1 32	06 19
09	1 33	06 23
13	1 34	06 27
17	1 35	06 31
21	1 36	06 35
25	1 37	06 39
29	1 38	06 44
33	1 39	06 48
37	1 40	06 52
06 41		06 56

Panel 3

SUN, etc. (m s)	° '	MOON (m s)
06 37	1 40	06 52
41	1 41	06 56
45	1 42	07 00
49	1 43	07 04
53	1 44	07 08
06 57	1 45	07 13
07 01	1 46	07 17
05	1 47	07 21
09	1 48	07 25
13	1 49	07 29
17	1 50	07 33
21	1 51	07 37
25	1 52	07 42
29	1 53	07 46
33	1 54	07 50
37	1 55	07 54
41	1 56	07 58
45	1 57	08 02
49	1 58	08 06
53	1 59	08 11
07 57	2 00	08 15
08 01	2 01	08 19
05	2 02	08 23
09	2 03	08 27
13	2 04	08 31
17	2 05	08 35
21	2 06	08 40
25	2 07	08 44
29	2 08	08 48
33	2 09	08 52
37	2 10	08 56
41	2 11	09 00
45	2 12	09 04
49	2 13	09 09
53	2 14	09 13
08 57	2 15	09 17
09 01	2 16	09 21
05	2 17	09 25
09	2 18	09 29
13	2 19	09 33
17	2 20	09 38
21	2 21	09 42
25	2 22	09 46
29	2 23	09 50
33	2 24	09 54
37	2 25	09 58
41	2 26	10 00
45	2 27	
49	2 28	
53	2 29	
09 57	2 30	

*Stars used in Pub. 249 (A.P. 3270) Vol. 1.
†Stars that may be used with Vols. 2 and 3.

INTERPOLATION OF MOONRISE, MOONSET

FOR LONGITUDE

Add if longitude *west*
Subtract if longitude *east*

Longitude	Diff.*					
tude	05	10	15	20	25	30
°	m	m	m	m	m	m
0	00	00	00	00	00	00
20	01	01	02	02	03	03
40	01	02	03	04	06	07
60	02	03	05	07	08	10
80	02	04	07	09	11	13
100	03	06	08	11	14	17
120	03	07	10	13	17	20
140	04	08	12	16	19	23
160	04	09	13	18	22	27
180	05	10	15	20	25	30

Longitude	Diff.*					
tude	35	40	45	50	55	60
°	m	m	m	m	m	m
0	00	00	00	00	00	00
15	03	03	04	04	05	05
30	06	07	08	08	09	10
45	09	10	11	12	14	15
60	12	13	15	17	18	20
75	15	17	19	21	23	25
90	18	20	22	25	28	30
105	20	23	26	29	32	35
120	23	27	30	33	37	40
135	26	30	34	38	41	45
150	29	33	38	42	46	50
165	32	37	41	46	50	55
180	35	40	45	50	55	60

Longitude	Diff.*					
tude	65	70	75	80	85	90
°	m	m	m	m	m	m
0	00	00	00	00	00	00
10	04	04	04	04	05	05
20	07	08	08	09	09	10
30	11	12	12	13	14	15
40	14	16	17	18	19	20
50	18	19	21	22	24	25
60	22	23	25	27	28	30
70	25	27	29	31	33	35
80	29	31	33	36	38	40
90	32	35	38	40	42	45
100	36	39	42	44	47	50
110	40	43	46	49	52	55
120	43	47	50	53	57	60
130	47	51	54	58	61	65
140	51	54	58	62	66	70
150	54	58	62	67	71	75
160	58	62	67	71	76	80
170	61	66	71	76	80	85
180	65	70	75	80	85	90

*When negative *subtract* correction if longitude *west*, and *add* if *east*.

STAR INDEX, JAN.—JUNE, 1978

No.	Name		Mag.	S.H.A.	Dec.
				° ′	° ′
1*	Alpheratz	†	2·2	358 11	N. 28 58
2	Ankaa		2·4	353 42	S. 42 26
3*	Schedar		2·5	350 11	N. 56 25
4*	Diphda	†	2·2	349 23	S. 18 06
5*	Achernar		0·6	335 47	S. 57 21
6*	Hamal	†	2·2	328 31	N. 23 21
7*	Acamar		3·1	315 39	S. 40 24
8*	Menkar	†	2·8	314 43	N. 4 00
9*	Mirfak		1·9	309 19	N. 49 47
10*	Aldebaran	†	1·1	291 20	N. 16 28
11*	Rigel	†	0·3	281 38	S. 8 14
12*	Capella		0·2	281 14	N. 45 59
13	Bellatrix	†	1·7	279 01	N. 6 20
14	Elnath	†	1·8	278 46	N. 28 35
15	Alnilam	†	1·8	276 13	S. 1 13
16*	Betelgeuse	†	0·1–1·2	271 30	N. 7 24
17*	Canopus		−0·9	264 08	S. 52 41
18*	Sirius	†	−1·6	258 57	S. 16 41
19	Adhara	†	1·6	255 33	S. 28 57
20*	Procyon	†	0·5	245 27	N. 5 17
21*	Pollux	†	1·2	244 00	N. 28 05
22	Avior		1·7	234 29	S. 59 27
23*	Suhail		2·2	223 12	S. 43 21
24*	Miaplacidus		1·8	221 45	S. 69 38
25*	Alphard	†	2·2	218 22	S. 8 34
26*	Regulus	†	1·3	208 12	N. 12 04
27*	Dubhe		2·0	194 24	N. 61 52
28*	Denebola	†	2·2	183 01	N. 14 42
29*	Gienah	†	2·8	176 19	S. 17 25
30*	Acrux		1·1	173 39	S. 62 59
31	Gacrux		1·6	172 30	S. 57 00
32*	Alioth		1·7	166 44	N. 56 05
33*	Spica	†	1·2	158 59	S. 11 03
34*	Alkaid		1·9	153 20	N. 49 25
35	Hadar		0·9	149 25	S. 60 16
36	Menkent		2·3	148 39	S. 36 16
37*	Arcturus	†	0·2	146 20	N. 19 18
38*	Rigil Kentaurus		0·1	140 28	S. 60 45
39	Zubenelgenubi	†	2·9	137 35	S. 15 57
40*	Kochab		2·2	137 18	N. 74 15
41*	Alphecca	†	2·3	126 33	N. 26 47
42*	Antares	†	1·2	112 59	S. 26 23
43	Atria		1·9	108 24	S. 68 59
44	Sabik	†	2·6	102 43	S. 15 42
45*	Shaula		1·7	96 58	S. 37 05
46*	Rasalhague	†	2·1	96 31	N. 12 35
47	Eltanin		2·4	90 58	N. 51 29
48	Kaus Australis		2·0	84 19	S. 34 24
49*	Vega		0·1	80 57	N. 38 46
50*	Nunki	†	2·1	76 31	S. 26 19
51*	Altair	†	0·9	62 34	N. 8 49
52*	Peacock		2·1	54 01	S. 56 48
53*	Deneb		1·3	49 50	N. 45 12
54*	Enif	†	2·5	34 13	N. 9 46
55	Al Na'ir		2·2	28 17	S. 47 04
56*	Fomalhaut	†	1·3	15 53	S. 29 44
57	Markab	†	2·6	14 05	N. 15 05

*Stars used in Pub. 249 (A.P. 3270) Vol. 1.
†Stars that may be used with Vols. 2 and 3.

(DAY 156) GREENWICH A. M. 1977 JUNE 5 (SUNDAY)

GMT	SUN GHA	SUN Dec.	ARIES GHA ♈	VENUS−4.1 GHA	VENUS Dec.	MARS 1.3 GHA	MARS Dec.	SATURN 0.6 GHA	SATURN Dec.	MOON GHA	MOON Dec.
h m	° ′	° ′	° ′	° ′	° ′	° ′	° ′	° ′	° ′	° ′	° ′
00 00	180 25.5	N22 30.4	253 18.4	225 38	N 8 57	225 49	N10 12	118 04	N18 00	313 54	S15 29
10	182 55.5	30.5	255 48.8	228 08		228 19		120 34		316 18	28
20	185 25.5	30.5	258 19.2	230 38		230 49		123 05		318 42	27
30	187 55.4 ·	30.6	260 49.6	233 08 ·	·	233 19 ·	·	125 35 ·	·	321 07 ·	25
40	190 25.4	30.6	263 20.0	235 38		235 49		128 06		323 31	24
50	192 55.4	30.6	265 50.4	238 08		238 20		130 36		325 55	23
01 00	195 25.4	N22 30.7	268 20.9	240 38	N 8 57	240 50	N10 13	133 06	N18 00	328 20	S15 22
10	197 55.4	30.7	270 51.3	243 08		243 20		135 37		330 44	21
20	200 25.4	30.8	273 21.7	245 38		245 50		138 07		333 08	20
30	202 55.3 ·	30.8	275 52.1	248 08 ·		248 20 ·		140 38 ·	·	335 33 ·	19
40	205 25.3	30.9	278 22.5	250 38		250 50		143 08		337 57	17
50	207 55.3	30.9	280 52.9	253 08		253 20		145 38		340 21	16
02 00	210 25.3	N22 31.0	283 23.3	255 38	N 8 58	255 50	N10 13	148 09	N18 00	342 46	S15 15
10	212 55.3	31.0	285 53.7	258 08		258 21		150 39		345 10	14
20	215 25.2	31.1	288 24.1	260 38		260 51		153 09		347 34	13
30	217 55.2 ·	31.1	290 54.6	263 08 ·		263 21 ·		155 40 ·	·	349 59 ·	12
40	220 25.2	31.2	293 25.0	265 39		265 51		158 10		352 23	10
50	222 55.2	31.2	295 55.4	268 09		268 21		160 41		354 47	09
03 00	225 25.2	N22 31.3	298 25.8	270 39	N 8 59	270 51	N10 14	163 11	N17 59	357 12	S15 08
10	227 55.2	31.3	300 56.2	273 09		273 21		165 41		359 36	07
20	230 25.1	31.3	303 26.6	275 39		275 51		168 12		2 00	06
30	232 55.1 ·	31.4	305 57.0	278 09 ·		278 21 ·		170 42 ·	·	4 25 ·	05
40	235 25.1	31.4	308 27.4	280 39		280 52		173 12		6 49	03
50	237 55.1	31.5	310 57.8	283 09		283 22		175 43		9 13	02
04 00	240 25.1	N22 31.5	313 28.3	285 39	N 8 59	285 52	N10 15	178 13	N17 59	11 38	S15 01
10	242 55.0	31.6	315 58.7	288 09		288 22		180 43		14 02	15 00
20	245 25.0	31.6	318 29.1	290 39		290 52		183 14		16 26	14 59
30	247 55.0 ·	31.7	320 59.5	293 09 ·		293 22 ·		185 44 ·	·	18 51 ·	58
40	250 25.0	31.7	323 29.9	295 39		295 52		188 15		21 15	56
50	252 55.0	31.8	326 00.3	298 09		298 22		190 45		23 40	55
05 00	255 25.0	N22 31.8	328 30.7	300 39	N 9 00	300 53	N10 15	193 15	N17 59	26 04	S14 54
10	257 54.9	31.9	331 01.1	303 09		303 23		195 46		28 28	53
20	260 24.9	31.9	333 31.5	305 39		305 53		198 16		30 53	51
30	262 54.9 ·	31.9	336 01.9	308 09 ·		308 23 ·		200 46 ·	·	33 17 ·	50
40	265 24.9	32.0	338 32.4	310 40		310 53		203 17		35 41	49
50	267 54.9	32.0	341 02.8	313 10		313 23		205 47		38 06	48
06 00	270 24.8	N22 32.1	343 33.2	315 40	N 9 01	315 53	N10 16	208 18	N17 59	40 30	S14 47
10	272 54.8	32.1	346 03.6	318 10		318 23		210 48		42 55	45
20	275 24.8	32.2	348 34.0	320 40		320 53		213 18		45 19	44
30	277 54.8 ·	32.2	351 04.4	323 10 ·		323 24 ·		215 49 ·	·	47 43 ·	43
40	280 24.8	32.3	353 34.8	325 40		325 54		218 19		50 08	42
50	282 54.8	32.3	356 05.2	328 10		328 24		220 49		52 32	41
07 00	285 24.7	N22 32.4	358 35.6	330 40	N 9 01	330 54	N10 17	223 20	N17 59	54 57	S14 39
10	287 54.7	32.4	1 06.1	333 10		333 24		225 50		57 21	38
20	290 24.7	32.4	3 36.5	335 40		335 54		228 21		59 45	37
30	292 54.7 ·	32.5	6 06.9	338 10 ·		338 24 ·		230 51 ·	·	62 10 ·	36
40	295 24.7	32.5	8 37.3	340 40		340 54		233 21		64 34	34
50	297 54.6	32.6	11 07.7	343 10		343 24		235 52		66 59	33
08 00	300 24.6	N22 32.6	13 38.1	345 40	N 9 02	345 55	N10 17	238 22	N17 59	69 23	S14 32
10	302 54.6	32.7	16 08.5	348 10		348 25		240 52		71 47	31
20	305 24.6	32.7	18 38.9	350 40		350 55		243 23		74 12	29
30	307 54.6 ·	32.8	21 09.3	353 11 ·		353 25 ·		245 53 ·	·	76 36 ·	28
40	310 24.6	32.8	23 39.8	355 41		355 55		248 24		79 01	27
50	312 54.5	32.9	26 10.2	358 11		358 25		250 54		81 25	26
09 00	315 24.5	N22 32.9	28 40.6	0 41	N 9 02	0 55	N10 18	253 24	N17 59	83 49	S14 24
10	317 54.5	33.0	31 11.0	3 11		3 25		255 55		86 14	23
20	320 24.5	33.0	33 41.4	5 41		5 56		258 25		88 38	22
30	322 54.5 ·	33.0	36 11.8	8 11 ·		8 26 ·		260 55 ·	·	91 03 ·	21
40	325 24.4	33.1	38 42.2	10 41		10 56		263 26		93 27	19
50	327 54.4	33.1	41 12.6	13 11		13 26		265 56		95 52	18
10 00	330 24.4	N22 33.2	43 43.0	15 41	N 9 03	15 56	N10 19	268 27	N17 59	98 16	S14 17
10	332 54.4	33.2	46 13.4	18 11		18 26		270 57		100 40	16
20	335 24.4	33.3	48 43.9	20 41		20 56		273 27		103 05	14
30	337 54.4 ·	33.3	51 14.3	23 11 ·		23 26 ·		275 58 ·	·	105 29 ·	13
40	340 24.3	33.4	53 44.7	25 41		25 56		278 28		107 54	12
50	342 54.3	33.4	56 15.1	28 11		28 27		280 58		110 18	10
11 00	345 24.3	N22 33.5	58 45.5	30 41	N 9 04	30 57	N10 19	283 29	N17 59	112 43	S14 09
10	347 54.3	33.5	61 15.9	33 11		33 27		285 59		115 07	08
20	350 24.3	33.5	63 46.3	35 42		35 57		288 30		117 32	07
30	352 54.2 ·	33.6	66 16.7	38 12 ·		38 27 ·		291 00 ·	·	119 56 ·	05
40	355 24.2	33.6	68 47.1	40 42		40 57		293 30		122 21	04
50	357 54.2	33.7	71 17.6	43 12		43 27		296 01		124 45	03
Rate	14 59.9	N0 00.3		15 00.3	N0 00.6	15 00.7	N0 00.7	15 02.3	S0 00.1	14 26.3	N0 07.3

Moon-rise

Lat.	Moon-rise	Diff.
N °	h m	m
72	01 02	−11
70	00 26	+03
68	00 00	08
66	23 57	07
64	23 46	10
62	23 36	11
60	23 28	13
58	23 20	14
56	23 14	15
54	23 08	16
52	23 03	17
50	22 58	18
45	22 47	19
40	22 39	20
35	22 31	21
30	22 24	23
20	22 13	24
10	22 03	26
0	21 54	27
10	21 44	28
20	21 34	30
30	21 22	31
35	21 16	32
40	21 08	33
45	20 59	35
50	20 48	36
52	20 43	37
54	20 38	38
56	20 32	39
58	20 25	40
60	20 17	41
S		

Moon's P. in A.

Alt. °	+ Corr.	Alt. °	+ Corr.
0	59	54	34
10	58	55	33
14	57	56	32
18	57	58	31
21	56	59	30
23	55	60	29
25	54	61	28
28	53	62	27
30	52	63	26
31	51	64	25
33	50	65	24
35	49	66	23
36	48	67	22
38	47	68	21
40	46	69	20
41	45	70	19
42	44	71	18
44	43	72	17
45	42	73	16
47	41	74	15
48	40	75	14
49	39	76	13
50	38	77	12
52	37	78	11
53	36	79	10
54	35	80	
55	34		

Sun SD 15.8
Moon SD 16′
Age 18d

(DAY 156) GREENWICH P. M. 1977 JUNE 5 (SUNDAY)

GMT	SUN GHA	SUN Dec.	ARIES GHA ♈	VENUS −4.1 GHA	VENUS Dec.	MARS 1.3 GHA	MARS Dec.	SATURN 0.6 GHA	SATURN Dec.	MOON GHA	MOON Dec.
h m	° ′	° ′	° ′	° ′	° ′	° ′	° ′	° ′	° ′	° ′	° ′
12 00	0 24.2	N22 33.7	73 48.0	45 42	N 9 04	45 57	N10 20	298 31	N17 59	127 10	S14 01
10	2 54.2	33.8	76 18.4	48 12		48 28		301 01		129 34	14 00
20	5 24.2	33.8	78 48.8	50 42		50 58		303 32		131 59	13 59
30	7 54.1 ·	33.9	81 19.2	53 12 ·	·	53 28 ·	·	306 02 ·	·	134 23 ·	57
40	10 24.1	33.9	83 49.6	55 42		55 58		308 33		136 47	56
50	12 54.1	34.0	86 20.0	58 12		58 28		311 03		139 12	55
13 00	15 24.1	N22 34.0	88 50.4	60 42	N 9 05	60 58	N10 21	313 33	N17 59	141 36	S13 54
10	17 54.1	34.0	91 20.8	63 12		63 28		316 04		144 01	52
20	20 24.0	34.1	93 51.3	65 42		65 58		318 34		146 25	51
30	22 54.0 ·	34.1	96 21.7	68 12 ·	·	68 28 ·	·	321 04 ·	·	148 50 ·	50
40	25 24.0	34.2	98 52.1	70 42		70 59		323 35		151 14	48
50	27 54.0	34.2	101 22.5	73 12		73 29		326 05		153 39	47
14 00	30 24.0	N22 34.3	103 52.9	75 42	N 9 06	75 59	N10 21	328 36	N17 59	156 03	S13 46
10	32 54.0	34.3	106 23.3	78 12		78 29		331 06		158 28	44
20	35 23.9	34.4	108 53.7	80 43		80 59		333 36		160 52	43
30	37 53.9 ·	34.4	111 24.1	83 13 ·	·	83 29 ·	·	336 07 ·	·	163 17 ·	42
40	40 23.9	34.4	113 54.5	85 43		85 59		338 37		165 41	40
50	42 53.9	34.5	116 24.9	88 13		88 29		341 07		168 06	39
15 00	45 23.9	N22 34.5	118 55.4	90 43	N 9 06	91 00	N10 22	343 38	N17 59	170 30	S13 38
10	47 53.8	34.6	121 25.8	93 13		93 30		346 08		172 55	36
20	50 23.8	34.6	123 56.2	95 43		96 00		348 39		175 20	35
30	52 53.8 ·	34.7	126 26.6	98 13 ·	·	98 30 ·	·	351 09 ·	·	177 44 ·	34
40	55 23.8	34.7	128 57.0	100 43		101 00		353 39		180 09	32
50	57 53.8	34.8	131 27.4	103 13		103 30		356 10		182 33	31
16 00	60 23.7	N22 34.8	133 57.8	105 43	N 9 07	106 00	N10 23	358 40	N17 59	184 58	S13 30
10	62 53.7	34.9	136 28.2	108 13		108 30		1 10		187 22	28
20	65 23.7	34.9	138 58.6	110 43		111 00		3 41		189 47	27
30	67 53.7 ·	34.9	141 29.1	113 13 ·	·	113 31 ·	·	6 11 ·	·	192 11 ·	26
40	70 23.7	35.0	143 59.5	115 43		116 01		8 42		194 36	24
50	72 53.7	35.0	146 29.9	118 13		118 31		11 12		197 00	23
17 00	75 23.6	N22 35.1	149 00.3	120 43	N 9 08	121 01	N10 23	13 42	N17 59	199 25	S13 22
10	77 53.6	35.1	151 30.7	123 13		123 31		16 13		201 49	20
20	80 23.6	35.2	154 01.1	125 44		126 01		18 43		204 14	19
30	82 53.6 ·	35.2	156 31.5	128 14 ·	·	128 31 ·	·	21 13 ·	·	206 39 ·	17
40	85 23.6	35.3	159 01.9	130 44		131 01		23 44		209 03	16
50	87 53.5	35.3	161 32.3	133 14		133 31		26 14		211 28	15
18 00	90 23.5	N22 35.3	164 02.8	135 44	N 9 08	136 02	N10 24	28 45	N17 59	213 52	S13 13
10	92 53.5	35.4	166 33.2	138 14		138 32		31 15		216 17	12
20	95 23.5	35.4	169 03.6	140 44		141 02		33 45		218 41	11
30	97 53.5 ·	35.5	171 34.0	143 14 ·	·	143 32 ·	·	36 16 ·	·	221 06 ·	09
40	100 23.5	35.5	174 04.4	145 44		146 02		38 46		223 30	08
50	102 53.4	35.6	176 34.8	148 14		148 32		41 16		225 55	06
19 00	105 23.4	N22 35.6	179 05.2	150 44	N 9 09	151 02	N10 25	43 47	N17 58	228 20	S13 05
10	107 53.4	35.7	181 35.6	153 14		153 32		46 17		230 44	04
20	110 23.4	35.7	184 06.0	155 44		156 03		48 48		233 09	02
30	112 53.4 ·	35.7	186 36.4	158 14 ·	·	158 33 ·	·	51 18 ·	·	235 33 ·	01
40	115 23.3	35.8	189 06.9	160 44		161 03		53 48		237 58	13 00
50	117 53.3	35.8	191 37.3	163 14		163 33		56 19		240 23	12 58
20 00	120 23.3	N22 35.9	194 07.7	165 44	N 9 09	166 03	N10 25	58 49	N17 58	242 47	S12 57
10	122 53.3	35.9	196 38.1	168 14		168 33		61 19		245 12	55
20	125 23.3	36.0	199 08.5	170 45		171 03		63 50		247 36	54
30	127 53.3 ·	36.0	201 38.9	173 15 ·	·	173 33 ·	·	66 20 ·	·	250 01 ·	53
40	130 23.2	36.1	204 09.3	175 45		176 03		68 51		252 26	51
50	132 53.2	36.1	206 39.7	178 15		178 34		71 21		254 50	50
21 00	135 23.2	N22 36.1	209 10.1	180 45	N 9 10	181 04	N10 26	73 51	N17 58	257 15	S12 48
10	137 53.2	36.2	211 40.6	183 15		183 34		76 22		259 39	47
20	140 23.2	36.2	214 11.0	185 45		186 04		78 52		262 04	46
30	142 53.1 ·	36.3	216 41.4	188 15 ·	·	188 34 ·	·	81 22 ·	·	264 29 ·	44
40	145 23.1	36.3	219 11.8	190 45		191 04		83 53		266 53	43
50	147 53.1	36.4	221 42.2	193 15		193 34		86 23		269 18	41
22 00	150 23.1	N22 36.4	224 12.6	195 45	N 9 11	196 04	N10 27	88 54	N17 58	271 42	S12 40
10	152 53.1	36.5	226 43.0	198 15		198 35		91 24		274 07	39
20	155 23.0	36.5	229 13.4	200 45		201 05		93 54		276 32	37
30	157 53.0 ·	36.5	231 43.8	203 15 ·	·	203 35 ·	·	96 25 ·	·	278 56 ·	36
40	160 23.0	36.6	234 14.2	205 45		206 05		98 55		281 21	34
50	162 53.0	36.6	236 44.7	208 15		208 35		101 25		283 46	33
23 00	165 23.0	N22 36.7	239 15.1	210 45	N 9 11	211 05	N10 27	103 56	N17 58	286 10	S12 31
10	167 53.0	36.7	241 45.5	213 15		213 35		106 26		288 35	30
20	170 22.9	36.8	244 15.9	215 45		216 05		108 56		290 59	29
30	172 52.9 ·	36.8	246 46.3	218 16 ·	·	218 35 ·	·	111 27 ·	·	293 24 ·	27
40	175 22.9	36.9	249 16.7	220 46		221 06		113 57		295 49	26
50	177 52.9	36.9	251 47.1	223 16		223 36		116 28		298 13	24
Rate	14 59.9	N0 00.3		15 00.3	N0 00.6	15 00.7	N0 00.7	15 02.2	S0 00.1	14 27.4	N0 08.2

Moonset / Diff.

Lat.	Moonset	Diff.
N	h m	m
72	05 35	70
70	06 10	70
68	06 35	56
66	06 54	51
64	07 09	47
62	07 22	45
60	07 33	43
58	07 42	41
56	07 50	40
54	07 58	39
52	08 04	38
50	08 10	37
45	08 22	37
40	08 33	35
35	08 42	34
30	08 49	33
20	09 03	32
10	09 14	30
0	09 25	29
10	09 36	28
20	09 47	27
30	10 00	25
35	10 07	24
40	10 16	23
45	10 26	22
50	10 38	21
52	10 43	19
54	10 49	19
56	10 56	18
58	11 03	17
60	11 12	16
S		15

Moon's P. in A.

Alt.	+ Corr.	Alt.	+ Corr.
°	′	°	′
0	59	54	34
7	58	55	33
12	57	56	32
16	57	57	32
19	56	58	31
22	55	60	30
24	54	61	29
27	53	62	28
29	52	63	27
31	51	64	26
32	50	65	25
34	49	66	24
36	48	67	23
38	47	68	22
39	46	69	21
41	45	70	20
42	44	71	19
43	43	72	18
	42	73	17
46	41	74	16
47	40	75	15
49	39	76	14
	38	77	13
51	37	78	12
53	36	79	11
54	35	80	10
55	34		

Sun SD 15.8
Moon SD 16′
Age 19d

SUNRISE

Lat.	May 17	May 20	May 23	May 26	May 29	Jun 1	Jun 4	Jun 7	Jun 10	Jun 13	Jun 16	Jun 19	Jun 22	Jun 25	Jun 28	Jul 1
	h m	h m	h m	h m	h m	h m	h m	h m	h m	h m	h m	h m	h m	h m	h m	h m
N 72°	□	□	□	□	□	□	□	□	□	□	□	□	□	□	□	□
70	□	□	□	□	□	□	□	□	□	□	□	□	□	□	□	□
68	01 37	01 18	00 56	00 21	□	□	□	□	□	□	□	□	□	□	□	□
66	02 15	02 03	01 51	01 39	01 26	01 13	01 00	00 46	00 30	□	□	□	□	□	□	00 16
64	02 42	02 32	02 23	02 14	02 06	01 58	01 51	01 45	01 40	01 35	01 32	01 31	01 31	01 33	01 36	01 41
62	03 02	02 54	02 47	02 40	02 33	02 28	02 22	02 18	02 14	02 12	02 10	02 09	02 09	02 11	02 13	02 16
N 60	03 18	03 12	03 05	03 00	02 54	02 50	02 45	02 42	02 39	02 37	02 36	02 35	02 36	02 37	02 39	02 42
58	03 32	03 26	03 21	03 10	03 11	03 07	03 04	03 01	02 59	02 57	02 56	02 56	02 56	02 57	02 59	03 02
56	03 44	03 39	03 34	03 30	03 26	03 22	03 19	03 17	03 15	03 14	03 13	03 13	03 13	03 14	03 16	03 18
54	03 54	03 50	03 45	03 42	03 38	03 35	03 32	03 30	03 29	03 28	03 27	03 27	03 27	03 29	03 30	03 32
52	04 04	03 59	03 55	03 52	03 49	03 46	03 44	03 42	03 41	03 40	03 39	03 39	03 40	03 41	03 42	03 44
N 50	04 12	04 08	04 04	04 01	03 58	03 56	03 54	03 52	03 51	03 50	03 50	03 50	03 51	03 52	03 53	03 55
45	04 29	04 26	04 23	04 21	04 18	04 17	04 15	04 14	04 13	04 13	04 13	04 13	04 13	04 14	04 15	04 17
40	04 43	04 41	04 38	04 36	04 35	04 33	04 32	04 31	04 31	04 30	04 30	04 31	04 31	04 32	04 33	04 35
35	04 55	04 53	04 51	04 50	04 48	04 47	04 46	04 46	04 45	04 45	04 46	04 46	04 46	04 47	04 48	04 49
30	05 06	05 04	05 02	05 01	05 00	04 59	04 59	04 58	04 58	04 58	04 58	04 59	04 59	05 00	05 01	05 02
N 20	05 23	05 22	05 21	05 21	05 20	05 20	05 20	05 20	05 20	05 20	05 20	05 21	05 22	05 22	05 23	05 24
N 10	05 39	05 38	05 38	05 38	05 38	05 38	05 38	05 38	05 38	05 39	05 39	05 40	05 41	05 41	05 42	05 43
0	05 53	05 53	05 53	05 53	05 54	05 54	05 55	05 55	05 56	05 56	05 57	05 57	05 58	05 59	05 59	06 00
S 10	06 07	06 08	06 08	06 09	06 10	06 10	06 11	06 12	06 13	06 13	06 14	06 15	06 16	06 16	06 17	06 17
20	06 22	06 23	06 24	06 25	06 26	06 28	06 29	06 30	06 31	06 32	06 33	06 33	06 34	06 35	06 35	06 36
S 30	06 39	06 41	06 42	06 44	06 46	06 47	06 49	06 50	06 52	06 53	06 54	06 55	06 56	06 56	06 56	06 56
35	06 49	06 51	06 53	06 55	06 57	06 59	07 01	07 02	07 04	07 05	07 06	07 07	07 08	07 08	07 09	07 08
40	07 00	07 03	07 05	07 08	07 10	07 12	07 14	07 16	07 18	07 19	07 20	07 21	07 22	07 23	07 23	07 23
45	07 13	07 16	07 19	07 22	07 25	07 28	07 30	07 32	07 34	07 36	07 37	07 38	07 39	07 39	07 39	07 39
50	07 29	07 33	07 37	07 40	07 44	07 47	07 50	07 52	07 54	07 56	07 58	07 59	08 00	08 00	08 00	07 59
S 52	07 37	07 41	07 45	07 49	07 52	07 56	07 59	08 02	08 04	08 06	08 08	08 09	08 10	08 10	08 10	08 09
54	07 45	07 50	07 54	07 58	08 02	08 06	08 09	08 12	08 15	08 17	08 19	08 20	08 21	08 21	08 21	08 20
56	07 54	07 59	08 04	08 09	08 13	08 17	08 21	08 24	08 27	08 30	08 31	08 33	08 33	08 34	08 33	08 32
58	08 05	08 11	08 16	08 21	08 26	08 30	08 35	08 38	08 41	08 44	08 46	08 47	08 48	08 48	08 48	08 47
S 60	08 17	08 23	08 30	08 35	08 41	08 46	08 51	08 55	08 58	09 01	09 03	09 05	09 06	09 06	09 05	09 04

SUNSET

Lat.	May 17	May 20	May 23	May 26	May 29	Jun 1	Jun 4	Jun 7	Jun 10	Jun 13	Jun 16	Jun 19	Jun 22	Jun 25	Jun 28	Jul 1
	h m	h m	h m	h m	h m	h m	h m	h m	h m	h m	h m	h m	h m	h m	h m	h m
N 72°	□	□	□	□	□	□	□	□	□	□	□	□	□	□	□	□
70	□	□	□	□	□	□	□	□	□	□	□	□	□	□	□	□
68	22 21	22 41	23 06	□	□	□	□	□	□	□	□	□	□	□	□	□
66	21 41	21 53	22 06	22 19	22 32	22 46	23 01	23 16	23 36	□	□	□	□	□	□	23 42
64	21 14	21 23	21 33	21 42	21 51	21 59	22 07	22 14	22 21	22 26	22 29	22 32	22 33	22 32	22 29	22 26
62	20 53	21 01	21 08	21 16	21 23	21 29	21 35	21 41	21 45	21 49	21 52	21 54	21 54	21 54	21 53	21 50
N 60	20 36	20 43	20 49	20 56	21 02	21 07	21 12	21 16	21 21	21 23	21 26	21 27	21 28	21 28	21 27	21 25
58	20 22	20 28	20 34	20 39	20 44	20 49	20 53	20 57	21 01	21 03	21 05	21 07	21 07	21 07	21 07	21 05
56	20 10	20 15	20 20	20 25	20 30	20 34	20 38	20 41	20 44	20 47	20 48	20 50	20 50	20 51	20 50	20 49
54	19 59	20 04	20 09	20 13	20 17	20 21	20 25	20 28	20 30	20 33	20 34	20 35	20 36	20 36	20 36	20 35
52	19 50	19 55	19 59	20 03	20 06	20 10	20 13	20 16	20 18	20 20	20 22	20 24	20 24	20 24	20 23	20 22
N 50	19 42	19 46	19 50	19 53	19 57	20 00	20 03	20 06	20 08	20 10	20 11	20 12	20 13	20 13	20 13	20 12
45	19 24	19 28	19 31	19 34	19 37	19 39	19 42	19 44	19 46	19 47	19 49	19 50	19 50	19 51	19 51	19 50
40	19 10	19 13	19 15	19 18	19 20	19 23	19 25	19 26	19 28	19 29	19 31	19 32	19 32	19 33	19 33	19 33
35	18 58	19 00	19 02	19 05	19 07	19 08	19 10	19 12	19 13	19 15	19 16	19 17	19 17	19 18	19 18	19 18
30	18 47	18 49	18 51	18 53	18 55	18 56	18 58	18 59	19 00	19 02	19 03	19 04	19 04	19 05	19 05	19 05
N 20	18 30	18 31	18 32	18 33	18 35	18 36	18 37	18 38	18 39	18 40	18 41	18 41	18 42	18 43	18 43	18 43
N 10	18 14	18 15	18 16	18 16	18 17	18 18	18 19	18 19	18 20	18 21	18 22	18 22	18 23	18 24	18 24	18 25
0	18 00	18 00	18 00	18 01	18 01	18 02	18 02	18 03	18 03	18 04	18 04	18 05	18 05	18 06	18 07	18 07
S 10	17 46	17 45	17 45	17 45	17 45	17 45	17 45	17 46	17 46	17 46	17 47	17 47	17 48	17 49	17 50	17 50
20	17 31	17 30	17 29	17 28	17 28	17 28	17 28	17 28	17 28	17 28	17 28	17 29	17 30	17 30	17 31	17 32
S 30	17 14	17 12	17 11	17 10	17 09	17 08	17 07	17 07	17 07	17 07	17 07	17 08	17 08	17 09	17 10	17 11
35	17 04	17 02	17 00	16 59	16 57	16 56	16 56	16 55	16 55	16 55	16 55	16 55	16 56	16 57	16 58	16 59
40	16 53	16 50	16 48	16 46	16 45	16 43	16 42	16 41	16 41	16 41	16 41	16 41	16 42	16 43	16 44	16 45
45	16 39	16 36	16 34	16 32	16 30	16 28	16 26	16 25	16 25	16 24	16 24	16 24	16 25	16 26	16 27	16 28
50	16 23	16 20	16 16	16 13	16 11	16 09	16 07	16 05	16 04	16 04	16 03	16 03	16 04	16 05	16 06	16 08
S 52	16 16	16 12	16 08	16 05	16 02	15 59	15 57	15 56	15 54	15 54	15 53	15 54	15 54	15 55	15 57	15 58
54	16 07	16 03	15 59	15 55	15 52	15 49	15 47	15 45	15 44	15 43	15 42	15 42	15 43	15 44	15 46	15 48
56	15 58	15 53	15 49	15 45	15 41	15 38	15 35	15 33	15 31	15 30	15 30	15 30	15 30	15 31	15 33	15 35
58	15 47	15 42	15 37	15 32	15 28	15 25	15 21	15 19	15 17	15 16	15 15	15 15	15 16	15 17	15 19	15 21
S 60	15 35	15 29	15 23	15 18	15 13	15 09	15 05	15 02	15 00	14 59	14 58	14 57	14 58	14 59	15 01	15 04

MORNING CIVIL TWILIGHT

Lat.	May 17	May 20	May 23	May 26	May 29	June 1	June 4	June 7	June 10	June 13	June 16	June 19	June 22	June 25	June 28	July 1
	h m	h m	h m	h m	h m	h m	h m	h m	h m	h m	h m	h m	h m	h m	h m	h m
N 72	☐	☐	☐	☐	☐	☐	☐	☐	☐	☐	☐	☐	☐	☐	☐	☐
70	☐	☐	☐	☐	☐	☐	☐	☐	☐	☐	☐	☐	☐	☐	☐	☐
68	////	////	////	////	☐	☐	☐	☐	☐	☐	☐	☐	☐	☐	☐	☐
66	////	////	////	////	////	////	////	////	////	☐	☐	☐	☐	☐	☐	////
64	00 54	00 18	////	////	////	////	////	////	////	////	////	////	////	////	////	////
62	01 44	01 30	01 16	01 00	00 41	00 01	////	////	////	////	////	////	////	////	////	////
N 60	02 13	02 04	01 54	01 45	01 36	01 27	01 18	01 10	01 03	00 57	00 52	00 49	00 49	00 51	00 56	01 02
58	36	28	02 21	02 13	02 07	02 01	01 55	01 50	01 46	01 43	01 41	01 40	01 41	01 42	01 44	01 48
56	02 54	02 47	41	35	30	25	02 21	02 17	02 14	02 12	02 11	02 10	02 11	02 12	02 14	02 17
54	03 08	03 03	02 57	02 52	02 48	02 44	41	38	35	34	33	32	33	34	36	38
52	21	16	03 11	03 07	03 03	03 00	02 57	02 54	02 53	02 51	02 51	02 50	02 51	02 52	02 54	02 56
N 50	03 32	03 28	03 23	03 20	03 16	03 13	03 11	03 09	03 07	03 06	03 06	03 06	03 06	03 07	03 09	03 10
45	03 55	03 51	03 48	03 45	03 43	03 40	03 39	37	36	35	35	35	36	37	03 38	03 40
40	04 12	04 10	04 07	04 05	04 03	04 01	04 00	03 59	03 58	03 58	03 58	03 58	03 59	04 00	04 02	
35	27	25	23	21	19	18	17	04 16	04 16	04 16	04 16	04 16	04 17	04 18	19	20
30	04 39	37	36	34	33	32	32	31	31	31	31	31	32	33	34	04 35
N 20	05 00	04 58	04 58	04 57	04 56	04 56	04 55	04 55	04 55	04 55	04 56	04 56	04 57	04 58	04 59	05 00
N 10	16	05 16	05 15	05 15	05 15	05 15	05 15	05 15	05 16	05 16	05 16	05 17	05 18	05 18	05 19	20
0	31	31	31	31	31	32	32	33	33	34	34	35	36	36	37	38
S 10	45	05 45	05 46	05 46	05 47	05 48	05 49	05 49	05 50	05 51	05 52	05 52	05 53	05 53	05 54	05 54
20	05 58	06 00	06 01	06 02	06 03	06 04	06 05	06 06	06 07	06 08	06 09	06 09	06 10	06 11	06 11	06 11
S 30	06 13	06 15	06 17	06 18	06 20	06 21	06 23	06 24	06 25	06 27	06 28	06 28	06 29	06 30	06 30	06 30
35	21	24	26	27	29	31	33	34	36	37	38	39	40	40	41	41
40	30	33	35	38	40	42	44	46	06 47	06 49	06 50	06 51	06 51	06 52	06 52	06 52
45	41	44	06 47	06 49	06 52	06 54	06 57	06 59	07 00	07 02	07 03	07 04	07 05	07 06	07 06	07 05
50	53	06 57	07 00	07 03	07 06	07 09	07 12	07 14	16	18	19	20	21	21	21	21
S 52	06 59	07 02	07 06	07 10	07 13	07 16	07 19	07 21	07 23	07 25	07 27	07 28	07 29	07 29	07 29	07 29
54	07 05	09	13	17	20	23	26	29	31	33	35	36	37	37	37	37
56	11	16	20	24	28	32	35	38	40	42	44	45	46	46	46	46
58	19	24	28	33	37	41	44	47	07 50	07 52	07 54	07 55	07 56	07 57	07 56	07 55
S 60	07 27	07 32	07 38	07 42	07 47	07 51	07 55	07 59	08 01	08 04	08 06	08 07	08 08	08 08	08 08	08 07

EVENING CIVIL TWILIGHT

Lat.	May 17	May 20	May 23	May 26	May 29	June 1	June 4	June 7	June 10	June 13	June 16	June 19	June 22	June 25	June 28	July 1
	h m	h m	h m	h m	h m	h m	h m	h m	h m	h m	h m	h m	h m	h m	h m	h m
N 72	☐	☐	☐	☐	☐	☐	☐	☐	☐	☐	☐	☐	☐	☐	☐	☐
70	☐	☐	☐	☐	☐	☐	☐	☐	☐	☐	☐	☐	☐	☐	☐	☐
68	////	////	////	☐	☐	☐	☐	☐	☐	☐	☐	☐	☐	☐	☐	☐
66	////	////	////	////	////	////	////	////	☐	☐	☐	☐	☐	☐	☐	////
64	23 07	////	////	////	////	////	////	////	////	////	////	////	////	////	////	////
62	22 13	22 27	22 42	23 00	23 22	////	////	////	////	////	////	////	////	////	////	////
N 60	21 42	21 52	22 02	22 12	22 22	22 31	22 41	22 50	22 58	23 05	23 10	23 14	23 15	23 13	23 09	23 03
58	19	27	21 35	21 42	21 50	21 57	22 03	22 09	22 14	22 18	22 21	22 23	22 23	22 23	22 21	22 18
56	21 01	21 08	21 14	21	26	32	21 37	21 42	21 45	21 49	21 51	21 52	21 53	21 53	21 52	21 50
54	20 46	20 52	20 57	21 03	21 08	21 13	17	21	24	27	29	30	31	31	30	29
52	33	38	43	20 48	20 52	20 57	21 00	21 04	21 07	21 09	21 11	21 12	21 13	21 13	21 12	21 11
N 50	20 22	20 26	20 31	20 35	20 39	20 43	20 46	20 49	20 52	20 54	20 56	20 57	20 58	20 58	20 57	20 57
45	19 59	20 02	20 06	20 09	20 13	20 16	20 18	20 21	23	25	26	27	28	28	28	27
40	41	19 44	19 47	19 50	19 52	19 55	19 57	19 59	20 01	20 02	20 04	20 05	20 05	20 06	20 06	20 05
35	26	29	31	33	36	38	40	41	19 43	19 44	19 45	19 46	19 47	19 47	19 48	19 47
30	19 14	19 16	19 18	19 20	19 22	23	25	27	28	29	30	31	32	32	32	32
N 20	18 53	18 55	18 56	18 57	18 59	19 00	19 01	19 02	19 03	19 04	19 05	19 06	19 07	19 08	19 08	19 08
N 10	37	37	38	39	40	18 41	18 42	18 42	18 43	18 44	18 45	18 46	18 46	18 47	18 47	18 48
0	22	22	22	23	23	24	24	25	25	26	27	27	28	29	29	30
S 10	18 08	18 08	18 07	18 07	18 07	18 08	18 08	18 08	18 09	18 09	18 10	18 10	18 11	18 12	18 12	18 13
20	17 54	17 53	17 53	17 52	17 52	17 51	17 51	17 51	17 52	17 52	17 53	17 53	17 54	17 54	17 55	17 56
S 30	17 39	17 38	17 36	17 35	17 35	17 34	17 34	17 33	17 33	17 33	17 34	17 34	17 35	17 35	17 36	17 37
35	31	29	27	26	25	24	24	23	23	23	23	23	24	25	26	27
40	22	19	18	16	14	13	12	17 12	17 11	17 11	17 11	17 12	17 12	13	14	15
45	17 11	17 09	17 06	17 04	17 02	17 00	16 59	16 58	16 58	16 58	16 58	16 59	17 00	17 01	17 02	
50	16 59	16 56	16 53	16 50	16 48	16 46	16 45	43	42	42	42	42	43	16 44	16 45	16 46
S 52	16 54	16 50	16 47	16 44	16 41	16 39	16 37	16 36	16 35	16 34	16 34	16 35	16 35	16 36	16 37	16 39
54	47	44	40	37	34	32	30	28	27	26	26	26	27	28	29	31
56	41	37	33	29	26	23	21	20	18	17	17	17	18	19	20	22
58	33	29	24	21	17	14	12	16 10	16 08	16 07	16 07	16 07	16 08	16 09	16 10	12
S 60	16 25	16 20	16 15	16 11	16 07	16 04	16 01	16 01	15 57	15 56	15 55	15 55	15 56	15 57	15 59	16 01

SUNLIGHT, TWILIGHT AND MOONLIGHT

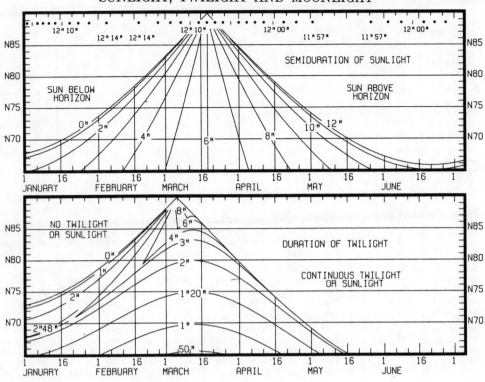

SEMIDURATION OF MOONLIGHT

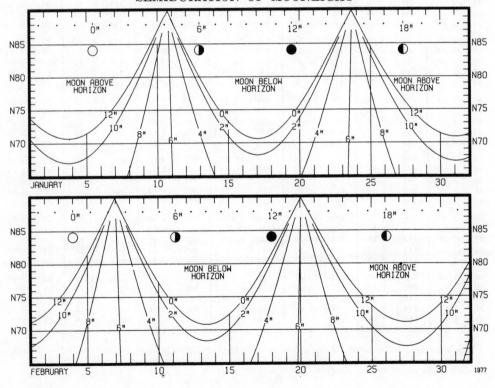

49

CONVERSION OF ARC TO TIME

o	h m	o	h m	o	h m	o	h m	o	h m	o	h m	'	m s
0	0 00	60	4 00	120	8 00	180	12 00	240	16 00	300	20 00	0	0 00
1	0 04	61	4 04	121	8 04	181	12 04	241	16 04	301	20 04	1	0 04
2	0 08	62	4 08	122	8 08	182	12 08	242	16 08	302	20 08	2	0 08
3	0 12	63	4 12	123	8 12	183	12 12	243	16 12	303	20 12	3	0 12
4	0 16	64	4 16	124	8 16	184	12 16	244	16 16	304	20 16	4	0 16
5	0 20	65	4 20	125	8 20	185	12 20	245	16 20	305	20 20	5	0 20
6	0 24	66	4 24	126	8 24	186	12 24	246	16 24	306	20 24	6	0 24
7	0 28	67	4 28	127	8 28	187	12 28	247	16 28	307	20 28	7	0 28
8	0 32	68	4 32	128	8 32	188	12 32	248	16 32	308	20 32	8	0 32
9	0 36	69	4 36	129	8 36	189	12 36	249	16 36	309	20 36	9	0 36
10	0 40	70	4 40	130	8 40	190	12 40	250	16 40	310	20 40	10	0 40
11	0 44	71	4 44	131	8 44	191	12 44	251	16 44	311	20 44	11	0 44
12	0 48	72	4 48	132	8 48	192	12 48	252	16 48	312	20 48	12	0 48
13	0 52	73	4 52	133	8 52	193	12 52	253	16 52	313	20 52	13	0 52
14	0 56	74	4 56	134	8 56	194	12 56	254	16 56	314	20 56	14	0 56
15	1 00	75	5 00	135	9 00	195	13 00	255	17 00	315	21 00	15	1 00
16	1 04	76	5 04	136	9 04	196	13 04	256	17 04	316	21 04	16	1 04
17	1 08	77	5 08	137	9 08	197	13 08	257	17 08	317	21 08	17	1 08
18	1 12	78	5 12	138	9 12	198	13 12	258	17 12	318	21 12	18	1 12
19	1 16	79	5 16	139	9 16	199	13 16	259	17 16	319	21 16	19	1 16
20	1 20	80	5 20	140	9 20	200	13 20	260	17 20	320	21 20	20	1 20
21	1 24	81	5 24	141	9 24	201	13 24	261	17 24	321	21 24	21	1 24
22	1 28	82	5 28	142	9 28	202	13 28	262	17 28	322	21 28	22	1 28
23	1 32	83	5 32	143	9 32	203	13 32	263	17 32	323	21 32	23	1 32
24	1 36	84	5 36	144	9 36	204	13 36	264	17 36	324	21 36	24	1 36
25	1 40	85	5 40	145	9 40	205	13 40	265	17 40	325	21 40	25	1 40
26	1 44	86	5 44	146	9 44	206	13 44	266	17 44	326	21 44	26	1 44
27	1 48	87	5 48	147	9 48	207	13 48	267	17 48	327	21 48	27	1 48
28	1 52	88	5 52	148	9 52	208	13 52	268	17 52	328	21 52	28	1 52
29	1 56	89	5 56	149	9 56	209	13 56	269	17 56	329	21 56	29	1 56
30	2 00	90	6 00	150	10 00	210	14 00	270	18 00	330	22 00	30	2 00
31	2 04	91	6 04	151	10 04	211	14 04	271	18 04	331	22 04	31	2 04
32	2 08	92	6 08	152	10 08	212	14 08	272	18 08	332	22 08	32	2 08
33	2 12	93	6 12	153	10 12	213	14 12	273	18 12	333	22 12	33	2 12
34	2 16	94	6 16	154	10 16	214	14 16	274	18 16	334	22 16	34	2 16
35	2 20	95	6 20	155	10 20	215	14 20	275	18 20	335	22 20	35	2 20
36	2 24	96	6 24	156	10 24	216	14 24	276	18 24	336	22 24	36	2 24
37	2 28	97	6 28	157	10 28	217	14 28	277	18 28	337	22 28	37	2 28
38	2 32	98	6 32	158	10 32	218	14 32	278	18 32	338	22 32	38	2 32
39	2 36	99	6 36	159	10 36	219	14 36	279	18 36	339	22 36	39	2 36
40	2 40	100	6 40	160	10 40	220	14 40	280	18 40	340	22 40	40	2 40
41	2 44	101	6 44	161	10 44	221	14 44	281	18 44	341	22 44	41	2 44
42	2 48	102	6 48	162	10 48	222	14 48	282	18 48	342	22 48	42	2 48
43	2 52	103	6 52	163	10 52	223	14 52	283	18 52	343	22 52	43	2 52
44	2 56	104	6 56	164	10 56	224	14 56	284	18 56	344	22 56	44	2 56
45	3 00	105	7 00	165	11 00	225	15 00	285	19 00	345	23 00	45	3 00
46	3 04	106	7 04	166	11 04	226	15 04	286	19 04	346	23 04	46	3 04
47	3 08	107	7 08	167	11 08	227	15 08	287	19 08	347	23 08	47	3 08
48	3 12	108	7 12	168	11 12	228	15 12	288	19 12	348	23 12	48	3 12
49	3 16	109	7 16	169	11 16	229	15 16	289	19 16	349	23 16	49	3 16
50	3 20	110	7 20	170	11 20	230	15 20	290	19 20	350	23 20	50	3 20
51	3 24	111	7 24	171	11 24	231	15 24	291	19 24	351	23 24	51	3 24
52	3 28	112	7 28	172	11 28	232	15 28	292	19 28	352	23 28	52	3 28
53	3 32	113	7 32	173	11 32	233	15 32	293	19 32	353	23 32	53	3 32
54	3 36	114	7 36	174	11 36	234	15 36	294	19 36	354	23 36	54	3 36
55	3 40	115	7 40	175	11 40	235	15 40	295	19 40	355	23 40	55	3 40
56	3 44	116	7 44	176	11 44	236	15 44	296	19 44	356	23 44	56	3 44
57	3 48	117	7 48	177	11 48	237	15 48	297	19 48	357	23 48	57	3 48
58	3 52	118	7 52	178	11 52	238	15 52	298	19 52	358	23 52	58	3 52
59	3 56	119	7 56	179	11 56	239	15 56	299	19 56	359	23 56	59	3 56

The above table is for converting expressions in arc to their equivalent in time; its main use in this Almanac is for the conversion of longitude for application to L.M.T. (*added* if *west*, *subtracted* if *east*) to give G.M.T., or vice versa, particularly in the case of sunrise, sunset, etc.

POLARIS (POLE STAR) TABLE, 1977
FOR DETERMINING THE LATITUDE FROM A SEXTANT ALTITUDE

L.H.A. ♈	Q	L.H.A. ♈	Q	L.H.A. ♈	Q	L.H.A. ♈	Q	L.H.A. ♈	Q	L.H.A. ♈	Q	L.H.A. ♈	Q	L.H.A. ♈	Q
° ′	′	° ′	′	° ′	′	° ′	′	° ′	′	° ′	′	° ′	′	° ′	′
358 24	−42	81 59	−32	114 43	− 6	144 59	+20	187 09	+46	268 23	+28	300 07	+ 2	330 47	−24
0 27	−43	83 27	−31	115 51	− 5	146 14	+21	189 59	+47	269 46	+27	301 16	+ 1	332 05	−25
2 38	−44	84 53	−30	117 00	− 4	147 29	+22	193 13	+48	271 07	+26	302 24	0	333 23	−26
4 58	−45	86 18	−29	118 09	− 3	148 46	+23	197 05	+49	272 27	+25	303 33	− 1	334 43	−27
7 31	−46	87 42	−28	119 17	− 2	150 03	+24	202 15	+50	273 46	+24	304 42	− 2	336 04	−28
10 19	−47	89 03	−27	120 25	− 1	151 21	+25	222 52	+49	275 04	+23	305 50	− 3	337 25	−29
13 30	−48	90 24	−26	121 34	0	152 40	+26	228 02	+48	276 21	+22	306 58	− 4	338 49	−30
17 18	−49	91 44	−25	122 43	+ 1	154 00	+27	231 54	+47	277 38	+21	308 07	− 5	340 14	−31
22 24	−50	93 02	−24	123 51	+ 2	155 21	+28	235 08	+46	278 53	+20	309 16	− 6	341 40	−32
42 43	−49	94 20	−23	125 00	+ 3	156 44	+29	237 58	+45	280 08	+19	310 24	− 7	343 08	−33
47 49	−48	95 36	−22	126 08	+ 4	158 08	+30	240 32	+44	281 22	+18	311 33	− 8	344 38	−34
51 37	−47	96 52	−21	127 17	+ 5	159 33	+31	242 54	+43	282 35	+17	312 42	− 9	346 10	−35
54 48	−46	98 07	−20	128 26	+ 6	161 01	+32	245 07	+42	283 48	+16	313 52	−10	347 45	−36
57 36	−45	99 21	−19	129 35	+ 7	162 30	+33	247 12	+41	285 00	+15	315 01	−11	349 23	−37
60 09	−44	100 35	−18	130 44	+ 8	164 01	+34	249 10	+40	286 12	+14	316 11	−12	351 03	−38
62 29	−43	101 48	−17	131 53	+ 9	165 34	+35	251 04	+39	287 23	+13	317 22	−13	352 47	−39
64 40	−42	103 00	−16	133 02	+10	167 10	+36	252 53	+38	288 34	+12	318 32	−14	354 34	−40
66 43	−41	104 12	−15	134 12	+11	168 48	+37	254 38	+37	289 45	+11	319 43	−15	356 26	−41
68 41	−40	105 24	−14	135 22	+12	170 29	+38	256 19	+36	290 55	+10	320 55	−16	358 24	−42
70 33	−39	106 35	−13	136 33	+13	172 14	+39	257 57	+35	292 05	+ 9	322 07	−17	0 27	−43
72 20	−38	107 45	−12	137 44	+14	174 03	+40	259 33	+34	293 14	+ 8	323 19	−18	2 38	−44
74 04	−37	108 56	−11	138 55	+15	175 57	+41	261 06	+33	294 23	+ 7	324 32	−19	4 58	−45
75 44	−36	110 06	−10	140 07	+16	177 55	+42	262 37	+32	295 32	+ 6	325 46	−20	7 31	−46
77 22	−35	111 15	− 9	141 19	+17	180 00	+43	264 06	+31	296 41	+ 5	327 00	−21	10 19	−47
78 57	−34	112 25	− 8	142 32	+18	182 13	+44	265 34	+30	297 50	+ 4	328 15	−22	13 30	−48
80 29	−33	113 34	− 7	143 45	+19	184 35	+45	266 59	+30	298 59	+ 3	329 31	−23	17 18	−49
81 59		114 43		144 59		187 09		268 23	+29	300 07		330 47		22 24	

Q, which does *not* include refraction, is to be applied to the corrected sextant altitude of *Polaris*.
Polaris: Mag. 2·1, S.H.A. 327° 26′, Dec. N. 89° 09′.7

STANDARD DOME REFRACTION

To be *subtracted* from sextant altitude when using sextant suspension in a perspex dome

Alt.	Refn.	Alt.	Refn.
°	′	°	′
10	8	50	4
20	7	60	4
30	6	70	3
40	5	80	3

This table must not be used if a calibration table is fitted to the dome, or if a flat glass plate is provided, or for non-standard domes.

BUBBLE SEXTANT ERROR

Sextant Number	Alt. °	Corr.

AZIMUTH OF *POLARIS*

L.H.A. ♈ 300°–120°	Latitude							L.H.A. ♈ 120°–300°
	0°	30°	50°	55°	60°	65°	70°	
°	°	°	°	°	°	°	°	°
300	0·8	1·0	1·3	1·5	1·7	2·0	2·4	300
310	0·8	0·9	1·3	1·4	1·6	1·9	2·4	290
320	0·8	0·9	1·2	1·3	1·5	1·8	2·3	280
330	0·7	0·8	1·1	1·2	1·4	1·7	2·1	270
340	0·6	0·7	1·0	1·1	1·2	1·5	1·8	260
350	0·5	0·6	0·8	0·9	1·0	1·2	1·5	250
0	0·4	0·4	0·6	0·7	0·8	0·9	1·1	240
10	0·3	0·3	0·4	0·4	0·5	0·6	0·7	230
20	0·1	0·1	0·2	0·2	0·2	0·3	0·3	220
30	0·0	0·0	0·1	0·1	0·1	0·1	0·1	210
40	359·9	359·9	359·8	359·8	359·8	359·7	359·7	200
50	359·7	359·7	359·6	359·6	359·5	359·4	359·3	190
60	359·6	359·6	359·4	359·3	359·2	359·1	358·9	180
70	359·5	359·4	359·2	359·1	359·0	358·8	358·5	170
80	359·4	359·3	359·0	358·9	358·8	358·5	358·2	160
90	359·3	359·2	358·9	358·8	358·6	358·3	357·9	150
100	359·2	359·1	358·8	358·7	358·5	358·2	357·7	140
110	359·2	359·1	358·7	358·6	358·4	358·1	357·6	130
120	359·2	359·0	358·7	358·5	358·3	358·0	357·6	120

When Cassiopeia is left (right), *Polaris* is west (east).

CORRECTIONS TO BE APPLIED TO SEXTANT ALTITUDE

REFRACTION

To be subtracted from sextant altitude (referred to as observed altitude in A.P. 3270)

R_0	Height above sea level in units of 1 000 ft.												R_0	$R = R_0 \times f$			
	0	5	10	15	20	25	30	35	40	45	50	55		f 0·9 1·0 1·1 1·2			
	Sextant Altitude													R			
	° ′	° ′	° ′	° ′	° ′	° ′	° ′	° ′	° ′	° ′	° ′	° ′	′	′ ′ ′ ′			
0	90	90	90	90	90	90	90	90	90	90	90	90	0	0 0 0 0			
1	63	59	55	5ı	46	41	36	31	26	20	17	13	1	1 1 1 1			
2	33	29	26	22	19	16	14	11	9	7	6	4	2	2 2 2 2			
3	21	19	16	14	12	10	8	7	5	4	2 40	1 40	3	3 3 3 4			
4	16	14	12	10	8	7	6	5	3 10	2 20	1 30	0 40	4	4 4 4 5			
5	12	11	9	8	7	5	4 00	3 10	2 10	1 30	0 39	+0 05	5	5 5 5 6			
6	10	9	7	5 50	4 50	3 50	3 10	2 20	1 30	0 49	+0 11	−0 19	6	5 6 7 7			
7	8 10	6 50	5 50	4 50	4 00	3 00	2 20	1 50	1 10	0 24	−0 11	−0 38	7	6 7 8 8			
8	6 50	5 50	5 00	4 00	3 10	2 30	1 50	1 20	0 38	+0 04	−0 28	−0 54	8	7 8 9 10			
9	6 00	5 10	4 10	3 20	2 40	2 00	1 30	1 00	0 19	−0 13	−0 42	−1 08	9	8 9 10 11			
10	5 20	4 30	3 40	2 50	2 10	1 40	1 10	0 35	+0 03	−0 27	−0 53	−1 18	10	9 10 11 12			
12	4 30	3 40	2 50	2 20	1 40	1 10	0 37	+0 11	−0 16	−0 43	−1 08	−1 31	12	11 12 13 14			
14	3 30	2 50	2 10	1 40	1 10	0 34	+0 09	−0 14	−0 37	−1 00	−1 23	−1 44	14	13 14 15 17			
16	2 50	2 10	1 40	1 10	0 37	+0 10	−0 13	−0 34	−0 53	−1 14	−1 35	−1 56	16	14 16 18 19			
18	2 20	1 40	1 20	0 43	+0 15	−0 08	−0 31	−0 52	−1 08	−1 27	−1 46	−2 05	18	16 18 20 22			
20	1 50	1 20	0 49	+0 23	−0 02	−0 26	−0 46	−1 06	−1 22	−1 39	−1 57	−2 14	20	18 20 22 24			
25	1 12	0 44	+0 19	−0 06	−0 28	−0 48	−1 09	−1 27	−1 42	−1 58	−2 14	−2 30	25	22 25 28 30			
30	0 34	+0 10	−0 13	−0 36	−0 55	−1 14	−1 32	−1 51	−2 06	−2 21	−2 34	−2 49	30	27 30 33 36			
35	+0 06	−0 16	−0 37	−0 59	−1 17	−1 33	−1 51	−2 07	−2 23	−2 37	−2 51	−3 04	35	31 35 38 42			
40	−0 18	−0 37	−0 58	−1 16	−1 34	−1 49	−2 06	−2 22	−2 35	−2 49	−3 03	−3 16	40	36 40 44 48			
45		−0 53	−1 14	−1 31	−1 47	−2 03	−2 18	−2 33	−2 47	−2 59	−3 13	−3 25	45	40 45 50 54			
50		−1 10	−1 28	−1 44	−1 59	−2 15	−2 28	−2 43	−2 56	−3 08	−3 22	−3 33	50	45 50 55 60			
55			−1 40	−1 53	−2 09	−2 24	−2 38	−2 52	−3 04	−3 17	−3 29	−3 41	55	49 55 60 66			
60				−2 03	−2 18	−2 33	−2 46	−3 01	−3 12	−3 25	−3 37	−3 48	60	54 60 66 72			
							−2 53	−3 07	−3 19	−3 31	−3 42	−3 53					

f	0	5	10	15	20	25	30	35	40	45	50	55	f	0·9 1·0 1·1 1·2
	Temperature in °C.													f
0·9	+47	+36	+27	+18	+10	+ 3	− 5	−13					0·9	Where R_0 is
1·0	+26	+16	+ 6	− 4	−13	−22	−31	−40	For these heights no temperature correction is necessary, so use $R = R_0$				1·0	less than 10′ or the height greater than 35 000 ft. use $R = R_0$
1·1	+ 5	− 5	−15	−25	−36	−46	−57	−68					1·1	
1·2	−16	−25	−36	−46	−58	−71	−83	−95					1·2	
	−37	−45	−56	−67	−81	−95								

Choose the column appropriate to height, in units of 1 000 ft., and find the range of altitude in which the sextant altitude lies; the corresponding value of R_0 is the refraction, to be subtracted from sextant altitude, unless conditions are extreme. In that case find f from the lower table, with critical argument temperature. Use the table on the right to form the refraction, $R = R_0 \times f$.

CORIOLIS (Z) CORRECTION

To be applied by moving the position line a distance Z to starboard (right) of the track in northern latitudes and to port (left) in southern latitudes.

G/S KNOTS	Latitude						G/S KNOTS	Latitude					
	0° 10°	20° 30°	40° 50°	60° 70°	80° 90°			0° 10°	20° 30°	40° 50°	60° 70°	80° 90°	
	′ ′	′ ′	′ ′	′ ′	′ ′			′ ′	′ ′	′ ′	′ ′	′ ′	
150	0 1	1 2	3 3	3 4	4 4		550	0 3	5 7	9 11	12 14	14 14	
200	0 1	2 3	3 4	5 5	5 5		600	0 3	5 8	10 12	14 15	16 16	
250	0 1	2 3	4 5	6 6	6 7		650	0 3	6 9	11 13	15 16	17 17	
300	0 1	3 4	5 6	7 7	8 8		700	0 3	6 9	12 14	16 17	18 18	
350	0 2	3 5	6 7	8 9	9 9		750	0 3	7 10	13 15	17 18	19 20	
400	0 2	4 5	7 8	9 10	10 10		800	0 4	7 10	13 16	18 20	21 21	
450	0 2	4 6	8 9	10 11	12 12		850	0 4	8 11	14 17	19 21	22 22	
500	0 2	4 7	8 10	11 12	13 13		900	0 4	8 12	15 18	20 22	23 24	

CORRECTIONS TO BE APPLIED TO MARINE SEXTANT ALTITUDES

MARINE SEXTANT ERROR	CORRECTIONS	CORRECTION FOR DIP OF THE HORIZON To be subtracted from sextant altitude								
Sextant Number	In addition to sextant error and dip, corrections are to be applied for:	Ht.	Dip	Ht.	Dip	Ht.	Dip	Ht.	Dip	Ht.	Dip
		Ft.	,	Ft.	,	Ft.	,	Ft.	,	Ft.	,
Index Error	Refraction	0	1	114	11	437	21	968	31	1 707	41
	Semi-diameter (for the	2	2	137	12	481	22	1 033	32	1 792	42
	Sun and Moon)	6		162		527		1 099		1 880	
	Parallax (for the Moon)	12	3	189	13	575	23	1 168	33	1 970	43
	Dome refraction (if	21	4	218	14	625	24	1 239	34	2 061	44
	applicable)	31	5	250	15	677	25	1 311	35	2 155	45
		43	6	283	16	731	26	1 386	36	2 251	46
		58	7	318	17	787	27	1 463	37	2 349	47
		75	8	356	18	845	28	1 543	38	2 449	48
		93	9	395	19	906	29	1 624	39	2 551	49
		114	10	437	20	968	30	1 707	40	2 655	50

INTERPOLATION TABLE

Dec. Inc.	Altitude Difference (d) Tens 10'	20'	30'	40'	50'	Decimals	Units 0'	1'	2'	3'	4'	5'	6'	7'	8'	9'	Double Second Diff. and Corr.
0.0	0.0	0.0	0.0	0.0	0.0	.0	0.0	0.0	0.0	0.0	0.0	0.0	0.0	0.1	0.1	0.1	0.0 0.0 48.2
0.1	0.0	0.0	0.0	0.0	0.1	.1	0.0	0.0	0.0	0.0	0.0	0.0	0.1	0.1	0.1	0.1	
0.2	0.0	0.0	0.1	0.1	0.1	.2	0.0	0.0	0.0	0.0	0.0	0.0	0.1	0.1	0.1	0.1	
0.3	0.0	0.1	0.1	0.2	0.2	.3	0.0	0.0	0.0	0.0	0.0	0.0	0.1	0.1	0.1	0.1	
0.4	0.1	0.1	0.2	0.3	0.3	.4	0.0	0.0	0.0	0.0	0.0	0.0	0.1	0.1	0.1	0.1	
0.5	0.1	0.2	0.3	0.3	0.4	.5	0.0	0.0	0.0	0.0	0.0	0.0	0.1	0.1	0.1	0.1	16.2 0.1 48.6
0.6	0.1	0.2	0.3	0.4	0.5	.6	0.0	0.0	0.0	0.0	0.0	0.0	0.1	0.1	0.1	0.1	
0.7	0.1	0.3	0.4	0.5	0.6	.7	0.0	0.0	0.0	0.0	0.0	0.0	0.1	0.1	0.1	0.1	
0.8	0.2	0.3	0.4	0.6	0.7	.8	0.0	0.0	0.0	0.0	0.0	0.0	0.1	0.1	0.1	0.1	
0.9	0.2	0.3	0.5	0.6	0.8	.9	0.0	0.0	0.0	0.0	0.0	0.0	0.1	0.1	0.1	0.1	
1.0	0.1	0.3	0.5	0.6	0.8	.0	0.0	0.0	0.0	0.1	0.1	0.1	0.1	0.2	0.2	0.2	8.2 0.1 24.6 0.2 41.0
1.1	0.2	0.3	0.5	0.7	0.9	.1	0.0	0.0	0.1	0.1	0.1	0.1	0.2	0.2	0.2	0.2	
1.2	0.2	0.4	0.6	0.8	1.0	.2	0.0	0.0	0.1	0.1	0.1	0.1	0.2	0.2	0.2	0.2	
1.3	0.2	0.4	0.6	0.9	1.1	.3	0.0	0.0	0.1	0.1	0.1	0.1	0.2	0.2	0.2	0.2	
1.4	0.2	0.5	0.7	0.9	1.2	.4	0.0	0.0	0.1	0.1	0.1	0.1	0.2	0.2	0.2	0.2	
1.5	0.3	0.5	0.8	1.0	1.3	.5	0.0	0.0	0.1	0.1	0.1	0.1	0.2	0.2	0.2	0.2	
1.6	0.3	0.5	0.8	1.1	1.3	.6	0.0	0.0	0.1	0.1	0.1	0.1	0.2	0.2	0.2	0.2	
1.7	0.3	0.6	0.9	1.2	1.4	.7	0.0	0.0	0.1	0.1	0.1	0.1	0.2	0.2	0.2	0.2	
1.8	0.3	0.6	0.9	1.2	1.5	.8	0.0	0.0	0.1	0.1	0.1	0.1	0.2	0.2	0.2	0.2	
1.9	0.4	0.7	1.0	1.3	1.6	.9	0.0	0.0	0.1	0.1	0.1	0.1	0.2	0.2	0.2	0.2	
2.0	0.3	0.6	1.0	1.3	1.6	.0	0.0	0.0	0.1	0.1	0.2	0.2	0.2	0.3	0.3	0.4	5.0 0.1 15.0 0.2 25.0 0.3 35.1
2.1	0.3	0.7	1.0	1.4	1.7	.1	0.0	0.0	0.1	0.1	0.2	0.2	0.3	0.3	0.3	0.4	
2.2	0.3	0.7	1.1	1.4	1.8	.2	0.0	0.0	0.1	0.1	0.2	0.2	0.3	0.3	0.3	0.4	
2.3	0.4	0.8	1.1	1.5	1.9	.3	0.0	0.1	0.1	0.1	0.2	0.2	0.3	0.3	0.3	0.4	
2.4	0.4	0.8	1.2	1.6	2.0	.4	0.0	0.1	0.1	0.1	0.2	0.2	0.3	0.3	0.3	0.4	
2.5	0.4	0.8	1.3	1.7	2.1	.5	0.0	0.1	0.1	0.1	0.2	0.2	0.3	0.3	0.4	0.4	
2.6	0.4	0.9	1.3	1.7	2.2	.6	0.0	0.1	0.1	0.1	0.2	0.2	0.3	0.3	0.4	0.4	
2.7	0.5	0.9	1.4	1.8	2.3	.7	0.0	0.1	0.1	0.2	0.2	0.2	0.3	0.3	0.4	0.4	
2.8	0.5	1.0	1.4	1.9	2.4	.8	0.0	0.1	0.1	0.2	0.2	0.2	0.3	0.3	0.4	0.4	
2.9	0.5	1.0	1.5	2.0	2.5	.9	0.0	0.1	0.1	0.2	0.2	0.2	0.3	0.3	0.4	0.4	
3.0	0.5	1.0	1.5	2.0	2.5	.0	0.0	0.1	0.1	0.2	0.2	0.3	0.3	0.4	0.5	0.5	3.6 0.1 10.9 0.2 18.2 0.3 25.5 0.4 32.8 0.5 40.1
3.1	0.5	1.0	1.5	2.0	2.6	.1	0.0	0.1	0.1	0.2	0.2	0.3	0.4	0.4	0.5	0.5	
3.2	0.5	1.0	1.6	2.1	2.6	.2	0.0	0.1	0.1	0.2	0.2	0.3	0.4	0.4	0.5	0.5	
3.3	0.5	1.1	1.6	2.2	2.7	.3	0.0	0.1	0.1	0.2	0.3	0.3	0.4	0.4	0.5	0.5	
3.4	0.6	1.1	1.7	2.3	2.8	.4	0.0	0.1	0.1	0.2	0.3	0.3	0.4	0.4	0.5	0.5	
3.5	0.6	1.2	1.8	2.3	2.9	.5	0.0	0.1	0.1	0.2	0.3	0.3	0.4	0.4	0.5	0.6	
3.6	0.6	1.2	1.8	2.4	3.0	.6	0.0	0.1	0.2	0.2	0.3	0.3	0.4	0.4	0.5	0.6	
3.7	0.6	1.3	1.9	2.5	3.1	.7	0.0	0.1	0.2	0.2	0.3	0.3	0.4	0.4	0.5	0.6	
3.8	0.7	1.3	1.9	2.6	3.2	.8	0.0	0.1	0.2	0.2	0.3	0.3	0.4	0.5	0.5	0.6	
3.9	0.7	1.3	2.0	2.6	3.3	.9	0.1	0.1	0.2	0.2	0.3	0.3	0.4	0.5	0.5	0.6	
4.0	0.6	1.3	2.0	2.6	3.3	.0	0.0	0.1	0.1	0.2	0.3	0.4	0.4	0.5	0.6	0.7	2.9 0.1 8.6 0.2 14.4 0.3 20.2 0.4 25.9 0.5 31.7 0.6 37.5
4.1	0.7	1.3	2.0	2.7	3.4	.1	0.0	0.1	0.2	0.2	0.3	0.4	0.5	0.5	0.6	0.7	
4.2	0.7	1.4	2.1	2.8	3.5	.2	0.0	0.1	0.2	0.2	0.3	0.4	0.5	0.5	0.6	0.7	
4.3	0.7	1.4	2.1	2.9	3.6	.3	0.0	0.1	0.2	0.2	0.3	0.4	0.5	0.5	0.6	0.7	
4.4	0.7	1.5	2.2	2.9	3.7	.4	0.0	0.1	0.2	0.3	0.3	0.4	0.5	0.6	0.6	0.7	
4.5	0.8	1.5	2.3	3.0	3.8	.5	0.0	0.1	0.2	0.3	0.3	0.4	0.5	0.6	0.6	0.7	
4.6	0.8	1.5	2.3	3.1	3.8	.6	0.0	0.1	0.2	0.3	0.3	0.4	0.5	0.6	0.6	0.7	
4.7	0.8	1.6	2.4	3.2	3.9	.7	0.1	0.1	0.2	0.3	0.4	0.4	0.5	0.6	0.7	0.7	
4.8	0.8	1.6	2.4	3.2	4.0	.8	0.1	0.1	0.2	0.3	0.4	0.4	0.5	0.6	0.7	0.7	
4.9	0.9	1.7	2.5	3.3	4.1	.9	0.1	0.1	0.2	0.3	0.4	0.4	0.5	0.6	0.7	0.7	
5.0	0.8	1.6	2.5	3.3	4.1	.0	0.0	0.1	0.2	0.3	0.4	0.5	0.5	0.6	0.7	0.8	2.4 0.1 7.2 0.2 12.0 0.3 16.8 0.4 21.6 0.5 26.4 0.6 31.2 0.7 36.0
5.1	0.8	1.7	2.5	3.4	4.2	.1	0.0	0.1	0.2	0.3	0.4	0.5	0.6	0.7	0.7	0.8	
5.2	0.8	1.7	2.6	3.4	4.3	.2	0.0	0.1	0.2	0.3	0.4	0.5	0.6	0.7	0.8	0.8	
5.3	0.9	1.8	2.6	3.5	4.4	.3	0.0	0.1	0.2	0.3	0.4	0.5	0.6	0.7	0.8	0.9	
5.4	0.9	1.8	2.7	3.6	4.5	.4	0.0	0.1	0.2	0.3	0.4	0.5	0.6	0.7	0.8	0.9	
5.5	0.9	1.8	2.8	3.7	4.6	.5	0.0	0.1	0.2	0.3	0.4	0.5	0.6	0.7	0.8	0.9	
5.6	0.9	1.9	2.8	3.7	4.7	.6	0.1	0.1	0.2	0.3	0.4	0.5	0.6	0.7	0.8	0.9	
5.7	1.0	1.9	2.9	3.8	4.8	.7	0.1	0.2	0.2	0.3	0.4	0.5	0.6	0.7	0.8	0.9	
5.8	1.0	2.0	2.9	3.9	4.9	.8	0.1	0.2	0.3	0.3	0.4	0.5	0.6	0.7	0.8	0.9	
5.9	1.0	2.0	3.0	4.0	5.0	.9	0.1	0.2	0.3	0.4	0.4	0.5	0.6	0.7	0.8	0.9	
6.0	1.0	2.0	3.0	4.0	5.0	.0	0.0	0.1	0.2	0.3	0.4	0.5	0.6	0.8	0.9	1.0	2.1 0.1 6.2 0.2 10.4 0.3 14.5 0.4 18.6 0.5 22.8 0.6 26.9 0.7 31.1 0.8 35.2
6.1	1.0	2.0	3.0	4.0	5.1	.1	0.0	0.1	0.2	0.3	0.4	0.6	0.7	0.8	0.9	1.0	
6.2	1.0	2.0	3.1	4.1	5.1	.2	0.0	0.1	0.2	0.3	0.5	0.6	0.7	0.8	0.9	1.0	
6.3	1.0	2.1	3.1	4.2	5.2	.3	0.0	0.1	0.2	0.4	0.5	0.6	0.7	0.8	0.9	1.0	
6.4	1.1	2.1	3.2	4.3	5.3	.4	0.0	0.2	0.3	0.4	0.5	0.6	0.7	0.8	0.9	1.0	
6.5	1.1	2.2	3.3	4.3	5.4	.5	0.1	0.2	0.3	0.4	0.5	0.6	0.7	0.8	0.9	1.0	
6.6	1.1	2.2	3.3	4.4	5.5	.6	0.1	0.2	0.3	0.4	0.5	0.6	0.7	0.8	0.9	1.0	
6.7	1.1	2.3	3.4	4.5	5.6	.7	0.1	0.2	0.3	0.4	0.5	0.6	0.7	0.8	0.9	1.1	
6.8	1.2	2.3	3.4	4.6	5.7	.8	0.1	0.2	0.3	0.4	0.5	0.6	0.7	0.8	1.0	1.1	
6.9	1.2	2.3	3.5	4.6	5.8	.9	0.1	0.2	0.3	0.4	0.5	0.6	0.7	0.9	1.0	1.1	
7.0	1.1	2.3	3.5	4.6	5.8	.0	0.0	0.1	0.2	0.4	0.5	0.6	0.7	0.9	1.0	1.1	1.8 0.1 5.5 0.2 9.1 0.3 12.8 0.4 16.5 0.5 20.1 0.6 23.8 0.7 27.4 0.8 31.1 0.9 34.7
7.1	1.2	2.3	3.5	4.7	5.9	.1	0.0	0.1	0.3	0.4	0.5	0.6	0.8	0.9	1.0	1.1	
7.2	1.2	2.4	3.6	4.8	6.0	.2	0.0	0.1	0.3	0.4	0.5	0.6	0.8	0.9	1.0	1.1	
7.3	1.2	2.4	3.6	4.9	6.1	.3	0.0	0.2	0.3	0.4	0.5	0.7	0.8	0.9	1.0	1.2	
7.4	1.2	2.5	3.7	4.9	6.2	.4	0.0	0.2	0.3	0.4	0.5	0.7	0.8	0.9	1.0	1.2	
7.5	1.3	2.5	3.8	5.0	6.3	.5	0.1	0.2	0.3	0.4	0.6	0.7	0.8	0.9	1.1	1.2	
7.6	1.3	2.5	3.8	5.1	6.3	.6	0.1	0.2	0.3	0.4	0.6	0.7	0.8	0.9	1.1	1.2	
7.7	1.3	2.6	3.9	5.2	6.4	.7	0.1	0.2	0.3	0.5	0.6	0.7	0.8	1.0	1.1	1.2	
7.8	1.3	2.6	3.9	5.2	6.5	.8	0.1	0.2	0.3	0.5	0.6	0.7	0.8	1.0	1.1	1.2	
7.9	1.4	2.7	4.0	5.3	6.6	.9	0.1	0.2	0.4	0.5	0.6	0.7	0.9	1.0	1.1	1.2	
	10'	20'	30'	40'	50'		0'	1'	2'	3'	4'	5'	6'	7'	8'	9'	

Dec. Inc.	Altitude Difference (d) Tens 10'	20'	30'	40'	50'	Decimals	Units 0'	1'	2'	3'	4'	5'	6'	7'	8'	9'	Double Second Diff. and Corr.
8.0	1.3	2.6	4.0	5.3	6.6	.0	0.0	0.1	0.3	0.4	0.6	0.7	0.8	1.0	1.1	1.3	1.6 0.1 4.8 0.2 8.0 0.3 11.2 0.4 14.5 0.5 17.7 0.6 20.9 0.7 24.1 0.8 27.3 0.9 30.5 1.0 33.7 1.1 36.9
8.1	1.3	2.7	4.0	5.4	6.7	.1	0.0	0.2	0.3	0.4	0.6	0.7	0.9	1.0	1.1	1.3	
8.2	1.3	2.7	4.1	5.4	6.8	.2	0.0	0.2	0.3	0.5	0.6	0.7	0.9	1.0	1.2	1.3	
8.3	1.4	2.8	4.1	5.5	6.9	.3	0.0	0.2	0.3	0.5	0.6	0.8	0.9	1.0	1.2	1.3	
8.4	1.4	2.8	4.2	5.6	7.0	.4	0.1	0.2	0.3	0.5	0.6	0.8	0.9	1.0	1.2	1.3	
8.5	1.4	2.8	4.3	5.7	7.1	.5	0.1	0.2	0.4	0.5	0.6	0.8	0.9	1.1	1.2	1.3	
8.6	1.4	2.9	4.3	5.7	7.2	.6	0.1	0.2	0.4	0.5	0.7	0.8	0.9	1.1	1.2	1.4	
8.7	1.5	2.9	4.4	5.8	7.3	.7	0.1	0.2	0.4	0.5	0.7	0.8	0.9	1.1	1.2	1.4	
8.8	1.5	3.0	4.4	5.9	7.4	.8	0.1	0.3	0.4	0.5	0.7	0.8	1.0	1.1	1.2	1.4	
8.9	1.5	3.0	4.5	6.0	7.5	.9	0.1	0.3	0.4	0.6	0.7	0.8	1.0	1.1	1.3	1.4	
9.0	1.5	3.0	4.5	6.0	7.5	.0	0.0	0.2	0.3	0.5	0.6	0.8	0.9	1.1	1.3	1.4	
9.1	1.5	3.0	4.5	6.0	7.6	.1	0.0	0.2	0.3	0.5	0.6	0.8	1.0	1.1	1.3	1.4	
9.2	1.5	3.0	4.6	6.1	7.6	.2	0.0	0.2	0.3	0.5	0.7	0.8	1.0	1.1	1.3	1.5	
9.3	1.5	3.1	4.6	6.2	7.7	.3	0.0	0.2	0.4	0.5	0.7	0.8	1.0	1.2	1.3	1.5	
9.4	1.6	3.1	4.7	6.3	7.8	.4	0.1	0.2	0.4	0.5	0.7	0.9	1.0	1.2	1.3	1.5	
9.5	1.6	3.2	4.8	6.3	7.9	.5	0.1	0.2	0.4	0.6	0.7	0.9	1.0	1.2	1.3	1.5	1.4 0.1 4.2 0.2 7.1 0.3 9.9 0.4 12.7 0.5 15.5 0.6 18.4 0.7 21.2 0.8 24.0 0.9 26.8 1.0 29.7 1.1 32.5 1.2 35.3
9.6	1.6	3.2	4.8	6.4	8.0	.6	0.1	0.3	0.4	0.6	0.7	0.9	1.0	1.2	1.4	1.5	
9.7	1.6	3.3	4.9	6.5	8.1	.7	0.1	0.3	0.4	0.6	0.7	0.9	1.1	1.2	1.4	1.5	
9.8	1.7	3.3	4.9	6.6	8.2	.8	0.1	0.3	0.4	0.6	0.8	0.9	1.1	1.2	1.4	1.6	
9.9	1.7	3.3	5.0	6.6	8.3	.9	0.1	0.3	0.5	0.6	0.8	0.9	1.1	1.3	1.4	1.6	
10.0	1.6	3.3	5.0	6.6	8.3	.0	0.0	0.2	0.3	0.5	0.7	0.9	1.0	1.2	1.4	1.6	
10.1	1.7	3.3	5.0	6.7	8.4	.1	0.0	0.2	0.4	0.5	0.7	0.9	1.1	1.2	1.4	1.6	
10.2	1.7	3.4	5.1	6.8	8.5	.2	0.0	0.2	0.4	0.6	0.7	0.9	1.1	1.3	1.4	1.6	
10.3	1.7	3.4	5.1	6.9	8.6	.3	0.1	0.2	0.4	0.6	0.8	0.9	1.1	1.3	1.5	1.6	
10.4	1.7	3.5	5.2	6.9	8.7	.4	0.1	0.2	0.4	0.6	0.8	0.9	1.1	1.3	1.5	1.6	
10.5	1.8	3.5	5.3	7.0	8.8	.5	0.1	0.3	0.4	0.6	0.8	1.0	1.1	1.3	1.5	1.7	
10.6	1.8	3.5	5.3	7.1	8.8	.6	0.1	0.3	0.5	0.6	0.8	1.0	1.2	1.3	1.5	1.7	
10.7	1.8	3.6	5.4	7.2	8.9	.7	0.1	0.3	0.5	0.6	0.8	1.0	1.2	1.3	1.5	1.7	
10.8	1.8	3.6	5.4	7.2	9.0	.8	0.1	0.3	0.5	0.7	0.8	1.0	1.2	1.4	1.5	1.7	
10.9	1.9	3.7	5.5	7.3	9.1	.9	0.2	0.3	0.5	0.7	0.9	1.0	1.2	1.4	1.6	1.7	
11.0	1.8	3.6	5.5	7.3	9.1	.0	0.0	0.2	0.4	0.6	0.8	1.0	1.1	1.3	1.5	1.7	1.3 0.1 3.8 0.2 6.3 0.3 8.9 0.4 11.4 0.5 14.0 0.6 16.5 0.7 19.0 0.8 21.6 0.9 24.1 1.0 26.7 1.1 29.2 1.2 31.7 1.3 34.3
11.1	1.8	3.7	5.5	7.4	9.2	.1	0.0	0.2	0.4	0.6	0.8	1.0	1.2	1.4	1.6	1.7	
11.2	1.8	3.7	5.6	7.4	9.3	.2	0.0	0.2	0.4	0.6	0.8	1.0	1.2	1.4	1.6	1.8	
11.3	1.9	3.8	5.6	7.5	9.4	.3	0.1	0.2	0.4	0.6	0.8	1.0	1.2	1.4	1.6	1.8	
11.4	1.9	3.8	5.7	7.6	9.5	.4	0.1	0.3	0.5	0.7	0.8	1.0	1.2	1.4	1.6	1.8	
11.5	1.9	3.8	5.8	7.7	9.6	.5	0.1	0.3	0.5	0.7	0.9	1.1	1.2	1.4	1.6	1.8	
11.6	1.9	3.9	5.8	7.7	9.7	.6	0.1	0.3	0.5	0.7	0.9	1.1	1.3	1.5	1.6	1.8	
11.7	2.0	3.9	5.9	7.8	9.8	.7	0.1	0.3	0.5	0.7	0.9	1.1	1.3	1.5	1.7	1.9	
11.8	2.0	4.0	5.9	7.9	9.9	.8	0.2	0.3	0.5	0.7	0.9	1.1	1.3	1.5	1.7	1.9	
11.9	2.0	4.0	6.0	8.0	10.0	.9	0.2	0.4	0.6	0.7	0.9	1.1	1.3	1.5	1.7	1.9	
12.0	2.0	4.0	6.0	8.0	10.0	.0	0.0	0.2	0.4	0.6	0.8	1.0	1.2	1.5	1.7	1.9	
12.1	2.0	4.0	6.0	8.0	10.1	.1	0.0	0.2	0.4	0.6	0.9	1.1	1.3	1.5	1.7	1.9	
12.2	2.0	4.0	6.1	8.1	10.1	.2	0.0	0.2	0.5	0.7	0.9	1.1	1.3	1.5	1.7	1.9	
12.3	2.0	4.1	6.1	8.2	10.2	.3	0.1	0.3	0.5	0.7	0.9	1.1	1.3	1.5	1.7	1.9	
12.4	2.1	4.1	6.2	8.3	10.3	.4	0.1	0.3	0.5	0.7	0.9	1.1	1.3	1.5	1.7	2.0	
12.5	2.1	4.2	6.3	8.3	10.4	.5	0.1	0.3	0.5	0.7	0.9	1.1	1.4	1.6	1.8	2.0	1.2 0.1 3.5 0.2 5.8 0.3 8.1 0.4 10.5 0.5 12.8 0.6 15.1 0.7 17.4 0.8 19.8 0.9 22.1 1.0 24.4 1.1 26.7 1.2 29.1 1.3 31.4 1.4 33.7 1.5 36.0
12.6	2.1	4.2	6.3	8.4	10.5	.6	0.1	0.3	0.5	0.7	1.0	1.2	1.4	1.6	1.8	2.0	
12.7	2.1	4.3	6.4	8.5	10.6	.7	0.1	0.4	0.6	0.8	1.0	1.2	1.4	1.6	1.8	2.0	
12.8	2.2	4.3	6.4	8.6	10.7	.8	0.2	0.4	0.6	0.8	1.0	1.2	1.4	1.6	1.8	2.0	
12.9	2.2	4.3	6.5	8.6	10.8	.9	0.2	0.4	0.6	0.8	1.0	1.2	1.4	1.6	1.9	2.1	
13.0	2.1	4.3	6.5	8.6	10.8	.0	0.0	0.2	0.4	0.7	0.9	1.1	1.3	1.6	1.8	2.0	
13.1	2.2	4.3	6.5	8.7	10.9	.1	0.0	0.2	0.5	0.7	0.9	1.1	1.4	1.6	1.8	2.0	
13.2	2.2	4.4	6.6	8.8	11.0	.2	0.0	0.3	0.5	0.7	0.9	1.2	1.4	1.6	1.8	2.1	
13.3	2.2	4.4	6.6	8.9	11.1	.3	0.1	0.3	0.5	0.7	1.0	1.2	1.4	1.6	1.9	2.1	
13.4	2.2	4.5	6.7	8.9	11.2	.4	0.1	0.3	0.5	0.8	1.0	1.2	1.4	1.7	1.9	2.1	
13.5	2.3	4.5	6.8	9.0	11.3	.5	0.1	0.3	0.6	0.8	1.0	1.2	1.5	1.7	1.9	2.1	
13.6	2.3	4.5	6.8	9.1	11.3	.6	0.1	0.4	0.6	0.8	1.0	1.3	1.5	1.7	1.9	2.2	
13.7	2.3	4.6	6.9	9.2	11.4	.7	0.2	0.4	0.6	0.8	1.1	1.3	1.5	1.7	2.0	2.2	
13.8	2.3	4.6	6.9	9.2	11.5	.8	0.2	0.4	0.6	0.9	1.1	1.3	1.5	1.8	2.0	2.2	
13.9	2.4	4.7	7.0	9.3	11.6	.9	0.2	0.4	0.7	0.9	1.1	1.3	1.6	1.8	2.0	2.2	
14.0	2.3	4.6	7.0	9.3	11.6	.0	0.0	0.2	0.5	0.7	1.0	1.2	1.4	1.7	1.9	2.2	1.1 0.1 3.2 0.2 5.3 0.3 7.5 0.4 9.6 0.5 11.7 0.6 13.9 0.7 16.0 0.8 18.1 0.9 20.3 1.0 22.4 1.1 24.5 1.2 26.7 1.3 28.8 1.4 30.9 1.5 33.1 1.6 35.2
14.1	2.3	4.7	7.0	9.4	11.7	.1	0.0	0.3	0.5	0.7	1.0	1.2	1.5	1.7	2.0	2.2	
14.2	2.3	4.7	7.1	9.4	11.8	.2	0.0	0.3	0.5	0.8	1.0	1.3	1.5	1.7	2.0	2.2	
14.3	2.4	4.8	7.1	9.5	11.9	.3	0.1	0.3	0.6	0.8	1.0	1.3	1.5	1.8	2.0	2.2	
14.4	2.4	4.8	7.2	9.6	12.0	.4	0.1	0.3	0.6	0.8	1.1	1.3	1.5	1.8	2.0	2.3	
14.5	2.4	4.8	7.3	9.7	12.1	.5	0.1	0.4	0.6	0.8	1.1	1.3	1.6	1.8	2.1	2.3	
14.6	2.4	4.9	7.3	9.7	12.2	.6	0.1	0.4	0.6	0.9	1.1	1.4	1.6	1.8	2.1	2.3	
14.7	2.5	4.9	7.4	9.8	12.3	.7	0.2	0.4	0.7	0.9	1.1	1.4	1.6	1.9	2.1	2.3	
14.8	2.5	5.0	7.4	9.9	12.4	.8	0.2	0.4	0.7	0.9	1.2	1.4	1.6	1.9	2.1	2.4	
14.9	2.5	5.0	7.5	10.0	12.5	.9	0.2	0.5	0.7	0.9	1.2	1.4	1.7	1.9	2.2	2.4	
15.0	2.5	5.0	7.5	10.0	12.5	.0	0.0	0.3	0.5	0.8	1.0	1.3	1.5	1.8	2.1	2.3	
15.1	2.5	5.0	7.5	10.0	12.6	.1	0.0	0.3	0.5	0.8	1.1	1.3	1.6	1.8	2.1	2.4	
15.2	2.5	5.0	7.6	10.1	12.6	.2	0.1	0.3	0.6	0.8	1.1	1.3	1.6	1.9	2.1	2.4	
15.3	2.5	5.1	7.6	10.2	12.7	.3	0.1	0.3	0.6	0.9	1.1	1.4	1.6	1.9	2.1	2.4	
15.4	2.6	5.1	7.7	10.3	12.8	.4	0.1	0.4	0.6	0.9	1.1	1.4	1.7	1.9	2.2	2.4	
15.5	2.6	5.2	7.8	10.3	12.9	.5	0.1	0.4	0.6	0.9	1.2	1.4	1.7	1.9	2.2	2.5	
15.6	2.6	5.2	7.8	10.4	13.0	.6	0.2	0.4	0.7	0.9	1.2	1.4	1.7	2.0	2.2	2.5	
15.7	2.6	5.3	7.9	10.5	13.1	.7	0.2	0.4	0.7	1.0	1.2	1.5	1.7	2.0	2.2	2.5	
15.8	2.7	5.3	7.9	10.6	13.2	.8	0.2	0.5	0.7	1.0	1.2	1.5	1.8	2.0	2.3	2.5	
15.9	2.7	5.3	8.0	10.6	13.3	.9	0.2	0.5	0.7	1.0	1.3	1.5	1.8	2.0	2.3	2.6	
	10'	20'	30'	40'	50'		0'	1'	2'	3'	4'	5'	6'	7'	8'	9'	

The Double-Second-Difference correction (Corr.) is always to be added to the tabulated altitude.

INTERPOLATION TABLE

Altitude Difference (d)

Dec. Inc.	Tens 10'	20'	30'	40'	50'	Decimals	Units 0'	1'	2'	3'	4'	5'	6'	7'	8'	9'
16.0	2.6	5.3	8.0	10.6	13.3	.0	0.0	0.3	0.5	0.8	1.1	1.4	1.6	1.9	2.2	2.5
16.1	2.7	5.3	8.0	10.7	13.4	.1	0.0	0.3	0.6	0.9	1.1	1.4	1.7	2.0	2.2	2.5
16.2	2.7	5.4	8.1	10.8	13.5	.2	0.1	0.3	0.6	0.9	1.2	1.4	1.7	2.0	2.3	2.5
16.3	2.7	5.4	8.1	10.9	13.6	.3	0.1	0.4	0.6	0.9	1.2	1.5	1.7	2.0	2.3	2.6
16.4	2.7	5.5	8.2	10.9	13.7	.4	0.1	0.4	0.7	0.9	1.2	1.5	1.8	2.0	2.3	2.6
16.5	2.8	5.5	8.3	11.0	13.8	.5	0.1	0.4	0.7	1.0	1.2	1.5	1.8	2.1	2.3	2.6
16.6	2.8	5.5	8.3	11.1	13.8	.6	0.2	0.4	0.7	1.0	1.3	1.5	1.8	2.1	2.4	2.6
16.7	2.8	5.6	8.4	11.2	13.9	.7	0.2	0.5	0.7	1.0	1.3	1.6	1.8	2.1	2.4	2.7
16.8	2.8	5.6	8.4	11.2	14.0	.8	0.2	0.5	0.8	1.0	1.3	1.6	1.9	2.1	2.4	2.7
16.9	2.9	5.7	8.5	11.3	14.1	.9	0.2	0.5	0.8	1.1	1.3	1.6	1.9	2.2	2.4	2.7
17.0	2.8	5.6	8.5	11.3	14.1	.0	0.0	0.3	0.6	0.9	1.2	1.5	1.7	2.0	2.3	2.6
17.1	2.8	5.7	8.5	11.4	14.2	.1	0.0	0.3	0.6	0.9	1.2	1.5	1.8	2.1	2.4	2.7
17.2	2.8	5.7	8.6	11.4	14.3	.2	0.1	0.3	0.6	0.9	1.2	1.5	1.8	2.1	2.4	2.7
17.3	2.9	5.8	8.6	11.5	14.4	.3	0.1	0.4	0.7	1.0	1.3	1.5	1.8	2.1	2.4	2.7
17.4	2.9	5.8	8.7	11.6	14.5	.4	0.1	0.4	0.7	1.0	1.3	1.6	1.9	2.2	2.4	2.7
17.5	2.9	5.8	8.8	11.7	14.6	.5	0.1	0.4	0.7	1.0	1.3	1.6	1.9	2.2	2.5	2.8
17.6	2.9	5.9	8.8	11.7	14.7	.6	0.2	0.5	0.8	1.0	1.3	1.6	1.9	2.2	2.5	2.8
17.7	3.0	5.9	8.9	11.8	14.8	.7	0.2	0.5	0.8	1.1	1.4	1.7	2.0	2.2	2.5	2.8
17.8	3.0	6.0	8.9	11.9	14.9	.8	0.2	0.5	0.8	1.1	1.4	1.7	2.0	2.3	2.6	2.9
17.9	3.0	6.0	9.0	12.0	15.0	.9	0.3	0.6	0.8	1.1	1.4	1.7	2.0	2.3	2.6	2.9
18.0	3.0	6.0	9.0	12.0	15.0	.0	0.0	0.3	0.6	0.9	1.2	1.5	1.8	2.2	2.5	2.8
18.1	3.0	6.0	9.0	12.0	15.1	.1	0.0	0.3	0.6	1.0	1.3	1.6	1.9	2.2	2.5	2.8
18.2	3.0	6.0	9.1	12.1	15.1	.2	0.1	0.4	0.7	1.0	1.3	1.6	1.9	2.2	2.5	2.8
18.3	3.0	6.1	9.1	12.2	15.2	.3	0.1	0.4	0.7	1.0	1.3	1.6	1.9	2.3	2.6	2.9
18.4	3.1	6.1	9.2	12.3	15.3	.4	0.1	0.4	0.7	1.0	1.4	1.7	2.0	2.3	2.6	2.9
18.5	3.1	6.2	9.3	12.3	15.4	.5	0.2	0.5	0.8	1.1	1.4	1.7	2.0	2.3	2.6	2.9
18.6	3.1	6.2	9.3	12.4	15.5	.6	0.2	0.5	0.8	1.1	1.4	1.7	2.0	2.3	2.7	3.0
18.7	3.1	6.3	9.4	12.5	15.6	.7	0.2	0.5	0.8	1.1	1.4	1.8	2.1	2.4	2.7	3.0
18.8	3.2	6.3	9.4	12.6	15.7	.8	0.2	0.6	0.9	1.2	1.5	1.8	2.1	2.4	2.7	3.0
18.9	3.2	6.3	9.5	12.6	15.8	.9	0.3	0.6	0.9	1.2	1.5	1.8	2.1	2.4	2.7	3.1
19.0	3.1	6.3	9.5	12.6	15.8	.0	0.0	0.3	0.6	1.0	1.3	1.6	1.9	2.3	2.6	2.9
19.1	3.2	6.3	9.5	12.7	15.9	.1	0.0	0.4	0.7	1.0	1.3	1.7	2.0	2.3	2.6	3.0
19.2	3.2	6.4	9.6	12.8	16.0	.2	0.1	0.4	0.7	1.0	1.4	1.7	2.0	2.3	2.7	3.0
19.3	3.2	6.4	9.6	12.9	16.1	.3	0.1	0.4	0.7	1.1	1.4	1.7	2.0	2.4	2.7	3.0
19.4	3.2	6.5	9.7	12.9	16.2	.4	0.1	0.5	0.8	1.1	1.4	1.8	2.1	2.4	2.7	3.1
19.5	3.3	6.5	9.8	13.0	16.3	.5	0.2	0.5	0.8	1.1	1.5	1.8	2.1	2.4	2.8	3.1
19.6	3.3	6.5	9.8	13.1	16.3	.6	0.2	0.5	0.8	1.2	1.5	1.8	2.1	2.5	2.8	3.1
19.7	3.3	6.6	9.9	13.2	16.4	.7	0.2	0.6	0.9	1.2	1.5	1.9	2.2	2.5	2.8	3.2
19.8	3.3	6.6	9.9	13.2	16.5	.8	0.3	0.6	0.9	1.2	1.6	1.9	2.2	2.5	2.9	3.2
19.9	3.4	6.7	10.0	13.3	16.6	.9	0.3	0.6	0.9	1.3	1.6	1.9	2.2	2.6	2.9	3.2
20.0	3.3	6.6	10.0	13.3	16.6	.0	0.0	0.3	0.7	1.0	1.4	1.7	2.0	2.4	2.7	3.1
20.1	3.3	6.7	10.0	13.4	16.7	.1	0.0	0.4	0.7	1.1	1.4	1.7	2.1	2.4	2.8	3.1
20.2	3.3	6.7	10.1	13.4	16.8	.2	0.1	0.4	0.8	1.1	1.4	1.8	2.1	2.5	2.8	3.1
20.3	3.4	6.8	10.1	13.5	16.9	.3	0.1	0.4	0.8	1.1	1.5	1.8	2.2	2.5	2.8	3.2
20.4	3.4	6.8	10.2	13.6	17.0	.4	0.1	0.5	0.8	1.2	1.5	1.8	2.2	2.5	2.9	3.2
20.5	3.4	6.8	10.3	13.7	17.1	.5	0.2	0.5	0.9	1.2	1.5	1.9	2.2	2.6	2.9	3.2
20.6	3.4	6.9	10.3	13.7	17.2	.6	0.2	0.5	0.9	1.2	1.6	1.9	2.3	2.6	2.9	3.3
20.7	3.5	6.9	10.4	13.8	17.3	.7	0.2	0.6	0.9	1.3	1.6	1.9	2.3	2.6	3.0	3.3
20.8	3.5	7.0	10.4	13.9	17.4	.8	0.3	0.6	1.0	1.3	1.6	2.0	2.3	2.7	3.0	3.3
20.9	3.5	7.0	10.5	14.0	17.5	.9	0.3	0.6	1.0	1.3	1.7	2.0	2.4	2.7	3.0	3.4
21.0	3.5	7.0	10.5	14.0	17.5	.0	0.0	0.4	0.7	1.1	1.4	1.8	2.1	2.5	2.9	3.2
21.1	3.5	7.0	10.5	14.0	17.6	.1	0.0	0.4	0.8	1.1	1.5	1.8	2.2	2.5	2.9	3.3
21.2	3.5	7.0	10.6	14.1	17.6	.2	0.1	0.4	0.8	1.1	1.5	1.9	2.2	2.6	2.9	3.3
21.3	3.5	7.1	10.6	14.2	17.7	.3	0.1	0.5	0.8	1.2	1.5	1.9	2.3	2.6	3.0	3.3
21.4	3.6	7.1	10.7	14.3	17.8	.4	0.1	0.5	0.9	1.2	1.6	1.9	2.3	2.7	3.0	3.4
21.5	3.6	7.2	10.8	14.3	17.9	.5	0.2	0.5	0.9	1.3	1.6	2.0	2.3	2.7	3.0	3.4
21.6	3.6	7.2	10.8	14.4	18.0	.6	0.2	0.6	0.9	1.3	1.6	2.0	2.4	2.7	3.1	3.4
21.7	3.6	7.3	10.9	14.5	18.1	.7	0.3	0.6	1.0	1.3	1.7	2.0	2.4	2.8	3.1	3.5
21.8	3.7	7.3	10.9	14.6	18.2	.8	0.3	0.6	1.0	1.4	1.7	2.1	2.4	2.8	3.2	3.5
21.9	3.7	7.3	11.0	14.6	18.3	.9	0.3	0.7	1.0	1.4	1.8	2.1	2.5	2.8	3.2	3.5
22.0	3.6	7.3	11.0	14.6	18.3	.0	0.0	0.4	0.7	1.1	1.5	1.9	2.2	2.6	3.0	3.4
22.1	3.7	7.3	11.0	14.7	18.4	.1	0.0	0.4	0.8	1.2	1.5	1.9	2.3	2.7	3.0	3.4
22.2	3.7	7.4	11.1	14.8	18.5	.2	0.1	0.4	0.8	1.2	1.6	1.9	2.3	2.7	3.1	3.4
22.3	3.7	7.4	11.1	14.9	18.6	.3	0.1	0.5	0.9	1.2	1.6	2.0	2.4	2.7	3.1	3.5
22.4	3.7	7.5	11.2	14.9	18.7	.4	0.1	0.5	0.9	1.3	1.6	2.0	2.4	2.8	3.1	3.5
22.5	3.8	7.5	11.3	15.0	18.8	.5	0.2	0.6	0.9	1.3	1.7	2.1	2.4	2.8	3.2	3.6
22.6	3.8	7.5	11.3	15.1	18.8	.6	0.2	0.6	1.0	1.3	1.7	2.1	2.5	2.8	3.2	3.6
22.7	3.8	7.6	11.4	15.2	18.9	.7	0.3	0.6	1.0	1.4	1.8	2.1	2.5	2.9	3.3	3.6
22.8	3.8	7.6	11.4	15.2	19.0	.8	0.3	0.7	1.0	1.4	1.8	2.2	2.5	2.9	3.3	3.7
22.9	3.9	7.7	11.5	15.3	19.1	.9	0.3	0.7	1.1	1.5	1.8	2.2	2.6	3.0	3.3	3.7
23.0	3.8	7.6	11.5	15.3	19.1	.0	0.0	0.4	0.8	1.2	1.6	2.0	2.3	2.7	3.1	3.5
23.1	3.8	7.7	11.5	15.4	19.2	.1	0.0	0.4	0.8	1.2	1.6	2.0	2.4	2.8	3.2	3.6
23.2	3.8	7.7	11.6	15.4	19.3	.2	0.1	0.5	0.9	1.3	1.6	2.0	2.4	2.8	3.2	3.6
23.3	3.9	7.8	11.6	15.5	19.4	.3	0.1	0.5	0.9	1.3	1.7	2.1	2.5	2.9	3.3	3.6
23.4	3.9	7.8	11.7	15.6	19.5	.4	0.2	0.5	0.9	1.3	1.7	2.1	2.5	2.9	3.3	3.7
23.5	3.9	7.8	11.8	15.7	19.6	.5	0.2	0.6	1.0	1.4	1.8	2.2	2.5	2.9	3.3	3.7
23.6	3.9	7.9	11.8	15.7	19.7	.6	0.2	0.6	1.0	1.4	1.8	2.2	2.6	3.0	3.4	3.8
23.7	4.0	7.9	11.9	15.8	19.8	.7	0.3	0.7	1.1	1.4	1.8	2.2	2.6	3.0	3.4	3.8
23.8	4.0	8.0	11.9	15.9	19.9	.8	0.3	0.7	1.1	1.5	1.9	2.3	2.7	3.1	3.4	3.8
23.9	4.0	8.0	12.0	16.0	20.0	.9	0.4	0.7	1.1	1.5	1.9	2.3	2.7	3.1	3.5	3.9
	10'	20'	30'	40'	50'		0'	1'	2'	3'	4'	5'	6'	7'	8'	9'

Double Second Diff. and Corr. (Dec. Inc. 16.0–17.9)

Double Second Diff.	Corr.
1.0	0.1
3.0	0.2
4.9	0.3
6.9	0.4
8.9	0.5
10.8	0.6
12.8	0.7
14.8	0.8
16.7	0.9
18.7	1.0
20.7	1.1
22.7	1.2
24.6	1.3
26.6	1.4
28.6	1.5
30.5	1.6
32.5	1.7
34.5	

Double Second Diff. and Corr. (Dec. Inc. 18.0–19.9)

Double Second Diff.	Corr.
0.9	0.1
2.8	0.2
4.6	0.3
6.5	0.4
8.3	0.5
10.2	0.6
12.0	0.7
13.9	0.8
15.7	0.9
17.6	1.0
19.4	1.1
21.3	1.2
23.1	1.3
25.0	1.4
26.8	1.5
28.7	1.6
30.5	1.7
32.3	1.8
34.2	

Double Second Diff. and Corr. (Dec. Inc. 20.0–21.9)

Double Second Diff.	Corr.
0.9	0.1
2.6	0.2
4.4	0.3
6.2	0.4
7.9	0.5
9.7	0.6
11.4	0.7
13.2	0.8
14.9	0.9
16.7	1.0
18.5	1.1
20.2	1.2
22.0	1.3
23.7	1.4
25.5	1.5
27.3	1.6
29.0	1.7
30.8	1.8
32.5	1.9
34.3	

Double Second Diff. and Corr. (Dec. Inc. 22.0–23.9)

Double Second Diff.	Corr.
0.8	0.1
2.5	0.2
4.2	0.3
5.9	0.4
7.6	0.5
9.3	0.6
11.0	0.7
12.7	0.8
14.4	0.9
16.1	1.0
17.8	1.1
19.5	1.2
21.2	1.3
22.8	1.4
24.5	1.5
26.2	1.6
27.9	1.7
29.6	1.8
31.3	1.9
33.0	2.0
34.7	

Altitude Difference (d)

Dec. Inc.	Tens 10'	20'	30'	40'	50'	Decimals	Units 0'	1'	2'	3'	4'	5'	6'	7'	8'	9'
24.0	4.0	8.0	12.0	16.0	20.0	.0	0.0	0.4	0.8	1.2	1.6	2.0	2.4	2.9	3.3	3.7
24.1	4.0	8.0	12.0	16.0	20.1	.1	0.0	0.4	0.9	1.3	1.7	2.1	2.5	2.9	3.3	3.7
24.2	4.0	8.0	12.1	16.1	20.1	.2	0.1	0.5	0.9	1.3	1.7	2.1	2.5	2.9	3.3	3.8
24.3	4.0	8.1	12.1	16.2	20.2	.3	0.1	0.5	0.9	1.3	1.8	2.2	2.6	3.0	3.4	3.8
24.4	4.1	8.1	12.2	16.3	20.3	.4	0.2	0.6	1.0	1.4	1.8	2.2	2.6	3.0	3.4	3.8
24.5	4.1	8.2	12.3	16.3	20.4	.5	0.2	0.6	1.0	1.4	1.8	2.2	2.7	3.1	3.5	3.9
24.6	4.1	8.2	12.3	16.4	20.5	.6	0.2	0.7	1.1	1.5	1.9	2.3	2.7	3.1	3.5	3.9
24.7	4.1	8.3	12.4	16.5	20.6	.7	0.3	0.7	1.1	1.5	1.9	2.3	2.7	3.1	3.6	4.0
24.8	4.2	8.3	12.4	16.6	20.7	.8	0.3	0.7	1.1	1.6	2.0	2.4	2.8	3.2	3.6	4.0
24.9	4.2	8.3	12.5	16.6	20.8	.9	0.4	0.8	1.2	1.6	2.0	2.4	2.8	3.2	3.6	4.0
25.0	4.1	8.3	12.5	16.6	20.8	.0	0.0	0.4	0.8	1.3	1.7	2.1	2.5	3.0	3.4	3.8
25.1	4.2	8.3	12.5	16.7	20.9	.1	0.0	0.5	0.9	1.3	1.7	2.2	2.6	3.0	3.4	3.9
25.2	4.2	8.4	12.6	16.8	21.0	.2	0.1	0.5	0.9	1.4	1.8	2.2	2.6	3.1	3.5	3.9
25.3	4.2	8.4	12.6	16.9	21.1	.3	0.1	0.6	1.0	1.4	1.8	2.3	2.7	3.1	3.5	4.0
25.4	4.2	8.5	12.7	16.9	21.2	.4	0.2	0.6	1.0	1.4	1.9	2.3	2.7	3.1	3.6	4.0
25.5	4.3	8.5	12.8	17.0	21.3	.5	0.2	0.6	1.1	1.5	1.9	2.3	2.8	3.2	3.6	4.0
25.6	4.3	8.5	12.8	17.1	21.3	.6	0.3	0.7	1.1	1.5	2.0	2.4	2.8	3.2	3.7	4.1
25.7	4.3	8.6	12.9	17.2	21.4	.7	0.3	0.7	1.1	1.6	2.0	2.4	2.8	3.3	3.7	4.1
25.8	4.3	8.6	12.9	17.2	21.5	.8	0.3	0.8	1.2	1.6	2.0	2.5	2.9	3.3	3.7	4.2
25.9	4.4	8.7	13.0	17.3	21.6	.9	0.4	0.8	1.2	1.7	2.1	2.5	2.9	3.4	3.8	4.2
26.0	4.3	8.6	13.0	17.3	21.6	.0	0.0	0.4	0.9	1.3	1.8	2.2	2.6	3.1	3.5	4.0
26.1	4.3	8.7	13.0	17.4	21.7	.1	0.0	0.5	0.9	1.4	1.8	2.3	2.7	3.1	3.6	4.0
26.2	4.3	8.7	13.1	17.4	21.8	.2	0.1	0.5	1.0	1.4	1.9	2.3	2.7	3.2	3.6	4.1
26.3	4.4	8.8	13.1	17.5	21.9	.3	0.1	0.6	1.0	1.5	1.9	2.3	2.8	3.2	3.7	4.1
26.4	4.4	8.8	13.2	17.6	22.0	.4	0.2	0.6	1.1	1.5	1.9	2.4	2.8	3.3	3.7	4.2
26.5	4.4	8.8	13.3	17.7	22.1	.5	0.2	0.7	1.1	1.5	2.0	2.4	2.9	3.3	3.8	4.2
26.6	4.4	8.9	13.3	17.7	22.2	.6	0.3	0.7	1.1	1.6	2.0	2.5	2.9	3.4	3.8	4.2
26.7	4.5	8.9	13.4	17.8	22.3	.7	0.3	0.8	1.2	1.6	2.1	2.5	3.0	3.4	3.8	4.3
26.8	4.5	9.0	13.4	17.9	22.4	.8	0.4	0.8	1.2	1.7	2.1	2.6	3.0	3.4	3.9	4.3
26.9	4.5	9.0	13.5	18.0	22.5	.9	0.4	0.8	1.3	1.7	2.2	2.6	3.0	3.5	3.9	4.4
27.0	4.5	9.0	13.5	18.0	22.5	.0	0.0	0.5	0.9	1.4	1.8	2.3	2.7	3.2	3.7	4.1
27.1	4.5	9.0	13.5	18.0	22.6	.1	0.0	0.5	1.0	1.4	1.9	2.3	2.8	3.3	3.7	4.2
27.2	4.5	9.0	13.6	18.1	22.6	.2	0.1	0.5	1.0	1.5	1.9	2.4	2.8	3.3	3.8	4.2
27.3	4.5	9.1	13.6	18.2	22.7	.3	0.1	0.6	1.1	1.5	2.0	2.4	2.9	3.3	3.8	4.3
27.4	4.6	9.1	13.7	18.3	22.8	.4	0.2	0.6	1.1	1.6	2.0	2.5	2.9	3.4	3.8	4.3
27.5	4.6	9.2	13.8	18.3	22.9	.5	0.2	0.7	1.1	1.6	2.1	2.5	3.0	3.4	3.9	4.4
27.6	4.6	9.2	13.8	18.4	23.0	.6	0.3	0.7	1.2	1.6	2.1	2.6	3.0	3.5	3.9	4.4
27.7	4.6	9.3	13.9	18.5	23.1	.7	0.3	0.8	1.2	1.7	2.2	2.6	3.1	3.5	4.0	4.4
27.8	4.7	9.3	13.9	18.6	23.2	.8	0.4	0.8	1.3	1.7	2.2	2.7	3.1	3.6	4.0	4.5
27.9	4.7	9.3	14.0	18.6	23.3	.9	0.4	0.9	1.3	1.8	2.2	2.7	3.2	3.6	4.1	4.5
28.0	4.6	9.3	14.0	18.6	23.3	.0	0.0	0.5	0.9	1.4	1.9	2.4	2.8	3.3	3.8	4.3
28.1	4.7	9.3	14.0	18.7	23.4	.1	0.0	0.5	1.0	1.5	1.9	2.4	2.9	3.4	3.8	4.3
28.2	4.7	9.4	14.1	18.8	23.5	.2	0.1	0.6	1.0	1.5	2.0	2.5	2.9	3.4	3.9	4.4
28.3	4.7	9.4	14.1	18.9	23.6	.3	0.1	0.6	1.1	1.6	2.0	2.5	3.0	3.5	3.9	4.4
28.4	4.7	9.5	14.2	18.9	23.7	.4	0.2	0.7	1.1	1.6	2.1	2.6	3.0	3.5	4.0	4.5
28.5	4.8	9.5	14.3	19.0	23.8	.5	0.2	0.7	1.2	1.7	2.1	2.6	3.1	3.6	4.0	4.5
28.6	4.8	9.5	14.3	19.1	23.8	.6	0.3	0.8	1.2	1.7	2.2	2.7	3.1	3.6	4.1	4.6
28.7	4.8	9.6	14.4	19.2	23.9	.7	0.3	0.8	1.3	1.8	2.2	2.7	3.2	3.7	4.1	4.6
28.8	4.8	9.6	14.4	19.2	24.0	.8	0.4	0.9	1.3	1.8	2.3	2.8	3.2	3.7	4.2	4.7
28.9	4.9	9.7	14.5	19.3	24.1	.9	0.4	0.9	1.4	1.9	2.3	2.8	3.3	3.8	4.2	4.7
29.0	4.8	9.6	14.5	19.3	24.1	.0	0.0	0.5	1.0	1.5	2.0	2.5	2.9	3.4	3.9	4.4
29.1	4.8	9.7	14.5	19.4	24.2	.1	0.0	0.5	1.0	1.5	2.0	2.5	3.0	3.5	4.0	4.5
29.2	4.8	9.7	14.6	19.4	24.3	.2	0.1	0.6	1.1	1.6	2.1	2.6	3.0	3.5	4.0	4.5
29.3	4.9	9.8	14.6	19.5	24.4	.3	0.1	0.6	1.1	1.6	2.1	2.6	3.1	3.6	4.1	4.6
29.4	4.9	9.8	14.7	19.6	24.5	.4	0.2	0.7	1.2	1.7	2.2	2.7	3.1	3.6	4.1	4.6
29.5	4.9	9.8	14.8	19.7	24.6	.5	0.2	0.7	1.2	1.7	2.2	2.7	3.2	3.7	4.2	4.7
29.6	4.9	9.9	14.8	19.7	24.7	.6	0.3	0.8	1.3	1.8	2.3	2.8	3.2	3.7	4.2	4.7
29.7	5.0	9.9	14.9	19.8	24.8	.7	0.3	0.8	1.3	1.8	2.3	2.8	3.3	3.8	4.3	4.8
29.8	5.0	10.0	14.9	19.9	24.9	.8	0.4	0.9	1.4	1.9	2.4	2.9	3.3	3.8	4.3	4.8
29.9	5.0	10.0	15.0	20.0	25.0	.9	0.4	0.9	1.4	1.9	2.4	2.9	3.4	3.9	4.4	4.9
30.0	5.0	10.0	15.0	20.0	25.0	.0	0.0	0.5	1.0	1.5	2.0	2.5	3.0	3.6	4.1	4.6
30.1	5.0	10.0	15.0	20.0	25.1	.1	0.1	0.6	1.1	1.6	2.1	2.6	3.1	3.6	4.1	4.6
30.2	5.0	10.0	15.1	20.1	25.1	.2	0.1	0.6	1.1	1.6	2.1	2.6	3.2	3.7	4.2	4.7
30.3	5.0	10.1	15.1	20.2	25.2	.3	0.2	0.7	1.2	1.7	2.2	2.7	3.2	3.7	4.2	4.7
30.4	5.1	10.1	15.2	20.3	25.3	.4	0.2	0.7	1.2	1.7	2.2	2.7	3.3	3.8	4.3	4.8
30.5	5.1	10.2	15.3	20.3	25.4	.5	0.3	0.8	1.3	1.8	2.3	2.8	3.3	3.8	4.3	4.8
30.6	5.1	10.2	15.3	20.4	25.5	.6	0.3	0.8	1.3	1.8	2.3	2.8	3.4	3.9	4.4	4.9
30.7	5.1	10.3	15.4	20.5	25.6	.7	0.4	0.9	1.4	1.9	2.4	2.9	3.4	3.9	4.4	4.9
30.8	5.2	10.3	15.4	20.6	25.7	.8	0.4	0.9	1.4	1.9	2.4	2.9	3.5	4.0	4.5	5.0
30.9	5.2	10.3	15.5	20.6	25.8	.9	0.5	1.0	1.5	2.0	2.5	3.0	3.5	4.0	4.5	5.0
31.0	5.1	10.3	15.5	20.6	25.8	.0	0.0	0.5	1.0	1.6	2.1	2.6	3.1	3.7	4.2	4.7
31.1	5.2	10.3	15.5	20.7	25.9	.1	0.1	0.6	1.1	1.6	2.2	2.7	3.2	3.7	4.3	4.8
31.2	5.2	10.4	15.6	20.8	26.0	.2	0.1	0.6	1.2	1.7	2.2	2.7	3.3	3.8	4.3	4.8
31.3	5.2	10.4	15.6	20.9	26.1	.3	0.2	0.7	1.2	1.7	2.3	2.8	3.3	3.8	4.4	4.9
31.4	5.2	10.5	15.7	20.9	26.2	.4	0.2	0.7	1.3	1.8	2.3	2.8	3.4	3.9	4.4	4.9
31.5	5.3	10.5	15.8	21.0	26.3	.5	0.3	0.8	1.3	1.8	2.4	2.9	3.4	3.9	4.5	5.0
31.6	5.3	10.5	15.8	21.1	26.3	.6	0.3	0.8	1.4	1.9	2.4	2.9	3.5	4.0	4.5	5.0
31.7	5.3	10.6	15.9	21.2	26.4	.7	0.4	0.9	1.4	1.9	2.5	3.0	3.5	4.0	4.6	5.1
31.8	5.3	10.6	15.9	21.2	26.5	.8	0.4	0.9	1.5	2.0	2.5	3.0	3.6	4.1	4.6	5.1
31.9	5.4	10.7	16.0	21.3	26.6	.9	0.5	1.0	1.5	2.0	2.6	3.1	3.6	4.1	4.7	5.2
	10'	20'	30'	40'	50'		0'	1'	2'	3'	4'	5'	6'	7'	8'	9'

Double Second Diff. and Corr. (Dec. Inc. 24.0–25.9)

Double Second Diff.	Corr.
0.8	0.1
2.5	0.2
4.1	0.3
5.8	0.4
7.4	0.5
9.1	0.6
10.7	0.7
12.3	0.8
14.0	0.9
15.6	1.0
17.3	1.1
18.9	1.2
20.6	1.3
22.2	1.4
23.9	1.5
25.5	1.6
27.2	1.7
28.8	1.8
30.4	1.9
32.1	2.0
33.7	2.1
35.4	

Double Second Diff. and Corr. (Dec. Inc. 26.0–27.9)

Double Second Diff.	Corr.
0.8	0.1
2.4	0.2
4.0	0.3
5.7	0.4
7.3	0.5
8.9	0.6
10.5	0.7
12.1	0.8
13.7	0.9
15.4	1.0
17.0	1.1
18.6	1.2
20.2	1.3
21.8	1.4
23.4	1.5
25.1	1.6
26.7	1.7
28.3	1.8
29.9	1.9
31.5	2.0
33.1	2.1
34.7	

Double Second Diff. and Corr. (Dec. Inc. 28.0–29.9)

Double Second Diff.	Corr.
0.8	0.1
2.4	0.2
4.0	0.3
5.6	0.4
7.2	0.5
8.8	0.6
10.4	0.7
12.0	0.8
13.6	0.9
15.2	1.0
16.8	1.1
18.4	1.2
20.0	1.3
21.6	1.4
23.2	1.5
24.8	1.6
26.4	1.7
28.0	1.8
29.6	1.9
31.2	2.0
32.8	2.1
34.4	

Double Second Diff. and Corr. (Dec. Inc. 30.0–31.9)

Double Second Diff.	Corr.
0.8	0.1
2.4	0.2
4.0	0.3
5.6	0.4
7.2	0.5
8.8	0.6
10.4	0.7
12.0	0.8
13.6	0.9
15.2	1.0
16.8	1.1
18.4	1.2
20.0	1.3
21.6	1.4
23.2	1.5
24.8	1.6
26.4	1.7
28.0	1.8
29.6	1.9
31.2	2.0
32.8	2.1
34.4	

The Double-Second-Difference correction (Corr.) is always to be added to the tabulated altitude.

INTERPOLATION TABLE

Dec. Inc.	Altitude Difference (d) Tens					Decimals	Units										Double Second Diff. and Corr.	
	10'	20'	30'	40'	50'		0'	1'	2'	3'	4'	5'	6'	7'	8'	9'		
28.0	4.6	9.3	14.0	18.6	23.3	.0	0.0	0.5	0.9	1.4	1.9	2.4	2.8	3.3	3.8	4.3	0.8	
28.1	4.7	9.3	14.0	18.7	23.4	.1	0.0	0.5	1.0	1.5	1.9	2.4	2.9	3.4	3.8	4.3	2.4	0.1
28.2	4.7	9.4	14.1	18.8	23.5	.2	0.1	0.6	1.0	1.5	2.0	2.5	2.9	3.4	3.9	4.4	4.0	0.2
28.3	4.7	9.4	14.1	18.9	23.6	.3	0.1	0.6	1.1	1.6	2.0	2.5	3.0	3.5	3.9	4.4	5.6	0.3
28.4	4.7	9.5	14.2	18.9	23.7	.4	0.2	0.7	1.1	1.6	2.1	2.6	3.0	3.5	4.0	4.5	7.2 / 8.8	0.4 / 0.5
28.5	4.8	9.5	14.3	19.0	23.8	.5	0.2	0.7	1.2	1.7	2.1	2.6	3.1	3.6	4.0	4.5	10.4	0.6
28.6	4.8	9.5	14.3	19.1	23.8	.6	0.3	0.8	1.2	1.7	2.2	2.7	3.1	3.6	4.1	4.6	12.0	0.7
28.7	4.8	9.6	14.4	19.2	23.9	.7	0.3	0.8	1.3	1.8	2.2	2.7	3.2	3.7	4.1	4.6	13.6	0.8
28.8	4.8	9.6	14.4	19.2	24.0	.8	0.4	0.9	1.3	1.8	2.3	2.8	3.2	3.7	4.2	4.7	15.2	0.9
28.9	4.9	9.7	14.5	19.3	24.1	.9	0.4	0.9	1.4	1.9	2.3	2.8	3.3	3.8	4.2	4.7	16.8 / 18.4	1.0 / 1.1
29.0	4.8	9.6	14.5	19.3	24.1	.0	0.0	0.5	1.0	1.5	2.0	2.5	2.9	3.4	3.9	4.4	20.0	1.2
29.1	4.8	9.7	14.5	19.4	24.2	.1	0.0	0.5	1.0	1.5	2.0	2.5	3.0	3.5	4.0	4.5	21.6	1.3
29.2	4.8	9.7	14.6	19.4	24.3	.2	0.1	0.6	1.1	1.6	2.1	2.6	3.0	3.5	4.0	4.5	23.2	1.4
29.3	4.9	9.8	14.6	19.5	24.4	.3	0.1	0.6	1.1	1.6	2.1	2.6	3.1	3.6	4.1	4.6	24.8	1.5
29.4	4.9	9.8	14.7	19.6	24.5	.4	0.2	0.7	1.2	1.7	2.2	2.7	3.1	3.6	4.1	4.6	26.4	1.6
29.5	4.9	9.8	14.8	19.7	24.6	.5	0.2	0.7	1.2	1.7	2.2	2.7	3.2	3.7	4.2	4.7	28.0	1.7
29.6	4.9	9.9	14.8	19.7	24.7	.6	0.3	0.8	1.3	1.8	2.3	2.8	3.2	3.7	4.2	4.7	29.6	1.8
29.7	5.0	9.9	14.9	19.8	24.8	.7	0.3	0.8	1.3	1.8	2.3	2.8	3.3	3.8	4.3	4.8	31.2	1.9
29.8	5.0	10.0	14.9	19.9	24.9	.8	0.4	0.9	1.4	1.9	2.4	2.9	3.3	3.8	4.3	4.8	32.8	2.0
29.9	5.0	10.0	15.0	20.0	25.0	.9	0.4	0.9	1.4	1.9	2.4	2.9	3.4	3.9	4.4	4.9	34.4	2.1
30.0	5.0	10.0	15.0	20.0	25.0	.0	0.0	0.5	1.0	1.5	2.0	2.5	3.0	3.6	4.1	4.6	0.8	
30.1	5.0	10.0	15.0	20.0	25.1	.1	0.1	0.6	1.1	1.6	2.1	2.6	3.1	3.6	4.1	4.6	2.4	0.1
30.2	5.0	10.0	15.1	20.1	25.1	.2	0.1	0.6	1.1	1.6	2.1	2.6	3.2	3.7	4.2	4.7	4.0	0.2
30.3	5.0	10.1	15.1	20.2	25.2	.3	0.2	0.7	1.2	1.7	2.2	2.7	3.2	3.7	4.2	4.7	5.6	0.3
30.4	5.1	10.1	15.2	20.3	25.3	.4	0.2	0.7	1.2	1.7	2.2	2.7	3.3	3.8	4.3	4.8	7.2 / 8.8	0.4 / 0.5
30.5	5.1	10.2	15.3	20.3	25.4	.5	0.3	0.8	1.3	1.8	2.3	2.8	3.3	3.8	4.3	4.8	10.4	0.6
30.6	5.1	10.2	15.3	20.4	25.5	.6	0.3	0.8	1.3	1.8	2.3	2.8	3.4	3.9	4.4	4.9	12.0	0.7
30.7	5.1	10.3	15.4	20.5	25.6	.7	0.4	0.9	1.4	1.9	2.4	2.9	3.4	3.9	4.4	4.9	13.6	0.8
30.8	5.2	10.3	15.4	20.6	25.7	.8	0.4	0.9	1.4	1.9	2.4	2.9	3.5	4.0	4.5	5.0	15.2	0.9
30.9	5.2	10.3	15.5	20.6	25.8	.9	0.5	1.0	1.5	2.0	2.5	3.0	3.5	4.0	4.5	5.0	16.8 / 18.4	1.0 / 1.1
31.0	5.1	10.3	15.5	20.6	25.8	.0	0.0	0.5	1.0	1.6	2.1	2.6	3.1	3.7	4.2	4.7	20.0	1.2
31.1	5.2	10.3	15.5	20.7	25.9	.1	0.1	0.6	1.1	1.6	2.2	2.7	3.2	3.7	4.3	4.8	21.6	1.3
31.2	5.2	10.4	15.6	20.8	26.0	.2	0.1	0.6	1.2	1.7	2.2	2.7	3.3	3.8	4.3	4.8	23.2	1.4
31.3	5.2	10.4	15.6	20.9	26.1	.3	0.2	0.7	1.2	1.7	2.3	2.8	3.3	3.8	4.4	4.9	24.8	1.5
31.4	5.2	10.5	15.7	20.9	26.2	.4	0.2	0.7	1.3	1.8	2.3	2.8	3.4	3.9	4.4	4.9	26.4	1.6
31.5	5.3	10.5	15.8	21.0	26.3	.5	0.3	0.8	1.3	1.8	2.4	2.9	3.4	3.9	4.5	5.0	28.0	1.7
31.6	5.3	10.5	15.8	21.1	26.3	.6	0.3	0.8	1.4	1.9	2.4	2.9	3.5	4.0	4.5	5.0	29.6	1.8
31.7	5.3	10.6	15.9	21.2	26.4	.7	0.4	0.9	1.4	1.9	2.5	3.0	3.5	4.0	4.6	5.1	31.2	1.9
31.8	5.3	10.6	15.9	21.2	26.5	.8	0.4	0.9	1.5	2.0	2.5	3.0	3.6	4.1	4.6	5.1	32.8	2.0
31.9	5.4	10.7	16.0	21.3	26.6	.9	0.5	1.0	1.5	2.0	2.6	3.1	3.6	4.1	4.7	5.2	34.4	2.1
32.0	5.3	10.6	16.0	21.3	26.6	.0	0.0	0.5	1.1	1.6	2.2	2.7	3.2	3.8	4.3	4.9	0.8	
32.1	5.3	10.7	16.0	21.4	26.7	.1	0.1	0.6	1.1	1.7	2.2	2.8	3.3	3.8	4.4	4.9	2.4	0.1
32.2	5.3	10.7	16.1	21.4	26.8	.2	0.1	0.6	1.2	1.7	2.3	2.8	3.4	3.9	4.4	5.0	4.0	0.2
32.3	5.4	10.8	16.1	21.5	26.9	.3	0.2	0.7	1.2	1.8	2.3	2.9	3.4	4.0	4.5	5.0	5.7	0.3
32.4	5.4	10.8	16.2	21.6	27.0	.4	0.2	0.8	1.3	1.8	2.4	2.9	3.5	4.0	4.5	5.1	7.3 / 8.9	0.4 / 0.5
32.5	5.4	10.8	16.3	21.7	27.1	.5	0.3	0.8	1.4	1.9	2.4	3.0	3.5	4.1	4.6	5.1	10.5	0.6
32.6	5.4	10.9	16.3	21.7	27.2	.6	0.3	0.9	1.4	1.9	2.5	3.0	3.6	4.1	4.7	5.2	12.1	0.7
32.7	5.5	10.9	16.4	21.8	27.3	.7	0.4	0.9	1.5	2.0	2.5	3.1	3.6	4.2	4.7	5.3	13.7	0.8
32.8	5.5	11.0	16.4	21.9	27.4	.8	0.4	1.0	1.5	2.1	2.6	3.1	3.7	4.2	4.8	5.3	15.4	0.9
32.9	5.5	11.0	16.5	22.0	27.5	.9	0.5	1.0	1.6	2.1	2.7	3.2	3.7	4.3	4.8	5.4	17.0 / 18.6	1.0 / 1.1
33.0	5.5	11.0	16.5	22.0	27.5	.0	0.0	0.6	1.1	1.7	2.2	2.8	3.3	3.9	4.5	5.0	20.2	1.2
33.1	5.5	11.0	16.5	22.0	27.6	.1	0.1	0.6	1.2	1.7	2.3	2.8	3.4	4.0	4.5	5.1	21.8	1.3
33.2	5.5	11.0	16.6	22.1	27.6	.2	0.1	0.7	1.2	1.8	2.3	2.9	3.5	4.0	4.6	5.1	23.4	1.4
33.3	5.5	11.1	16.6	22.2	27.7	.3	0.2	0.7	1.3	1.8	2.4	3.0	3.5	4.1	4.6	5.2	25.1	1.5
33.4	5.6	11.1	16.7	22.3	27.8	.4	0.2	0.8	1.3	1.9	2.5	3.0	3.6	4.1	4.7	5.2	26.7	1.6
33.5	5.6	11.2	16.8	22.3	27.9	.5	0.3	0.8	1.4	2.0	2.5	3.1	3.6	4.2	4.7	5.3	28.3	1.7
33.6	5.6	11.2	16.8	22.4	28.0	.6	0.3	0.9	1.5	2.0	2.6	3.1	3.7	4.2	4.8	5.4	29.9	1.8
33.7	5.6	11.3	16.9	22.5	28.1	.7	0.4	0.9	1.5	2.1	2.6	3.2	3.7	4.3	4.9	5.4	31.5	1.9
33.8	5.7	11.3	16.9	22.6	28.2	.8	0.4	1.0	1.6	2.1	2.7	3.2	3.8	4.4	4.9	5.5	33.1	2.0
33.9	5.7	11.3	17.0	22.6	28.3	.9	0.5	1.1	1.6	2.2	2.7	3.3	3.9	4.4	5.0	5.5	34.7	2.1
34.0	5.6	11.3	17.0	22.6	28.3	.0	0.0	0.6	1.1	1.7	2.3	2.9	3.4	4.0	4.6	5.2	0.8	
34.1	5.7	11.3	17.0	22.7	28.4	.1	0.1	0.6	1.2	1.8	2.4	2.9	3.5	4.1	4.7	5.2	2.5	0.1
34.2	5.7	11.4	17.1	22.8	28.5	.2	0.1	0.7	1.3	1.8	2.4	3.0	3.6	4.1	4.7	5.3	4.1	0.2
34.3	5.7	11.4	17.1	22.9	28.6	.3	0.2	0.7	1.3	1.9	2.5	3.0	3.6	4.2	4.8	5.3	5.8	0.3
34.4	5.7	11.5	17.2	22.9	28.7	.4	0.2	0.8	1.4	2.0	2.5	3.1	3.7	4.3	4.8	5.4	7.4 / 9.1	0.4 / 0.5
34.5	5.8	11.5	17.3	23.0	28.8	.5	0.3	0.9	1.4	2.0	2.6	3.2	3.7	4.3	4.9	5.5	10.7	0.6
34.6	5.8	11.5	17.3	23.1	28.8	.6	0.3	0.9	1.5	2.1	2.6	3.2	3.8	4.4	4.9	5.5	12.3	0.7
34.7	5.8	11.6	17.4	23.2	28.9	.7	0.4	1.0	1.6	2.1	2.7	3.3	3.9	4.4	5.0	5.6	14.0	0.8
34.8	5.8	11.6	17.4	23.2	29.0	.8	0.5	1.0	1.6	2.2	2.8	3.3	3.9	4.5	5.1	5.6	15.6	0.9
34.9	5.9	11.7	17.5	23.3	29.1	.9	0.5	1.1	1.7	2.2	2.8	3.4	4.0	4.5	5.1	5.7	17.3 / 18.9	1.0 / 1.1
35.0	5.8	11.6	17.5	23.3	29.1	.0	0.0	0.6	1.2	1.8	2.4	3.0	3.5	4.1	4.7	5.3	20.6	1.2
35.1	5.8	11.7	17.5	23.4	29.2	.1	0.1	0.7	1.2	1.8	2.4	3.0	3.6	4.2	4.8	5.4	22.2	1.3
35.2	5.8	11.7	17.6	23.4	29.3	.2	0.1	0.7	1.3	1.9	2.5	3.1	3.7	4.3	4.9	5.4	23.9	1.4
35.3	5.9	11.8	17.6	23.5	29.4	.3	0.2	0.8	1.4	2.0	2.5	3.1	3.7	4.3	4.9	5.5	25.5	1.5
35.4	5.9	11.8	17.7	23.6	29.5	.4	0.2	0.8	1.4	2.0	2.6	3.2	3.8	4.4	5.0	5.6	27.2	1.6
35.5	5.9	11.8	17.8	23.7	29.6	.5	0.3	0.9	1.5	2.1	2.7	3.3	3.8	4.4	5.0	5.6	28.8	1.7
35.6	5.9	11.9	17.8	23.7	29.7	.6	0.4	0.9	1.5	2.1	2.7	3.3	3.9	4.5	5.1	5.7	30.4	1.8
35.7	6.0	11.9	17.9	23.8	29.8	.7	0.4	1.0	1.6	2.2	2.8	3.4	4.0	4.6	5.1	5.7	32.1	1.9
35.8	6.0	12.0	17.9	23.9	29.9	.8	0.5	1.1	1.7	2.2	2.8	3.4	4.0	4.6	5.2	5.8	33.7	2.0
35.9	6.0	12.0	18.0	24.0	30.0	.9	0.5	1.1	1.7	2.3	2.9	3.5	4.1	4.7	5.3	5.9	35.4	2.1
	10'	20'	30'	40'	50'		0'	1'	2'	3'	4'	5'	6'	7'	8'	9'		

Dec. Inc.	Altitude Difference (d) Tens					Decimals	Units										Double Second Diff. and Corr.	
	10'	20'	30'	40'	50'		0'	1'	2'	3'	4'	5'	6'	7'	8'	9'		
36.0	6.0	12.0	18.0	24.0	30.0	.0	0.0	0.6	1.2	1.8	2.4	3.0	3.6	4.3	4.9	5.5		
36.1	6.0	12.0	18.0	24.0	30.1	.1	0.1	0.7	1.3	1.9	2.5	3.1	3.7	4.3	4.9	5.5	0.8	
36.2	6.0	12.0	18.1	24.1	30.1	.2	0.1	0.7	1.3	1.9	2.6	3.2	3.8	4.4	5.0	5.6	2.5	0.1
36.3	6.0	12.1	18.1	24.2	30.2	.3	0.2	0.8	1.4	2.0	2.6	3.2	3.8	4.4	5.0	5.7	4.2	0.2
36.4	6.1	12.1	18.2	24.3	30.3	.4	0.2	0.9	1.5	2.1	2.7	3.3	3.9	4.5	5.1	5.7	5.9 / 7.6	0.3 / 0.4
36.5	6.1	12.2	18.3	24.3	30.4	.5	0.3	0.9	1.5	2.1	2.7	3.3	4.0	4.6	5.2	5.8	9.3	0.5
36.6	6.1	12.2	18.3	24.4	30.5	.6	0.4	1.0	1.6	2.2	2.8	3.4	4.0	4.6	5.2	5.8	11.0	0.6
36.7	6.1	12.3	18.4	24.5	30.6	.7	0.4	1.0	1.6	2.3	2.9	3.5	4.1	4.7	5.3	5.9	12.7	0.7
36.8	6.2	12.3	18.4	24.6	30.7	.8	0.5	1.1	1.7	2.3	2.9	3.5	4.1	4.7	5.4	6.0	14.4	0.8
36.9	6.2	12.3	18.5	24.6	30.8	.9	0.5	1.2	1.8	2.4	3.0	3.6	4.2	4.8	5.4	6.0	16.1 / 17.8	0.9 / 1.0
37.0	6.1	12.3	18.5	24.6	30.8	.0	0.0	0.6	1.2	1.9	2.5	3.1	3.7	4.4	5.0	5.6	19.5	1.1
37.1	6.2	12.3	18.5	24.7	30.9	.1	0.1	0.7	1.3	1.9	2.6	3.2	3.8	4.4	5.1	5.7	21.2	1.2
37.2	6.2	12.4	18.6	24.8	31.0	.2	0.1	0.7	1.4	2.0	2.6	3.2	3.9	4.5	5.1	5.7	22.8	1.3
37.3	6.2	12.4	18.6	24.9	31.1	.3	0.2	0.8	1.4	2.1	2.7	3.3	3.9	4.6	5.2	5.8	24.5	1.4
37.4	6.2	12.5	18.7	24.9	31.2	.4	0.2	0.9	1.5	2.1	2.7	3.4	4.0	4.6	5.2	5.9	26.2 / 27.9	1.5 / 1.6
37.5	6.3	12.5	18.8	25.0	31.3	.5	0.3	0.9	1.6	2.2	2.8	3.4	4.1	4.7	5.3	5.9	29.6	1.7
37.6	6.3	12.5	18.8	25.1	31.3	.6	0.4	1.0	1.6	2.2	2.9	3.5	4.1	4.7	5.4	6.0	31.3	1.8
37.7	6.3	12.6	18.9	25.2	31.4	.7	0.4	1.1	1.7	2.3	2.9	3.6	4.2	4.8	5.4	6.1	33.0	1.9
37.8	6.3	12.6	18.9	25.2	31.5	.8	0.5	1.1	1.7	2.4	3.0	3.6	4.2	4.9	5.5	6.1	34.7	2.0
37.9	6.4	12.7	19.0	25.3	31.6	.9	0.6	1.2	1.8	2.4	3.1	3.7	4.3	4.9	5.6	6.2		
38.0	6.3	12.6	19.0	25.3	31.6	.0	0.0	0.6	1.3	1.9	2.6	3.2	3.8	4.5	5.1	5.8		
38.1	6.3	12.7	19.0	25.4	31.7	.1	0.1	0.7	1.3	2.0	2.6	3.3	3.9	4.6	5.2	5.8		
38.2	6.3	12.7	19.1	25.4	31.8	.2	0.1	0.8	1.4	2.1	2.7	3.3	4.0	4.6	5.3	5.9	0.9	
38.3	6.4	12.8	19.1	25.5	31.9	.3	0.2	0.8	1.5	2.1	2.8	3.4	4.0	4.7	5.3	6.0	2.6	0.1
38.4	6.4	12.8	19.2	25.6	32.0	.4	0.3	0.9	1.5	2.2	2.8	3.5	4.1	4.7	5.4	6.0	4.4 / 6.2	0.2 / 0.3
38.5	6.4	12.8	19.3	25.7	32.1	.5	0.3	1.0	1.6	2.2	2.9	3.5	4.2	4.8	5.5	6.1	7.9	0.4
38.6	6.4	12.9	19.3	25.7	32.2	.6	0.4	1.0	1.7	2.3	3.0	3.6	4.2	4.9	5.5	6.2	9.7	0.5
38.7	6.5	12.9	19.4	25.8	32.3	.7	0.4	1.1	1.7	2.4	3.0	3.7	4.3	4.9	5.6	6.2	11.4	0.6
38.8	6.5	13.0	19.4	25.9	32.4	.8	0.5	1.2	1.8	2.4	3.1	3.7	4.4	5.0	5.6	6.3	13.2	0.7
38.9	6.5	13.0	19.5	26.0	32.5	.9	0.6	1.2	1.9	2.5	3.1	3.8	4.4	5.1	5.7	6.4	14.9 / 16.7	0.8 / 0.9
39.0	6.5	13.0	19.5	26.0	32.5	.0	0.0	0.7	1.3	2.0	2.6	3.3	3.9	4.6	5.3	5.9	18.5	1.0
39.1	6.5	13.0	19.5	26.0	32.6	.1	0.1	0.7	1.4	2.0	2.7	3.4	4.0	4.7	5.3	6.0	20.2	1.1
39.2	6.5	13.0	19.6	26.1	32.6	.2	0.1	0.8	1.4	2.1	2.8	3.4	4.1	4.7	5.4	6.1	22.0	1.2
39.3	6.5	13.1	19.6	26.2	32.7	.3	0.2	0.9	1.5	2.2	2.8	3.5	4.1	4.8	5.5	6.1	23.7	1.3
39.4	6.6	13.1	19.7	26.3	32.8	.4	0.3	0.9	1.6	2.2	2.9	3.6	4.2	4.9	5.5	6.2	25.5 / 27.3	1.4 / 1.5
39.5	6.6	13.2	19.8	26.3	32.9	.5	0.3	1.0	1.6	2.3	3.0	3.6	4.3	4.9	5.6	6.3	29.0	1.6
39.6	6.6	13.2	19.8	26.4	33.0	.6	0.4	1.1	1.7	2.4	3.0	3.7	4.3	5.0	5.7	6.3	30.8	1.7
39.7	6.6	13.3	19.9	26.5	33.1	.7	0.5	1.1	1.8	2.4	3.1	3.8	4.4	5.1	5.7	6.4	32.5	1.8
39.8	6.7	13.3	19.9	26.6	33.2	.8	0.5	1.2	1.8	2.5	3.2	3.8	4.5	5.1	5.8	6.5	34.3	1.9
39.9	6.7	13.3	20.0	26.6	33.3	.9	0.6	1.3	1.9	2.6	3.2	3.9	4.5	5.2	5.9	6.5		
40.0	6.6	13.3	20.0	26.6	33.3	.0	0.0	0.7	1.3	2.0	2.7	3.4	4.0	4.7	5.4	6.1		
40.1	6.7	13.3	20.0	26.7	33.4	.1	0.1	0.7	1.4	2.1	2.8	3.4	4.1	4.8	5.5	6.1		
40.2	6.7	13.4	20.1	26.8	33.5	.2	0.1	0.8	1.5	2.2	2.8	3.5	4.2	4.9	5.5	6.2	0.9	
40.3	6.7	13.4	20.1	26.9	33.6	.3	0.2	0.9	1.6	2.2	2.9	3.6	4.3	4.9	5.6	6.3	2.8	0.1
40.4	6.7	13.5	20.2	26.9	33.7	.4	0.3	0.9	1.6	2.3	3.0	3.6	4.3	5.0	5.7	6.3	4.6 / 6.5	0.2 / 0.3
40.5	6.8	13.5	20.3	27.0	33.8	.5	0.3	1.0	1.7	2.4	3.0	3.7	4.4	5.1	5.7	6.4	8.3	0.4
40.6	6.8	13.5	20.3	27.1	33.8	.6	0.4	1.1	1.8	2.4	3.1	3.8	4.5	5.1	5.8	6.5	10.2	0.5
40.7	6.8	13.6	20.4	27.2	33.9	.7	0.5	1.1	1.8	2.5	3.2	3.8	4.5	5.2	5.9	6.5	12.0	0.6
40.8	6.8	13.6	20.4	27.2	34.0	.8	0.5	1.2	1.9	2.6	3.2	3.9	4.6	5.3	5.9	6.6	13.9	0.7
40.9	6.9	13.7	20.5	27.3	34.1	.9	0.6	1.3	2.0	2.6	3.3	4.0	4.7	5.3	6.0	6.7	15.7 / 17.6	0.8 / 0.9
41.0	6.8	13.6	20.5	27.3	34.1	.0	0.0	0.7	1.4	2.1	2.8	3.5	4.1	4.8	5.5	6.2	19.4	1.0
41.1	6.8	13.7	20.5	27.4	34.2	.1	0.1	0.8	1.5	2.1	2.8	3.5	4.2	4.9	5.6	6.3	21.3	1.1
41.2	6.8	13.7	20.6	27.4	34.3	.2	0.1	0.8	1.5	2.2	2.9	3.6	4.3	5.0	5.7	6.4	23.1	1.2
41.3	6.9	13.8	20.6	27.5	34.4	.3	0.2	0.9	1.6	2.3	3.0	3.7	4.4	5.0	5.7	6.4	25.0	1.3
41.4	6.9	13.8	20.7	27.6	34.5	.4	0.3	1.0	1.7	2.4	3.0	3.7	4.4	5.1	5.8	6.5	26.8 / 28.7	1.4 / 1.5
41.5	6.9	13.8	20.8	27.7	34.6	.5	0.3	1.0	1.7	2.4	3.1	3.8	4.5	5.2	5.9	6.6	30.5	1.6
41.6	6.9	13.9	20.8	27.7	34.7	.6	0.4	1.1	1.8	2.5	3.2	3.9	4.6	5.3	5.9	6.6	32.3	1.7
41.7	7.0	13.9	20.9	27.8	34.8	.7	0.5	1.2	1.9	2.6	3.3	3.9	4.6	5.3	6.0	6.7	34.2	1.8
41.8	7.0	14.0	20.9	27.9	34.9	.8	0.6	1.2	1.9	2.6	3.3	4.0	4.7	5.4	6.1	6.8		
41.9	7.0	14.0	21.0	28.0	35.0	.9	0.6	1.3	2.0	2.7	3.4	4.1	4.8	5.5	6.2	6.8		
42.0	7.0	14.0	21.0	28.0	35.0	.0	0.0	0.7	1.4	2.1	2.8	3.5	4.2	5.0	5.7	6.4		
42.1	7.0	14.0	21.0	28.0	35.1	.1	0.1	0.8	1.5	2.2	2.9	3.6	4.3	5.0	5.7	6.4		
42.2	7.0	14.0	21.1	28.1	35.1	.2	0.1	0.8	1.6	2.3	3.0	3.7	4.4	5.1	5.8	6.5		
42.3	7.0	14.1	21.1	28.2	35.2	.3	0.2	0.9	1.6	2.3	3.0	3.8	4.5	5.2	5.9	6.6	1.0	
42.4	7.1	14.1	21.2	28.3	35.3	.4	0.3	1.0	1.7	2.4	3.1	3.8	4.5	5.2	5.9	6.7	3.0 / 4.9	0.1 / 0.2
42.5	7.1	14.2	21.3	28.3	35.4	.5	0.4	1.1	1.8	2.5	3.2	3.9	4.6	5.3	6.0	6.7	6.9	0.3
42.6	7.1	14.2	21.3	28.4	35.5	.6	0.4	1.1	1.8	2.5	3.3	4.0	4.7	5.4	6.1	6.8	8.9	0.4
42.7	7.1	14.3	21.4	28.5	35.6	.7	0.5	1.2	1.9	2.6	3.3	4.0	4.7	5.5	6.2	6.9	10.8	0.5
42.8	7.2	14.3	21.4	28.6	35.7	.8	0.6	1.3	2.0	2.7	3.4	4.1	4.8	5.5	6.2	6.9	12.8	0.6
42.9	7.2	14.3	21.5	28.6	35.8	.9	0.6	1.3	2.1	2.8	3.5	4.2	4.9	5.6	6.3	7.0	14.8 / 16.7	0.7 / 0.8
43.0	7.1	14.3	21.5	28.6	35.8	.0	0.0	0.7	1.4	2.2	2.9	3.6	4.3	5.1	5.8	6.5	18.7	0.9
43.1	7.2	14.3	21.5	28.7	35.9	.1	0.1	0.8	1.5	2.2	3.0	3.7	4.4	5.1	5.9	6.6	20.7	1.0
43.2	7.2	14.4	21.6	28.8	36.0	.2	0.1	0.9	1.6	2.3	3.0	3.8	4.5	5.2	5.9	6.7	22.7	1.1
43.3	7.2	14.4	21.6	28.9	36.1	.3	0.2	0.9	1.7	2.4	3.1	3.8	4.6	5.3	6.0	6.7	24.6	1.2
43.4	7.2	14.5	21.7	28.9	36.2	.4	0.3	1.0	1.7	2.5	3.2	3.9	4.6	5.4	6.1	6.8	26.6 / 28.6	1.3 / 1.4
43.5	7.3	14.5	21.8	29.0	36.3	.5	0.4	1.1	1.8	2.5	3.3	4.0	4.7	5.4	6.2	6.9	30.5	1.5
43.6	7.3	14.5	21.8	29.1	36.3	.6	0.4	1.2	1.9	2.6	3.3	4.1	4.8	5.5	6.2	7.0	32.5	1.6
43.7	7.3	14.6	21.9	29.2	36.4	.7	0.5	1.2	2.0	2.7	3.4	4.1	4.9	5.6	6.3	7.0	34.5	1.7
43.8	7.3	14.6	21.9	29.2	36.5	.8	0.6	1.3	2.0	2.8	3.5	4.2	4.9	5.7	6.4	7.1		
43.9	7.4	14.7	22.0	29.3	36.6	.9	0.7	1.4	2.1	2.8	3.6	4.3	5.0	5.7	6.5	7.2		
	10'	20'	30'	40'	50'		0'	1'	2'	3'	4'	5'	6'	7'	8'	9'		

The Double-Second-Difference correction (Corr.) is always to be added to the tabulated altitude.

INTERPOLATION TABLE

Altitude Difference (d)

Dec. Inc.	Tens 10'	20'	30'	40'	50'	Decimals	Units 0'	1'	2'	3'	4'	5'	6'	7'	8'	9'	Double Second Diff. and Corr.
44.0	7.3	14.6	22.0	29.3	36.6	**.0**	0.0	0.7	1.5	2.2	3.0	3.7	4.4	5.2	5.9	6.7	1.1 0.1 3.2 0.2 5.3 0.3 7.5 0.4 9.6 0.5 11.7 0.6 13.9 0.7 16.0 0.8 18.1 0.9 20.3 1.0 22.4 1.1 24.5 1.2 26.7 1.3 28.8 1.4 30.9 1.5 33.1 1.6 35.2
44.1	7.3	14.7	22.0	29.4	36.7	**.1**	0.1	0.8	1.6	2.3	3.0	3.8	4.5	5.3	6.0	6.7	
44.2	7.3	14.7	22.1	29.4	36.8	**.2**	0.1	0.9	1.6	2.4	3.1	3.9	4.6	5.3	6.1	6.8	
44.3	7.4	14.8	22.1	29.5	36.9	**.3**	0.2	1.0	1.7	2.4	3.2	3.9	4.7	5.4	6.2	6.9	
44.4	7.4	14.8	22.2	29.6	37.0	**.4**	0.3	1.0	1.8	2.5	3.3	4.0	4.7	5.5	6.2	7.0	
44.5	7.4	14.8	22.3	29.7	37.1	**.5**	0.4	1.1	1.9	2.6	3.3	4.1	4.8	5.6	6.3	7.0	
44.6	7.4	14.9	22.3	29.7	37.2	**.6**	0.4	1.2	1.9	2.7	3.4	4.2	4.9	5.6	6.4	7.1	
44.7	7.5	14.9	22.4	29.8	37.3	**.7**	0.5	1.3	2.0	2.7	3.5	4.2	5.0	5.7	6.5	7.2	
44.8	7.5	15.0	22.4	29.9	37.4	**.8**	0.6	1.3	2.1	2.8	3.6	4.3	5.0	5.8	6.5	7.3	
44.9	7.5	15.0	22.5	30.0	37.5	**.9**	0.7	1.4	2.2	2.9	3.6	4.4	5.1	5.9	6.6	7.3	
45.0	7.5	15.0	22.5	30.0	37.5	**.0**	0.0	0.8	1.5	2.3	3.0	3.8	4.5	5.3	6.1	6.8	
45.1	7.5	15.0	22.5	30.0	37.6	**.1**	0.1	0.8	1.6	2.4	3.1	3.9	4.6	5.4	6.1	6.9	
45.2	7.5	15.0	22.6	30.1	37.6	**.2**	0.2	0.9	1.7	2.4	3.2	3.9	4.7	5.5	6.2	7.0	
45.3	7.5	15.1	22.6	30.2	37.7	**.3**	0.2	1.0	1.7	2.5	3.3	4.0	4.8	5.5	6.3	7.1	
45.4	7.6	15.1	22.7	30.3	37.8	**.4**	0.3	1.1	1.8	2.6	3.3	4.1	4.9	5.6	6.4	7.1	
45.5	7.6	15.2	22.8	30.3	37.9	**.5**	0.4	1.1	1.9	2.7	3.4	4.2	4.9	5.7	6.4	7.2	
45.6	7.6	15.2	22.8	30.4	38.0	**.6**	0.5	1.2	2.0	2.7	3.5	4.2	5.0	5.8	6.5	7.3	
45.7	7.6	15.3	22.9	30.5	38.1	**.7**	0.5	1.3	2.0	2.8	3.6	4.3	5.1	5.8	6.6	7.4	
45.8	7.7	15.3	22.9	30.6	38.2	**.8**	0.6	1.4	2.1	2.9	3.6	4.4	5.2	5.9	6.7	7.4	
45.9	7.7	15.3	23.0	30.6	38.3	**.9**	0.7	1.4	2.2	3.0	3.7	4.5	5.2	6.0	6.7	7.5	
46.0	7.6	15.3	23.0	30.6	38.3	**.0**	0.0	0.8	1.5	2.3	3.1	3.9	4.6	5.4	6.2	7.0	1.2 0.1 3.5 0.2 5.8 0.3 8.1 0.4 10.5 0.5 12.8 0.6 15.1 0.7 17.4 0.8 19.8 0.9 22.1 1.0 24.4 1.1 26.7 1.2 29.1 1.3 31.4 1.4 33.7 1.5 36.0
46.1	7.7	15.3	23.0	30.7	38.4	**.1**	0.1	0.9	1.6	2.4	3.2	4.0	4.7	5.5	6.3	7.1	
46.2	7.7	15.4	23.1	30.8	38.5	**.2**	0.2	0.9	1.7	2.5	3.3	4.0	4.8	5.6	6.4	7.1	
46.3	7.7	15.4	23.1	30.9	38.6	**.3**	0.2	1.0	1.8	2.6	3.3	4.1	4.9	5.7	6.4	7.2	
46.4	7.7	15.5	23.2	30.9	38.7	**.4**	0.3	1.1	1.9	2.6	3.4	4.2	5.0	5.7	6.5	7.3	
46.5	7.8	15.5	23.3	31.0	38.8	**.5**	0.4	1.2	1.9	2.7	3.5	4.3	5.0	5.8	6.6	7.4	
46.6	7.8	15.5	23.3	31.1	38.8	**.6**	0.5	1.2	2.0	2.8	3.6	4.3	5.1	5.9	6.7	7.4	
46.7	7.8	15.6	23.4	31.2	38.9	**.7**	0.5	1.3	2.1	2.9	3.6	4.4	5.2	6.0	6.7	7.5	
46.8	7.8	15.6	23.4	31.2	39.0	**.8**	0.6	1.4	2.2	2.9	3.7	4.5	5.3	6.0	6.8	7.6	
46.9	7.9	15.7	23.5	31.3	39.1	**.9**	0.7	1.5	2.2	3.0	3.8	4.6	5.3	6.1	6.9	7.7	
47.0	7.8	15.6	23.5	31.3	39.1	**.0**	0.0	0.8	1.6	2.4	3.2	4.0	4.7	5.5	6.3	7.1	
47.1	7.8	15.7	23.5	31.4	39.2	**.1**	0.1	0.9	1.7	2.5	3.2	4.0	4.8	5.6	6.4	7.2	
47.2	7.8	15.7	23.6	31.4	39.3	**.2**	0.2	0.9	1.7	2.5	3.3	4.1	4.9	5.7	6.5	7.3	
47.3	7.9	15.8	23.6	31.5	39.4	**.3**	0.2	1.0	1.8	2.6	3.4	4.2	5.0	5.8	6.6	7.4	
47.4	7.9	15.8	23.7	31.6	39.5	**.4**	0.3	1.1	1.9	2.7	3.5	4.3	5.1	5.9	6.6	7.4	
47.5	7.9	15.8	23.8	31.7	39.6	**.5**	0.4	1.2	2.0	2.8	3.6	4.4	5.1	5.9	6.7	7.5	1.3 0.1 3.8 0.2 6.3 0.3 8.9 0.4 11.4 0.5 14.0 0.6 16.5 0.7 19.0 0.8 21.6 0.9 24.1 1.0 26.7 1.1 29.2 1.2 31.7 1.3 34.3
47.6	7.9	15.9	23.8	31.7	39.7	**.6**	0.5	1.3	2.1	2.8	3.6	4.4	5.2	6.0	6.8	7.6	
47.7	8.0	15.9	23.9	31.8	39.8	**.7**	0.6	1.3	2.1	2.9	3.7	4.5	5.3	6.1	6.9	7.7	
47.8	8.0	16.0	23.9	31.9	39.9	**.8**	0.6	1.4	2.2	3.0	3.8	4.6	5.4	6.2	7.0	7.8	
47.9	8.0	16.0	24.0	32.0	40.0	**.9**	0.7	1.5	2.3	3.1	3.9	4.7	5.5	6.3	7.0	7.8	
48.0	8.0	16.0	24.0	32.0	40.0	**.0**	0.0	0.8	1.6	2.4	3.2	4.0	4.8	5.7	6.5	7.3	
48.1	8.0	16.0	24.0	32.0	40.1	**.1**	0.1	0.9	1.7	2.5	3.3	4.1	4.9	5.7	6.5	7.4	
48.2	8.0	16.0	24.1	32.1	40.1	**.2**	0.2	1.0	1.8	2.6	3.4	4.2	5.0	5.8	6.6	7.4	
48.3	8.0	16.1	24.1	32.2	40.2	**.3**	0.2	1.1	1.9	2.7	3.5	4.3	5.1	5.9	6.7	7.5	
48.4	8.1	16.1	24.2	32.3	40.3	**.4**	0.3	1.1	1.9	2.7	3.6	4.4	5.2	6.0	6.8	7.6	
48.5	8.1	16.2	24.3	32.3	40.4	**.5**	0.4	1.2	2.0	2.8	3.6	4.4	5.3	6.1	6.9	7.7	
48.6	8.1	16.2	24.3	32.4	40.5	**.6**	0.5	1.3	2.1	2.9	3.7	4.5	5.3	6.1	7.0	7.8	
48.7	8.1	16.3	24.4	32.5	40.6	**.7**	0.6	1.4	2.2	3.0	3.8	4.6	5.4	6.2	7.0	7.8	
48.8	8.2	16.3	24.4	32.6	40.7	**.8**	0.6	1.5	2.3	3.1	3.9	4.7	5.5	6.3	7.1	7.9	
48.9	8.2	16.3	24.5	32.6	40.8	**.9**	0.7	1.5	2.3	3.2	4.0	4.8	5.6	6.4	7.2	8.0	
49.0	8.1	16.3	24.5	32.6	40.8	**.0**	0.0	0.8	1.6	2.5	3.3	4.1	4.9	5.8	6.6	7.4	1.4 0.1 4.2 0.2 7.1 0.3 9.9 0.4 12.7 0.5 15.5 0.6 18.4 0.7 21.2 0.8 24.0 0.9 26.8 1.0 29.7 1.1 32.5 1.2 35.3
49.1	8.2	16.3	24.5	32.7	40.9	**.1**	0.1	0.9	1.7	2.6	3.4	4.2	5.0	5.9	6.7	7.5	
49.2	8.2	16.4	24.6	32.8	41.0	**.2**	0.2	1.0	1.8	2.6	3.5	4.3	5.1	5.9	6.8	7.6	
49.3	8.2	16.4	24.6	32.9	41.1	**.3**	0.2	1.1	1.9	2.7	3.5	4.4	5.2	6.0	6.8	7.7	
49.4	8.2	16.5	24.7	32.9	41.2	**.4**	0.3	1.2	2.0	2.8	3.6	4.5	5.3	6.1	6.9	7.8	
49.5	8.3	16.5	24.8	33.0	41.3	**.5**	0.4	1.2	2.1	2.9	3.7	4.5	5.4	6.2	7.0	7.8	
49.6	8.3	16.5	24.8	33.1	41.3	**.6**	0.5	1.3	2.1	3.0	3.8	4.6	5.4	6.3	7.1	7.9	
49.7	8.3	16.6	24.9	33.2	41.4	**.7**	0.6	1.4	2.2	3.1	3.9	4.7	5.5	6.4	7.2	8.0	
49.8	8.3	16.6	24.9	33.2	41.5	**.8**	0.7	1.5	2.3	3.1	4.0	4.8	5.6	6.4	7.3	8.1	
49.9	8.4	16.7	25.0	33.3	41.6	**.9**	0.7	1.6	2.4	3.2	4.0	4.9	5.7	6.5	7.3	8.2	
50.0	8.3	16.6	25.0	33.3	41.6	**.0**	0.0	0.8	1.7	2.5	3.4	4.2	5.0	5.9	6.7	7.6	
50.1	8.3	16.7	25.0	33.4	41.7	**.1**	0.1	0.9	1.8	2.6	3.5	4.3	5.1	6.0	6.8	7.7	
50.2	8.3	16.7	25.1	33.4	41.8	**.2**	0.2	1.0	1.9	2.7	3.5	4.4	5.2	6.1	6.9	7.7	
50.3	8.4	16.8	25.1	33.5	41.9	**.3**	0.3	1.1	1.9	2.8	3.6	4.5	5.3	6.1	7.0	7.8	
50.4	8.4	16.8	25.2	33.6	42.0	**.4**	0.3	1.2	2.0	2.9	3.7	4.5	5.4	6.2	7.1	7.9	
50.5	8.4	16.8	25.3	33.7	42.1	**.5**	0.4	1.3	2.1	2.9	3.8	4.6	5.5	6.3	7.2	8.0	1.6 0.1 4.8 0.2 8.0 0.3 11.2 0.4 14.5 0.5 17.7 0.6 20.9 0.7 24.1 0.8 27.3 0.9 30.5 1.0 33.7 1.1 36.9
50.6	8.4	16.9	25.3	33.7	42.2	**.6**	0.5	1.3	2.2	3.0	3.9	4.7	5.6	6.4	7.2	8.1	
50.7	8.5	16.9	25.4	33.8	42.3	**.7**	0.6	1.4	2.3	3.1	4.0	4.8	5.6	6.5	7.3	8.2	
50.8	8.5	17.0	25.4	33.9	42.4	**.8**	0.7	1.5	2.4	3.2	4.0	4.9	5.7	6.6	7.4	8.2	
50.9	8.5	17.0	25.5	34.0	42.5	**.9**	0.8	1.6	2.4	3.3	4.1	5.0	5.8	6.6	7.5	8.3	
51.0	8.5	17.0	25.5	34.0	42.5	**.0**	0.0	0.9	1.7	2.6	3.4	4.3	5.1	6.0	6.9	7.7	
51.1	8.5	17.0	25.5	34.0	42.6	**.1**	0.1	0.9	1.8	2.7	3.5	4.4	5.2	6.1	7.0	7.8	
51.2	8.5	17.0	25.6	34.1	42.6	**.2**	0.2	1.0	1.9	2.7	3.6	4.5	5.3	6.2	7.0	7.9	
51.3	8.5	17.1	25.6	34.2	42.7	**.3**	0.3	1.1	2.0	2.8	3.7	4.5	5.4	6.3	7.1	8.0	
51.4	8.6	17.1	25.7	34.3	42.8	**.4**	0.3	1.2	2.1	2.9	3.8	4.6	5.5	6.4	7.2	8.1	
51.5	8.6	17.2	25.8	34.3	42.9	**.5**	0.4	1.3	2.1	3.0	3.9	4.7	5.6	6.4	7.3	8.2	
51.6	8.6	17.2	25.8	34.4	43.0	**.6**	0.5	1.4	2.2	3.1	3.9	4.8	5.7	6.5	7.4	8.2	
51.7	8.6	17.3	25.9	34.5	43.1	**.7**	0.6	1.5	2.3	3.2	4.0	4.9	5.8	6.6	7.5	8.3	
51.8	8.7	17.3	25.9	34.6	43.2	**.8**	0.7	1.5	2.4	3.3	4.1	5.0	5.8	6.7	7.6	8.4	
51.9	8.7	17.3	26.0	34.6	43.3	**.9**	0.8	1.6	2.5	3.3	4.2	5.1	5.9	6.8	7.7	8.5	
	10'	20'	30'	40'	50'		0'	1'	2'	3'	4'	5'	6'	7'	8'	9'	

Dec. Inc.	Tens 10'	20'	30'	40'	50'	Decimals	Units 0'	1'	2'	3'	4'	5'	6'	7'	8'	9'	Double Second Diff. and Corr.
52.0	8.6	17.3	26.0	34.6	43.3	**.0**	0.0	0.9	1.7	2.6	3.5	4.4	5.2	6.1	7.0	7.9	1.8 0.1 5.5 0.2 9.1 0.3 12.8 0.4 16.5 0.5 20.1 0.6 23.8 0.7 27.4 0.8 31.1 0.9 34.7
52.1	8.7	17.3	26.0	34.7	43.4	**.1**	0.1	1.0	1.8	2.7	3.6	4.5	5.3	6.2	7.1	8.0	
52.2	8.7	17.4	26.1	34.8	43.5	**.2**	0.2	1.0	1.9	2.8	3.7	4.5	5.4	6.3	7.2	8.0	
52.3	8.7	17.4	26.1	34.9	43.6	**.3**	0.3	1.1	2.0	2.9	3.8	4.6	5.5	6.4	7.3	8.1	
52.4	8.7	17.5	26.2	34.9	43.7	**.4**	0.3	1.2	2.1	3.0	3.8	4.7	5.6	6.5	7.3	8.2	
52.5	8.8	17.5	26.3	35.0	43.8	**.5**	0.4	1.3	2.2	3.1	3.9	4.8	5.7	6.6	7.4	8.3	
52.6	8.8	17.5	26.3	35.1	43.8	**.6**	0.5	1.4	2.3	3.1	4.0	4.9	5.8	6.6	7.5	8.4	
52.7	8.8	17.6	26.4	35.2	43.9	**.7**	0.6	1.5	2.4	3.2	4.1	5.0	5.9	6.7	7.6	8.5	
52.8	8.8	17.6	26.4	35.2	44.0	**.8**	0.7	1.6	2.4	3.3	4.2	5.1	5.9	6.8	7.7	8.6	
52.9	8.9	17.7	26.5	35.3	44.1	**.9**	0.8	1.7	2.5	3.4	4.3	5.2	6.0	6.9	7.8	8.7	
53.0	8.8	17.6	26.5	35.3	44.1	**.0**	0.0	0.9	1.8	2.7	3.6	4.5	5.3	6.2	7.1	8.0	2.1 0.1 6.2 0.2 10.4 0.3 14.5 0.4 18.6 0.5 22.8 0.6 26.9 0.7 31.1 0.8 35.2
53.1	8.8	17.7	26.5	35.4	44.2	**.1**	0.1	1.0	1.9	2.8	3.7	4.5	5.4	6.3	7.2	8.1	
53.2	8.8	17.7	26.6	35.4	44.3	**.2**	0.2	1.1	2.0	2.9	3.7	4.6	5.5	6.4	7.3	8.2	
53.3	8.9	17.8	26.6	35.5	44.4	**.3**	0.3	1.2	2.1	2.9	3.8	4.7	5.6	6.5	7.4	8.3	
53.4	8.9	17.8	26.7	35.6	44.5	**.4**	0.4	1.2	2.1	3.0	3.9	4.8	5.7	6.6	7.5	8.4	
53.5	8.9	17.8	26.8	35.7	44.6	**.5**	0.4	1.3	2.2	3.1	4.0	4.9	5.8	6.7	7.6	8.5	
53.6	8.9	17.9	26.8	35.7	44.7	**.6**	0.5	1.4	2.3	3.2	4.1	5.0	5.9	6.8	7.7	8.6	
53.7	9.0	17.9	26.9	35.8	44.8	**.7**	0.6	1.5	2.4	3.3	4.2	5.1	6.0	6.9	7.8	8.6	
53.8	9.0	18.0	26.9	35.9	44.9	**.8**	0.7	1.6	2.5	3.4	4.3	5.2	6.1	7.0	7.8	8.7	
53.9	9.0	18.0	27.0	36.0	45.0	**.9**	0.8	1.7	2.6	3.5	4.4	5.3	6.2	7.0	7.9	8.8	
54.0	9.0	18.0	27.0	36.0	45.0	**.0**	0.0	0.9	1.8	2.7	3.6	4.5	5.4	6.4	7.3	8.2	2.4 0.1 7.2 0.2 12.0 0.3 16.8 0.4 21.6 0.5 26.4 0.6 31.2 0.7 36.0
54.1	9.0	18.0	27.0	36.0	45.1	**.1**	0.1	1.0	1.9	2.8	3.7	4.6	5.5	6.4	7.4	8.3	
54.2	9.0	18.0	27.1	36.1	45.1	**.2**	0.2	1.1	2.0	2.9	3.8	4.7	5.6	6.5	7.4	8.4	
54.3	9.0	18.1	27.1	36.2	45.2	**.3**	0.3	1.2	2.1	3.0	3.9	4.8	5.7	6.6	7.5	8.4	
54.4	9.1	18.1	27.2	36.3	45.3	**.4**	0.4	1.3	2.2	3.1	4.0	4.9	5.8	6.7	7.6	8.5	
54.5	9.1	18.2	27.3	36.3	45.4	**.5**	0.5	1.4	2.3	3.2	4.1	5.0	5.9	6.8	7.7	8.6	
54.6	9.1	18.2	27.3	36.4	45.5	**.6**	0.5	1.5	2.4	3.3	4.2	5.1	6.0	6.9	7.8	8.7	
54.7	9.1	18.3	27.4	36.5	45.6	**.7**	0.6	1.5	2.5	3.4	4.3	5.2	6.1	7.0	7.9	8.8	
54.8	9.2	18.3	27.4	36.6	45.7	**.8**	0.7	1.6	2.5	3.5	4.4	5.3	6.2	7.1	8.0	8.9	
54.9	9.2	18.3	27.5	36.6	45.8	**.9**	0.8	1.7	2.6	3.5	4.5	5.4	6.3	7.2	8.1	9.0	
55.0	9.1	18.3	27.5	36.6	45.8	**.0**	0.0	0.9	1.8	2.8	3.7	4.6	5.5	6.5	7.4	8.3	2.9 0.1 8.6 0.2 14.4 0.3 20.2 0.4 25.9 0.5 31.7 0.6 37.5
55.1	9.2	18.3	27.5	36.7	45.9	**.1**	0.1	1.0	1.9	2.9	3.8	4.7	5.6	6.6	7.5	8.4	
55.2	9.2	18.4	27.6	36.8	46.0	**.2**	0.2	1.1	2.0	3.0	3.9	4.8	5.7	6.7	7.6	8.5	
55.3	9.2	18.4	27.6	36.9	46.1	**.3**	0.3	1.2	2.1	3.1	4.0	4.9	5.8	6.8	7.7	8.6	
55.4	9.2	18.5	27.7	36.9	46.2	**.4**	0.4	1.3	2.2	3.1	4.1	5.0	5.9	6.8	7.8	8.7	
55.5	9.3	18.5	27.8	37.0	46.3	**.5**	0.5	1.4	2.3	3.2	4.2	5.1	6.0	6.9	7.9	8.8	
55.6	9.3	18.5	27.8	37.1	46.3	**.6**	0.6	1.5	2.4	3.3	4.3	5.2	6.1	7.0	8.0	8.9	
55.7	9.3	18.6	27.9	37.2	46.4	**.7**	0.6	1.6	2.5	3.4	4.3	5.3	6.2	7.1	8.0	9.0	
55.8	9.3	18.6	27.9	37.2	46.5	**.8**	0.7	1.7	2.6	3.5	4.4	5.4	6.3	7.2	8.1	9.1	
55.9	9.4	18.7	28.0	37.3	46.6	**.9**	0.8	1.8	2.7	3.6	4.5	5.5	6.4	7.3	8.2	9.2	
56.0	9.3	18.6	28.0	37.3	46.6	**.0**	0.0	0.9	1.9	2.8	3.8	4.7	5.6	6.6	7.5	8.5	3.6 0.1 10.9 0.2 18.2 0.3 25.5 0.4 32.8 0.5 40.1
56.1	9.3	18.7	28.0	37.4	46.7	**.1**	0.1	1.0	2.0	2.9	3.9	4.8	5.7	6.7	7.6	8.6	
56.2	9.3	18.7	28.1	37.4	46.8	**.2**	0.2	1.1	2.1	3.0	4.0	4.9	5.8	6.8	7.7	8.7	
56.3	9.4	18.8	28.1	37.5	46.9	**.3**	0.3	1.2	2.2	3.1	4.0	5.0	5.9	6.9	7.8	8.8	
56.4	9.4	18.8	28.2	37.6	47.0	**.4**	0.4	1.3	2.3	3.2	4.1	5.1	6.0	7.0	7.9	8.9	
56.5	9.4	18.8	28.3	37.7	47.1	**.5**	0.5	1.4	2.4	3.3	4.2	5.2	6.1	7.1	8.0	8.9	
56.6	9.4	18.9	28.3	37.7	47.2	**.6**	0.6	1.5	2.4	3.4	4.3	5.3	6.2	7.2	8.1	9.0	
56.7	9.5	18.9	28.4	37.8	47.3	**.7**	0.7	1.6	2.5	3.5	4.4	5.4	6.3	7.3	8.2	9.1	
56.8	9.5	19.0	28.4	37.9	47.4	**.8**	0.8	1.7	2.6	3.6	4.5	5.5	6.4	7.4	8.3	9.2	
56.9	9.5	19.0	28.5	38.0	47.5	**.9**	0.8	1.8	2.7	3.7	4.6	5.6	6.5	7.4	8.4	9.3	
57.0	9.5	19.0	28.5	38.0	47.5	**.0**	0.0	1.0	1.9	2.9	3.8	4.8	5.7	6.7	7.7	8.6	5.0 0.1 15.0 0.2 25.0 0.3 35.1
57.1	9.5	19.0	28.5	38.0	47.6	**.1**	0.1	1.1	2.0	3.0	3.9	4.9	5.8	6.8	7.8	8.7	
57.2	9.5	19.0	28.6	38.1	47.6	**.2**	0.2	1.1	2.1	3.1	4.0	5.0	5.9	6.9	7.9	8.8	
57.3	9.5	19.1	28.6	38.2	47.7	**.3**	0.3	1.2	2.2	3.2	4.1	5.1	6.0	7.0	8.0	8.9	
57.4	9.6	19.1	28.7	38.3	47.8	**.4**	0.4	1.3	2.3	3.3	4.2	5.2	6.1	7.1	8.0	9.0	
57.5	9.6	19.2	28.8	38.3	47.9	**.5**	0.5	1.4	2.4	3.4	4.3	5.3	6.2	7.2	8.1	9.1	
57.6	9.6	19.2	28.8	38.4	48.0	**.6**	0.6	1.5	2.5	3.4	4.4	5.4	6.3	7.3	8.2	9.2	
57.7	9.6	19.3	28.9	38.5	48.1	**.7**	0.7	1.6	2.6	3.5	4.5	5.5	6.4	7.4	8.3	9.3	
57.8	9.7	19.3	28.9	38.6	48.2	**.8**	0.8	1.7	2.7	3.6	4.6	5.6	6.5	7.5	8.4	9.4	
57.9	9.7	19.3	29.0	38.6	48.3	**.9**	0.9	1.8	2.8	3.7	4.7	5.7	6.6	7.6	8.5	9.5	
58.0	9.6	19.3	29.0	38.6	48.3	**.0**	0.0	1.0	1.9	2.9	3.9	4.9	5.8	6.8	7.8	8.8	8.2 0.1 24.6 0.2 41.0
58.1	9.7	19.3	29.0	38.7	48.4	**.1**	0.1	1.1	2.0	3.0	4.0	5.0	5.9	6.9	7.9	8.9	
58.2	9.7	19.4	29.1	38.8	48.5	**.2**	0.2	1.2	2.1	3.1	4.1	5.1	6.0	7.0	8.0	9.0	
58.3	9.7	19.4	29.1	38.9	48.6	**.3**	0.3	1.3	2.2	3.2	4.2	5.2	6.1	7.1	8.1	9.1	
58.4	9.7	19.5	29.2	38.9	48.7	**.4**	0.4	1.4	2.3	3.3	4.3	5.3	6.2	7.2	8.2	9.2	
58.5	9.8	19.5	29.3	39.0	48.8	**.5**	0.5	1.5	2.4	3.4	4.4	5.4	6.3	7.3	8.3	9.3	
58.6	9.8	19.5	29.3	39.1	48.8	**.6**	0.6	1.6	2.5	3.5	4.5	5.5	6.4	7.4	8.4	9.4	
58.7	9.8	19.6	29.4	39.2	48.9	**.7**	0.7	1.7	2.6	3.6	4.6	5.6	6.5	7.5	8.5	9.5	
58.8	9.8	19.6	29.4	39.2	49.0	**.8**	0.8	1.8	2.7	3.7	4.7	5.7	6.6	7.6	8.6	9.6	
58.9	9.9	19.7	29.5	39.3	49.1	**.9**	0.9	1.9	2.8	3.8	4.8	5.8	6.7	7.7	8.7	9.7	
59.0	9.8	19.6	29.5	39.3	49.1	**.0**	0.0	1.0	2.0	3.0	4.0	5.0	5.9	6.9	7.9	8.9	16.2 0.1 48.6
59.1	9.8	19.7	29.5	39.4	49.2	**.1**	0.1	1.1	2.1	3.1	4.1	5.1	6.0	7.0	8.0	9.0	
59.2	9.8	19.7	29.6	39.4	49.3	**.2**	0.2	1.2	2.2	3.2	4.2	5.2	6.1	7.1	8.1	9.1	
59.3	9.9	19.8	29.6	39.5	49.4	**.3**	0.3	1.3	2.3	3.3	4.3	5.3	6.2	7.2	8.2	9.2	
59.4	9.9	19.8	29.7	39.6	49.5	**.4**	0.4	1.4	2.4	3.4	4.4	5.4	6.3	7.3	8.3	9.3	
59.5	9.9	19.8	29.8	39.7	49.6	**.5**	0.5	1.5	2.5	3.5	4.5	5.5	6.4	7.4	8.4	9.4	0.0 0.0 48.2
59.6	9.9	19.9	29.8	39.7	49.6	**.6**	0.6	1.6	2.6	3.6	4.6	5.6	6.5	7.5	8.5	9.5	
59.7	10.0	19.9	29.9	39.8	49.8	**.7**	0.7	1.7	2.7	3.7	4.7	5.7	6.6	7.6	8.6	9.6	
59.8	10.0	20.0	29.9	39.9	49.9	**.8**	0.8	1.8	2.8	3.8	4.8	5.8	6.7	7.7	8.7	9.7	
59.9	10.0	20.0	30.0	40.0	50.0	**.9**	0.9	1.9	2.9	3.9	4.9	5.9	6.8	7.8	8.8	9.8	
	10'	20'	30'	40'	50'		0'	1'	2'	3'	4'	5'	6'	7'	8'	9'	

The Double-Second-Difference correction (Corr.) is always to be added to the tabulated altitude.

14°, 346° L.H.A. LATITUDE SAME NAME AS DECLINATION

N. Lat. { L.H.A. greater than 180°......Zn=Z
L.H.A. less than 180°............Zn=360°−Z

Dec.	30° Hc	d	Z	31° Hc	d	Z	32° Hc	d	Z	33° Hc	d	Z	34° Hc	d	Z	35° Hc	d	Z	36° Hc	d	Z	37° Hc	d	Z	Dec.
°	° ′	′	°	° ′	′	°	° ′	′	°	° ′	′	°	° ′	′	°	° ′	′	°	° ′	′	°	° ′	′	°	°
0	57 10.3	+55.2	153.5	56 16.5	+55.5	154.2	55 22.3	+55.9	154.8	54 27.9	+56.1	155.4	53 33.2	+56.4	156.0	52 38.3	+56.6	156.5	51 43.2	+56.8	157.0	50 47.8	+57.1	157.5	0
1	58 05.5	55.0	152.8	57 12.0	55.3	153.5	56 18.2	55.6	154.2	55 24.0	56.0	154.8	54 29.6	56.2	155.4	53 34.9	56.5	156.0	52 40.0	56.7	156.5	51 44.9	56.9	157.0	1
2	59 00.5	54.6	152.0	58 07.3	55.1	152.8	57 13.8	55.4	153.5	56 20.0	55.7	154.1	55 25.8	56.1	154.8	54 31.4	56.3	155.4	53 36.7	56.6	155.9	52 41.8	56.8	156.5	2
3	59 55.1	54.4	151.2	59 02.4	54.7	152.0	58 09.2	55.1	152.8	57 15.7	55.5	153.5	56 21.9	55.8	154.1	55 27.7	56.1	154.8	54 33.3	56.4	155.4	53 38.6	56.7	155.9	3
4	60 49.5	54.0	150.3	59 57.1	54.5	151.2	59 04.3	54.9	152.0	58 11.2	55.2	152.8	57 17.7	55.6	153.5	56 23.8	56.0	154.1	55 29.7	56.2	154.8	54 35.3	56.5	155.4	4
5	61 43.5	+53.6	149.4	60 51.6	+54.1	150.3	59 59.2	+54.6	151.2	59 06.4	+55.0	152.0	58 13.3	+55.3	152.8	57 19.8	+55.6	153.5	56 25.9	+56.0	154.2	55 31.8	+56.3	154.8	5
6	62 37.1	53.2	148.5	61 45.7	53.7	149.4	60 53.8	54.2	150.4	60 01.4	54.7	151.2	59 08.6	55.1	152.0	58 15.4	55.5	152.8	57 21.9	55.8	153.5	56 28.1	56.1	154.2	6
7	63 30.3	52.7	147.4	62 39.4	53.4	148.5	61 48.0	53.9	149.5	60 56.1	54.3	150.4	60 03.7	54.8	151.2	59 10.9	55.2	152.1	58 17.7	55.6	152.8	57 24.2	55.9	153.5	7
8	64 23.0	52.2	146.4	63 32.8	52.8	147.5	62 41.9	53.4	148.5	61 50.4	54.0	149.5	60 58.5	54.5	150.4	60 06.1	54.9	151.3	59 13.3	55.3	152.1	58 20.1	55.6	152.8	8
9	65 15.2	51.7	145.2	64 25.6	52.4	146.4	63 35.3	53.0	147.5	62 44.4	53.6	148.6	61 53.0	54.1	149.5	61 01.0	54.6	150.5	60 08.6	55.0	151.3	59 15.7	55.5	152.1	9
10	66 06.9	+51.0	144.0	65 18.0	+51.8	145.2	64 28.3	+52.5	146.4	63 38.0	+53.2	147.6	62 47.1	+53.7	148.6	61 55.6	+54.2	149.6	61 03.6	+54.7	150.5	60 11.2	+55.1	151.4	10
11	66 57.9	50.3	142.6	66 09.8	51.2	144.0	65 20.8	52.0	145.3	64 31.2	52.6	146.5	63 40.8	53.3	147.6	62 49.8	53.9	148.7	61 58.3	54.4	149.6	61 06.3	54.8	150.6	11
12	67 48.2	49.5	141.2	67 01.0	50.4	142.7	66 12.8	51.3	144.1	65 23.8	52.1	145.4	64 34.1	52.8	146.6	63 43.7	53.4	147.7	62 52.7	54.0	148.7	62 01.1	54.5	149.7	12
13	68 37.7	48.7	139.7	67 51.4	49.7	141.3	67 04.1	50.7	142.8	66 15.9	51.5	144.2	65 26.9	52.3	145.4	64 37.1	53.0	146.6	63 46.7	53.6	147.8	62 55.6	54.2	148.8	13
14	69 26.4	47.6	138.1	68 41.1	48.9	139.8	67 54.8	49.9	141.4	67 07.4	50.9	142.9	66 19.2	51.6	144.2	65 30.1	52.4	145.5	64 40.3	53.1	146.7	63 49.8	53.7	147.8	14
15	70 14.0	+46.5	136.3	69 30.0	+47.8	138.1	68 44.7	+49.0	139.9	67 58.3	+50.0	141.5	67 10.8	+51.0	142.9	66 22.5	+51.9	144.3	65 33.4	+52.6	145.6	64 43.5	+53.3	146.8	15
16	71 00.5	45.3	134.4	70 17.8	46.7	136.4	69 33.7	48.0	138.2	68 48.3	49.2	140.0	68 01.8	50.3	141.6	67 14.4	51.1	143.1	66 26.0	52.0	144.4	65 36.8	52.7	145.7	16
17	71 45.8	43.8	132.3	71 04.5	45.5	134.5	70 21.7	47.0	136.5	69 37.5	48.3	138.4	68 52.1	49.4	140.1	68 05.5	50.5	141.7	67 18.0	51.4	143.2	66 29.5	52.2	144.5	17
18	72 29.6	42.2	130.1	71 50.0	44.1	132.4	71 08.7	45.7	134.6	70 25.8	47.2	136.6	69 41.5	48.5	138.5	68 56.0	49.6	140.2	68 09.4	50.6	141.8	67 21.7	51.6	143.3	18
19	73 11.8	40.4	127.7	72 34.1	42.4	130.2	71 54.4	44.3	132.6	71 13.0	45.9	134.7	70 30.0	47.4	136.7	69 45.6	48.7	138.6	69 00.0	49.9	140.3	68 13.3	50.9	141.9	19
20	73 52.2	+38.3*	125.1	73 16.5	+40.7	127.8	72 38.7	+42.7	130.3	71 58.9	+44.6	132.7	71 17.4	+46.2	134.9	70 34.3	+47.7	136.9	69 49.9	+48.9	138.8	69 04.2	+50.0	140.5	20
21	74 30.5	36.0*	122.3	73 57.2	38.6*	125.2	73 21.4	41.0	127.9	72 43.5	43.0	130.5	72 03.6	44.8	132.8	71 22.0	46.4	135.0	70 38.8	47.9	137.0	69 54.2	49.1	138.9	21
22	75 06.5	33.4*	119.2	74 35.8	36.3*	122.4	74 02.4	38.9*	125.3	73 26.5	41.2	128.1	72 48.4	43.3	130.6	72 08.4	45.1	133.0	71 26.7	46.6	135.2	70 43.3	48.2	137.2	22
23	75 39.9	30.5*	115.9	75 12.1	33.7*	119.3	74 41.3	36.5*	122.5	74 07.7	39.2*	125.5	73 31.7	41.5	128.2	72 53.5	43.5	130.8	72 13.3	45.4	133.2	71 31.5	46.9	135.4	23
24	76 10.4	27.1*	112.4	75 45.8	30.7*	116.0	75 17.8	34.0*	119.5	74 46.9	36.8*	122.7	74 13.2	39.4*	125.6	73 37.0	41.8	128.4	72 58.7	43.8	131.0	72 18.4	45.6	133.3	24
25	76 37.5	+23.6*	108.6	76 16.5	+27.5*	112.5	75 51.8	+31.0*	116.1	75 23.7	+34.3*	119.6	74 52.6	+37.2*	122.8	74 18.8	+39.8*	125.8	73 42.5	+42.1	128.6	73 04.0	+44.1	131.2	25
26	77 01.1	19.6*	104.5	76 44.0	23.8*	108.7	76 22.8	27.8*	112.6	75 58.0	31.3*	116.3	75 29.8	34.6*	119.7	74 58.6	37.5*	123.0	74 24.6	40.1*	126.0	73 48.1	42.4	128.8	26
27	77 20.7	15.4*	100.3	77 07.8	19.9*	104.6	76 50.6	24.1*	108.7	76 29.3	28.1*	112.7	76 04.4	31.6*	116.4	75 36.1	34.9*	119.9	75 04.7	37.8*	123.2	74 30.5	40.4*	126.2	27
28	77 36.1	10.8*	95.8	77 27.7	15.5*	100.3	77 14.7	20.1*	104.7	76 57.4	24.4*	108.8	76 36.0	28.4*	112.8	76 11.0	31.9*	116.6	75 42.5	35.2*	120.1	75 10.9	38.1*	123.4	28
29	77 46.9	6.1*	91.2	77 43.2	11.0*	95.8	77 34.8	15.8*	100.3	77 21.8	20.4*	104.7	77 04.4	24.7*	108.9	76 42.9	28.7*	113.0	76 17.7	32.3*	116.7	75 49.0	35.6*	120.3	29
30	77 53.0	+1.2*	86.5	77 54.2	+6.3*	91.1	77 50.6	+11.2*	95.8	77 42.2	+16.0*	100.4	77 29.1	+20.6*	104.8	77 11.6	+25.0*	109.1	76 50.0	+29.0*	113.1	76 24.6	+32.6*	116.9	30
31	77 54.2	-3.6*	81.7	78 00.5	+1.3*	86.4	78 01.8	6.3*	91.1	77 58.2	11.3*	95.8	77 49.7	16.3*	100.4	77 36.6	20.9*	104.9	77 19.0	25.2*	109.2	76 57.2	29.3*	113.3	31
32	77 50.6	8.4*	77.0	78 01.8	-3.6*	81.6	78 08.1	+1.4*	86.3	78 09.5	6.5*	91.0	78 06.0	11.5*	95.8	77 57.5	16.5*	100.5	77 44.2	21.2*	105.0	77 26.5	25.6*	109.3	32
33	77 42.2	13.1*	72.3	77 58.2	8.5*	76.8	78 09.5	-3.5*	81.4	78 16.0	+1.5*	86.2	78 17.5	6.7*	91.0	78 14.0	11.7*	95.8	78 05.4	16.8*	100.5	77 52.1	21.5*	105.1	33
34	77 29.1	17.5*	67.7	77 49.7	13.1*	72.0	78 06.0	8.5*	76.6	78 17.5	-3.5*	81.3	78 24.2	+1.5*	86.1	78 25.7	6.8*	91.0	78 22.2	11.9*	95.8	78 13.6	17.0*	100.6	34
35	77 11.6	-21.6*	63.4	77 36.6	-17.6*	67.4	77 57.5	-13.3*	71.8	78 14.0	-8.6*	76.3	78 25.7	-3.5*	81.1	78 32.5	+1.6*	86.0	78 34.1	+6.9*	90.9	78 30.6	+12.1*	95.8	35
36	76 50.0	25.4*	59.2	77 19.0	21.8*	63.0	77 44.2	17.7*	67.1	78 05.4	13.3*	71.5	78 22.2	8.6*	76.1	78 34.1	-3.5*	80.9	78 41.0	+1.7*	85.9	78 42.7	7.1*	90.9	36
37	76 24.6	28.8*	55.3	76 57.2	25.5*	58.9	77 26.5	21.9*	62.7	77 52.1	17.8*	66.8	78 13.6	13.4*	71.2	78 30.6	8.6*	75.9	78 42.7	-3.5*	80.8	78 49.8	+1.7*	85.8	37
38	75 55.8	32.0*	51.6	76 31.7	29.1*	54.9	77 04.6	25.7*	58.5	77 34.3	22.1*	62.3	78 00.2	18.0*	66.5	78 22.0	13.6*	71.0	78 39.2	8.7*	75.7	78 51.5	-3.5*	80.6	38
39	75 23.8	34.7*	48.2	76 02.6	32.1*	51.2	76 38.9	29.3*	54.5	77 12.2	26.0*	58.1	77 42.2	22.3*	62.0	78 08.4	18.1*	66.2	78 30.5	13.6*	70.7	78 48.0	8.8*	75.5	39
40	74 49.1	-37.2*	45.0	75 30.5	-34.9*	47.8	76 09.6	-32.3*	50.8	76 46.2	-29.4*	54.1	77 19.9	-26.1*	57.7	77 50.3	-22.5*	61.6	78 16.9	-18.4*	65.8	78 39.2	-13.7*	70.4	40
41	74 11.9	39.3*	42.1	74 55.6	37.4*	44.6	75 37.3	35.2*	47.3	76 16.8	32.6*	50.3	76 53.8	29.7*	53.6	77 27.8	26.4*	57.3	77 58.5	22.6*	61.2	78 25.5	18.6*	65.5	41
42	73 32.6	41.4	39.4	74 18.2	39.6*	41.6	75 02.1	37.6*	44.1	75 44.2	35.4*	46.9	76 24.1	32.8*	49.9	77 01.4	29.9*	53.2	77 35.9	26.7*	56.8	78 06.9	22.9*	60.8	42
43	72 51.2	43.0	36.9	73 38.6	41.5	38.9	74 24.5	39.8*	41.2	75 08.8	37.8*	43.6	75 51.3	35.7*	46.4	76 31.5	33.1*	49.4	77 09.2	30.1*	52.7	77 44.0	26.8*	56.4	43
44	72 08.2	44.6	34.6	72 57.1	43.3	36.4	73 44.7	41.7	38.4	74 31.0	40.1*	40.7	75 15.6	38.1*	43.2	75 58.4	35.9*	45.9	76 39.1	33.4*	48.9	77 17.2	30.5*	52.3	44
45	71 23.6	-45.8	32.4	72 13.8	-44.7	34.1	73 03.0	-43.5	35.9	73 50.9	-41.9	37.9	74 37.5	-40.2*	40.2	75 22.5	-38.3*	42.7	76 05.7	-36.2*	45.4	76 46.7	-33.6*	48.4	45
46	70 37.8	47.1	30.4	71 29.1	46.1	32.0	72 19.5	44.9	33.6	73 09.0	43.7	35.4	73 57.3	42.3	37.4	74 44.2	40.6*	39.7	75 29.5	38.6*	42.1	76 13.1	36.5*	44.9	46
47	69 50.7	48.2	28.6	70 43.0	47.3	30.0	71 34.6	46.3	31.5	72 25.3	45.1	33.1	73 15.0	43.8	34.9	74 03.6	42.4	36.9	74 50.9	40.8*	39.1	75 36.6	38.9*	41.6	47
48	69 02.5	49.1	26.9	69 55.7	48.3	28.1	70 48.3	47.4	29.5	71 40.2	46.5	31.0	72 31.2	45.4	32.6	73 21.2	44.1	34.4	74 10.1	42.7	36.4	74 57.7	41.1*	38.6	48
49	68 13.4	49.9	25.3	69 07.4	49.2	26.4	70 00.9	48.5	27.7	70 53.7	47.7	29.0	71 45.8	46.7	30.5	72 37.1	45.6	32.1	73 27.4	44.4	33.9	74 16.6	42.9	35.9	49
50	67 23.5	-50.6	23.9	68 18.2	-50.1	24.9	69 12.4	-49.4	26.0	70 06.0	-48.6	27.2	70 59.1	-47.8	28.5	71 51.5	-46.9	30.0	72 43.0	-45.8	31.6	73 33.7	-44.7	33.3	50
51	66 32.9	51.4	22.5	67 28.1	50.8	23.4	68 23.0	50.3	24.4	69 17.4	49.6	25.5	70 11.3	48.9	26.7	71 04.6	48.1	28.0	71 57.2	47.1	29.4	72 49.0	46.1	31.0	51
52	65 41.5	51.9	21.2	66 37.3	51.5	22.0	67 32.7	50.9	23.0	68 27.8	50.4	23.9	69 22.4	49.8	25.0	70 16.5	49.0	26.2	71 10.1	48.3	27.5	72 02.9	47.3	28.9	52
53	64 49.6	52.5	20.0	65 45.8	52.0	20.8	66 41.8	51.6	21.6	67 37.4	51.1	22.5	68 32.6	50.5	23.5	69 27.5	50.0	24.5	70 21.8	49.3	25.7	71 15.6	48.5	26.9	53
54	63 57.1	53.0	18.9	64 53.8	52.6	19.6	65 50.2	52.2	20.3	66 46.3	51.8	21.1	67 42.1	51.3	22.0	68 37.5	50.7	23.0	69 32.5	50.1	24.0	70 27.1	49.4	25.1	54
55	63 04.1	-53.4	17.8	64 01.2	-53.1	18.5	64 58.0	-52.8	19.1	65 54.5	-52.3	19.9	66 50.8	-51.9	20.7	67 46.8	-51.5	21.5	68 42.4	-50.9	22.5	69 37.7	-50.4	23.5	55
56	62 10.7	53.8	16.8	63 08.1	53.5	17.4	64 05.2	53.2	18.0	65 02.2	52.9	18.7	65 58.9	52.5	19.4	66 55.3	52.0	20.2	67 51.5	51.6	21.0	68 47.3	51.1	22.0	56
57	61 16.9	54.1	15.9	62 14.6	54.0	16.4	63 12.0	53.6	17.0	64 09.3	53.3	17.6	65 06.4	53.0	18.2	66 03.3	52.7	18.9	66 59.9	52.2	19.7	67 56.2	51.8	20.5	57
58	60 22.8	54.6	15.0	61 20.6	54.2	15.5	62 18.4	54.0	16.0	63 16.0	53.8	16.6	64 13.4	53.5	17.1	65 10.6	53.1	17.8	66 07.7	52.8	18.5	67 04.4	52.3	19.2	58
59	59 28.2	54.8	14.2	60 26.4	54.6	14.6	61 24.4	54.4	15.1	62 22.2	54.1	15.6	63 19.9	53.8	16.1	64 17.5	53.6	16.7	65 14.9	53.3	17.3	66 12.1	53.0	18.0	59
60	58 33.4	-55.0	13.4	59 31.8	-54.9	13.8	60 30.0	-54.7	14.2	61 28.1	-54.5	14.7	62 26.1	-54.3	15.2	63 23.9	-54.0	15.7	64 21.6	-53.7	16.2	65 19.1	-53.4	16.8	60
61	57 38.4	55.4	12.7	58 36.9	55.2	13.0	59 35.3	55.0	13.4	60 33.6	54.8	13.8	61 31.8	54.6	14.2	62 29.9	54.4	14.7	63 27.9	54.2	15.2	64 25.7	53.9	15.8	61
62	56 43.0	55.5	11.9	57 41.7	55.4	12.3	58 40.3	55.3	12.6	59 38.8	55.1	13.0	60 37.2	54.9	13.4	61 35.5	54.7	13.8	62 33.7	54.5	14.3	63 31.8	54.2	14.8	62
63	55 47.5	55.8	11.3	56 46.3	55.7	11.6	57 45.0	55.5	11.9	58 43.7	55.4	12.2	59 42.3	55.2	12.6	60 40.8	55.0	13.0	61 39.2	54.8	13.4	62 37.6	54.7	13.8	63
64	54 51.7	56.0	10.6	55 50.6	55.8	10.9	56 49.5	55.7	11.2	57 48.3	55.6	11.5	58 47.1	55.4	11.8	59 45.8	55.3	12.2	60 44.4	55.1	12.5	61 42.9	54.9	12.9	64
65	53 55.7	-56.2	10.0	54 54.8	-56.1	10.2	55 53.8	-56.0	10.5	56 52.7	-55.8	10.8	57 51.7	-55.7	11.1	58 50.5	-55.5	11.4	59 49.3	-55.4	11.7	60 48.0	-55.2	12.1	65
66	52 59.5	56.3	9.4	53 58.7	56.2	9.6	54 57.8	56.1	9.9	55 56.9	56.0	10.1	56 56.0	55.9	10.4	57 55.0	55.8	10.7	58 53.9	55.7	11.0	59 52.8	55.5	11.3	66
67	52 03.2	56.5	8.8	53 02.5	56.4	9.0	54 01.7	56.3	9.3	55 00.9	56.2	9.5	56 00.1	56.1	9.7	56 59.2	56.0	10.0	57 58.2	55.8	10.3	58 57.3	55.8	10.6	67
68	51 06.7	56.6	8.3	52 06.1	56.6	8.5	53 05.4	56.5	8.7	54 04.7	56.4	8.9	55 04.0	56.3	9.1	56 03.2	56.2	9.3	57 02.4	56.1	9.6	58 01.5	56.0	9.8	68
69	50 10.1	56.8	7.8	51 09.5	56.7	7.9	52 08.9	56.6	8.1	53 08.3	56.5	8.3	54 07.7	56.5	8.5	55 07.0	56.4	8.7	56 06.3	56.3	8.9	57 05.5	56.1	9.2	69
70	49 13.3	-56.9	7.3	50 12.8	-56.8	7.4	51 12.3	-56.7	7.6	52 11.8	-56.7	7.8	53 11.2	-56.6	7.9	54 10.6	-56.5	8.1	55 10.0	-56.4	8.3	56 09.4	-56.4	8.5	70
71	48 16.4	57.0	6.8	49 16.0	56.9	6.9	50 15.6	56.9	7.1	51 15.1	56.8	7.2	52 14.6	56.8	7.4	53 14.1	56.7	7.6	54 13.6	56.7	7.7	55 13.0	56.5	7.9	71
72	47 19.4	57.1	6.3	48 19.1	57.1	6.5	49 18.7	57.0	6.6	50 18.3	57.0	6.7	51 17.8	56.9	6.9	52 17.4	56.8	7.0	53 16.9	56.7	7.2	54 16.5	56.7	7.4	72
73	46 22.3	57.2	5.9	47 22.0	57.2	6.0	48 21.7	57.2	6.1	49 21.3	57.1	6.2	50 20.9	57.0	6.4	51 20.6	57.0	6.5	52 20.2	56.9	6.6	53 19.8	56.9	6.8	73
74	45 25.1	57.3	5.5	46 24.8	57.3	5.6	47 24.5	57.2	5.7	48 24.2	57.2	5.8	49 23.9	57.1	5.9	50 23.6	57.1	6.0	51 23.3	57.1	6.1	52 22.9	57.0	6.3	74
75	44 27.8	-57.4	5.0	45 27.5	-57.3	5.1	46 27.3	-57.3	5.2	47 27.0	-57.2	5.3	48 26.8	-57.3	5.4	49 26.5	-57.2	5.5	50 26.2	-57.1	5.6	51 25.9	-57.1	5.8	75
76	43 30.4	57.5	4.6	44 30.2	57.5	4.7	45 30.0	57.4	4.8	46 29.8	57.4	4.9	47 29.5	57.3	5.0	48 29.3	57.3	5.1	49 29.1	57.3	5.2	50 28.8	57.2	5.3	76
77	42 32.9	57.6	4.2	43 32.7	57.5	4.3	44 32.6	57.5	4.4	45 32.4	57.5	4.5	46 32.2	57.4	4.5	47 32.0	57.4	4.6	48 31.8	57.4	4.7	49 31.6	57.3	4.8	77
78	41 35.3	57.6	3.9	42 35.2	57.6	3.9	43 35.1	57.6	4.0	44 34.9	57.5	4.0	45 34.8	57.6	4.1	46 34.6	57.5	4.2	47 34.4	57.4	4.3	48 34.3	57.5	4.4	78
79	40 37.7	57.7	3.5	41 37.6	57.7	3.5	42 37.5	57.7	3.6	43 37.4	57.7	3.7	44 37.2	57.6	3.7	45 37.1	57.6	3.8	46 37.0	57.6	3.9	47 36.8	57.5	3.9	79
80	39 40.0	-57.8	3.1	40 39.9	-57.7	3.2	41 39.8	-57.7	3.2	42 39.7	-57.7	3.3	43 39.6	-57.7	3.3	44 39.5	-57.6	3.4	45 39.4	-57.6	3.4	46 39.3	-57.6	3.5	80
81	38 42.2	57.8	2.8	39 42.2	57.8	2.8	40 42.1	57.8	2.9	41 42.0	57.8	2.9	42 41.9	57.7	3.0	43 41.9	57.8	3.0	44 41.8	57.7	3.1	45 41.7	57.7	3.1	81
82	37 44.4	57.9	2.4	38 44.4	57.9	2.5	39 44.3	57.9	2.5	40 44.2	57.8	2.5	41 44.2	57.8	2.6	42 44.1	57.8	2.6	43 44.1	57.8	2.7	44 44.0	57.8	2.7	82
83	36 46.5	57.9	2.1	37 46.5	57.9	2.1	38 46.4	57.9	2.2	39 46.4	57.9	2.2	40 46.4	57.9	2.2	41 46.3	57.9	2.3	42 46.3	57.9	2.3	43 46.2	57.8	2.3	83
84	35 48.6	58.0	1.8	36 48.6	58.0	1.8	37 48.5	57.9	1.8	38 48.5	58.0	1.9	39 48.5	58.0	1.9	40 48.4	57.9	1.9	41 48.4	57.9	1.9	42 48.4	58.0	2.0	84
85	34 50.6	-58.0	1.5	35 50.6	-58.0	1.5	36 50.6	-58.1	1.5	37 50.5	-58.0	1.5	38 50.5	-58.0	1.6	39 50.5	-58.0	1.6	40 50.5	-58.0	1.6	41 50.4	-57.9	1.6	85
86	33 52.6	58.1	1.2	34 52.6	58.1	1.2	35 52.5	58.0	1.2	36 52.5	58.0	1.2	37 52.5	58.0	1.2	38 52.5	58.1	1.2	39 52.5	58.1	1.3	40 52.5	58.1	1.3	86
87	32 54.5	58.1	0.9	33 54.5	58.1	0.9	34 54.5	58.1	0.9	35 54.5	58.1	0.9	36 54.5	58.2	0.9	37 54.4	58.1	0.9	38 54.4	58.1	0.9	39 54.4	58.1	0.9	87
88	31 56.4	58.2	0.6	32 56.4	58.2	0.6	33 56.4	58.2	0.6	34 56.4	58.2	0.6	35 56.3	58.1	0.6	36 56.3	58.1	0.6	37 56.3	58.1	0.6	38 56.3	58.1	0.6	88
89	30 58.2	58.2	0.3	31 58.2	58.2	0.3	32 58.2	58.2	0.3	33 58.2	58.2	0.3	34 58.2	58.2	0.3	35 58.2	58.2	0.3	36 58.2	58.2	0.3	37 58.2	58.2	0.3	89
90	30 00.0	-58.2	0.0	31 00.0	-58.2	0.0	32 00.0	-58.2	0.0	33 00.0	-58.2	0.0	34 00.0	-58.2	0.0	35 00.0	-58.2	0.0	36 00.0	-58.2	0.0	37 00.0	-58.2	0.0	90
	30°			31°			32°			33°			34°			35°			36°			37°			

14°, 346° L.H.A. LATITUDE SAME NAME AS DECLINATION

58

14°, 346° L.H.A. LATITUDE SAME NAME AS DECLINATION

N. Lat. { L.H.A. greater than 180°......Zn=Z ; L.H.A. less than 180°............Zn=360°−Z }

Dec.	38°			39°			40°			41°		
	Hc	d	Z	Hc	d	Z	Hc	d	Z	Hc	d	Z
°	° ′	′	°	° ′	′	°	° ′	′	°	° ′	′	°
0	49 52.3	+57.3	158.0	48 56.6	+57.4	158.4	48 00.7	+57.7	158.8	47 04.7	+57.8	159.2
1	50 49.6	57.1	157.5	49 54.0	57.4	157.9	48 58.4	57.5	158.4	48 02.5	57.7	158.8
2	51 46.7	57.0	157.0	50 51.4	57.2	157.5	49 55.9	57.4	157.9	49 00.2	57.5	158.4
3	52 43.7	56.9	156.5	51 48.6	57.1	157.0	50 53.3	57.3	157.5	49 57.7	57.5	157.9
4	53 40.6	56.7	156.0	52 45.7	57.0	156.5	51 50.6	57.1	157.0	50 55.2	57.4	157.5
5	54 37.3	+56.6	155.4	53 42.7	+56.8	156.0	52 47.7	+57.1	156.5	51 52.6	+57.3	157.0
6	55 33.9	56.4	154.8	54 39.5	56.6	155.4	53 44.8	56.9	156.0	52 49.9	57.1	156.5
7	56 30.3	56.2	154.2	55 36.1	56.5	154.8	54 41.7	56.7	155.5	53 47.0	57.0	156.0
8	57 26.5	56.0	153.6	56 32.6	56.3	154.2	55 38.4	56.6	154.9	54 44.0	56.8	155.5
9	58 22.5	55.8	152.9	57 28.9	56.1	153.6	56 35.0	56.4	154.3	55 40.8	56.7	154.9
10	59 18.3	+55.5	152.2	58 25.0	+55.9	152.9	57 31.4	+56.3	153.7	56 37.5	+56.5	154.3
11	60 13.8	55.3	151.4	59 20.9	55.7	152.2	58 27.7	55.9	153.0	57 34.0	56.3	153.7
12	61 09.1	55.0	150.6	60 16.6	55.4	151.5	59 23.6	55.8	152.3	58 30.3	56.1	153.1
13	62 04.1	54.6	149.8	61 12.0	55.1	150.7	60 19.4	55.5	151.6	59 26.4	55.9	152.4
14	62 58.7	54.3	148.9	62 07.1	54.7	149.9	61 14.9	55.2	150.8	60 22.3	55.7	151.7
15	63 53.0	+53.8	147.9	63 01.8	+54.4	149.0	62 10.1	+54.9	150.0	61 18.0	+55.3	150.9
16	64 46.8	53.5	146.9	63 56.2	54.1	148.0	63 05.0	54.6	149.1	62 13.3	55.1	150.1
17	65 40.3	52.9	145.8	64 50.3	53.6	147.0	63 59.6	54.2	148.2	63 08.4	54.7	149.2
18	66 33.2	52.4	144.7	65 43.9	53.1	146.0	64 53.8	53.7	147.2	64 03.1	54.3	148.3
19	67 25.6	51.7	143.4	66 37.0	52.5	144.8	65 47.5	53.3	146.1	64 57.4	53.9	147.3
20	68 17.3	+51.1	142.1	67 29.5	+52.0	143.6	66 40.8	+52.8	145.0	65 51.3	+53.5	146.2
21	69 08.4	50.3	140.6	68 21.5	51.2	142.2	67 33.6	52.1	143.7	66 44.8	52.9	145.1
22	69 58.7	49.3	139.1	69 12.7	50.5	140.8	68 25.7	51.5	142.4	67 37.7	52.3	143.9
23	70 48.0	48.4	137.4	70 03.2	49.6	139.2	69 17.2	50.7	141.0	68 30.0	51.7	142.6
24	71 36.4	47.2	135.5	70 52.8	48.6	137.6	70 07.9	49.8	139.4	69 21.7	50.9	141.2
25	72 23.6	+45.9	133.5	71 41.4	+47.5	135.7	70 57.7	+48.9	137.8	70 12.6	+50.1	139.6
26	73 09.5	44.4	131.4	72 28.9	46.2	133.7	71 46.6	47.7	135.9	71 02.7	49.1	138.0
27	73 53.9	42.7	129.0	73 15.1	44.7	131.6	72 34.3	46.5	134.0	71 51.8	48.1	136.2
28	74 36.6	40.7•	126.4	73 59.8	43.0	129.2	73 20.8	45.0	131.8	72 39.9	46.7	134.2
29	75 17.3	38.5•	123.6	74 42.8	41.0•	126.6	74 05.8	43.3	129.4	73 26.6	45.3	132.1
30	75 55.8	+35.9•	120.5	75 23.8	+38.8•	123.8	74 49.1	+41.4•	126.9	74 11.9	+43.7	129.7
31	76 31.7	32.9•	117.1	76 02.6	36.3•	120.7	75 30.5	39.1•	124.0	74 55.6	41.7•	127.1
32	77 04.6	29.7•	113.5	76 38.9	33.3•	117.3	76 09.6	36.6•	120.9	75 37.3	39.5•	124.3
33	77 34.3	25.9•	109.5	77 12.2	30.0•	113.6	76 46.2	33.7•	117.6	76 16.8	37.0•	121.2
34	78 00.2	21.8•	105.2	77 42.2	26.2•	109.7	77 19.9	30.4•	113.9	76 53.8	34.0•	117.8
35	78 22.0	+17.2•	100.7	78 08.4	+22.1•	105.4	77 50.3	+26.6•	109.8	77 27.8	+30.7•	114.1
36	78 39.2	12.3•	95.9	78 30.5	17.5•	100.8	78 16.9	22.3•	105.5	77 58.5	27.0•	110.0
37	78 51.5	7.2•	90.8	78 48.0	12.5•	95.9	78 39.2	17.8•	100.9	78 25.5	22.7•	105.7
38	78 58.7	+ 1.8•	85.7	79 00.5	7.3•	90.8	78 57.0	12.7•	95.9	78 48.2	18.0•	101.0
39	79 00.5	− 3.5•	80.4	79 07.8	+ 1.9•	85.6	79 09.7	7.5•	90.8	79 06.2	12.9•	96.0
40	78 57.0	− 8.8•	75.2	79 09.7	− 3.5•	80.3	79 17.2	+ 1.9•	85.5	79 19.1	+ 7.6•	90.8
41	78 48.2	14.0•	70.1	79 06.2	8.9•	75.0	79 19.1	− 3.5•	80.1	79 26.7	+ 2.0•	85.4
42	78 34.2	18.7•	65.1	78 57.3	14.1•	69.8	79 15.6	9.1•	74.7	79 28.7	− 3.6•	79.9
43	78 15.5	23.1•	60.4	78 43.2	19.0•	64.8	79 06.5	14.2•	69.5	79 25.1	9.1•	74.5
44	77 52.4	27.2•	55.9	78 24.2	23.4•	60.0	78 52.3	19.2•	64.4	79 16.0	14.5•	69.1
45	77 25.2	−30.7•	51.8	78 00.8	−27.4•	55.5	78 33.1	−23.7•	59.5	79 01.5	−19.4•	64.0
46	76 54.5	33.9•	47.9	77 33.4	31.0•	51.3	78 09.4	27.7•	55.0	78 42.1	23.9•	59.1
47	76 20.6	36.8•	44.3	77 02.4	34.3•	47.4	77 41.7	31.4•	50.7	78 18.2	28.1•	54.5
48	75 43.8	39.2•	41.1	76 28.1	37.0•	43.8	77 10.3	34.5•	46.8	77 50.1	31.7•	50.2
49	75 04.6	41.4•	38.0	75 51.1	39.6•	40.5	76 35.8	37.4•	43.2	77 18.4	34.9•	46.2
50	74 23.2	−43.2	35.3	75 11.5	−41.6•	37.5	75 58.4	−39.9•	39.9	76 43.5	−37.7•	42.6
51	73 40.0	44.9	32.8	74 29.9	43.6	34.7	75 18.5	41.9•	36.9	76 05.8	40.2•	39.3
52	72 55.1	46.4	30.5	73 46.3	45.1	32.2	74 36.6	43.9	34.1	75 25.6	42.3•	36.3
53	72 08.7	47.6	28.4	73 01.2	46.6	29.9	73 52.7	45.4	31.6	74 43.3	44.2	33.5
54	71 21.1	48.7	26.4	72 14.6	47.9	27.8	73 07.3	46.9	29.3	73 59.1	45.7	31.0
55	70 32.4	−49.6	24.6	71 26.7	−48.9	25.9	72 20.4	−48.1	27.2	73 13.4	−47.1	28.7
56	69 42.8	50.6	23.0	70 37.8	49.9	24.1	71 32.3	49.1	25.3	72 26.3	48.4	26.6
57	68 52.2	51.2	21.4	69 47.9	50.7	22.4	70 43.2	50.2	23.5	71 37.9	49.4	24.7
58	68 01.0	52.0	20.0	68 57.2	51.5	20.9	69 53.0	50.9	21.9	70 48.5	50.3	23.0
59	67 09.0	52.6	18.7	68 05.7	52.1	19.5	69 02.1	51.7	20.4	69 58.2	51.2	21.3
60	66 16.4	−53.1	17.5	67 13.6	−52.8	18.2	68 10.4	−52.3	19.0	69 07.0	−51.9	19.8
61	65 23.3	53.5	16.4	66 20.8	53.2	17.0	67 18.1	52.9	17.7	68 15.1	52.5	18.5
62	64 29.8	54.0	15.3	65 27.6	53.8	15.9	66 25.2	53.4	16.5	67 22.6	53.1	17.2
63	63 35.8	54.4	14.3	64 33.8	54.1	14.8	65 31.8	53.9	15.4	66 29.5	53.6	16.0
64	62 41.4	54.8	13.4	63 39.7	54.5	13.8	64 37.9	54.3	14.3	65 35.9	54.0	14.9
65	61 46.6	−55.0	12.5	62 45.2	−54.9	12.9	63 43.6	−54.7	13.4	64 41.9	−54.4	13.8
66	60 51.6	55.4	11.7	61 50.3	55.2	12.0	62 48.9	55.0	12.4	63 47.5	54.8	12.9
67	59 56.2	55.6	10.9	60 55.1	55.5	11.2	61 53.9	55.3	11.6	62 52.7	55.2	12.0
68	59 00.6	55.9	10.1	59 59.6	55.7	10.4	60 58.6	55.6	10.8	61 57.5	55.4	11.1
69	58 04.7	56.0	9.4	59 03.9	55.9	9.7	60 03.0	55.8	10.0	61 02.1	55.7	10.3
70	57 08.7	−56.3	8.8	58 08.0	−56.2	9.0	59 07.2	−56.1	9.3	60 06.4	−56.0	9.6
71	56 12.4	56.5	8.1	57 11.8	56.4	8.4	58 11.1	56.2	8.6	59 10.4	56.1	8.8
72	55 15.9	56.6	7.5	56 15.4	56.5	7.7	57 14.9	56.5	7.9	58 14.3	56.4	8.2
73	54 19.3	56.8	7.0	55 18.9	56.7	7.1	56 18.4	56.6	7.3	57 17.9	56.6	7.5
74	53 22.5	56.9	6.4	54 22.2	56.9	6.6	55 21.8	56.8	6.7	56 21.3	56.7	6.9
75	52 25.6	−57.0	5.9	53 25.3	−57.0	6.0	54 25.0	−57.0	6.2	55 24.6	−56.9	6.3
76	51 28.6	57.2	5.4	52 28.3	57.1	5.5	53 28.0	57.1	5.6	54 27.7	57.0	5.8
77	50 31.4	57.3	4.9	51 31.2	57.3	5.0	52 30.9	57.2	5.1	53 30.7	57.2	5.3
78	49 34.1	57.4	4.4	50 33.9	57.4	4.5	51 33.7	57.3	4.6	52 33.5	57.3	4.7
79	48 36.7	57.5	4.0	49 36.5	57.4	4.1	50 36.4	57.5	4.2	51 36.2	57.4	4.3
80	47 39.2	−57.6	3.6	48 39.1	−57.6	3.6	49 38.9	−57.5	3.7	50 38.8	−57.5	3.8
81	46 41.6	57.7	3.2	47 41.5	57.7	3.2	48 41.4	57.6	3.3	49 41.3	57.6	3.4
82	45 43.9	57.7	2.8	46 43.8	57.7	2.8	47 43.8	57.7	2.9	48 43.7	57.7	2.9
83	44 46.2	57.9	2.4	45 46.1	57.8	2.4	46 46.1	57.9	2.5	47 46.0	57.8	2.5
84	43 48.3	57.9	2.0	44 48.3	57.9	2.0	45 48.2	57.8	2.1	46 48.2	57.9	2.1
85	42 50.4	−57.9	1.6	43 50.4	−58.0	1.7	44 50.4	−58.0	1.7	45 50.3	−57.9	1.7
86	41 52.5	58.1	1.3	42 52.4	58.0	1.3	43 52.4	58.0	1.3	44 52.4	58.0	1.4
87	40 54.4	58.1	1.0	41 54.4	58.1	1.0	42 54.4	58.1	1.0	43 54.4	58.1	1.0
88	39 56.3	58.1	0.6	40 56.3	58.1	0.6	41 56.3	58.1	0.7	42 56.3	58.1	0.7
89	38 58.2	58.2	0.3	39 58.2	58.2	0.3	40 58.2	58.2	0.3	41 58.2	58.2	0.3
90	38 00.0	−58.2	0.0	39 00.0	−58.2	0.0	40 00.0	−58.2	0.0	41 00.0	−58.2	0.0
	38°			39°			40°			41°		

42°			43°			44°			45°			Dec.
Hc	d	Z	Hc	d	Z	Hc	d	Z	Hc	d	Z	
° ′	′	°	° ′	′	°	° ′	′	°	° ′	′	°	°
46 08.6	+57.9	159.6	45 12.3	+58.0	159.9	44 15.9	+58.1	160.3	43 19.3	+58.3	160.6	0
47 06.5	57.8	159.2	46 10.3	58.0	159.6	45 14.0	58.1	159.9	44 17.6	58.3	160.2	1
48 04.3	57.8	158.8	47 08.3	57.9	159.2	46 12.1	58.1	159.6	45 15.9	58.1	159.9	2
49 02.1	57.6	158.4	48 06.2	57.8	158.8	47 10.2	57.9	159.2	46 14.0	58.1	159.6	3
49 59.7	57.6	158.0	49 04.0	57.7	158.4	48 08.1	57.9	158.8	47 12.1	58.1	159.2	4
50 57.3	+57.4	157.5	50 01.7	+57.7	158.0	49 06.0	+57.8	158.4	48 10.2	+57.9	158.8	5
51 54.7	57.4	157.0	50 59.4	57.5	157.5	50 03.8	57.7	158.0	49 08.1	57.9	158.4	6
52 52.1	57.2	156.6	51 56.9	57.4	157.1	51 01.5	57.6	157.6	50 06.0	57.8	158.0	7
53 49.3	57.0	156.1	52 54.3	57.3	156.6	51 59.1	57.5	157.1	51 03.8	57.7	157.6	8
54 46.3	57.0	155.5	53 51.6	57.2	156.1	52 56.6	57.4	156.6	52 01.5	57.5	157.2	9
55 43.3	+56.8	155.0	54 48.8	+57.0	155.6	53 54.0	+57.3	156.1	52 59.0	+57.5	156.7	10
56 40.1	56.6	154.4	55 45.8	56.9	155.0	54 51.3	57.1	155.6	53 56.5	57.4	156.2	11
57 36.7	56.4	153.8	56 42.7	56.7	154.5	55 48.4	57.0	155.1	54 53.9	57.2	155.7	12
58 33.1	56.2	153.1	57 39.4	56.5	153.9	56 45.4	56.8	154.5	55 51.1	57.0	155.2	13
59 29.3	56.0	152.5	58 35.9	56.4	153.2	57 42.2	56.6	153.9	56 48.1	57.0	154.6	14
60 25.3	+55.8	151.7	59 32.3	+56.1	152.6	58 38.8	+56.5	153.3	57 45.1	+56.7	154.0	15
61 21.1	55.5	151.0	60 28.4	55.9	151.8	59 35.3	56.2	152.7	58 41.8	56.6	153.4	16
62 16.6	55.1	150.2	61 24.3	55.6	151.1	60 31.5	56.0	152.0	59 38.4	56.3	152.8	17
63 11.7	54.9	149.3	62 19.9	55.3	150.3	61 27.5	55.8	151.2	60 34.7	56.1	152.1	18
64 06.6	54.5	148.4	63 15.2	55.0	149.5	62 23.3	55.4	150.4	61 30.8	55.9	151.3	19
65 01.1	+54.1	147.4	64 10.2	+54.6	148.5	63 18.7	+55.2	149.6	62 26.7	+55.6	150.6	20
65 55.2	53.6	146.4	65 04.8	54.3	147.6	64 13.9	54.8	148.7	63 22.3	55.3	149.7	21
66 48.8	53.1	145.3	65 59.1	53.8	146.6	65 08.7	54.4	147.7	64 17.6	55.0	148.9	22
67 41.9	52.5	144.1	66 52.9	53.3	145.4	66 03.1	54.0	146.7	65 12.6	54.6	147.9	23
68 34.4	51.9	142.8	67 46.2	52.7	144.3	66 57.1	53.5	145.6	66 07.2	54.1	146.9	24
69 26.3	+51.2	141.4	68 38.9	+52.1	143.0	67 50.6	+52.9	144.5	67 01.3	+53.7	145.8	25
70 17.5	50.3	139.9	69 31.0	51.4	141.6	68 43.5	52.3	143.2	67 55.0	53.2	144.7	26
71 07.8	49.4	138.2	70 22.4	50.6	140.1	69 35.8	51.7	141.8	68 48.2	52.5	143.4	27
71 57.2	48.3	136.4	71 13.0	49.7	138.4	70 27.5	50.8	140.3	69 40.7	51.9	142.0	28
72 45.5	47.1	134.5	72 02.7	48.5	136.7	71 18.3	49.9	138.7	70 32.6	51.0	140.6	29
73 32.6	+45.6	132.3	72 51.2	+47.4	134.7	72 08.2	+48.9	136.9	71 23.6	+50.2	139.0	30
74 18.2	43.9	130.0	73 38.6	45.9	132.6	72 57.1	47.6	135.0	72 13.8	49.2	137.2	31
75 02.1	42.1•	127.4	74 24.5	44.3	130.2	73 44.7	46.3	132.9	73 03.0	47.9	135.3	32
75 44.2	39.9•	124.6	75 08.8	42.5•	127.7	74 31.0	44.6	130.5	73 50.9	46.6	133.2	33
76 24.1	37.3•	121.5	75 51.3	40.2•	124.8	75 15.6	42.8	128.0	74 37.5	45.0	130.8	34
77 01.4	+34.5•	118.0	76 31.5	+37.7•	121.7	75 58.4	+40.7•	125.1	75 22.5	+43.2•	128.3	35
77 35.9	31.0•	114.3	77 09.2	34.8•	118.3	76 39.1	38.1•	122.0	76 05.7	41.0•	125.5	36
78 06.9	27.3•	110.3	77 44.0	31.5•	114.6	77 17.2	35.2•	118.6	76 46.7	38.5•	122.4	37
78 34.2	23.1•	105.8	78 15.5	27.7•	110.5	77 52.4	31.8•	114.8	77 25.2	35.6•	118.9	38
78 57.3	18.3•	101.1	78 43.2	23.3•	106.0	78 24.2	28.1•	110.7	78 00.8	32.3•	115.1	39
79 15.6	+13.1•	96.1	79 06.5	+18.6•	101.2	78 52.3	+23.7•	106.2	78 33.1	+28.4•	111.0	40
79 28.7	7.8•	90.8	79 25.1	13.4•	96.1	79 16.0	18.9•	101.4	79 01.5	24.1•	106.4	41
79 36.5	+ 2.0•	85.3	79 38.5	7.9•	90.8	79 34.9	13.6•	96.2	79 25.6	19.2•	101.5	42
79 38.5	− 3.6•	79.8	79 46.4	+ 2.1•	85.2	79 48.5	8.0•	90.8	79 44.8	13.8•	96.3	43
79 34.9	9.3•	74.2	79 48.5	− 3.7•	79.6	79 56.5	+ 2.1•	85.1	79 58.6	8.2•	90.8	44
79 25.6	−14.7•	68.8	79 44.8	− 9.4•	73.9	79 58.6	− 3.7•	79.4	80 06.8	+ 2.2•	85.0	45
79 10.9	19.6•	63.6	79 35.4	14.9•	68.4	79 54.9	9.6•	73.7	80 09.0	− 3.9•	79.2	46
78 51.3	24.3•	58.6	79 20.5	19.9•	63.1	79 45.3	15.1•	68.1	80 05.1	9.7•	73.4	47
78 27.0	28.4•	53.9	79 00.6	24.6•	58.1	79 30.2	20.2•	62.7	79 55.4	15.3•	67.7	48
77 58.6	32.0•	49.6	78 36.0	28.8•	53.4	79 10.0	25.0•	57.6	79 40.1	20.6•	62.2	49
77 26.6	−35.3•	45.7	78 07.2	−32.4•	49.1	78 45.0	−29.1•	52.9	79 19.5	−25.3•	57.1	50
76 51.3	38.1•	42.0	77 34.8	35.7•	45.1	78 15.9	32.8•	48.5	78 54.2	29.5•	52.3	51
76 13.2	40.5•	38.7	76 59.1	38.4•	41.4	77 43.1	36.1•	44.4	78 24.7	33.2•	47.9	52
75 32.7	42.7	35.7	76 20.7	40.9•	38.1	77 07.0	38.8•	40.8	77 51.5	36.5•	43.8	53
74 50.0	44.4	32.9	75 39.8	43.0	35.0	76 28.2	41.2•	37.4	77 15.0	39.2•	40.1	54
74 05.6	−46.1	30.4	74 56.8	−44.7	32.3	75 47.0	−43.4	34.4	76 35.8	−41.7•	36.8	55
73 19.5	47.4	28.1	74 12.1	46.4	29.8	75 03.6	45.1	31.7	75 54.1	43.7	33.7	56
72 32.1	48.6	26.0	73 25.7	47.7	27.5	74 18.5	46.6	29.2	75 10.4	45.4	31.0	57
71 43.5	49.6	24.1	72 38.0	48.9	25.4	73 31.9	48.0	26.9	74 25.0	47.0	28.5	58
70 53.9	50.6	22.4	71 49.1	49.9	23.5	72 43.9	49.2	24.8	73 38.0	48.3	26.2	59
70 03.3	−51.4	20.8	70 59.2	−50.8	21.8	71 54.7	−50.2	22.9	72 49.7	−49.5	24.2	60
69 11.9	52.1	19.3	70 08.4	51.6	20.2	71 04.5	51.0	21.2	72 00.2	50.4	22.3	61
68 19.8	52.7	17.9	69 16.8	52.3	18.7	70 13.5	51.9	19.6	71 09.8	51.3	20.6	62
67 27.1	53.2	16.6	68 24.5	52.9	17.4	69 21.6	52.5	18.2	70 18.5	52.0	19.0	63
66 33.9	53.8	15.5	67 31.6	53.5	16.1	68 29.1	53.1	16.8	69 26.5	52.8	17.6	64
65 40.1	−54.2	14.4	66 38.1	−53.9	14.9	67 36.0	−53.6	15.6	68 33.7	−53.3	16.2	65
64 45.9	54.6	13.3	65 44.2	54.3	13.9	66 42.4	54.1	14.4	67 40.4	53.8	15.0	66
63 51.3	54.9	12.4	64 49.9	54.8	12.8	65 48.3	54.5	13.3	66 46.6	54.3	13.9	67
62 56.4	55.3	11.5	63 55.1	55.1	11.9	64 53.8	54.9	12.3	65 52.3	54.7	12.8	68
62 01.1	55.6	10.6	63 00.0	55.4	11.0	63 58.9	55.3	11.4	64 57.6	55.0	11.8	69
61 05.5	−55.8	9.9	62 04.6	−55.7	10.2	63 03.6	−55.5	10.5	64 02.6	−55.4	10.9	70
60 09.7	56.1	9.1	61 08.9	55.9	9.4	62 08.1	55.8	9.7	63 07.2	55.7	10.0	71
59 13.6	56.2	8.4	60 13.0	56.2	8.7	61 12.3	56.1	8.9	62 11.5	55.9	9.2	72
58 17.4	56.5	7.7	59 16.8	56.4	8.0	60 16.2	56.3	8.2	61 15.6	56.2	8.5	73
57 20.9	56.7	7.1	58 20.4	56.6	7.3	59 19.9	56.5	7.5	60 19.4	56.4	7.7	74
56 24.2	−56.8	6.5	57 23.8	−56.7	6.7	58 23.4	−56.7	6.9	59 23.0	−56.6	7.1	75
55 27.4	57.0	5.9	56 27.1	57.0	6.1	57 26.7	56.8	6.2	58 26.4	56.8	6.4	76
54 30.4	57.1	5.4	55 30.1	57.0	5.5	56 29.9	57.1	5.7	57 29.6	57.0	5.8	77
53 33.3	57.2	4.9	54 33.1	57.2	5.0	55 32.8	57.1	5.1	56 32.6	57.1	5.2	78
52 36.1	57.4	4.4	53 35.9	57.4	4.5	54 35.7	57.3	4.6	55 35.5	57.3	4.7	79
51 38.7	−57.5	3.9	52 38.5	−57.4	4.0	53 38.4	−57.4	4.1	54 38.2	−57.3	4.2	80
50 41.2	57.6	3.4	51 41.1	57.6	3.5	52 41.0	57.6	3.6	53 40.9	57.5	3.7	81
49 43.6	57.7	3.0	50 43.5	57.6	3.0	51 43.4	57.6	3.1	52 43.4	57.7	3.2	82
48 45.9	57.7	2.6	49 45.9	57.8	2.6	50 45.8	57.7	2.7	51 45.7	57.7	2.7	83
47 48.2	57.9	2.2	48 48.1	57.8	2.2	49 48.1	57.8	2.2	50 48.0	57.8	2.3	84
46 50.3	−57.9	1.8	47 50.3	−57.9	1.8	48 50.3	−57.9	1.8	49 50.2	−57.9	1.9	85
45 52.4	58.0	1.4	46 52.4	58.0	1.4	47 52.4	58.0	1.4	48 52.3	57.9	1.5	86
44 54.4	58.1	1.0	45 54.4	58.1	1.0	46 54.4	58.1	1.1	47 54.4	58.1	1.1	87
43 56.3	58.1	0.7	44 56.3	58.1	0.7	45 56.3	58.1	0.7	46 56.3	58.1	0.7	88
42 58.2	58.2	0.3	43 58.2	58.2	0.3	44 58.2	58.2	0.3	45 58.2	58.2	0.3	89
42 00.0	−58.2	0.0	43 00.0	−58.2	0.0	44 00.0	−58.2	0.0	45 00.0	−58.2	0.0	90
42°			43°			44°			45°			

14°, 346° L.H.A. LATITUDE SAME NAME AS DECLINATION

LATITUDE CONTRARY NAME TO DECLINATION L.H.A. 35°, 325°

Dec.	38°			39°			40°			41°		
	Hc	d	Z	Hc	d	Z	Hc	d	Z	Hc	d	Z
°	° ′	′	°	° ′	′	°	° ′	′	°	° ′	′	°
0	40 12.2	−48.5	131.3	39 32.3	−49.1	131.9	38 52.0	−49.7	132.6	38 11.2	−50.2	133.1
1	39 23.7	48.8	132.1	38 43.2	49.4	132.7	38 02.3	49.9	133.3	37 21.0	50.5	133.8
2	38 34.9	49.1	132.8	37 53.8	49.6	133.4	37 12.4	50.2	134.0	36 30.5	50.6	134.5
3	37 45.8	49.4	133.6	37 04.2	49.9	134.1	36 22.2	50.4	134.7	35 39.9	50.9	135.2
4	36 56.4	49.6	134.3	36 14.3	50.1	134.8	35 31.8	50.6	135.3	34 49.0	51.1	135.8
5	36 06.8	−49.8	135.0	35 24.2	−50.3	135.5	34 41.2	−50.8	136.0	33 57.9	−51.3	136.5
6	35 17.0	50.1	135.7	34 33.9	50.6	136.2	33 50.4	51.0	136.6	33 06.6	51.4	137.1
7	34 26.9	50.3	136.3	33 43.3	50.7	136.8	32 59.4	51.2	137.3	32 15.2	51.6	137.7
8	33 36.6	50.5	137.0	32 52.6	51.0	137.4	32 08.2	51.4	137.9	31 23.6	51.8	138.3
9	32 46.1	50.7	137.6	32 01.6	51.1	138.1	31 16.8	51.5	138.5	30 31.8	52.0	138.9
10	31 55.4	−50.9	138.3	31 10.5	−51.3	138.7	30 25.3	−51.7	139.1	29 39.8	−52.1	139.5
11	31 04.5	51.0	138.9	30 19.2	51.5	139.3	29 33.6	51.9	139.7	28 47.7	52.2	140.0
12	30 13.5	51.2	139.5	29 27.7	51.6	139.9	28 41.7	52.0	140.2	27 55.5	52.4	140.6
13	29 22.3	51.4	140.1	28 36.1	51.8	140.5	27 49.7	52.1	140.8	27 03.1	52.5	141.1
14	28 30.9	51.5	140.7	27 44.3	51.9	141.0	26 57.6	52.3	141.4	26 10.6	52.6	141.7
15	27 39.4	−51.7	141.3	26 52.4	−52.0	141.6	26 05.3	−52.4	141.9	25 18.0	−52.7	142.2
16	26 47.7	51.8	141.9	26 00.4	52.2	142.2	25 12.9	52.5	142.5	24 25.3	52.9	142.7
17	25 55.9	52.0	142.4	25 08.2	52.2	142.7	24 20.4	52.6	143.0	23 32.4	52.9	143.3
18	25 03.9	52.0	143.0	24 16.0	52.4	143.2	23 27.8	52.7	143.5	22 39.5	53.1	143.8
19	24 11.9	52.2	143.5	23 23.6	52.5	143.8	22 35.1	52.8	144.0	21 46.4	53.1	144.3
20	23 19.7	−52.3	144.1	22 31.1	−52.6	144.3	21 42.3	−53.0	144.5	20 53.3	−53.2	144.8
21	22 27.4	52.4	144.6	21 38.5	52.7	144.8	20 49.3	53.0	145.0	20 00.1	53.3	145.3
22	21 35.0	52.4	145.1	20 45.8	52.8	145.3	19 56.3	53.0	145.5	19 06.8	53.4	145.7
23	20 42.6	52.6	145.6	19 53.0	52.9	145.8	19 03.3	53.2	146.0	18 13.4	53.4	146.2
24	19 50.0	52.7	146.1	19 00.1	53.0	146.3	18 10.1	53.2	146.5	17 20.0	53.5	146.7
25	18 57.3	−52.7	146.7	18 07.1	−53.0	146.8	17 16.9	−53.3	147.0	16 26.5	−53.6	147.2
26	18 04.6	52.8	147.2	17 14.1	53.1	147.3	16 23.6	53.4	147.5	15 32.9	53.6	147.6
27	17 11.8	52.9	147.7	16 21.0	53.1	147.8	15 30.2	53.4	148.0	14 39.3	53.7	148.1
28	16 18.9	53.0	148.2	15 27.9	53.3	148.3	14 36.8	53.5	148.4	13 45.6	53.7	148.6
29	15 25.9	53.0	148.6	14 34.6	53.3	148.8	13 43.3	53.6	148.9	12 51.9	53.8	149.0
30	14 32.9	−53.1	149.1	13 41.3	−53.3	149.3	12 49.7	−53.5	149.4	11 58.1	−53.8	149.5
31	13 39.8	53.2	149.6	12 48.0	53.4	149.7	11 56.2	53.7	149.8	11 04.3	53.9	149.9
32	12 46.6	53.1	150.1	11 54.6	53.4	150.2	11 02.5	53.6	150.3	10 10.4	53.9	150.4
33	11 53.5	53.3	150.6	11 01.2	53.5	150.7	10 08.9	53.8	150.7	9 16.5	54.0	150.8
34	11 00.2	53.3	151.0	10 07.7	53.5	151.1	9 15.1	53.7	151.2	8 22.5	53.9	151.3
35	10 06.9	−53.3	151.5	9 14.2	−53.6	151.6	8 21.4	−53.8	151.6	7 28.6	−54.0	151.7
36	9 13.6	53.3	152.0	8 20.6	53.5	152.0	7 27.6	53.8	152.1	6 34.6	54.0	152.2
37	8 20.3	53.4	152.4	7 27.1	53.7	152.5	6 33.8	53.8	152.5	5 40.6	54.1	152.6
38	7 26.9	53.5	152.9	6 33.4	53.6	152.9	5 40.0	53.8	153.0	4 46.5	54.0	153.0
39	6 33.4	53.4	153.3	5 39.8	53.6	153.4	4 46.2	53.9	153.4	3 52.5	54.1	153.5
40	5 40.0	−53.5	153.8	4 46.2	−53.7	153.8	3 52.3	−53.9	153.9	2 58.4	−54.0	153.9
41	4 46.5	53.4	154.3	3 52.5	53.7	154.3	2 58.4	53.9	154.3	2 04.4	54.1	154.3
42	3 53.1	53.5	154.7	2 58.8	53.7	154.7	2 04.5	53.9	154.8	1 10.3	54.1	154.8
43	2 59.6	53.5	155.2	2 05.1	53.7	155.2	1 10.6	53.8	155.2	0 16.2	−54.1	155.2
44	2 06.1	53.6	155.6	1 11.4	53.7	155.6	0 16.8	−53.9	155.6	0 37.9	+54.1	24.4
45	1 12.5	−53.5	156.1	0 17.7	−53.7	156.1	0 37.1	+53.9	23.9	1 32.0	+54.1	23.9
46	0 19.0	−53.5	156.5	0 36.0	+53.7	23.5	1 31.0	53.9	23.5	2 26.1	54.0	23.5
47	0 34.5	+53.5	23.0	1 29.7	53.7	23.0	2 24.9	53.9	23.0	3 20.1	54.1	23.1
48	1 28.0	53.5	22.6	2 23.4	53.7	22.6	3 18.8	53.9	22.6	4 14.2	54.0	22.6
49	2 21.5	53.5	22.1	3 17.1	53.7	22.1	4 12.7	53.8	22.2	5 08.2	54.1	22.2
50	3 15.0	+53.5	21.7	4 10.8	+53.7	21.7	5 06.5	+53.9	21.7	6 02.3	+54.0	21.8
51	4 08.5	53.5	21.2	5 04.5	53.6	21.2	6 00.4	53.8	21.3	6 56.3	54.0	21.3
52	5 02.0	53.5	20.8	5 58.1	53.6	20.8	6 54.2	53.8	20.8	7 50.3	53.9	20.9
53	5 55.5	53.4	20.3	6 51.7	53.6	20.3	7 48.0	53.7	20.4	8 44.2	53.9	20.4
54	6 48.9	53.4	19.8	7 45.3	53.6	19.9	8 41.7	53.8	19.9	9 38.1	53.9	20.0
55	7 42.3	+53.4	19.4	8 38.9	+53.5	19.4	9 35.5	+53.7	19.5	10 32.0	+53.9	19.5
56	8 35.7	53.3	18.9	9 32.4	53.5	19.0	10 29.2	53.6	19.0	11 25.9	53.8	19.1
57	9 29.0	53.4	18.5	10 25.9	53.5	18.5	11 22.8	53.6	18.6	12 19.7	53.8	18.6
58	10 22.4	53.2	18.0	11 19.4	53.4	18.1	12 16.4	53.6	18.1	13 13.5	53.7	18.2
59	11 15.6	53.2	17.5	12 12.8	53.4	17.6	13 10.0	53.5	17.7	14 07.2	53.6	17.7
60	12 08.8	+53.2	17.1	13 06.2	+53.3	17.1	14 03.5	+53.5	17.2	15 00.8	+53.6	17.3
61	13 02.0	53.1	16.6	13 59.5	53.3	16.7	14 57.0	53.4	16.7	15 54.4	53.6	16.8
62	13 55.1	53.1	16.1	14 52.8	53.2	16.2	15 50.4	53.3	16.3	16 48.0	53.5	16.3
63	14 48.2	53.0	15.6	15 46.0	53.1	15.7	16 43.7	53.3	15.8	17 41.5	53.4	15.9
64	15 41.2	53.0	15.1	16 39.1	53.1	15.2	17 37.0	53.2	15.3	18 34.9	53.3	15.4
65	16 34.2	+52.8	14.6	17 32.2	+53.0	14.7	18 30.2	+53.2	14.8	19 28.2	+53.3	14.9
66	17 27.0	52.8	14.2	18 25.2	52.9	14.2	19 23.4	53.0	14.3	20 21.5	53.2	14.4
67	18 19.8	52.8	13.7	19 18.1	52.9	13.7	20 16.4	53.0	13.8	21 14.7	53.1	13.9
68	19 12.6	52.6	13.2	20 11.0	52.7	13.2	21 09.4	52.9	13.3	22 07.8	53.0	13.4
69	20 05.2	52.6	12.6	21 03.7	52.7	12.7	22 02.3	52.7	12.8	23 00.8	52.9	12.9
70	20 57.8	+52.4	12.1	21 56.4	+52.6	12.2	22 55.0	+52.7	12.3	23 53.7	+52.7	12.4
71	21 50.2	52.4	11.6	22 49.0	52.4	11.7	23 47.7	52.6	11.8	24 46.4	52.7	11.9
72	22 42.6	52.2	11.1	23 41.4	52.4	11.2	24 40.3	52.5	11.2	25 39.1	52.6	11.3
73	23 34.8	52.2	10.5	24 33.8	52.2	10.6	25 32.8	52.3	10.7	26 31.7	52.5	10.8
74	24 27.0	52.0	10.0	25 26.0	52.2	10.1	26 25.1	52.2	10.2	27 24.2	52.3	10.3
75	25 19.0	+51.9	9.5	26 18.2	+52.0	9.5	27 17.3	+52.1	9.6	28 16.5	+52.2	9.7
76	26 10.9	51.7	8.9	27 10.2	51.8	9.0	28 09.4	52.0	9.1	29 08.7	52.0	9.1
77	27 02.6	51.7	8.3	28 02.0	51.7	8.4	29 01.4	51.8	8.5	30 00.7	51.9	8.6
78	27 54.3	51.5	7.8	28 53.7	51.6	7.8	29 53.2	51.6	7.9	30 52.6	51.7	8.0
79	28 45.8	51.3	7.2	29 45.3	51.4	7.2	30 44.8	51.5	7.3	31 44.3	51.6	7.4
80	29 37.1	+51.2	6.6	30 36.7	+51.2	6.6	31 36.3	+51.3	6.7	32 35.9	+51.4	6.8
81	30 28.3	51.0	6.0	31 27.9	51.1	6.0	32 27.6	51.1	6.1	33 27.3	51.2	6.2
82	31 19.3	50.8	5.4	32 19.0	50.9	5.4	33 18.7	51.0	5.5	34 18.5	51.0	5.5
83	32 10.1	50.6	4.7	33 09.9	50.7	4.8	34 09.7	50.7	4.8	35 09.5	50.7	4.9
84	33 00.7	50.5	4.1	34 00.6	50.5	4.1	35 00.4	50.5	4.2	36 00.2	50.6	4.3
85	33 51.2	+50.2	3.5	34 51.1	+50.2	3.5	35 50.9	+50.3	3.5	36 50.8	+50.4	3.6
86	34 41.4	50.0	2.8	35 41.3	50.1	2.8	36 41.2	50.1	2.9	37 41.2	50.1	2.9
87	35 31.4	49.8	2.1	36 31.4	49.8	2.1	37 31.3	49.8	2.2	38 31.3	49.8	2.2
88	36 21.2	49.5	1.4	37 21.2	49.5	1.4	38 21.1	49.6	1.5	39 21.1	49.6	1.5
89	37 10.7	49.3	0.7	38 10.7	49.3	0.7	39 10.7	49.3	0.7	40 10.7	49.3	0.8
90	38 00.0	+49.0	0.0	39 00.0	+49.0	0.0	40 00.0	+49.0	0.0	41 00.0	+49.0	0.0
	38°			39°			40°			41°		

42°			43°			44°			45°			Dec.
Hc	d	Z	Hc	d	Z	Hc	d	Z	Hc	d	Z	
° ′	′	°	° ′	′	°	° ′	′	°	° ′	′	°	°
37 29.9	−50.7	133.7	36 48.3	−51.2	134.2	36 06.2	−51.7	134.8	35 23.8	−52.2	135.3	0
36 39.2	50.9	134.4	35 57.1	51.4	134.9	35 14.5	51.8	135.4	34 31.6	52.3	135.9	1
35 48.3	51.2	135.0	35 05.7	51.7	135.5	34 22.7	52.1	136.0	33 39.3	52.4	136.5	2
34 57.1	51.3	135.7	34 14.0	51.7	136.1	33 30.6	52.2	136.6	32 46.9	52.7	137.1	3
34 05.8	51.5	136.3	33 22.3	52.0	136.8	32 38.4	52.4	137.2	31 54.2	52.8	137.6	4
33 14.3	−51.7	136.9	32 30.3	−52.1	137.3	31 46.0	−52.5	137.8	31 01.4	−52.9	138.2	5
32 22.6	51.9	137.5	31 38.2	52.3	137.9	30 53.5	52.7	138.3	30 08.5	53.0	138.7	6
31 30.7	52.1	138.1	30 45.9	52.5	138.5	30 00.8	52.8	138.9	29 15.5	53.2	139.3	7
30 38.6	52.2	138.7	29 53.4	52.5	139.1	29 08.0	53.0	139.4	28 22.3	53.3	139.8	8
29 46.4	52.3	139.3	29 00.9	52.8	139.6	28 15.0	53.0	140.0	27 29.0	53.5	140.3	9
28 54.1	−52.5	139.8	28 08.1	−52.8	140.2	27 22.0	−53.2	140.5	26 35.5	−53.5	140.8	10
28 01.6	52.6	140.4	27 15.3	53.0	140.7	26 28.8	53.3	141.0	25 42.0	53.6	141.3	11
27 09.0	52.7	140.9	26 22.3	53.0	141.2	25 35.5	53.4	141.5	24 48.4	53.7	141.8	12
26 16.3	52.9	141.4	25 29.3	53.2	141.7	24 42.1	53.5	142.0	23 54.7	53.9	142.3	13
25 23.4	52.9	142.0	24 36.1	53.3	142.3	23 48.6	53.6	142.5	23 00.8	53.9	142.8	14
24 30.5	−53.1	142.5	23 42.8	−53.4	142.8	22 55.0	−53.7	143.0	22 06.9	−53.9	143.3	15
23 37.4	53.1	143.0	22 49.4	53.4	143.3	22 01.3	53.8	143.5	21 13.0	54.1	143.7	16
22 44.3	53.3	143.5	21 56.0	53.6	143.7	21 07.5	53.9	144.0	20 18.9	54.1	144.2	17
21 51.0	53.3	144.0	21 02.4	53.6	144.2	20 13.6	53.9	144.5	19 24.8	54.2	144.7	18
20 57.7	53.5	144.5	20 08.8	53.8	144.7	19 19.7	54.0	144.9	18 30.6	54.3	145.1	19
20 04.2	−53.5	145.0	19 15.0	−53.7	145.2	18 25.7	−54.0	145.4	17 36.3	−54.3	145.6	20
19 10.7	53.5	145.5	18 21.3	53.9	145.7	17 31.7	54.2	145.8	16 42.0	54.4	146.0	21
18 17.2	53.7	145.9	17 27.4	53.9	146.1	16 37.5	54.1	146.3	15 47.6	54.5	146.4	22
17 23.5	53.7	146.4	16 33.5	54.0	146.6	15 43.4	54.3	146.7	14 53.1	54.4	146.9	23
16 29.8	53.8	146.9	15 39.5	54.0	147.0	14 49.1	54.3	147.2	13 58.7	54.6	147.3	24
15 36.0	−53.8	147.3	14 45.5	−54.1	147.5	13 54.8	−54.3	147.6	13 04.1	−54.5	147.7	25
14 42.2	53.9	147.8	13 51.4	54.1	147.9	13 00.5	54.4	148.1	12 09.6	54.6	148.2	26
13 48.3	53.9	148.2	12 57.3	54.2	148.4	12 06.1	54.4	148.5	11 15.0	54.7	148.6	27
12 54.4	54.0	148.7	12 03.1	54.2	148.8	11 11.7	54.4	148.9	10 20.3	54.7	149.0	28
12 00.4	54.0	149.1	11 08.9	54.3	149.2	10 17.3	54.5	149.3	9 25.6	54.7	149.4	29
11 06.4	−54.1	149.6	10 14.6	−54.3	149.7	9 22.8	−54.5	149.8	8 30.9	−54.7	149.8	30
10 12.3	54.1	150.0	9 20.3	54.3	150.1	8 28.3	54.6	150.2	7 36.2	54.8	150.3	31
9 18.2	54.1	150.5	8 26.0	54.4	150.5	7 33.7	54.5	150.6	6 41.4	54.8	150.7	32
8 24.1	54.2	150.9	7 31.6	54.3	151.0	6 39.2	54.6	151.0	5 46.6	54.8	151.1	33
7 29.9	54.2	151.3	6 37.3	54.4	151.4	5 44.6	54.6	151.5	4 51.8	54.8	151.5	34
6 35.7	−54.2	151.8	5 42.9	−54.5	151.8	4 50.0	−54.7	151.9	3 57.0	−54.8	151.9	35
5 41.5	54.2	152.2	4 48.4	54.4	152.2	3 55.3	54.6	152.3	3 02.2	54.8	152.3	36
4 47.3	54.2	152.6	3 54.0	54.4	152.7	3 00.7	54.6	152.7	2 07.4	54.9	152.7	37
3 53.1	54.3	153.1	2 59.6	54.5	153.1	2 06.1	54.7	153.1	1 12.5	54.8	153.1	38
2 58.8	54.3	153.5	2 05.1	54.5	153.5	1 11.4	54.6	153.5	0 17.7	−54.8	153.5	39
2 04.5	−54.2	153.9	1 10.6	−54.4	153.9	0 16.8	−54.7	153.9	0 37.1	+54.9	26.1	40
1 10.3	54.3	154.3	0 16.2	−54.5	154.3	0 37.9	+54.7	25.7	1 32.0	54.8	25.7	41
0 16.0	−54.3	154.8	0 38.3	+54.4	25.2	1 32.6	54.6	25.2	2 26.8	54.9	25.3	42
0 38.3	+54.3	24.8	1 32.7	54.5	24.8	2 27.2	54.6	24.8	3 21.7	54.8	24.8	43
1 32.6	54.2	24.4	2 27.2	54.5	24.4	3 21.8	54.7	24.4	4 16.5	54.8	24.4	44
2 26.8	+54.3	24.0	3 21.7	+54.4	24.0	4 16.5	+54.6	24.0	5 11.3	+54.8	24.0	45
3 21.1	54.2	23.5	4 16.1	54.4	23.5	5 11.1	54.6	23.6	6 06.1	54.7	23.6	46
4 15.3	54.3	23.1	5 10.5	54.4	23.1	6 05.7	54.6	23.2	7 00.8	54.8	23.2	47
5 09.6	54.2	22.7	6 04.9	54.4	22.7	7 00.3	54.5	22.7	7 55.6	54.7	22.8	48
6 03.8	54.2	22.2	6 59.3	54.4	22.3	7 54.8	54.6	22.3	8 50.3	54.7	22.4	49
6 58.0	+54.2	21.8	7 53.7	+54.3	21.9	8 49.4	+54.5	21.9	9 45.0	+54.7	22.0	50
7 52.2	54.1	21.4	8 48.0	54.3	21.4	9 43.9	54.4	21.5	10 39.7	54.6	21.5	51
8 46.3	54.1	20.9	9 42.3	54.3	21.0	10 38.3	54.5	21.1	11 34.3	54.6	21.1	52
9 40.4	54.1	20.5	10 36.6	54.3	20.6	11 32.8	54.4	20.6	12 28.9	54.6	20.7	53
10 34.5	54.1	20.1	11 30.9	54.2	20.1	12 27.2	54.3	20.2	13 23.5	54.5	20.3	54
11 28.6	+54.0	19.6	12 25.1	+54.1	19.7	13 21.5	+54.4	19.8	14 18.0	+54.5	19.8	55
12 22.6	53.9	19.2	13 19.2	54.1	19.2	14 15.9	54.2	19.3	15 12.5	54.4	19.4	56
13 16.5	53.9	18.7	14 13.3	54.1	18.8	15 10.1	54.2	18.9	16 06.9	54.3	19.0	57
14 10.4	53.9	18.3	15 07.4	54.0	18.4	16 04.3	54.2	18.4	17 01.2	54.3	18.5	58
15 04.3	53.8	17.8	16 01.4	54.0	17.9	16 58.5	54.1	18.0	17 55.5	54.3	18.1	59
15 58.1	+53.8	17.4	16 55.4	+53.9	17.4	17 52.6	+54.0	17.5	18 49.8	+54.2	17.6	60
16 51.9	53.7	16.9	17 49.3	53.8	17.0	18 46.6	54.0	17.1	19 44.0	54.1	17.2	61
17 45.6	53.6	16.4	18 43.1	53.7	16.5	19 40.6	53.9	16.6	20 38.1	54.0	16.7	62
18 39.2	53.5	16.0	19 36.8	53.7	16.0	20 34.5	53.8	16.1	21 32.1	54.0	16.3	63
19 32.7	53.5	15.5	20 30.5	53.6	15.6	21 28.3	53.8	15.7	22 26.1	53.8	15.8	64
20 26.2	+53.4	15.0	21 24.1	+53.6	15.1	22 22.1	+53.6	15.2	23 19.9	+53.8	15.3	65
21 19.6	53.3	14.5	22 17.7	53.4	14.6	23 15.7	53.6	14.7	24 13.7	53.7	14.8	66
22 12.9	53.2	14.0	23 11.1	53.3	14.1	24 09.3	53.4	14.2	25 07.4	53.6	14.3	67
23 06.1	53.1	13.5	24 04.4	53.3	13.6	25 02.7	53.4	13.7	26 01.0	53.5	13.8	68
23 59.2	53.0	13.0	24 57.7	53.1	13.1	25 56.1	53.3	13.2	26 54.5	53.4	13.3	69
24 52.2	+53.0	12.5	25 50.8	+53.0	12.6	26 49.4	+53.1	12.7	27 47.9	+53.2	12.8	70
25 45.2	52.8	12.0	26 43.8	53.0	12.1	27 42.5	53.0	12.2	28 41.1	53.2	12.3	71
26 38.0	52.6	11.4	27 36.8	52.7	11.5	28 35.5	52.9	11.6	29 34.3	53.0	11.8	72
27 30.6	52.6	10.9	28 29.5	52.7	11.0	29 28.4	52.8	11.1	30 27.3	52.9	11.2	73
28 23.2	52.4	10.4	29 22.2	52.5	10.5	30 21.2	52.6	10.6	31 20.2	52.7	10.7	74
29 15.6	+52.3	9.8	30 14.7	+52.4	9.9	31 13.8	+52.5	10.0	32 12.9	+52.6	10.1	75
30 07.9	52.1	9.2	31 07.1	52.2	9.3	32 06.3	52.3	9.4	33 05.5	52.4	9.5	76
31 00.0	52.0	8.7	31 59.3	52.1	8.8	32 58.6	52.2	8.8	33 57.9	52.2	8.9	77
31 52.0	51.8	8.1	32 51.4	51.9	8.2	33 50.8	52.0	8.3	34 50.1	52.1	8.4	78
32 43.8	51.6	7.5	33 43.3	51.7	7.6	34 42.8	51.8	7.7	35 42.2	51.9	7.7	79
33 35.4	+51.5	6.9	34 35.0	+51.5	6.9	35 34.6	+51.6	7.0	36 34.1	+51.7	7.1	80
34 26.9	51.3	6.2	35 26.5	51.4	6.3	36 26.2	51.4	6.4	37 25.8	51.5	6.5	81
35 18.2	51.0	5.6	36 17.9	51.1	5.7	37 17.6	51.2	5.8	38 17.3	51.2	5.8	82
36 09.2	50.9	5.0	37 09.0	50.9	5.0	38 08.8	50.9	5.1	39 08.5	51.1	5.2	83
37 00.1	50.6	4.3	37 59.9	50.7	4.4	38 59.7	50.8	4.4	39 59.6	50.7	4.5	84
37 50.7	+50.4	3.6	38 50.6	+50.4	3.7	39 50.5	+50.4	3.7	40 50.3	+50.5	3.8	85
38 41.1	50.1	2.9	39 41.0	50.2	3.0	40 40.9	50.2	3.0	41 40.8	50.3	3.1	86
39 31.2	49.9	2.2	40 31.2	49.9	2.3	41 31.1	50.0	2.3	42 31.1	49.9	2.3	87
40 21.1	49.6	1.5	41 21.1	49.6	1.5	42 21.1	49.6	1.6	43 21.0	49.7	1.6	88
41 10.7	49.3	0.8	42 10.7	49.3	0.8	43 10.7	49.3	0.8	44 10.7	49.3	0.8	89
42 00.0	+49.0	0.0	43 00.0	+49.0	0.0	44 00.0	+49.0	0.0	45 00.0	+49.0	0.0	90
42°			43°			44°			45°			

S. Lat. { L.H.A. greater than 180°......Zn=180°−Z
L.H.A. less than 180°............Zn=180°+Z

LATITUDE SAME NAME AS DECLINATION L.H.A. 145°, 215°

LATITUDE CONTRARY NAME TO DECLINATION   L.H.A. 46°, 314°

Dec.	38°			39°			40°			41°			42°			43°			44°			45°			Dec.
	Hc	d	Z	Hc	d	Z	Hc	d	Z	Hc	d	Z	Hc	d	Z	Hc	d	Z	Hc	d	Z	Hc	d	Z	
°	° ′	′	°	° ′	′	°	° ′	′	°	° ′	′	°	° ′	′	°	° ′	′	°	° ′	′	°	° ′	′	°	°
0	33 11.3	−44.3	120.7	32 40.4	−45.0	121.3	32 09.0	−45.7	121.8	31 37.1	−46.3	122.4	31 04.8	−47.0	122.9	30 32.0	−47.6	123.4	29 58.8	−48.2	123.9	29 25.2	−48.8	124.3	0
1	32 27.0	44.6	121.5	31 55.4	45.3	122.1	31 23.3	45.9	122.6	30 50.8	46.6	123.1	30 17.8	47.2	123.6	29 44.4	47.9	124.1	29 10.6	48.5	124.5	28 36.4	49.0	125.0	1
2	31 42.4	44.9	122.3	31 10.1	45.5	122.8	30 37.4	46.2	123.3	30 04.2	46.9	123.8	29 30.6	47.5	124.3	28 56.5	48.0	124.8	28 22.1	48.6	125.2	27 47.4	49.2	125.6	2
3	30 57.5	45.1	123.1	30 24.6	45.9	123.6	29 51.2	46.5	124.1	29 17.3	47.0	124.5	28 43.1	47.7	125.0	28 08.5	48.3	125.4	27 33.5	48.8	125.9	26 58.2	49.4	126.3	3
4	30 12.4	45.4	123.9	29 38.7	46.0	124.3	29 04.7	46.7	124.8	28 30.3	47.3	125.3	27 55.4	47.8	125.7	27 20.2	48.4	126.1	26 44.7	49.0	126.5	26 08.8	49.5	126.9	4
5	29 27.0	−45.7	124.6	28 52.7	−46.3	125.1	28 18.0	−46.9	125.5	27 43.0	−47.5	126.0	27 07.6	−48.1	126.4	26 31.8	−48.6	126.8	25 55.7	−49.1	127.2	25 19.3	−49.7	127.6	5
6	28 41.3	45.9	125.4	28 06.4	46.5	125.8	27 31.1	47.1	126.2	26 55.5	47.7	126.6	26 19.5	48.3	127.0	25 43.2	48.8	127.4	25 06.6	49.4	127.8	24 29.6	49.8	128.2	6
7	27 55.4	46.1	126.1	27 19.9	46.8	126.5	26 44.0	47.3	126.9	26 07.8	47.9	127.3	25 31.2	48.4	127.7	24 54.4	49.0	128.1	24 17.2	49.4	128.4	23 39.8	50.0	128.8	7
8	27 09.3	46.4	126.8	26 33.1	46.9	127.2	25 56.7	47.5	127.6	25 19.9	48.1	128.0	24 42.8	48.6	128.4	24 05.4	49.1	128.7	23 27.8	49.6	129.1	22 49.8	50.1	129.4	8
9	26 22.9	46.6	127.5	25 46.2	47.1	127.9	25 09.2	47.7	128.3	24 31.8	48.2	128.7	23 54.2	48.7	129.0	23 16.3	49.2	129.3	22 38.2	49.8	129.7	21 59.7	50.2	130.0	9
10	25 36.3	−46.7	128.2	24 59.1	−47.4	128.6	24 21.5	−47.9	129.0	23 43.6	−48.4	129.3	23 05.5	−48.9	129.6	22 27.1	−49.4	130.0	21 48.4	−49.9	130.3	21 09.5	−50.3	130.6	10
11	24 49.6	47.0	128.9	24 11.7	47.5	129.3	23 33.6	48.0	129.6	22 55.2	48.5	129.9	22 16.6	49.1	130.3	21 37.7	49.6	130.6	20 58.5	50.0	130.9	20 19.2	50.5	131.2	11
12	24 02.6	47.1	129.6	23 24.2	47.6	129.9	22 45.6	48.2	130.3	22 06.7	48.7	130.6	21 27.5	49.2	130.9	20 48.1	49.6	131.2	20 08.5	50.1	131.5	19 28.7	50.6	131.7	12
13	23 15.5	47.3	130.3	22 36.6	47.9	130.6	21 57.4	48.3	130.9	21 18.0	48.8	131.2	20 38.3	49.3	131.5	19 58.5	49.8	131.8	19 18.4	50.2	132.0	18 38.1	50.7	132.3	13
14	22 28.2	47.5	130.9	21 48.7	47.9	131.3	21 09.1	48.5	131.5	20 29.2	49.0	131.8	19 49.0	49.4	132.1	19 08.7	49.9	132.4	18 28.2	50.4	132.6	17 47.4	50.7	132.9	14
15	21 40.7	−47.6	131.6	21 00.8	−48.2	131.9	20 20.6	−48.6	132.2	19 40.2	−49.1	132.4	18 59.6	−49.5	132.7	18 18.8	−50.0	133.0	17 37.8	−50.4	133.2	16 56.7	−50.9	133.4	15
16	20 53.1	47.8	132.3	20 12.6	48.2	132.5	19 32.0	48.8	132.8	18 51.1	49.2	133.1	18 10.1	49.7	133.3	17 28.8	50.1	133.5	16 47.4	50.5	133.8	16 05.8	50.9	134.0	16
17	20 05.3	47.9	132.9	19 24.4	48.4	133.2	18 43.2	48.8	133.4	18 01.9	49.3	133.7	17 20.4	49.8	133.9	16 38.7	50.2	134.1	15 56.9	50.6	134.3	15 14.9	51.0	134.5	17
18	19 17.4	48.0	133.5	18 36.0	48.5	133.8	17 54.4	49.0	134.0	17 12.6	49.4	134.3	16 30.6	49.8	134.5	15 48.5	50.3	134.7	15 06.3	50.7	134.9	14 23.9	51.1	135.1	18
19	18 29.4	48.2	134.2	17 47.5	48.6	134.4	17 05.4	49.1	134.6	16 23.2	49.5	134.9	15 40.8	50.0	135.1	14 58.2	50.3	135.2	14 15.6	50.8	135.4	13 32.8	51.2	135.6	19
20	17 41.2	−48.3	134.8	16 58.9	−48.8	135.0	16 16.3	−49.1	135.2	15 33.7	−49.7	135.4	14 50.8	−50.0	135.6	14 07.9	−50.5	135.8	13 24.8	−50.8	136.0	12 41.6	−51.2	136.1	20
21	16 52.9	48.4	135.4	16 10.1	48.8	135.6	15 27.2	49.3	135.8	14 44.0	49.7	136.0	14 00.8	50.1	136.2	13 17.4	50.5	136.4	12 34.0	51.0	136.5	11 50.4	51.3	136.7	21
22	16 04.5	48.5	136.0	15 21.3	49.0	136.2	14 37.9	49.4	136.4	13 54.3	49.7	136.6	13 10.7	50.2	136.8	12 26.9	50.6	136.9	11 43.0	50.9	137.1	10 59.1	51.4	137.2	22
23	15 16.0	48.6	136.7	14 32.3	49.0	136.8	13 48.5	49.4	137.0	13 04.6	49.9	137.2	12 20.5	50.2	137.3	11 36.3	50.6	137.5	10 52.1	51.0	137.6	10 07.7	51.4	137.7	23
24	14 27.4	48.6	137.3	13 43.3	49.1	137.4	12 59.1	49.6	137.6	12 14.7	49.9	137.7	11 30.3	50.4	137.9	10 45.7	50.7	138.0	10 01.1	51.1	138.1	9 16.3	51.4	138.3	24
25	13 38.8	−48.8	137.9	12 54.2	−49.2	138.0	12 09.5	−49.5	138.2	11 24.8	−50.0	138.3	10 39.9	−50.3	138.4	9 55.0	−50.7	138.6	9 10.0	−51.1	138.7	8 24.9	−51.5	138.8	25
26	12 50.0	48.9	138.5	12 05.0	49.2	138.6	11 20.0	49.7	138.7	10 34.8	50.0	138.9	9 49.6	50.5	139.0	9 04.3	50.8	139.1	8 18.9	51.2	139.2	7 33.4	51.5	139.3	26
27	12 01.1	48.9	139.1	11 15.8	49.4	139.2	10 30.3	49.7	139.3	9 44.8	50.1	139.4	8 59.1	50.4	139.5	8 13.5	50.9	139.6	7 27.7	51.2	139.7	6 41.9	51.6	139.8	27
28	11 12.2	49.0	139.6	10 26.4	49.4	139.8	9 40.6	49.8	139.9	8 54.7	50.2	140.0	8 08.7	50.6	140.1	7 22.6	50.9	140.2	6 36.5	51.2	140.3	5 50.3	51.5	140.3	28
29	10 23.2	49.1	140.2	9 37.0	49.4	140.3	8 50.8	49.8	140.5	8 04.5	50.2	140.5	7 18.1	50.5	140.6	6 31.7	50.9	140.7	5 45.3	51.3	140.8	4 58.8	51.6	140.8	29
30	9 34.1	−49.1	140.8	8 47.6	−49.5	140.9	8 01.0	−49.9	141.0	7 14.3	−50.2	141.1	6 27.6	−50.6	141.2	5 40.8	−50.9	141.2	4 54.0	−51.3	141.3	4 07.2	−51.7	141.3	30
31	8 45.0	49.2	141.4	7 58.1	49.6	141.5	7 11.1	49.9	141.6	6 24.1	50.3	141.7	5 37.0	50.6	141.7	4 49.9	51.0	141.8	4 02.7	51.3	141.8	3 15.5	51.6	141.9	31
32	7 55.8	49.2	142.0	7 08.5	49.6	142.1	6 21.2	50.0	142.1	5 33.8	50.3	142.2	4 46.4	50.7	142.3	3 58.9	51.0	142.3	3 11.4	51.3	142.3	2 23.9	51.6	142.4	32
33	7 06.6	49.3	142.6	6 18.9	49.6	142.6	5 31.2	49.9	142.7	4 43.5	50.3	142.7	3 55.7	50.7	142.8	3 07.9	51.0	142.8	2 20.1	51.3	142.9	1 32.3	51.7	142.9	33
34	6 17.3	49.3	143.1	5 29.3	49.7	143.2	4 41.3	50.1	143.2	3 53.2	50.4	143.3	3 05.0	50.6	143.3	2 16.9	51.0	143.4	1 28.8	51.4	143.4	0 40.6	−51.6	143.4	34
35	5 28.0	−49.3	143.7	4 39.6	−49.6	143.8	3 51.2	−50.0	143.8	3 02.8	−50.4	143.8	2 14.4	−50.7	143.9	1 25.9	−51.0	143.9	0 37.4	−51.3	143.9	0 11.0	+51.7	36.1	35
36	4 38.7	49.4	144.3	3 50.0	49.7	144.3	3 01.2	50.0	144.4	2 12.4	50.3	144.4	1 23.7	50.7	144.4	0 34.9	−51.0	144.4	0 13.9	+51.4	35.6	1 02.7	51.7	35.6	36
37	3 49.3	49.4	144.8	3 00.3	49.8	144.9	2 11.2	50.1	144.9	1 22.1	50.4	144.9	0 33.0	−50.7	144.9	0 16.1	+51.1	35.1	1 05.3	51.3	35.1	1 54.4	51.6	35.1	37
38	2 59.9	49.4	145.4	2 10.5	49.7	145.4	1 21.1	50.1	145.5	0 31.7	−50.4	145.5	0 17.7	+50.8	34.5	1 07.2	51.0	34.5	1 56.6	51.3	34.6	2 46.0	51.6	34.6	38
39	2 10.5	49.4	146.0	1 20.8	49.8	146.0	0 31.0	−50.0	146.0	0 18.7	+50.4	34.0	1 08.5	50.6	34.0	1 58.2	51.0	34.0	2 47.9	51.3	34.0	3 37.6	51.6	34.1	39
40	1 21.1	−49.4	146.6	0 31.0	−49.7	146.6	0 19.0	+50.1	33.4	1 09.1	+50.4	33.4	1 59.1	+50.7	33.5	2 49.2	+51.0	33.5	3 39.2	+51.3	33.5	4 29.2	+51.6	33.6	40
41	0 31.7	−49.4	147.1	0 18.7	+49.8	32.9	1 09.1	50.0	32.9	1 59.5	50.3	32.9	2 49.8	50.7	32.9	3 40.2	51.0	33.0	4 30.5	51.3	33.0	5 20.8	51.6	33.0	41
42	0 17.7	+49.5	32.3	1 08.5	49.7	32.3	1 59.1	50.1	32.3	2 49.8	50.4	32.4	3 40.5	50.7	32.4	4 31.2	50.9	32.4	5 21.8	51.2	32.5	6 12.4	51.5	32.5	42
43	1 07.2	49.4	31.7	1 58.2	49.7	31.8	2 49.2	50.0	31.8	3 40.2	50.3	31.8	4 31.2	50.6	31.9	5 22.1	50.9	31.9	6 13.0	51.3	32.0	7 03.9	51.5	32.0	43
44	1 56.6	49.4	31.2	2 47.9	49.7	31.2	3 39.2	50.0	31.2	4 30.5	50.3	31.3	5 21.8	50.6	31.3	6 13.0	50.9	31.4	7 04.3	51.1	31.4	7 55.4	51.5	31.5	44
45	2 46.0	+49.4	30.6	3 37.6	+49.7	30.6	4 29.2	+50.0	30.7	5 20.8	+50.3	30.7	6 12.4	+50.6	30.8	7 03.9	+50.9	30.8	7 55.4	+51.2	30.9	8 46.9	+51.4	31.0	45
46	3 35.4	49.4	30.0	4 27.3	49.7	30.1	5 19.2	50.0	30.1	6 11.1	50.3	30.2	7 03.0	50.5	30.2	7 54.8	50.8	30.3	8 46.6	51.1	30.4	9 38.3	51.4	30.5	46
47	4 24.8	49.3	29.5	5 17.0	49.6	29.5	6 09.2	49.9	29.6	7 01.4	50.2	29.6	7 53.5	50.5	29.7	8 45.6	50.8	29.8	9 37.7	51.0	29.8	10 29.7	51.3	29.9	47
48	5 14.1	49.3	28.9	6 06.6	49.6	29.0	6 59.1	49.9	29.0	7 51.6	50.1	29.1	8 44.0	50.4	29.1	9 36.4	50.7	29.2	10 28.7	51.0	29.3	11 21.0	51.3	29.4	48
49	6 03.4	49.3	28.3	6 56.2	49.6	28.4	7 49.0	49.8	28.4	8 41.7	50.2	28.5	9 34.4	50.4	28.6	10 27.1	50.7	28.7	11 19.7	51.0	28.8	12 12.3	51.2	28.9	49
50	6 52.7	+49.2	27.8	7 45.8	+49.5	27.8	8 38.8	+49.8	27.9	9 31.9	+50.0	28.0	10 24.8	+50.4	28.0	11 17.8	+50.6	28.1	12 10.7	+50.8	28.2	13 03.5	+51.1	28.3	50
51	7 41.9	49.2	27.2	8 35.3	49.5	27.2	9 28.6	49.8	27.3	10 21.9	50.0	27.4	11 15.2	50.2	27.5	12 08.4	50.5	27.6	13 01.5	50.8	27.7	13 54.6	51.1	27.8	51
52	8 31.1	49.2	26.6	9 24.8	49.4	26.7	10 18.4	49.6	26.8	11 11.9	50.0	26.8	12 05.4	50.2	26.9	12 58.9	50.5	27.0	13 52.3	50.8	27.1	14 45.7	51.0	27.3	52
53	9 20.3	49.1	26.0	10 14.2	49.3	26.1	11 08.0	49.6	26.2	12 01.9	49.8	26.3	12 55.6	50.2	26.4	13 49.4	50.4	26.5	14 43.1	50.6	26.6	15 36.7	50.9	26.7	53
54	10 09.4	49.0	25.4	11 03.5	49.3	25.5	11 57.6	49.6	25.6	12 51.7	49.8	25.7	13 45.8	50.0	25.8	14 39.8	50.3	25.9	15 33.7	50.6	26.0	16 27.6	50.8	26.2	54
55	10 58.4	+48.9	24.9	11 52.8	+49.2	24.9	12 47.2	+49.5	25.0	13 41.5	+49.8	25.1	14 35.8	+50.0	25.2	15 30.1	+50.2	25.4	16 24.3	+50.4	25.5	17 18.4	+50.7	25.6	55
56	11 47.3	48.9	24.3	12 42.0	49.1	24.4	13 36.7	49.3	24.4	14 31.3	49.6	24.6	15 25.8	49.9	24.7	16 20.3	50.1	24.8	17 14.7	50.4	24.9	18 09.1	50.7	25.0	56
57	12 36.2	48.8	23.7	13 31.1	49.1	23.8	14 26.0	49.3	23.9	15 20.9	49.5	24.0	16 15.7	49.8	24.1	17 10.4	50.1	24.2	18 05.1	50.3	24.3	18 59.8	50.5	24.5	57
58	13 25.0	48.7	23.1	14 20.2	48.9	23.2	15 15.3	49.2	23.3	16 10.4	49.5	23.4	17 05.5	49.7	23.5	18 00.5	49.9	23.6	18 55.4	50.2	23.8	19 50.3	50.4	23.9	58
59	14 13.7	48.7	22.5	15 09.1	48.9	22.6	16 04.5	49.1	22.7	16 59.9	49.3	22.8	17 55.2	49.5	22.9	18 50.4	49.8	23.0	19 45.6	50.0	23.2	20 40.7	50.3	23.3	59
60	15 02.4	+48.5	21.9	15 58.0	+48.8	22.0	16 53.6	+49.0	22.1	17 49.2	+49.2	22.2	18 44.7	+49.5	22.3	19 40.2	+49.7	22.5	20 35.6	+50.0	22.6	21 31.0	+50.2	22.7	60
61	15 50.9	48.4	21.3	16 46.8	48.6	21.4	17 42.6	48.9	21.5	18 38.4	49.2	21.6	19 34.2	49.4	21.7	20 29.9	49.6	21.9	21 25.6	49.8	22.0	22 21.2	50.0	22.2	61
62	16 39.3	48.3	20.6	17 35.4	48.6	20.7	18 31.5	48.8	20.9	19 27.6	49.0	21.0	20 23.6	49.2	21.1	21 19.5	49.5	21.3	22 15.4	49.7	21.4	23 11.2	49.9	21.6	62
63	17 27.6	48.2	20.0	18 24.0	48.4	20.1	19 20.3	48.6	20.2	20 16.6	48.8	20.4	21 12.8	49.1	20.5	22 09.0	49.3	20.6	23 05.1	49.5	20.8	24 01.1	49.8	20.9	63
64	18 15.8	48.1	19.4	19 12.4	48.3	19.5	20 08.9	48.5	19.6	21 05.4	48.7	19.8	22 01.9	48.9	19.9	22 58.3	49.1	20.0	23 54.6	49.4	20.2	24 50.9	49.6	20.3	64
65	19 03.9	+47.9	18.8	20 00.7	+48.1	18.9	20 57.4	+48.4	19.0	21 54.1	+48.6	19.1	22 50.8	+48.8	19.3	23 47.4	+49.0	19.4	24 44.0	+49.2	19.6	25 40.5	+49.5	19.7	65
66	19 51.8	47.8	18.1	20 48.8	48.1	18.2	21 45.8	48.2	18.4	22 42.7	48.5	18.5	23 39.6	48.7	18.6	24 36.4	48.9	18.8	25 33.2	49.1	18.9	26 30.0	49.2	19.1	66
67	20 39.6	47.7	17.5	21 36.9	47.8	17.6	22 34.0	48.1	17.7	23 31.2	48.2	17.9	24 28.3	48.4	18.0	25 25.3	48.7	18.1	26 22.3	48.9	18.3	27 19.2	49.1	18.4	67
68	21 27.3	47.5	16.8	22 24.7	47.7	16.9	23 22.1	47.9	17.1	24 19.4	48.1	17.2	25 16.7	48.3	17.3	26 14.0	48.5	17.5	27 11.2	48.7	17.6	28 08.3	49.0	17.8	68
69	22 14.8	47.4	16.2	23 12.4	47.6	16.3	24 10.0	47.7	16.4	25 07.5	48.0	16.5	26 05.0	48.2	16.7	27 02.5	48.3	16.8	27 59.9	48.5	17.0	28 57.3	48.7	17.1	69
70	23 02.2	+47.1	15.5	24 00.0	+47.3	15.6	24 57.7	+47.6	15.7	25 55.5	+47.7	15.9	26 53.2	+47.9	16.0	27 50.8	+48.1	16.2	28 48.4	+48.3	16.3	29 46.0	+48.5	16.5	70
71	23 49.3	47.1	14.8	24 47.3	47.2	14.9	25 45.3	47.3	15.1	26 43.2	47.6	15.2	27 41.1	47.7	15.3	28 38.9	47.9	15.5	29 36.7	48.1	15.6	30 34.5	48.3	15.8	71
72	24 36.4	46.8	14.2	25 34.5	47.0	14.3	26 32.6	47.2	14.4	27 30.8	47.3	14.5	28 28.8	47.5	14.6	29 26.8	47.8	14.8	30 24.8	47.9	14.9	31 22.8	48.1	15.1	72
73	25 23.2	46.6	13.5	26 21.5	46.8	13.6	27 19.8	47.0	13.7	28 18.1	47.1	13.8	29 16.3	47.3	14.0	30 14.6	47.4	14.1	31 12.7	47.7	14.2	32 10.9	47.8	14.4	73
74	26 09.8	46.4	12.8	27 08.3	46.6	12.9	28 06.8	46.7	13.0	29 05.2	46.9	13.1	30 03.6	47.1	13.2	31 02.0	47.3	13.4	32 00.4	47.4	13.5	32 58.7	47.6	13.7	74
75	26 56.2	+46.2	12.1	27 54.9	+46.3	12.2	28 53.5	+46.5	12.3	29 52.1	+46.7	12.4	30 50.7	+46.8	12.5	31 49.3	+47.0	12.7	32 47.8	+47.1	12.8	33 46.3	+47.3	12.9	75
76	27 42.4	46.0	11.3	28 41.2	46.1	11.4	29 40.0	46.3	11.6	30 38.8	46.4	11.7	31 37.5	46.6	11.8	32 36.3	46.7	11.9	33 34.9	46.9	12.1	34 33.6	47.1	12.2	76
77	28 28.4	45.7	10.6	29 27.3	45.9	10.7	30 26.3	46.0	10.8	31 25.2	46.2	10.9	32 24.1	46.3	11.0	33 23.0	46.4	11.2	34 21.8	46.6	11.3	35 20.7	46.7	11.4	77
78	29 14.1	45.5	9.9	30 13.2	45.6	10.0	31 12.3	45.8	10.1	32 11.4	45.9	10.2	33 10.4	46.0	10.3	34 09.4	46.2	10.4	35 08.4	46.4	10.5	36 07.4	46.5	10.7	78
79	29 59.6	45.2	9.1	30 58.8	45.4	9.2	31 58.1	45.4	9.3	32 57.3	45.6	9.4	33 56.4	45.8	9.5	34 55.6	45.9	9.6	35 54.8	46.0	9.8	36 53.9	46.1	9.9	79
80	30 44.8	+45.0	8.4	31 44.2	+45.1	8.4	32 43.5	+45.2	8.5	33 42.9	+45.3	8.6	34 42.2	+45.4	8.7	35 41.5	+45.5	8.8	36 40.8	+45.6	9.0	37 40.0	+45.8	9.1	80
81	31 29.8	44.7	7.6	32 29.3	44.8	7.7	33 28.7	44.9	7.8	34 28.2	45.0	7.8	35 27.6	45.1	7.9	36 27.0	45.2	8.0	37 26.4	45.4	8.1	38 25.8	45.5	8.3	81
82	32 14.5	44.4	6.8	33 14.1	44.4	6.9	34 13.6	44.6	7.0	35 13.2	44.6	7.0	36 12.7	44.8	7.1	37 12.2	44.9	7.2	38 11.8	44.9	7.3	39 11.3	45.1	7.4	82
83	32 58.9	44.0	6.0	33 58.5	44.2	6.1	34 58.2	44.2	6.1	35 57.8	44.4	6.2	36 57.5	44.4	6.3	37 57.1	44.5	6.4	38 56.7	44.6	6.5	39 56.4	44.7	6.6	83
84	33 42.9	43.8	5.2	34 42.7	43.8	5.2	35 42.4	43.9	5.3	36 42.2	43.9	5.4	37 41.9	44.0	5.5	38 41.6	44.2	5.5	39 41.3	44.3	5.6	40 41.1	44.2	5.7	84
85	34 26.7	+43.4	4.4	35 26.5	+43.5	4.4	36 26.3	+43.6	4.5	37 26.1	+43.6	4.5	38 25.9	+43.7	4.6	39 25.8	+43.7	4.7	40 25.6	+43.7	4.7	41 25.3	+43.9	4.8	85
86	35 10.1	43.0	3.5	36 10.0	43.1	3.6	37 09.9	43.1	3.6	38 09.7	43.2	3.7	39 09.6	43.3	3.7	40 09.5	43.3	3.8	41 09.3	43.4	3.8	42 09.2	43.4	3.9	86
87	35 53.1	42.7	2.7	36 53.1	42.7	2.7	37 53.0	42.8	2.7	38 52.9	42.8	2.8	39 52.9	42.8	2.8	40 52.8	42.9	2.9	41 52.7	42.9	2.9	42 52.6	43.0	2.9	87
88	36 35.8	42.3	1.8	37 35.8	42.3	1.8	38 35.8	42.3	1.8	39 35.7	42.4	1.9	40 35.7	42.4	1.9	41 35.7	42.4	1.9	42 35.6	42.5	2.0	43 35.6	42.5	2.0	88
89	37 18.1	41.9	0.9	38 18.1	41.9	0.9	39 18.1	41.9	0.9	40 18.1	41.9	0.9	41 18.1	41.9	1.0	42 18.1	41.9	1.0	43 18.1	41.9	1.0	44 18.1	41.9	1.0	89
90	38 00.0	+41.5	0.0	39 00.0	+41.5	0.0	40 00.0	+41.4	0.0	41 00.0	+41.4	0.0	42 00.0	+41.4	0.0	43 00.0	+41.4	0.0	44 00.0	+41.4	0.0	45 00.0	+41.4	0.0	90
	38°			39°			40°			41°			42°			43°			44°			45°			

S. Lat. { L.H.A. greater than 180°......Zn=180°−Z
L.H.A. less than 180°............Zn=180°+Z

LATITUDE SAME NAME AS DECLINATION   L.H.A. 134°, 226°

LATITUDE CONTRARY NAME TO DECLINATION L.H.A. 62°, 298°

Dec.	38°			39°			40°			41°		
	Hc	d	Z	Hc	d	Z	Hc	d	Z	Hc	d	Z
°	° ′	′	°	° ′	′	°	° ′	′	°	° ′	′	°
0	21 42.7	−39.8	108.1	21 23.9	−40.7	108.5	21 04.7	−41.5	108.9	20 45.1	−42.2	109.2
1	21 02.9	40.1	108.9	20 43.2	40.8	109.3	20 23.2	41.6	109.6	20 02.9	42.4	110.0
2	20 22.8	40.3	109.7	20 02.4	41.1	110.1	19 41.6	41.8	110.4	19 20.5	42.6	110.7
3	19 42.5	40.6	110.5	19 21.3	41.3	110.8	18 59.8	42.1	111.2	18 37.9	42.7	111.5
4	19 01.9	40.7	111.3	18 40.0	41.5	111.6	18 17.7	42.2	111.9	17 55.2	42.9	112.2
5	18 21.2	−40.9	112.1	17 58.5	−41.6	112.4	17 35.5	−42.3	112.7	17 12.3	−43.1	113.0
6	17 40.3	41.1	112.8	17 16.9	41.8	113.1	16 53.2	42.5	113.4	16 29.2	43.2	113.7
7	16 59.2	41.2	113.6	16 35.1	42.0	113.9	16 10.7	42.7	114.1	15 46.0	43.4	114.4
8	16 18.0	41.4	114.4	15 53.1	42.1	114.6	15 28.0	42.8	114.9	15 02.6	43.5	115.1
9	15 36.6	41.6	115.1	15 11.0	42.3	115.4	14 45.2	43.0	115.6	14 19.1	43.6	115.8
10	14 55.0	−41.7	115.9	14 28.7	−42.4	116.1	14 02.2	−43.0	116.3	13 35.5	−43.7	116.5
11	14 13.3	41.8	116.6	13 46.3	42.5	116.8	13 19.2	43.2	117.0	12 51.8	43.9	117.2
12	13 31.5	42.0	117.3	13 03.8	42.6	117.6	12 36.0	43.3	117.8	12 07.9	43.9	117.9
13	12 49.5	42.1	118.1	12 21.2	42.8	118.3	11 52.7	43.5	118.5	11 24.0	44.1	118.6
14	12 07.4	42.2	118.8	11 38.4	42.9	119.0	11 09.2	43.5	119.2	10 39.9	44.1	119.3
15	11 25.2	−42.3	119.5	10 55.5	−42.9	119.7	10 25.7	−43.6	119.9	9 55.8	−44.2	120.0
16	10 42.9	42.4	120.3	10 12.6	43.1	120.4	9 42.1	43.7	120.6	9 11.6	44.3	120.7
17	10 00.5	42.5	121.0	9 29.5	43.1	121.1	8 58.4	43.7	121.3	8 27.3	44.4	121.4
18	9 18.0	42.6	121.7	8 46.4	43.2	121.8	8 14.7	43.8	122.0	7 42.9	44.5	122.1
19	8 35.4	42.7	122.4	8 03.2	43.3	122.5	7 30.9	43.9	122.6	6 58.4	44.5	122.7
20	7 52.7	−42.7	123.1	7 19.9	−43.4	123.2	6 47.0	−44.0	123.3	6 13.9	−44.5	123.4
21	7 10.0	42.8	123.8	6 36.5	43.4	123.9	6 03.0	44.0	124.0	5 29.4	44.6	124.1
22	6 27.2	42.9	124.5	5 53.1	43.5	124.6	5 19.0	44.1	124.7	4 44.8	44.6	124.8
23	5 44.3	42.9	125.2	5 09.6	43.5	125.3	4 34.9	44.1	125.4	4 00.2	44.7	125.4
24	5 01.4	43.0	125.9	4 26.1	43.5	126.0	3 50.8	44.1	126.1	3 15.5	44.7	126.1
25	4 18.4	−43.0	126.6	3 42.6	−43.6	126.7	3 06.7	−44.1	126.7	2 30.8	−44.7	126.8
26	3 35.4	43.0	127.3	2 59.0	43.6	127.4	2 22.6	44.2	127.4	1 46.1	44.7	127.4
27	2 52.4	43.1	128.0	2 15.4	43.6	128.1	1 38.4	44.2	128.1	1 01.4	44.8	128.1
28	2 09.3	43.1	128.7	1 31.8	43.7	128.8	0 54.2	44.2	128.8	0 16.6	−44.7	128.8
29	1 26.2	43.0	129.4	0 48.1	43.6	129.4	0 10.0	−44.2	129.4	0 28.1	+44.7	50.6
30	0 43.2	−43.1	130.1	0 04.5	−43.7	130.1	0 34.2	+44.2	49.9	1 12.8	+44.8	49.9
31	0 00.1	−43.1	130.8	0 39.2	+43.6	49.2	1 18.4	44.1	49.2	1 57.6	44.7	49.2
32	0 43.0	+43.1	48.5	1 22.8	43.6	48.5	2 02.5	44.2	48.5	2 42.3	44.6	48.6
33	1 26.1	43.1	47.8	2 06.4	43.6	47.8	2 46.7	44.1	47.8	3 26.9	44.7	47.9
34	2 09.2	43.1	47.1	2 50.0	43.6	47.1	3 30.8	44.1	47.2	4 11.6	44.6	47.2
35	2 52.3	+43.0	46.4	3 33.6	+43.6	46.4	4 14.9	+44.1	46.5	4 56.2	+44.6	46.5
36	3 35.3	43.0	45.7	4 17.2	43.5	45.8	4 59.0	44.0	45.8	5 40.8	44.5	45.9
37	4 18.3	42.9	45.0	5 00.7	43.5	45.1	5 43.0	44.0	45.1	6 25.3	44.5	45.2
38	5 01.2	43.0	44.3	5 44.2	43.4	44.4	6 27.0	43.9	44.4	7 09.8	44.5	44.5
39	5 44.2	42.8	43.6	6 27.6	43.3	43.7	7 10.9	43.9	43.8	7 54.3	44.3	43.8
40	6 27.0	+42.8	42.9	7 10.9	+43.4	43.0	7 54.8	+43.8	43.1	8 38.6	+44.3	43.2
41	7 09.8	42.8	42.2	7 54.3	43.2	42.3	8 38.6	43.7	42.4	9 22.9	44.2	42.5
42	7 52.6	42.6	41.5	8 37.5	43.1	41.6	9 22.3	43.7	41.7	10 07.1	44.1	41.8
43	8 35.2	42.6	40.8	9 20.6	43.1	40.9	10 06.0	43.5	41.0	10 51.2	44.1	41.1
44	9 17.8	42.5	40.1	10 03.7	43.0	40.2	10 49.5	43.5	40.3	11 35.3	43.9	40.4
45	10 00.3	+42.5	39.3	10 46.7	+42.9	39.5	11 33.0	+43.3	39.6	12 19.2	+43.8	39.7
46	10 42.8	42.3	38.6	11 29.6	42.8	38.7	12 16.3	43.3	38.9	13 03.0	43.7	39.0
47	11 25.1	42.2	37.9	12 12.4	42.6	38.0	12 59.6	43.1	38.2	13 46.7	43.6	38.3
48	12 07.3	42.1	37.2	12 55.0	42.6	37.3	13 42.7	43.0	37.5	14 30.3	43.5	37.6
49	12 49.4	41.9	36.4	13 37.6	42.4	36.6	14 25.7	42.9	36.7	15 13.8	43.3	36.9
50	13 31.3	+41.9	35.7	14 20.0	+42.3	35.9	15 08.6	+42.7	36.0	15 57.1	+43.2	36.2
51	14 13.2	41.7	35.0	15 02.3	42.2	35.1	15 51.3	42.6	35.3	16 40.3	43.0	35.5
52	14 54.9	41.6	34.2	15 44.5	42.0	34.4	16 33.9	42.5	34.6	17 23.3	42.9	34.7
53	15 36.5	41.4	33.5	16 26.5	41.8	33.6	17 16.4	42.2	33.8	18 06.2	42.7	34.0
54	16 17.9	41.2	32.7	17 08.3	41.7	32.9	17 58.6	42.1	33.1	18 48.9	42.5	33.2
55	16 59.1	+41.1	32.0	17 50.0	+41.5	32.1	18 40.7	+41.9	32.3	19 31.4	+42.3	32.5
56	17 40.2	40.9	31.2	18 31.5	41.3	31.4	19 22.6	41.8	31.6	20 13.7	42.2	31.7
57	18 21.1	40.7	30.4	19 12.8	41.1	30.6	20 04.4	41.5	30.8	20 55.9	41.9	31.0
58	19 01.8	40.5	29.7	19 53.9	40.9	29.8	20 45.9	41.3	30.0	21 37.8	41.7	30.2
59	19 42.3	40.4	28.9	20 34.8	40.7	29.1	21 27.2	41.1	29.2	22 19.5	41.5	29.4
60	20 22.7	+40.1	28.1	21 15.5	+40.5	28.3	22 08.3	+40.9	28.5	23 01.0	+41.3	28.7
61	21 02.8	39.8	27.3	21 56.0	40.3	27.5	22 49.2	40.6	27.7	23 42.3	41.0	27.9
62	21 42.6	39.7	26.5	22 36.3	40.0	26.7	23 29.8	40.4	26.9	24 23.3	40.8	27.1
63	22 22.3	39.4	25.7	23 16.3	39.8	25.9	24 10.2	40.2	26.1	25 04.1	40.5	26.3
64	23 01.7	39.1	24.9	23 56.1	39.5	25.1	24 50.4	39.8	25.2	25 44.6	40.2	25.4
65	23 40.8	+38.9	24.0	24 35.6	+39.2	24.2	25 30.2	+39.6	24.4	26 24.8	+40.0	24.6
66	24 19.7	38.6	23.2	25 14.8	38.9	23.4	26 09.8	39.3	23.6	27 04.8	39.6	23.8
67	24 58.3	38.3	22.4	25 53.7	38.7	22.6	26 49.1	39.0	22.7	27 44.4	39.3	22.9
68	25 36.6	38.0	21.5	26 32.4	38.3	21.7	27 28.1	38.7	21.9	28 23.7	39.0	22.1
69	26 14.6	37.7	20.7	27 10.7	38.1	20.8	28 06.8	38.3	21.0	29 02.7	38.7	21.2
70	26 52.3	+37.4	19.8	27 48.8	+37.7	20.0	28 45.1	+38.0	20.1	29 41.4	+38.3	20.3
71	27 29.7	37.1	18.9	28 26.5	37.3	19.1	29 23.1	37.7	19.3	30 19.7	38.0	19.5
72	28 06.8	36.7	18.0	29 03.8	37.0	18.2	30 00.8	37.2	18.4	30 57.7	37.6	18.6
73	28 43.5	36.3	17.1	29 40.8	36.6	17.3	30 38.0	36.9	17.5	31 35.3	37.1	17.6
74	29 19.8	36.0	16.2	30 17.4	36.2	16.4	31 14.9	36.5	16.5	32 12.4	36.8	16.7
75	29 55.8	+35.5	15.3	30 53.6	+35.9	15.4	31 51.4	+36.1	15.6	32 49.2	+36.3	15.8
76	30 31.3	35.2	14.4	31 29.5	35.4	14.5	32 27.5	35.7	14.7	33 25.5	35.9	14.8
77	31 06.5	34.8	13.4	32 04.9	34.9	13.6	33 03.2	35.2	13.7	34 01.4	35.5	13.9
78	31 41.3	34.3	12.5	32 39.8	34.6	12.6	33 38.4	34.7	12.7	34 36.9	35.0	12.9
79	32 15.6	33.9	11.5	33 14.4	34.1	11.6	34 13.1	34.3	11.8	35 11.9	34.4	11.9
80	32 49.5	+33.4	10.5	33 48.5	+33.5	10.6	34 47.4	+33.8	10.8	35 46.3	+34.0	10.9
81	33 22.9	32.9	9.5	34 22.0	33.1	9.6	35 21.2	33.3	9.8	36 20.3	33.5	9.9
82	33 55.8	32.5	8.5	34 55.1	32.6	8.6	35 54.5	32.7	8.7	36 53.8	32.9	8.8
83	34 28.3	31.9	7.5	35 27.7	32.1	7.6	36 27.2	32.2	7.7	37 26.7	32.3	7.8
84	35 00.2	31.4	6.5	35 59.8	31.5	6.6	36 59.4	31.6	6.6	37 59.0	31.7	6.7
85	35 31.6	+30.8	5.4	36 31.3	+30.9	5.5	37 31.0	+31.1	5.6	38 30.7	+31.2	5.6
86	36 02.4	30.3	4.4	37 02.2	30.4	4.4	38 02.1	30.4	4.5	39 01.9	30.5	4.5
87	36 32.7	29.7	3.3	37 32.6	29.8	3.3	38 32.5	29.8	3.4	39 32.4	29.9	3.4
88	37 02.4	29.1	2.2	38 02.4	29.1	2.2	39 02.3	29.2	2.3	40 02.3	29.2	2.3
89	37 31.5	28.5	1.1	38 31.5	28.5	1.1	39 31.5	28.5	1.1	40 31.5	28.5	1.2
90	38 00.0	+27.8	0.0	39 00.0	+27.8	0.0	40 00.0	+27.8	0.0	41 00.0	+27.8	0.0
	38°			39°			40°			41°		

42°			43°			44°			45°			Dec.
Hc	d	Z	Hc	d	Z	Hc	d	Z	Hc	d	Z	
° ′	′	°	° ′	′	°	° ′	′	°	° ′	′	°	°
20 25.1	−42.9	109.6	20 04.9	−43.7	109.9	19 44.2	−44.3	110.3	19 23.3	−45.1	110.6	0
19 42.2	43.1	110.3	19 21.2	43.8	110.7	18 59.9	44.5	111.0	18 38.2	45.2	111.3	1
18 59.1	43.3	111.1	18 37.4	44.0	111.4	18 15.4	44.7	111.7	17 53.0	45.3	112.0	2
18 15.8	43.4	111.8	17 53.4	44.2	112.1	17 30.7	44.9	112.4	17 07.7	45.5	112.7	3
17 32.4	43.7	112.5	17 09.2	44.3	112.8	16 45.8	44.9	113.1	16 22.2	45.6	113.4	4
16 48.7	−43.7	113.2	16 24.9	−44.4	113.5	16 00.9	−45.1	113.8	15 36.6	−45.8	114.0	5
16 05.0	43.9	114.0	15 40.5	44.6	114.2	15 15.8	45.3	114.5	14 50.8	45.9	114.7	6
15 21.1	44.0	114.7	14 55.9	44.7	114.9	14 30.5	45.3	115.1	14 04.9	45.9	115.4	7
14 37.1	44.2	115.4	14 11.2	44.8	115.6	13 45.2	45.4	115.8	13 19.0	46.1	116.0	8
13 52.9	44.3	116.1	13 26.4	44.9	116.3	12 59.8	45.6	116.5	12 32.9	46.2	116.7	9
13 08.6	−44.4	116.8	12 41.5	−45.0	117.0	12 14.2	−45.6	117.2	11 46.7	−46.2	117.3	10
12 24.2	44.5	117.4	11 56.5	45.1	117.6	11 28.6	45.8	117.8	11 00.5	46.4	118.0	11
11 39.7	44.6	118.1	11 11.4	45.3	118.3	10 42.8	45.8	118.5	10 14.1	46.4	118.6	12
10 55.1	44.6	118.8	10 26.1	45.2	119.0	9 57.0	45.9	119.1	9 27.7	46.5	119.3	13
10 10.5	44.8	119.5	9 40.9	45.4	119.6	9 11.1	46.0	119.8	8 41.2	46.5	119.9	14
9 25.7	−44.8	120.2	8 55.5	−45.5	120.3	8 25.1	−46.0	120.4	7 54.7	−46.6	120.6	15
8 40.9	45.0	120.8	8 10.0	45.5	121.0	7 39.1	46.1	121.1	7 08.1	46.7	121.2	16
7 55.9	44.9	121.5	7 24.5	45.5	121.6	6 53.0	46.1	121.7	6 21.4	46.7	121.8	17
7 11.0	45.1	122.2	6 39.0	45.6	122.3	6 06.9	46.2	122.4	5 34.7	46.7	122.5	18
6 25.9	45.0	122.8	5 53.4	45.7	122.9	5 20.7	46.2	123.0	4 48.0	46.8	123.1	19
5 40.9	−45.2	123.5	5 07.7	−45.7	123.6	4 34.5	−46.3	123.7	4 01.2	−46.8	123.7	20
4 55.7	45.1	124.2	4 22.0	45.7	124.2	3 48.2	46.3	124.3	3 14.4	46.9	124.3	21
4 10.6	45.2	124.8	3 36.3	45.8	124.9	3 01.9	46.3	124.9	2 27.5	46.8	125.0	22
3 25.4	45.3	125.5	2 50.5	45.8	125.5	2 15.6	46.3	125.6	1 40.7	46.9	125.6	23
2 40.1	45.2	126.1	2 04.7	45.8	126.2	1 29.3	46.3	126.2	0 53.8	46.8	126.2	24
1 54.9	−45.3	126.8	1 18.9	−45.8	126.8	0 43.0	−46.4	126.8	0 07.0	−46.9	126.8	25
1 09.6	45.3	127.5	0 33.1	−45.8	127.5	0 03.4	+46.3	52.5	0 39.9	+46.9	52.5	26
0 24.3	−45.2	128.1	0 12.7	+45.8	51.9	0 49.7	46.4	51.9	1 26.8	46.8	51.9	27
0 20.9	+45.3	51.2	0 58.5	45.8	51.2	1 36.1	46.3	51.3	2 13.6	46.9	51.3	28
1 06.2	45.3	50.6	1 44.3	45.8	50.6	2 22.4	46.3	50.6	3 00.5	46.8	50.7	29
1 51.5	+45.2	49.9	2 30.1	+45.8	49.9	3 08.7	+46.3	50.0	3 47.3	+46.8	50.0	30
2 36.7	45.3	49.3	3 15.9	45.7	49.3	3 55.0	46.2	49.3	4 34.1	46.7	49.4	31
3 22.0	45.2	48.6	4 01.6	45.7	48.6	4 41.2	46.3	48.7	5 20.8	46.7	48.8	32
4 07.2	45.1	47.9	4 47.3	45.7	48.0	5 27.5	46.1	48.1	6 07.5	46.7	48.1	33
4 52.3	45.2	47.3	5 33.0	45.7	47.3	6 13.6	46.2	47.4	6 54.2	46.6	47.5	34
5 37.5	+45.1	46.6	6 18.7	+45.5	46.7	6 59.8	+46.1	46.8	7 40.8	+46.6	46.9	35
6 22.6	45.0	46.0	7 04.2	45.6	46.0	7 45.9	46.0	46.1	8 27.4	46.5	46.2	36
7 07.6	45.0	45.3	7 49.8	45.4	45.4	8 31.9	45.9	45.5	9 13.9	46.4	45.6	37
7 52.6	44.9	44.6	8 35.2	45.4	44.7	9 17.8	45.9	44.8	10 00.3	46.4	45.0	38
8 37.5	44.8	43.9	9 20.6	45.4	44.1	10 03.7	45.8	44.2	10 46.7	46.3	44.3	39
9 22.3	+44.8	43.3	10 06.0	+45.2	43.4	10 49.5	+45.8	43.5	11 33.0	+46.2	43.7	40
10 07.1	44.7	42.6	10 51.2	45.2	42.7	11 35.3	45.6	42.9	12 19.2	46.1	43.0	41
10 51.8	44.6	41.9	11 36.4	45.1	42.1	12 20.9	45.5	42.2	13 05.3	46.0	42.3	42
11 36.4	44.5	41.2	12 21.5	44.9	41.4	13 06.4	45.5	41.5	13 51.3	45.9	41.7	43
12 20.9	44.4	40.6	13 06.4	44.9	40.7	13 51.9	45.3	40.9	14 37.2	45.8	41.0	44
13 05.3	+44.3	39.9	13 51.3	+44.7	40.0	14 37.2	+45.2	40.2	15 23.0	+45.6	40.4	45
13 49.6	44.1	39.2	14 36.0	44.7	39.3	15 22.4	45.1	39.5	16 08.6	45.6	39.7	46
14 33.7	44.1	38.5	15 20.7	44.5	38.6	16 07.5	44.9	38.8	16 54.2	45.3	39.0	47
15 17.8	43.9	37.8	16 05.2	44.3	37.9	16 52.4	44.8	38.1	17 39.5	45.3	38.3	48
16 01.7	43.8	37.1	16 49.5	44.2	37.2	17 37.2	44.7	37.4	18 24.8	45.1	37.6	49
16 45.5	+43.6	36.4	17 33.7	+44.1	36.5	18 21.9	+44.5	36.7	19 09.9	+44.9	36.9	50
17 29.1	43.4	35.6	18 17.8	43.9	35.8	19 06.4	44.3	36.0	19 54.8	44.8	36.2	51
18 12.5	43.4	34.9	19 01.7	43.7	35.1	19 50.7	44.2	35.3	20 39.6	44.6	35.5	52
18 55.9	43.1	34.2	19 45.4	43.6	34.4	20 34.9	44.0	34.6	21 24.2	44.4	34.8	53
19 39.0	42.9	33.4	20 29.0	43.4	33.6	21 18.9	43.8	33.9	22 08.6	44.3	34.1	54
20 21.9	+42.8	32.7	21 12.4	+43.1	32.9	22 02.7	+43.6	33.1	22 52.9	+44.0	33.3	55
21 04.7	42.5	31.9	21 55.5	43.0	32.2	22 46.3	43.4	32.4	23 36.9	43.8	32.6	56
21 47.2	42.4	31.2	22 38.5	42.8	31.4	23 29.7	43.1	31.6	24 20.7	43.6	31.9	57
22 29.6	42.1	30.4	23 21.3	42.5	30.6	24 12.8	43.0	30.9	25 04.3	43.3	31.1	58
23 11.7	41.9	29.7	24 03.8	42.3	29.9	24 55.8	42.7	30.1	25 47.6	43.1	30.3	59
23 53.6	+41.7	28.9	24 46.1	+42.1	29.1	25 38.5	+42.4	29.3	26 30.7	+42.9	29.6	60
24 35.3	41.4	28.1	25 28.2	41.8	28.3	26 20.9	42.2	28.5	27 13.6	42.6	28.8	61
25 16.7	41.2	27.3	26 10.0	41.5	27.5	27 03.1	42.0	27.7	27 56.2	42.3	28.0	62
25 57.9	40.8	26.5	26 51.5	41.3	26.7	27 45.1	41.6	26.9	28 38.5	42.0	27.2	63
26 38.7	40.6	25.7	27 32.8	40.9	25.9	28 26.7	41.3	26.1	29 20.5	41.7	26.4	64
27 19.3	+40.3	24.8	28 13.7	+40.7	25.1	29 08.0	+41.1	25.3	30 02.2	+41.4	25.5	65
27 59.6	40.0	24.0	28 54.4	40.3	24.2	29 49.1	40.7	24.5	30 43.6	41.1	24.7	66
28 39.6	39.7	23.2	29 34.7	40.1	23.4	30 29.8	40.4	23.6	31 24.7	40.7	23.8	67
29 19.3	39.3	22.3	30 14.8	39.7	22.5	31 10.2	40.0	22.7	32 05.4	40.4	23.0	68
29 58.6	39.0	21.4	30 54.5	39.3	21.6	31 50.2	39.6	21.9	32 45.8	40.0	22.1	69
30 37.6	+38.7	20.5	31 33.8	+38.9	20.8	32 29.8	+39.3	21.0	33 25.8	+39.6	21.2	70
31 16.3	38.2	19.7	32 12.7	38.6	19.9	33 09.1	38.9	20.1	34 05.4	39.3	20.3	71
31 54.5	37.9	18.7	32 51.3	38.2	19.0	33 48.0	38.5	19.2	34 44.7	38.8	19.4	72
32 32.4	37.5	17.8	33 29.5	37.7	18.0	34 26.5	38.1	18.2	35 23.5	38.3	18.5	73
33 09.9	37.0	16.9	34 07.2	37.4	17.1	35 04.6	37.6	17.3	36 01.8	37.9	17.5	74
33 46.9	+36.6	16.0	34 44.6	+36.8	16.1	35 42.2	+37.1	16.3	36 39.7	+37.5	16.6	75
34 23.5	36.2	15.0	35 21.4	36.5	15.2	36 19.3	36.7	15.4	37 17.2	36.9	15.6	76
34 59.7	35.7	14.0	35 57.9	35.9	14.2	36 56.0	36.2	14.4	37 54.1	36.4	14.6	77
35 35.4	35.2	13.0	36 33.8	35.4	13.2	37 32.2	35.6	13.4	38 30.5	35.9	13.6	78
36 10.6	34.6	12.0	37 09.2	34.9	12.2	38 07.8	35.2	12.4	39 06.4	35.4	12.5	79
36 45.2	+34.2	11.0	37 44.1	+34.4	11.2	38 43.0	+34.5	11.3	39 41.8	+34.8	11.5	80
37 19.4	33.6	10.0	38 18.5	33.8	10.1	39 17.5	34.0	10.3	40 16.6	34.1	10.4	81
37 53.0	33.1	9.0	38 52.3	33.2	9.1	39 51.5	33.4	9.2	40 50.7	33.6	9.3	82
38 26.1	32.5	7.9	39 25.5	32.6	8.0	40 24.9	32.8	8.1	41 24.3	32.9	8.2	83
38 58.6	31.8	6.8	39 58.1	32.0	6.9	40 57.7	32.1	7.0	41 57.2	32.3	7.1	84
39 30.4	+31.3	5.7	40 30.1	+31.4	5.8	41 29.8	+31.5	5.9	42 29.5	+31.6	6.0	85
40 01.7	30.6	4.6	41 01.5	30.7	4.7	42 01.3	30.8	4.8	43 01.1	30.8	4.8	86
40 32.3	29.9	3.5	41 32.2	30.0	3.5	42 32.1	30.0	3.6	43 31.9	30.2	3.7	87
41 02.2	29.3	2.3	42 02.2	29.3	2.4	43 02.1	29.3	2.4	44 02.1	29.3	2.5	88
41 31.5	28.5	1.2	42 31.5	28.5	1.2	43 31.4	28.6	1.2	44 31.4	28.6	1.2	89
42 00.0	+27.8	0.0	43 00.0	+27.8	0.0	44 00.0	+27.8	0.0	45 00.0	+27.8	0.0	90
42°			43°			44°			45°			

S. Lat. { L.H.A. greater than 180°......Zn=180°−Z
L.H.A. less than 180°............Zn=180°+Z

LATITUDE SAME NAME AS DECLINATION L.H.A. 118°, 242°

LATITUDE CONTRARY NAME TO DECLINATION — L.H.A. 63°, 297°

Dec.	38° Hc	38° d	38° Z	39° Hc	39° d	39° Z	40° Hc	40° d	40° Z	41° Hc	41° d	41° Z	42° Hc	42° d	42° Z	43° Hc	43° d	43° Z	44° Hc	44° d	44° Z	45° Hc	45° d	45° Z	Dec.
°	° ′	′	°	° ′	′	°	° ′	′	°	° ′	′	°	° ′	′	°	° ′	′	°	° ′	′	°	° ′	′	°	°
0	20 57.7	−39.6	107.4	20 39.6	−40.5	107.8	20 21.1	−41.3	108.1	20 02.2	−42.0	108.5	19 43.0	−42.7	108.8	19 23.5	−43.5	109.2	19 03.7	−44.2	109.5	18 43.5	−44.9	109.8	0
1	20 18.1	39.9	108.2	19 59.1	40.6	108.6	19 39.8	41.4	108.9	19 20.2	42.1	109.2	19 00.3	42.9	109.6	18 40.0	43.6	109.9	18 19.5	44.4	110.2	17 58.6	45.0	110.5	1
2	19 38.2	40.1	109.0	19 18.5	40.9	109.3	18 58.4	41.6	109.7	18 38.1	42.4	110.0	18 17.4	43.1	110.3	17 56.4	43.8	110.6	17 35.1	44.4	110.9	17 13.6	45.2	111.2	2
3	18 58.1	40.3	109.8	18 37.6	41.1	110.1	18 16.8	41.8	110.4	17 55.7	42.5	110.7	17 34.3	43.2	111.0	17 12.6	43.9	111.3	16 50.7	44.7	111.6	16 28.4	45.3	111.9	3
4	18 17.8	40.5	110.6	17 56.5	41.2	110.9	17 35.0	42.0	111.2	17 13.2	42.7	111.5	16 51.1	43.4	111.8	16 28.7	44.1	112.0	16 06.0	44.7	112.3	15 43.1	45.4	112.6	4
5	17 37.3	−40.7	111.4	17 15.3	−41.4	111.7	16 53.0	−42.1	111.9	16 30.5	−42.9	112.2	16 07.7	−43.6	112.5	15 44.6	−44.2	112.7	15 21.3	−44.9	113.0	14 57.7	−45.6	113.3	5
6	16 56.6	40.8	112.1	16 33.9	41.6	112.4	16 10.9	42.3	112.7	15 47.6	43.0	112.9	15 24.1	43.7	113.2	15 00.4	44.4	113.4	14 36.4	45.0	113.7	14 12.1	45.6	113.9	6
7	16 15.8	41.0	112.9	15 52.3	41.7	113.2	15 28.6	42.4	113.4	15 04.6	43.1	113.7	14 40.4	43.8	113.9	14 16.0	44.5	114.1	13 51.4	45.2	114.4	13 26.5	45.8	114.6	7
8	15 34.8	41.2	113.7	15 10.6	41.9	113.9	14 46.2	42.6	114.1	14 21.5	43.2	114.4	13 56.6	43.9	114.6	13 31.5	44.5	114.8	13 06.2	45.2	115.1	12 40.7	45.8	115.3	8
9	14 53.6	41.3	114.4	14 28.7	42.0	114.6	14 03.6	42.7	114.9	13 38.3	43.4	115.1	13 12.7	44.0	115.3	12 47.0	44.7	115.5	12 21.0	45.3	115.7	11 54.9	46.0	115.9	9
10	14 12.3	−41.4	115.2	13 46.7	−42.1	115.4	13 20.9	−42.8	115.6	12 54.9	−43.5	115.8	12 28.7	−44.2	116.0	12 02.3	−44.8	116.2	11 35.7	−45.4	116.4	11 08.9	−46.0	116.6	10
11	13 30.9	41.6	115.9	13 04.6	42.3	116.1	12 38.1	42.9	116.3	12 11.4	43.6	116.5	11 44.5	44.2	116.7	11 17.5	44.9	116.9	10 50.3	45.5	117.1	10 22.9	46.1	117.2	11
12	12 49.3	41.7	116.6	12 22.3	42.3	116.8	11 55.2	43.1	117.0	11 27.8	43.7	117.2	11 00.3	44.4	117.4	10 32.6	45.0	117.6	10 04.8	45.6	117.7	9 36.8	46.2	117.9	12
13	12 07.6	41.8	117.4	11 40.0	42.5	117.6	11 12.1	43.1	117.7	10 44.1	43.8	117.9	10 15.9	44.4	118.1	9 47.6	45.0	118.2	9 19.2	45.7	118.4	8 50.6	46.3	118.5	13
14	11 25.8	41.9	118.1	10 57.5	42.6	118.3	10 29.0	43.3	118.5	10 00.3	43.9	118.6	9 31.5	44.5	118.8	9 02.6	45.1	118.9	8 33.5	45.7	119.0	8 04.3	46.3	119.2	14
15	10 43.9	−42.0	118.8	10 14.9	−42.7	119.0	9 45.7	−43.3	119.2	9 16.4	−43.9	119.3	8 47.0	−44.6	119.4	8 17.5	−45.2	119.6	7 47.8	−45.8	119.7	7 18.0	−46.4	119.8	15
16	10 01.9	42.1	119.6	9 32.2	42.7	119.7	9 02.4	43.4	119.9	8 32.5	44.0	120.0	8 02.4	44.6	120.1	7 32.3	45.3	120.2	7 02.0	45.8	120.3	6 31.6	46.4	120.4	16
17	9 19.8	42.2	120.3	8 49.5	42.9	120.4	8 19.0	43.5	120.6	7 48.5	44.1	120.7	7 17.8	44.7	120.8	6 47.0	45.3	120.9	6 16.2	45.9	121.0	5 45.2	46.4	121.1	17
18	8 37.6	42.3	121.0	8 06.6	42.9	121.1	7 35.5	43.5	121.3	7 04.4	44.2	121.4	6 33.1	44.8	121.5	6 01.7	45.3	121.6	5 30.3	45.9	121.6	4 58.8	46.5	121.7	18
19	7 55.3	42.4	121.7	7 23.7	43.0	121.8	6 52.0	43.6	121.9	6 20.2	44.2	122.0	5 48.3	44.8	122.1	5 16.4	45.4	122.2	4 44.4	46.0	122.3	4 12.3	46.5	122.4	19
20	7 12.9	−42.4	122.4	6 40.7	−43.0	122.5	6 08.4	−43.7	122.6	5 36.0	−44.3	122.7	5 03.5	−44.8	122.8	4 31.0	−45.4	122.9	3 58.4	−46.0	122.9	3 25.8	−46.6	123.0	20
21	6 30.5	42.5	123.2	5 57.7	43.1	123.2	5 24.7	43.7	123.3	4 51.7	44.3	123.4	4 18.7	44.9	123.5	3 45.6	45.5	123.5	3 12.4	46.0	123.6	2 39.2	46.6	123.6	21
22	5 48.0	42.5	123.9	5 14.6	43.2	123.9	4 41.0	43.7	124.0	4 07.4	44.3	124.1	3 33.8	44.9	124.1	3 00.1	45.5	124.2	2 26.4	46.0	124.2	1 52.6	46.6	124.3	22
23	5 05.5	42.6	124.6	4 31.4	43.1	124.6	3 57.3	43.8	124.7	3 23.1	44.3	124.8	2 48.9	44.9	124.8	2 14.6	45.5	124.8	1 40.4	46.1	124.9	1 06.0	46.5	124.9	23
24	4 22.9	42.6	125.3	3 48.3	43.3	125.3	3 13.5	43.8	125.4	2 38.8	44.4	125.4	2 04.0	45.0	125.5	1 29.1	45.5	125.5	0 54.3	46.0	125.5	0 19.5	−46.6	125.5	24
25	3 40.3	−42.6	126.0	3 05.0	−43.2	126.0	2 29.7	−43.8	126.1	1 54.4	−44.4	126.1	1 19.0	−44.9	126.1	0 43.6	−45.5	126.1	0 08.3	−46.1	126.1	0 27.1	+46.6	53.9	25
26	2 57.7	42.7	126.7	2 21.8	43.3	126.7	1 45.9	43.8	126.8	1 10.0	44.4	126.8	0 34.1	−45.0	126.8	0 01.9	+45.5	53.2	0 37.8	+46.1	53.2	1 13.7	46.6	53.2	26
27	2 15.0	42.7	127.4	1 38.5	43.3	127.4	1 02.1	43.9	127.4	0 25.6	−44.4	127.4	0 10.9	+45.0	52.6	0 47.4	45.5	52.6	1 23.9	46.0	52.6	2 00.3	46.6	52.6	27
28	1 32.3	42.7	128.1	0 55.2	43.2	128.1	0 18.2	−43.8	128.1	0 18.8	+44.4	51.9	0 55.9	44.9	51.9	1 32.9	45.5	51.9	2 09.9	46.0	51.9	2 46.9	46.5	52.0	28
29	0 49.6	42.8	128.8	0 12.0	−43.3	128.8	0 25.6	+43.9	51.2	1 03.2	44.4	51.2	1 40.8	45.0	51.2	2 18.4	45.5	51.3	2 55.9	46.0	51.3	3 33.4	46.5	51.3	29
30	0 06.8	−42.7	129.5	0 31.3	+43.3	50.5	1 09.5	+43.8	50.5	1 47.6	+44.4	50.5	2 25.8	+44.9	50.6	3 03.9	+45.4	50.6	3 41.9	+46.0	50.6	4 19.9	+46.5	50.7	30
31	0 35.9	+42.7	49.8	1 14.6	43.3	49.8	1 53.3	43.8	49.8	2 32.0	44.4	49.9	3 10.7	44.9	49.9	3 49.3	45.4	49.9	4 27.9	45.9	50.0	5 06.4	46.5	50.1	31
32	1 18.6	42.7	49.1	1 57.9	43.2	49.1	2 37.1	43.8	49.1	3 16.4	44.3	49.2	3 55.6	44.8	49.2	4 34.7	45.4	49.3	5 13.8	45.9	49.4	5 52.9	46.4	49.4	32
33	2 01.3	42.7	48.4	2 41.1	43.3	48.4	3 20.9	43.8	48.5	4 00.7	44.3	48.5	4 40.4	44.9	48.6	5 20.1	45.4	48.6	5 59.7	45.9	48.7	6 39.3	46.4	48.8	33
34	2 44.0	42.7	47.7	3 24.4	43.2	47.7	4 04.7	43.7	47.8	4 45.0	44.3	47.8	5 25.3	44.7	47.9	6 05.5	45.2	48.0	6 45.6	45.8	48.1	7 25.7	46.3	48.2	34
35	3 26.7	+42.6	47.0	4 07.6	+43.1	47.0	4 48.4	+43.7	47.1	5 29.3	+44.2	47.2	6 10.0	+44.8	47.2	6 50.7	+45.3	47.3	7 31.4	+45.7	47.4	8 12.0	+46.2	47.5	35
36	4 09.3	42.6	46.3	4 50.7	43.2	46.3	5 32.1	43.7	46.4	6 13.5	44.1	46.5	6 54.8	44.6	46.6	7 36.0	45.2	46.7	8 17.1	45.7	46.8	8 58.2	46.2	46.9	36
37	4 51.9	42.5	45.6	5 33.9	43.0	45.6	6 15.8	43.6	45.7	6 57.6	44.1	45.8	7 39.4	44.7	45.9	8 21.2	45.1	46.0	9 02.8	45.6	46.1	9 44.4	46.1	46.2	37
38	5 34.4	42.5	44.9	6 16.9	43.0	44.9	6 59.4	43.5	45.0	7 41.7	44.1	45.1	8 24.1	44.5	45.2	9 06.3	45.0	45.3	9 48.4	45.6	45.4	10 30.5	46.0	45.6	38
39	6 16.9	42.5	44.2	6 59.9	43.0	44.2	7 42.9	43.5	44.3	8 25.8	44.0	44.4	9 08.6	44.5	44.5	9 51.3	45.0	44.7	10 34.0	45.4	44.8	11 16.5	45.9	44.9	39
40	6 59.4	+42.3	43.4	7 42.9	+42.9	43.5	8 26.4	+43.4	43.6	9 09.8	+43.8	43.7	9 53.1	+44.3	43.9	10 36.3	+44.9	44.0	11 19.4	+45.4	44.1	12 02.4	+45.9	44.3	40
41	7 41.7	42.4	42.7	8 25.8	42.8	42.8	9 09.8	43.3	42.9	9 53.6	43.8	43.0	10 37.4	44.3	43.1	11 21.2	44.7	43.3	12 04.8	45.2	43.4	12 48.3	45.7	43.6	41
42	8 24.1	42.2	42.0	9 08.6	42.7	42.1	9 53.1	43.2	42.2	10 37.4	43.8	42.4	11 21.7	44.2	42.5	12 05.9	44.7	42.6	12 50.0	45.2	42.8	13 34.0	45.7	42.9	42
43	9 06.3	42.1	41.3	9 51.3	42.7	41.4	10 36.3	43.1	41.5	11 21.2	43.6	41.7	12 05.9	44.1	41.8	12 50.6	44.6	41.9	13 35.2	45.0	42.1	14 19.7	45.5	42.3	43
44	9 48.4	42.1	40.6	10 34.0	42.5	40.7	11 19.4	43.0	40.8	12 04.8	43.5	41.0	12 50.0	44.0	41.1	13 35.2	44.5	41.3	14 20.2	45.0	41.4	15 05.2	45.4	41.6	44
45	10 30.5	+41.9	39.9	11 16.5	+42.4	40.0	12 02.4	+42.9	40.1	12 48.3	+43.4	40.2	13 34.0	+43.9	40.4	14 19.7	+44.3	40.6	15 05.2	+44.8	40.7	15 50.6	+45.3	40.9	45
46	11 12.4	41.9	39.1	11 58.9	42.4	39.3	12 45.3	42.8	39.4	13 31.7	43.2	39.5	14 17.9	43.7	39.7	15 04.0	44.2	39.9	15 50.0	44.7	40.0	16 35.9	45.1	40.2	46
47	11 54.3	41.7	38.4	12 41.3	42.2	38.5	13 28.1	42.7	38.7	14 14.9	43.2	38.8	15 01.6	43.6	39.0	15 48.2	44.1	39.2	16 34.7	44.5	39.3	17 21.0	45.0	39.5	47
48	12 36.0	41.6	37.7	13 23.5	42.0	37.8	14 10.8	42.6	37.9	14 58.1	43.0	38.1	15 45.2	43.5	38.3	16 32.3	43.9	38.5	17 19.2	44.4	38.6	18 06.0	44.9	38.8	48
49	13 17.6	41.5	36.9	14 05.5	42.0	37.1	14 53.4	42.4	37.2	15 41.1	42.9	37.4	16 28.7	43.3	37.6	17 16.2	43.8	37.7	18 03.6	44.2	37.9	18 50.9	44.6	38.1	49
50	13 59.1	+41.3	36.2	14 47.5	+41.8	36.3	15 35.8	+42.2	36.5	16 24.0	+42.7	36.7	17 12.0	+43.2	36.8	18 00.0	+43.6	37.0	18 47.8	+44.1	37.2	19 35.5	+44.6	37.4	50
51	14 40.4	41.2	35.4	15 29.3	41.6	35.6	16 18.0	42.1	35.7	17 06.7	42.5	35.9	17 55.2	43.0	36.1	18 43.6	43.5	36.3	19 31.9	43.9	36.5	20 20.1	44.3	36.7	51
52	15 21.6	41.1	34.7	16 10.9	41.5	34.8	17 00.1	42.0	35.0	17 49.2	42.4	35.2	18 38.2	42.8	35.4	19 27.1	43.3	35.6	20 15.8	43.7	35.8	21 04.4	44.2	36.0	52
53	16 02.7	40.9	33.9	16 52.4	41.4	34.1	17 42.1	41.8	34.3	18 31.6	42.2	34.4	19 21.0	42.7	34.6	20 10.4	43.0	34.8	20 59.5	43.6	35.1	21 48.6	44.0	35.3	53
54	16 43.6	40.7	33.2	17 33.8	41.1	33.3	18 23.9	41.5	33.5	19 13.8	42.1	33.7	20 03.7	42.5	33.9	20 53.4	42.9	34.1	21 43.1	43.3	34.3	22 32.6	43.7	34.5	54
55	17 24.3	+40.5	32.4	18 14.9	+41.0	32.6	19 05.4	+41.4	32.7	19 55.9	+41.8	32.9	20 46.2	+42.2	33.1	21 36.3	+42.7	33.3	22 26.4	+43.1	33.6	23 16.3	+43.6	33.8	55
56	18 04.8	40.4	31.6	18 55.9	40.8	31.8	19 46.8	41.2	32.0	20 37.7	41.6	32.2	21 28.4	42.1	32.4	22 19.0	42.5	32.6	23 09.5	42.9	32.8	23 59.9	43.3	33.1	56
57	18 45.2	40.2	30.8	19 36.7	40.5	31.0	20 28.0	41.0	31.2	21 19.3	41.4	31.4	22 10.5	41.8	31.6	23 01.5	42.3	31.8	23 52.4	42.7	32.1	24 43.2	43.1	32.3	57
58	19 25.4	39.9	30.0	20 17.2	40.4	30.2	21 09.0	40.8	30.4	22 00.7	41.2	30.6	22 52.3	41.6	30.8	23 43.8	42.0	31.0	24 35.1	42.5	31.3	25 26.3	42.9	31.5	58
59	20 05.3	39.7	29.3	20 57.6	40.2	29.4	21 49.8	40.6	29.6	22 41.9	41.0	29.8	23 33.9	41.4	30.0	24 25.8	41.8	30.3	25 17.6	42.1	30.5	26 09.2	42.6	30.7	59
60	20 45.0	+39.6	28.5	21 37.8	+39.9	28.6	22 30.4	+40.3	28.8	23 22.9	+40.7	29.0	24 15.3	+41.1	29.3	25 07.6	+41.5	29.5	25 59.7	+42.0	29.7	26 51.8	+42.3	30.0	60
61	21 24.6	39.2	27.6	22 17.7	39.6	27.8	23 10.7	40.0	28.0	24 03.6	40.5	28.2	24 56.4	40.9	28.5	25 49.1	41.3	28.7	26 41.7	41.6	28.9	27 34.1	42.1	29.2	61
62	22 03.8	39.1	26.8	22 57.3	39.5	27.0	23 50.7	39.9	27.2	24 44.1	40.2	27.4	25 37.3	40.6	27.6	26 30.4	40.9	27.9	27 23.3	41.4	28.1	28 16.2	41.8	28.4	62
63	22 42.9	38.8	26.0	23 36.8	39.1	26.2	24 30.6	39.5	26.4	25 24.3	39.9	26.6	26 17.9	40.3	26.8	27 11.3	40.7	27.0	28 04.7	41.1	27.3	28 58.0	41.5	27.5	63
64	23 21.7	38.5	25.2	24 15.9	38.9	25.4	25 10.1	39.3	25.6	26 04.2	39.6	25.8	26 58.2	40.0	26.0	27 52.0	40.4	26.2	28 45.8	40.8	26.5	29 39.5	41.1	26.7	64
65	24 00.2	+38.2	24.3	24 54.8	+38.6	24.5	25 49.4	+38.9	24.7	26 43.8	+39.3	24.9	27 38.2	+39.7	25.2	28 32.4	+40.1	25.4	29 26.6	+40.4	25.6	30 20.6	+40.9	25.9	65
66	24 38.4	38.0	23.5	25 33.4	38.3	23.7	26 28.3	38.7	23.9	27 23.1	39.1	24.1	28 17.9	39.4	24.3	29 12.5	39.8	24.5	30 07.0	40.2	24.8	31 01.5	40.5	25.0	66
67	25 16.4	37.7	22.6	26 11.7	38.0	22.8	27 07.0	38.3	23.0	28 02.2	38.7	23.2	28 57.3	39.0	23.4	29 52.3	39.4	23.7	30 47.2	39.7	23.9	31 42.0	40.1	24.2	67
68	25 54.1	37.3	21.8	26 49.7	37.7	22.0	27 45.3	38.1	22.2	28 40.9	38.3	22.4	29 36.3	38.7	22.6	30 31.7	39.0	22.8	31 26.9	39.5	23.0	32 22.1	39.8	23.3	68
69	26 31.4	37.0	20.9	27 27.4	37.4	21.1	28 23.4	37.6	21.3	29 19.2	38.1	21.5	30 15.0	38.4	21.7	31 10.7	38.7	21.9	32 06.4	39.0	22.1	33 01.9	39.4	22.4	69
70	27 08.4	+36.7	20.0	28 04.8	+37.0	20.2	29 01.0	+37.4	20.4	29 57.3	+37.6	20.6	30 53.4	+38.0	20.8	31 49.4	+38.3	21.0	32 45.4	+38.6	21.2	33 41.3	+39.0	21.5	70
71	27 45.1	36.4	19.1	28 41.8	36.6	19.3	29 38.4	36.9	19.5	30 34.9	37.3	19.7	31 31.4	37.5	19.9	32 27.7	38.0	20.1	33 24.0	38.3	20.3	34 20.3	38.5	20.6	71
72	28 21.5	36.0	18.2	29 18.4	36.3	18.4	30 15.3	36.6	18.6	31 12.2	36.9	18.8	32 08.9	37.2	19.0	33 05.7	37.5	19.2	34 02.3	37.8	19.4	34 58.8	38.2	19.6	72
73	28 57.5	35.6	17.3	29 54.7	35.9	17.5	30 51.9	36.2	17.7	31 49.1	36.4	17.9	32 46.1	36.8	18.0	33 43.2	37.0	18.3	34 40.1	37.4	18.5	35 37.0	37.7	18.7	73
74	29 33.1	35.2	16.4	30 30.6	35.5	16.6	31 28.1	35.8	16.7	32 25.5	36.1	16.9	33 22.9	36.3	17.1	34 20.2	36.6	17.3	35 17.5	36.9	17.5	36 14.7	37.2	17.7	74
75	30 08.3	+34.8	15.5	31 06.1	+35.1	15.6	32 03.9	+35.3	15.8	33 01.6	+35.6	16.0	33 59.2	+35.9	16.1	34 56.8	+36.2	16.3	35 54.4	+36.4	16.5	36 51.9	+36.7	16.8	75
76	30 43.1	34.4	14.5	31 41.2	34.7	14.7	32 39.2	34.9	14.8	33 37.2	35.2	15.0	34 35.1	35.4	15.2	35 33.0	35.7	15.4	36 30.8	36.0	15.6	37 28.6	36.2	15.8	76
77	31 17.5	34.0	13.6	32 15.9	34.2	13.7	33 14.1	34.5	13.9	34 12.4	34.6	14.0	35 10.5	35.0	14.2	36 08.7	35.2	14.4	37 06.8	35.4	14.6	38 04.8	35.7	14.8	77
78	31 51.5	33.6	12.6	32 50.1	33.7	12.7	33 48.6	33.9	12.9	34 47.0	34.2	13.0	35 45.5	34.4	13.2	36 43.9	34.6	13.4	37 42.2	34.9	13.5	38 40.5	35.2	13.7	78
79	32 25.1	33.0	11.6	33 23.8	33.3	11.7	34 22.5	33.5	11.9	35 21.2	33.7	12.0	36 19.9	33.9	12.2	37 18.5	34.2	12.3	38 17.1	34.4	12.5	39 15.7	34.6	12.7	79
80	32 58.1	+32.6	10.6	33 57.1	+32.8	10.7	34 56.0	+33.0	10.9	35 54.9	+33.2	11.0	36 53.8	+33.4	11.2	37 52.7	+33.6	11.3	38 51.5	+33.8	11.5	39 50.3	+34.0	11.6	80
81	33 30.7	32.2	9.6	34 29.9	32.3	9.7	35 29.0	32.5	9.9	36 28.1	32.7	10.0	37 27.2	32.8	10.1	38 26.3	33.0	10.3	39 25.3	33.2	10.4	40 24.3	33.4	10.5	81
82	34 02.9	31.6	8.6	35 02.2	31.7	8.7	36 01.5	31.9	8.8	37 00.8	32.0	8.9	38 00.0	32.2	9.1	38 59.3	32.4	9.2	39 58.5	32.6	9.3	40 57.7	32.7	9.5	82
83	34 34.5	31.0	7.6	35 33.9	31.1	7.7	36 33.4	31.3	7.8	37 32.8	31.5	7.9	38 32.2	31.7	8.0	39 31.7	31.7	8.1	40 31.1	31.9	8.2	41 30.4	32.1	8.3	83
84	35 05.5	30.6	6.5	36 05.1	30.7	6.6	37 04.7	30.8	6.7	38 04.3	30.9	6.8	39 03.9	31.0	6.9	40 03.4	31.2	7.0	41 03.0	31.3	7.1	42 02.5	31.5	7.2	84
85	35 36.1	+29.9	5.5	36 35.8	+30.1	5.6	37 35.5	+30.2	5.6	38 35.2	+30.3	5.7	39 34.9	+30.4	5.8	40 34.6	+30.5	5.9	41 34.3	+30.6	6.0	42 34.0	+30.7	6.1	85
86	36 06.0	29.4	4.4	37 05.9	29.4	4.5	38 05.7	29.5	4.5	39 05.5	29.6	4.6	40 05.3	29.7	4.7	41 05.1	29.8	4.7	42 04.9	29.9	4.8	43 04.7	30.0	4.9	86
87	36 35.4	28.8	3.3	37 35.3	28.9	3.4	38 35.2	29.0	3.4	39 35.1	29.0	3.5	40 35.0	29.1	3.5	41 34.9	29.1	3.6	42 34.8	29.1	3.6	43 34.7	29.2	3.7	87
88	37 04.2	28.2	2.2	38 04.2	28.2	2.3	39 04.2	28.2	2.3	40 04.1	28.3	2.3	41 04.1	28.3	2.4	42 04.0	28.4	2.4	43 03.9	28.5	2.4	44 03.9	28.4	2.5	88
89	37 32.4	27.6	1.1	38 32.4	27.6	1.1	39 32.4	27.6	1.2	40 32.4	27.6	1.2	41 32.4	27.6	1.2	42 32.4	27.6	1.2	43 32.4	27.6	1.2	44 32.3	27.7	1.3	89
90	38 00.0	+26.9	0.0	39 00.0	+26.9	0.0	40 00.0	+26.9	0.0	41 00.0	+26.9	0.0	42 00.0	+26.9	0.0	43 00.0	+26.8	0.0	44 00.0	+26.8	0.0	45 00.0	+26.8	0.0	90
	38°			39°			40°			41°			42°			43°			44°			45°			

S. Lat. { L.H.A. greater than 180°......Zn=180°−Z; L.H.A. less than 180°...........Zn=180°+Z }

LATITUDE SAME NAME AS DECLINATION — L.H.A. 117°, 243°

Dec.	38° Hc	d	Z	39° Hc	d	Z	40° Hc	d	Z	41° Hc	d	Z	42° Hc	d	Z	43° Hc	d	Z	44° Hc	d	Z	45° Hc	d	Z	Dec.
°	° ′	′	°	° ′	′	°	° ′	′	°	° ′	′	°	° ′	′	°	° ′	′	°	° ′	′	°	° ′	′	°	°
0	18 41.6	-39.1	105.3	18 25.6	-39.9	105.7	18 09.3	-40.7	106.0	17 52.6	-41.5	106.3	17 35.6	-42.2	106.6	17 18.3	-42.9	106.9	17 00.8	-43.7	107.2	16 42.9	-44.4	107.5	0
1	18 02.5	39.3	106.1	17 45.7	40.1	106.4	17 28.6	40.9	106.7	17 11.1	41.6	107.0	16 53.4	42.3	107.3	16 35.4	43.1	107.6	16 17.1	43.8	107.9	15 58.5	44.5	108.2	1
2	17 23.2	39.4	106.9	17 05.6	40.2	107.2	16 47.7	41.0	107.5	16 29.5	41.7	107.8	16 11.1	42.6	108.1	15 52.3	43.2	108.3	15 33.3	44.0	108.6	15 14.0	44.6	108.9	2
3	16 43.8	39.7	107.7	16 25.4	40.5	108.0	16 06.7	41.2	108.3	15 47.8	42.0	108.5	15 28.5	42.6	108.8	15 09.1	43.4	109.1	14 49.3	44.0	109.3	14 29.4	44.8	109.6	3
4	16 04.1	39.8	108.5	15 44.9	40.5	108.8	15 25.5	41.3	109.0	15 05.8	42.0	109.3	14 45.9	42.8	109.5	14 25.7	43.5	109.8	14 05.3	44.2	110.0	13 44.6	44.8	110.3	4
5	15 24.3	-40.0	109.3	15 04.4	-40.8	109.5	14 44.2	-41.5	109.8	14 23.8	-42.3	110.0	14 03.1	-42.9	110.3	13 42.2	-43.6	110.5	13 21.1	-44.3	110.7	12 59.8	-45.0	110.9	5
6	14 44.3	40.1	110.0	14 23.6	40.9	110.3	14 02.7	41.6	110.5	13 41.5	42.3	110.8	13 20.2	43.1	111.0	12 58.6	43.7	111.2	12 36.8	44.4	111.4	12 14.8	45.1	111.6	6
7	14 04.2	40.3	110.8	13 42.7	41.0	111.0	13 21.1	41.8	111.3	12 59.2	42.5	111.5	12 37.1	43.1	111.7	12 14.9	43.9	111.9	11 52.4	44.5	112.1	11 29.7	45.1	112.3	7
8	13 23.9	40.5	111.6	13 01.7	41.2	111.8	12 39.3	41.8	112.0	12 16.7	42.5	112.2	11 54.0	43.3	112.4	11 31.0	43.9	112.6	11 07.9	44.6	112.8	10 44.6	45.3	113.0	8
9	12 43.4	40.5	112.3	12 20.5	41.2	112.5	11 57.5	42.0	112.7	11 34.2	42.7	112.9	11 10.7	43.3	113.1	10 47.1	44.1	113.3	10 23.3	44.7	113.5	9 59.3	45.3	113.6	9
10	12 02.9	-40.7	113.1	11 39.3	-41.4	113.3	11 15.5	-42.1	113.5	10 51.5	-42.8	113.6	10 27.4	-43.5	113.8	10 03.0	-44.1	114.0	9 38.6	-44.8	114.1	9 14.0	-45.4	114.3	10
11	11 22.2	40.8	113.8	10 57.9	41.5	114.0	10 33.4	42.2	114.2	10 08.7	42.8	114.4	9 43.9	43.5	114.5	9 18.9	44.2	114.7	8 53.8	44.8	114.8	8 28.6	45.5	115.0	11
12	10 41.4	40.9	114.6	10 16.4	41.6	114.8	9 51.2	42.3	114.9	9 25.9	43.0	115.1	9 00.4	43.7	115.2	8 34.7	44.2	115.4	8 09.0	44.9	115.5	7 43.1	45.5	115.6	12
13	10 00.5	40.9	115.3	9 34.8	41.7	115.5	9 08.9	42.3	115.6	8 42.9	43.0	115.8	8 16.7	43.6	115.9	7 50.5	44.4	116.0	7 24.1	45.0	116.2	6 57.6	45.6	116.3	13
14	9 19.6	41.1	116.1	8 53.1	41.7	116.2	8 26.6	42.5	116.3	7 59.9	43.1	116.5	7 33.1	43.8	116.6	7 06.1	44.4	116.7	6 39.1	45.0	116.8	6 12.0	45.6	116.9	14
15	8 38.5	-41.2	116.8	8 11.4	-41.9	116.9	7 44.1	-42.5	117.1	7 16.8	-43.2	117.2	6 49.3	-43.8	117.3	6 21.7	-44.4	117.4	5 54.1	-45.1	117.5	5 26.4	-45.7	117.6	15
16	7 57.3	41.2	117.5	7 29.5	41.9	117.7	7 01.6	42.6	117.8	6 33.6	43.2	117.9	6 05.5	43.9	118.0	5 37.3	44.5	118.1	5 09.0	45.1	118.1	4 40.7	45.7	118.2	16
17	7 16.1	41.3	118.3	6 47.6	42.0	118.4	6 19.0	42.6	118.5	5 50.4	43.3	118.6	5 21.6	43.9	118.7	4 52.8	44.5	118.7	4 23.9	45.1	118.8	3 55.0	45.8	118.9	17
18	6 34.8	41.4	119.0	6 05.6	42.0	119.1	5 36.4	42.7	119.2	5 07.1	43.3	119.3	4 37.7	43.9	119.3	4 08.3	44.6	119.4	3 38.8	45.2	119.5	3 09.2	45.7	119.5	18
19	5 53.4	41.5	119.7	5 23.6	42.1	119.8	4 53.7	42.7	119.9	4 23.8	43.4	120.0	3 53.8	44.0	120.0	3 23.7	44.6	120.1	2 53.6	45.2	120.1	2 23.5	45.8	120.2	19
20	5 11.9	-41.4	120.5	4 41.5	-42.1	120.5	4 11.0	-42.8	120.6	3 40.4	-43.4	120.7	3 09.8	-44.0	120.7	2 39.1	-44.6	120.8	2 08.4	-45.2	120.8	1 37.7	-45.8	120.8	20
21	4 30.5	41.6	121.2	3 59.4	42.2	121.2	3 28.2	42.8	121.3	2 57.0	43.4	121.4	2 25.8	44.0	121.4	1 54.5	44.6	121.4	1 23.2	45.2	121.4	0 51.9	45.8	121.5	21
22	3 48.9	41.5	121.9	3 17.2	42.2	122.0	2 45.4	42.8	122.0	2 13.6	43.4	122.0	1 41.8	44.1	122.1	1 09.9	44.7	122.1	0 38.0	-45.2	122.1	0 06.1	-45.8	122.1	22
23	3 07.4	41.6	122.6	2 35.0	42.2	122.7	2 02.6	42.9	122.7	1 30.2	43.5	122.7	0 57.7	44.0	122.7	0 25.2	-44.6	122.8	0 07.2	+45.2	57.2	0 39.7	+45.8	57.2	23
24	2 25.8	41.6	123.4	1 52.8	42.3	123.4	1 19.7	42.8	123.4	0 46.7	43.5	123.4	0 13.7	-44.1	123.4	0 19.4	+44.6	56.6	0 52.4	45.3	56.6	1 25.5	45.8	56.6	24
25	1 44.2	-41.7	124.1	1 10.5	-42.2	124.1	0 36.9	-42.9	124.1	0 03.2	-43.4	124.1	0 30.4	+44.0	55.9	1 04.0	+44.7	55.9	1 37.7	+45.2	55.9	2 11.3	+45.7	56.0	25
26	1 02.5	41.6	124.8	0 28.3	-42.3	124.8	0 06.0	+42.8	55.2	0 40.2	+43.5	55.2	1 14.4	44.1	55.2	1 48.7	44.6	55.2	2 22.9	45.2	55.3	2 57.0	45.8	55.3	26
27	0 20.9	-41.7	125.5	0 14.0	+42.2	54.5	0 48.8	42.9	54.5	1 23.7	43.4	54.5	1 58.5	44.0	54.5	2 33.3	44.6	54.6	3 08.1	45.1	54.6	3 42.8	45.7	54.7	27
28	0 20.8	+41.6	53.8	0 56.2	42.3	53.8	1 31.7	42.8	53.8	2 07.1	43.4	53.8	2 42.5	44.0	53.9	3 17.9	44.6	53.9	3 53.2	45.1	53.9	4 28.5	45.7	54.0	28
29	1 02.4	41.6	53.0	1 38.5	42.2	53.1	2 14.5	42.8	53.1	2 50.5	43.4	53.1	3 26.5	44.0	53.2	4 02.5	44.5	53.2	4 38.3	45.1	53.3	5 14.2	45.6	53.4	29
30	1 44.0	+41.7	52.3	2 20.7	+42.2	52.4	2 57.3	+42.8	52.4	3 33.9	+43.4	52.4	4 10.5	+43.9	52.5	4 47.0	+44.5	52.6	5 23.4	+45.1	52.6	5 59.8	+45.6	52.7	30
31	2 25.7	41.5	51.6	3 02.9	42.2	51.6	3 40.1	42.8	51.7	4 17.3	43.3	51.7	4 54.4	43.9	51.8	5 31.5	44.4	51.9	6 08.5	45.0	52.0	6 45.4	45.6	52.0	31
32	3 07.2	41.6	50.9	3 45.1	42.1	50.9	4 22.9	42.7	51.0	5 00.6	43.3	51.1	5 38.3	43.9	51.1	6 15.9	44.4	51.2	6 53.5	44.9	51.3	7 31.0	45.5	51.4	32
33	3 48.8	41.5	50.2	4 27.2	42.1	50.2	5 05.6	42.7	50.3	5 43.9	43.2	50.4	6 22.2	43.7	50.4	7 00.3	44.4	50.5	7 38.4	44.9	50.6	8 16.5	45.4	50.7	33
34	4 30.3	41.5	49.4	5 09.3	42.1	49.5	5 48.3	42.6	49.6	6 27.1	43.2	49.7	7 05.9	43.8	49.7	7 44.7	44.2	49.8	8 23.3	44.8	50.0	9 01.9	45.3	50.1	34
35	5 11.8	+41.5	48.7	5 51.4	+42.0	48.8	6 30.9	+42.5	48.9	7 10.3	+43.1	49.0	7 49.7	+43.6	49.1	8 28.9	+44.3	49.2	9 08.1	+44.8	49.3	9 47.2	+45.3	49.4	35
36	5 53.3	41.3	48.0	6 33.4	41.9	48.1	7 13.4	42.5	48.2	7 53.4	43.1	48.3	8 33.3	43.6	48.4	9 13.2	44.1	48.5	9 52.9	44.6	48.6	10 32.5	45.2	48.7	36
37	6 34.6	41.3	47.3	7 15.3	41.9	47.3	7 55.9	42.5	47.4	8 36.5	42.9	47.6	9 16.9	43.5	47.7	9 57.3	44.0	47.8	10 37.5	44.6	47.9	11 17.7	45.1	48.1	37
38	7 15.9	41.3	46.5	7 57.2	41.8	46.6	8 38.4	42.3	46.7	9 19.4	42.9	46.8	10 00.4	43.4	47.0	10 41.3	44.0	47.1	11 22.1	44.5	47.2	12 02.8	45.0	47.4	38
39	7 57.2	41.2	45.8	8 39.0	41.7	45.9	9 20.7	42.2	46.0	10 02.3	42.8	46.1	10 43.8	43.4	46.3	11 25.3	43.8	46.4	12 06.6	44.4	46.6	12 47.8	44.9	46.7	39
40	8 38.4	+41.0	45.1	9 20.7	+41.6	45.2	10 02.9	+42.2	45.3	10 45.1	+42.7	45.4	11 27.2	+43.2	45.6	12 09.1	+43.8	45.7	12 51.0	+44.2	45.9	13 32.7	+44.8	46.0	40
41	9 19.4	41.0	44.3	10 02.3	41.5	44.4	10 45.1	42.1	44.6	11 27.8	42.6	44.7	12 10.4	43.1	44.9	12 52.9	43.6	45.0	13 35.2	44.2	45.2	14 17.5	44.6	45.4	41
42	10 00.4	40.9	43.6	10 43.8	41.5	43.7	11 27.2	41.9	43.8	12 10.4	42.5	44.0	12 53.5	43.0	44.1	13 36.5	43.5	44.3	14 19.4	44.0	44.5	15 02.1	44.6	44.7	42
43	10 41.3	40.8	42.8	11 25.3	41.3	43.0	12 09.1	41.9	43.1	12 52.9	42.3	43.3	13 36.5	42.9	43.4	14 20.0	43.4	43.6	15 03.4	43.9	43.8	15 46.7	44.4	44.0	43
44	11 22.1	40.7	42.1	12 06.6	41.2	42.2	12 51.0	41.7	42.4	13 35.2	42.3	42.5	14 19.4	42.7	42.7	15 03.4	43.3	42.9	15 47.3	43.8	43.1	16 31.1	44.2	43.3	44
45	12 02.8	+40.5	41.3	12 47.8	+41.0	41.5	13 32.7	+41.6	41.6	14 17.5	+42.0	41.8	15 02.1	+42.6	42.0	15 46.7	+43.1	42.2	16 31.1	+43.6	42.4	17 15.3	+44.1	42.6	45
46	12 43.3	40.4	40.6	13 28.8	41.0	40.7	14 14.3	41.4	40.9	14 59.5	42.0	41.1	15 44.7	42.5	41.2	16 29.8	42.9	41.4	17 14.7	43.4	41.6	17 59.4	44.0	41.9	46
47	13 23.7	40.3	39.8	14 09.8	40.8	40.0	14 55.7	41.3	40.2	15 41.5	41.8	40.3	16 27.2	42.3	40.5	17 12.7	42.8	40.7	17 58.1	43.3	40.9	18 43.4	43.8	41.1	47
48	14 04.0	40.2	39.1	14 50.6	40.6	39.2	15 37.0	41.1	39.4	16 23.3	41.6	39.6	17 09.5	42.1	39.8	17 55.5	42.7	40.0	18 41.4	43.2	40.2	19 27.2	43.6	40.4	48
49	14 44.2	40.0	38.3	15 31.2	40.5	38.5	16 18.1	41.0	38.6	17 04.9	41.5	38.8	17 51.6	42.0	39.0	18 38.2	42.4	39.2	19 24.6	42.9	39.5	20 10.8	43.4	39.7	49
50	15 24.2	+39.8	37.5	16 11.7	+40.3	37.7	16 59.1	+40.8	37.9	17 46.4	+41.3	38.1	18 33.6	+41.8	38.3	19 20.6	+42.3	38.5	20 07.5	+42.8	38.7	20 54.2	+43.3	38.9	50
51	16 04.0	39.7	36.7	16 52.0	40.2	36.9	17 39.9	40.7	37.1	18 27.7	41.1	37.3	19 15.4	41.6	37.5	20 02.9	42.1	37.7	20 50.3	42.5	38.0	21 37.5	43.0	38.2	51
52	16 43.7	39.4	36.0	17 32.2	39.9	36.1	18 20.6	40.4	36.3	19 08.8	40.9	36.5	19 57.0	41.4	36.8	20 45.0	41.8	37.0	21 32.8	42.4	37.2	22 20.5	42.9	37.5	52
53	17 23.1	39.3	35.2	18 12.1	39.8	35.4	19 01.0	40.2	35.6	19 49.7	40.8	35.8	20 38.4	41.2	36.0	21 26.8	41.7	36.2	22 15.2	42.1	36.4	23 03.4	42.6	36.7	53
54	18 02.4	39.1	34.4	18 51.9	39.6	34.6	19 41.2	40.1	34.8	20 30.5	40.5	35.0	21 19.6	40.9	35.2	22 08.5	41.5	35.4	22 57.3	41.9	35.7	23 46.0	42.4	35.9	54
55	18 41.5	+38.9	33.6	19 31.5	+39.3	33.8	20 21.3	+39.8	34.0	21 11.0	+40.2	34.2	22 00.5	+40.8	34.4	22 50.0	+41.2	34.6	23 39.2	+41.7	34.9	24 28.4	+42.1	35.1	55
56	19 20.4	38.7	32.8	20 10.8	39.1	33.0	21 01.1	39.6	33.2	21 51.2	40.1	33.4	22 41.3	40.5	33.6	23 31.2	40.9	33.9	24 20.9	41.5	34.1	25 10.5	41.9	34.4	56
57	19 59.1	38.5	32.0	20 49.9	38.9	32.2	21 40.7	39.3	32.4	22 31.3	39.8	32.6	23 21.8	40.2	32.8	24 12.1	40.8	33.1	25 02.4	41.1	33.3	25 52.4	41.7	33.6	57
58	20 37.6	38.2	31.1	21 28.8	38.7	31.3	22 20.0	39.1	31.6	23 11.1	39.6	31.8	24 02.0	40.0	32.0	24 52.9	40.4	32.3	25 43.5	40.9	32.5	26 34.1	41.3	32.8	58
59	21 15.8	38.0	30.3	22 07.5	38.4	30.5	22 59.1	38.9	30.7	23 50.7	39.2	31.0	24 42.0	39.8	31.2	25 33.3	40.2	31.4	26 24.4	40.7	31.7	27 15.4	41.1	32.0	59
60	21 53.8	+37.7	29.5	22 45.9	+38.2	29.7	23 38.0	+38.6	29.9	24 29.9	+39.1	30.1	25 21.8	+39.4	30.4	26 13.5	+39.9	30.6	27 05.1	+40.3	30.9	27 56.5	+40.8	31.1	60
61	22 31.5	37.4	28.7	23 24.1	37.9	28.9	24 16.6	38.3	29.1	25 09.0	38.7	29.3	26 01.2	39.2	29.5	26 53.4	39.6	29.8	27 45.4	40.0	30.0	28 37.3	40.4	30.3	61
62	23 08.9	37.2	27.8	24 02.0	37.6	28.0	24 54.9	38.0	28.2	25 47.7	38.4	28.4	26 40.4	38.9	28.7	27 33.0	39.3	28.9	28 25.4	39.7	29.2	29 17.7	40.2	29.5	62
63	23 46.1	36.9	26.9	24 39.6	37.3	27.2	25 32.9	37.7	27.4	26 26.1	38.2	27.6	27 19.3	38.5	27.8	28 12.3	38.9	28.1	29 05.1	39.4	28.3	29 57.9	39.8	28.6	63
64	24 23.0	36.6	26.1	25 16.9	37.0	26.3	26 10.6	37.4	26.5	27 04.3	37.8	26.7	27 57.8	38.2	27.0	28 51.2	38.6	27.2	29 44.5	39.1	27.5	30 37.7	39.5	27.7	64
65	24 59.6	+36.3	25.2	25 53.9	+36.7	25.4	26 48.0	+37.1	25.6	27 42.1	+37.4	25.9	28 36.0	+37.9	26.1	29 29.8	+38.3	26.3	30 23.6	+38.6	26.6	31 17.2	+39.1	26.9	65
66	25 35.9	36.0	24.3	26 30.6	36.3	24.5	27 25.1	36.7	24.7	28 19.5	37.2	25.0	29 13.9	37.5	25.2	30 08.1	37.9	25.4	31 02.2	38.4	25.7	31 56.3	38.7	26.0	66
67	26 11.9	35.7	23.4	27 06.9	36.0	23.6	28 01.8	36.4	23.9	28 56.7	36.7	24.1	29 51.4	37.2	24.3	30 46.0	37.6	24.5	31 40.6	37.9	24.8	32 35.0	38.3	25.1	67
68	26 47.6	35.3	22.5	27 42.9	35.7	22.7	28 38.2	36.1	22.9	29 33.4	36.4	23.2	30 28.6	36.7	23.4	31 23.6	37.1	23.6	32 18.5	37.5	23.9	33 13.3	37.9	24.1	68
69	27 22.9	34.9	21.6	28 18.6	35.3	21.8	29 14.3	35.6	22.0	30 09.8	36.0	22.3	31 05.3	36.4	22.5	32 00.7	36.8	22.7	32 56.0	37.1	23.0	33 51.2	37.5	23.2	69
70	27 57.8	+34.6	20.7	28 53.9	+34.9	20.9	29 49.9	+35.3	21.1	30 45.8	+35.7	21.3	31 41.7	+36.0	21.5	32 37.5	+36.3	21.8	33 33.1	+36.7	22.0	34 28.7	+37.1	22.3	70
71	28 32.4	34.2	19.8	29 28.8	34.5	20.0	30 25.2	34.8	20.2	31 21.5	35.1	20.4	32 17.7	35.5	20.6	33 13.8	35.9	20.8	34 09.8	36.2	21.1	35 05.8	36.5	21.3	71
72	29 06.6	33.8	18.9	30 03.3	34.2	19.0	31 00.0	34.5	19.2	31 56.6	34.8	19.4	32 53.2	35.1	19.6	33 49.7	35.4	19.9	34 46.0	35.8	20.1	35 42.3	36.2	20.3	72
73	29 40.4	33.4	17.9	30 37.5	33.6	18.1	31 34.5	34.0	18.3	32 31.4	34.3	18.5	33 28.3	34.6	18.7	34 25.1	34.9	18.9	35 21.8	35.3	19.1	36 18.5	35.6	19.4	73
74	30 13.8	32.9	16.9	31 11.1	33.3	17.1	32 08.5	33.5	17.3	33 05.7	33.9	17.5	34 02.9	34.2	17.7	35 00.0	34.5	17.9	35 57.1	34.8	18.1	36 54.1	35.1	18.4	74
75	30 46.7	+32.6	16.0	31 44.4	+32.8	16.1	32 42.0	+33.1	16.3	33 39.6	+33.3	16.5	34 37.1	+33.6	16.7	35 34.5	+34.0	16.9	36 31.9	+34.2	17.1	37 29.2	+34.6	17.3	75
76	31 19.3	32.0	15.0	32 17.2	32.3	15.2	33 15.1	32.6	15.3	34 12.9	32.9	15.5	35 10.7	33.2	15.7	36 08.5	33.4	15.9	37 06.1	33.8	16.1	38 03.8	34.0	16.3	76
77	31 51.3	31.7	14.0	32 49.5	31.9	14.2	33 47.7	32.1	14.3	34 45.8	32.4	14.5	35 43.9	32.6	14.7	36 41.9	32.9	14.9	37 39.9	33.1	15.0	38 37.8	33.4	15.3	77
78	32 23.0	31.1	13.0	33 21.4	31.4	13.1	34 19.8	31.6	13.3	35 18.2	31.8	13.5	36 16.5	32.1	13.6	37 14.8	32.3	13.8	38 13.0	32.6	14.0	39 11.2	32.9	14.2	78
79	32 54.1	30.6	12.0	33 52.8	30.8	12.1	34 51.4	31.1	12.3	35 50.0	31.3	12.4	36 48.6	31.5	12.6	37 47.1	31.8	12.7	38 45.6	32.0	12.9	39 44.1	32.2	13.1	79
80	33 24.7	+30.1	11.0	34 23.6	+30.3	11.1	35 22.5	+30.5	11.2	36 21.3	+30.7	11.4	37 20.1	+31.0	11.5	38 18.9	+31.1	11.7	39 17.6	+31.4	11.8	40 16.3	+31.6	12.0	80
81	33 54.8	29.6	9.9	34 53.9	29.8	10.0	35 53.0	29.9	10.2	36 52.0	30.2	10.3	37 51.1	30.3	10.4	38 50.0	30.6	10.6	39 49.0	30.8	10.7	40 47.9	31.0	10.9	81
82	34 24.4	29.0	8.9	35 23.7	29.2	9.0	36 22.9	29.4	9.1	37 22.2	29.5	9.2	38 21.4	29.7	9.3	39 20.6	29.9	9.5	40 19.8	30.0	9.6	41 18.9	30.3	9.7	82
83	34 53.4	28.5	7.8	35 52.9	28.6	7.9	36 52.3	28.8	8.0	37 51.7	28.9	8.1	38 51.1	29.1	8.2	39 50.5	29.2	8.3	40 49.8	29.4	8.5	41 49.2	29.5	8.6	83
84	35 21.9	27.9	6.7	36 21.5	28.0	6.8	37 21.1	28.1	6.9	38 20.6	28.3	7.0	39 20.2	28.4	7.1	40 19.7	28.6	7.2	41 19.2	28.7	7.3	42 18.7	28.9	7.4	84
85	35 49.8	+27.3	5.6	36 49.5	+27.4	5.7	37 49.2	+27.5	5.8	38 48.9	+27.6	5.9	39 48.6	+27.7	5.9	40 48.3	+27.8	6.0	41 47.9	+28.0	6.1	42 47.6	+28.1	6.2	85
86	36 17.1	26.7	4.5	37 16.9	26.8	4.6	38 16.7	26.9	4.7	39 16.5	27.0	4.7	40 16.3	27.0	4.8	41 16.1	27.1	4.9	42 15.9	27.2	4.9	43 15.7	27.3	5.0	86
87	36 43.8	26.0	3.4	37 43.7	26.1	3.5	38 43.6	26.2	3.5	39 43.5	26.2	3.6	40 43.3	26.3	3.6	41 43.2	26.4	3.7	42 43.1	26.4	3.7	43 43.0	26.5	3.8	87
88	37 09.8	25.5	2.3	38 09.8	25.4	2.3	39 09.8	25.4	2.4	40 09.7	25.5	2.4	41 09.6	25.6	2.4	42 09.6	25.6	2.5	43 09.5	25.7	2.5	44 09.5	25.7	2.5	88
89	37 35.3	24.7	1.2	38 35.2	24.8	1.2	39 35.2	24.8	1.2	40 35.2	24.8	1.2	41 35.2	24.8	1.2	42 35.2	24.8	1.2	43 35.2	24.8	1.3	44 35.2	24.8	1.3	89
90	38 00.0	+24.1	0.0	39 00.0	+24.0	0.0	40 00.0	+24.0	0.0	41 00.0	+24.0	0.0	42 00.0	+24.0	0.0	43 00.0	+24.0	0.0	44 00.0	+24.0	0.0	45 00.0	+24.0	0.0	90
	38°			39°			40°			41°			42°			43°			44°			45°			

S. Lat. { L.H.A. greater than 180°......Zn=180°−Z
L.H.A. less than 180°............Zn=180°+Z

Dec.	38° Hc	d	Z	39° Hc	d	Z	40° Hc	d	Z	41° Hc	d	Z	Dec.
°	° ′	′	°	° ′	′	°	° ′	′	°	° ′	′	°	°
0	6 17.8	−37.2	94.9	6 12.5	−38.0	95.1	6 07.2	−38.8	95.2	6 01.8	−39.7	95.3	0
1	5 40.6	37.3	95.7	5 34.5	38.0	95.8	5 28.4	38.9	95.9	5 22.1	39.6	96.0	1
2	5 03.3	37.3	96.5	4 56.5	38.2	96.6	4 49.5	38.9	96.7	4 42.5	39.7	96.8	2
3	4 26.0	37.4	97.3	4 18.3	38.2	97.4	4 10.6	39.0	97.5	4 02.8	39.8	97.5	3
4	3 48.6	37.4	98.1	3 40.1	38.2	98.2	3 31.6	39.0	98.2	3 23.0	39.8	98.3	4
5	3 11.2	−37.4	98.9	3 01.9	−38.2	98.9	2 52.6	−39.0	99.0	2 43.2	−39.8	99.0	5
6	2 33.8	37.5	99.7	2 23.7	38.3	99.7	2 13.6	39.1	99.7	2 03.4	39.9	99.8	6
7	1 56.3	37.5	100.4	1 45.4	38.3	100.5	1 34.5	39.1	100.5	1 23.5	39.8	100.5	7
8	1 18.8	37.5	101.2	1 07.1	38.3	101.2	0 55.4	39.1	101.3	0 43.7	39.9	101.3	8
9	0 41.3	37.5	102.0	0 28.8	−38.3	102.0	0 16.3	−39.1	102.0	0 03.8	−39.8	102.0	9
10	0 03.8	−37.6	102.8	0 09.5	+38.3	77.2	0 22.8	+39.1	77.2	0 36.0	+39.9	77.2	10
11	0 33.8	+37.5	76.4	0 47.8	38.3	76.5	1 01.9	39.0	76.5	1 15.9	39.8	76.5	11
12	1 11.3	37.5	75.7	1 26.1	38.3	75.7	1 40.9	39.1	75.7	1 55.7	39.9	75.7	12
13	1 48.8	37.5	74.9	2 04.4	38.3	74.9	2 20.0	39.0	74.9	2 35.6	39.8	75.0	13
14	2 26.3	37.4	74.1	2 42.7	38.2	74.1	2 59.0	39.0	74.2	3 15.4	39.7	74.2	14
15	3 03.7	+37.4	73.3	3 20.9	+38.2	73.4	3 38.0	+39.0	73.4	3 55.1	+39.8	73.5	15
16	3 41.1	37.4	72.5	3 59.1	38.2	72.6	4 17.0	38.9	72.7	4 34.9	39.6	72.7	16
17	4 18.5	37.3	71.7	4 37.3	38.1	71.8	4 55.9	38.9	71.9	5 14.5	39.7	72.0	17
18	4 55.8	37.3	71.0	5 15.4	38.0	71.0	5 34.8	38.8	71.1	5 54.2	39.5	71.2	18
19	5 33.1	37.2	70.2	5 53.4	38.0	70.3	6 13.6	38.8	70.4	6 33.7	39.5	70.5	19
20	6 10.3	+37.2	69.4	6 31.4	+37.9	69.5	6 52.4	+38.6	69.6	7 13.2	+39.4	69.7	20
21	6 47.5	37.0	68.6	7 09.3	37.8	68.7	7 31.0	38.6	68.8	7 52.6	39.4	69.0	21
22	7 24.5	37.0	67.8	7 47.1	37.8	67.9	8 09.6	38.5	68.1	8 32.0	39.2	68.2	22
23	8 01.5	36.9	67.0	8 24.9	37.6	67.1	8 48.1	38.4	67.3	9 11.2	39.2	67.4	23
24	8 38.4	36.8	66.2	9 02.5	37.6	66.4	9 26.5	38.3	66.5	9 50.4	39.0	66.7	24
25	9 15.2	+36.7	65.4	9 40.1	+37.4	65.6	10 04.8	+38.2	65.7	10 29.4	+38.9	65.9	25
26	9 51.9	36.5	64.6	10 17.5	37.3	64.8	10 43.0	38.1	64.9	11 08.3	38.9	65.1	26
27	10 28.4	36.5	63.8	10 54.8	37.2	64.0	11 21.1	37.9	64.2	11 47.2	38.6	64.3	27
28	11 04.9	36.3	63.0	11 32.0	37.1	63.2	11 59.0	37.8	63.4	12 25.8	38.6	63.6	28
29	11 41.2	36.2	62.2	12 09.1	36.9	62.4	12 36.8	37.7	62.6	13 04.4	38.4	62.8	29
30	12 17.4	+36.0	61.4	12 46.0	+36.8	61.6	13 14.5	+37.5	61.8	13 42.8	+38.3	62.0	30
31	12 53.4	35.9	60.5	13 22.8	36.6	60.8	13 52.0	37.4	61.0	14 21.1	38.1	61.2	31
32	13 29.3	35.7	59.7	13 59.4	36.5	59.9	14 29.4	37.2	60.2	14 59.2	37.9	60.4	32
33	14 05.0	35.6	58.9	14 35.9	36.3	59.1	15 06.6	37.0	59.3	15 37.1	37.7	59.6	33
34	14 40.6	35.3	58.1	15 12.2	36.1	58.3	15 43.6	36.9	58.5	16 14.8	37.6	58.8	34
35	15 15.9	+35.2	57.2	15 48.3	+35.9	57.5	16 20.5	+36.6	57.7	16 52.4	+37.4	58.0	35
36	15 51.1	35.0	56.4	16 24.2	35.7	56.6	16 57.1	36.5	56.9	17 29.8	37.2	57.1	36
37	16 26.1	34.8	55.5	16 59.9	35.6	55.8	17 33.6	36.2	56.0	18 07.0	36.9	56.3	37
38	17 00.9	34.6	54.7	17 35.5	35.3	54.9	18 09.8	36.0	55.2	18 43.9	36.8	55.5	38
39	17 35.5	34.3	53.8	18 10.8	35.0	54.1	18 45.8	35.8	54.4	19 20.7	36.5	54.6	39
40	18 09.8	+34.1	53.0	18 45.8	+34.9	53.2	19 21.6	+35.6	53.5	19 57.2	+36.2	53.8	40
41	18 43.9	33.9	52.1	19 20.7	34.5	52.4	19 57.2	35.3	52.7	20 33.4	36.0	53.0	41
42	19 17.8	33.6	51.2	19 55.2	34.4	51.5	20 32.5	35.0	51.8	21 09.4	35.8	52.1	42
43	19 51.4	33.4	50.4	20 29.6	34.1	50.6	21 07.5	34.8	50.9	21 45.2	35.5	51.2	43
44	20 24.8	33.1	49.5	21 03.7	33.8	49.8	21 42.3	34.5	50.1	22 20.7	35.2	50.4	44
45	20 57.9	+32.8	48.6	21 37.5	+33.5	48.9	22 16.8	+34.2	49.2	22 55.9	+34.9	49.5	45
46	21 30.7	32.5	47.7	22 11.0	33.2	48.0	22 51.0	33.9	48.3	23 30.8	34.6	48.6	46
47	22 03.2	32.2	46.8	22 44.2	32.9	47.1	23 24.9	33.6	47.4	24 05.4	34.3	47.7	47
48	22 35.4	31.9	45.9	23 17.1	32.6	46.2	23 58.5	33.3	46.5	24 39.7	34.0	46.8	48
49	23 07.3	31.6	44.9	23 49.7	32.3	45.3	24 31.8	33.0	45.6	25 13.7	33.6	45.9	49
50	23 38.9	+31.3	44.0	24 22.0	+31.9	44.3	25 04.8	+32.6	44.7	25 47.3	+33.3	45.0	50
51	24 10.2	30.9	43.1	24 53.9	31.6	43.4	25 37.4	32.2	43.7	26 20.6	32.9	44.1	51
52	24 41.1	30.6	42.1	25 25.5	31.2	42.5	26 09.6	31.9	42.8	26 53.5	32.6	43.1	52
53	25 11.7	30.1	41.2	25 56.7	30.8	41.5	26 41.5	31.5	41.8	27 26.1	32.2	42.2	53
54	25 41.8	29.9	40.2	26 27.5	30.5	40.6	27 13.0	31.1	40.9	27 58.3	31.7	41.2	54
55	26 11.7	+29.4	39.3	26 58.0	+30.1	39.6	27 44.1	+30.7	39.9	28 30.0	+31.4	40.3	55
56	26 41.1	29.0	38.3	27 28.1	29.6	38.6	28 14.8	30.3	38.9	29 01.4	30.9	39.3	56
57	27 10.1	28.6	37.3	27 57.7	29.3	37.6	28 45.1	29.9	38.0	29 32.3	30.5	38.3	57
58	27 38.7	28.2	36.3	28 27.0	28.7	36.6	29 15.0	29.4	37.0	30 02.8	30.1	37.3	58
59	28 06.9	27.7	35.3	28 55.7	28.4	35.6	29 44.4	29.0	36.0	30 32.9	29.5	36.3	59
60	28 34.6	+27.3	34.3	29 24.1	+27.9	34.6	30 13.4	+28.5	35.0	31 02.4	+29.1	35.3	60
61	29 01.9	26.9	33.3	29 52.0	27.4	33.6	30 41.9	28.0	33.9	31 31.5	28.6	34.3	61
62	29 28.8	26.3	32.3	30 19.4	26.9	32.6	31 09.9	27.5	32.9	32 00.1	28.1	33.2	62
63	29 55.1	25.9	31.2	30 46.3	26.5	31.5	31 37.4	27.0	31.9	32 28.2	27.6	32.2	63
64	30 21.0	25.3	30.2	31 12.8	25.9	30.5	32 04.4	26.4	30.8	32 55.8	27.1	31.1	64
65	30 46.3	+24.9	29.1	31 38.7	+25.4	29.4	32 30.8	+26.0	29.8	33 22.9	+26.4	30.1	65
66	31 11.2	24.3	28.1	32 04.1	24.8	28.4	32 56.8	25.4	28.7	33 49.3	25.9	29.0	66
67	31 35.5	23.8	27.0	32 28.9	24.3	27.3	33 22.2	24.8	27.6	34 15.2	25.4	27.9	67
68	31 59.3	23.2	25.9	32 53.2	23.7	26.2	33 47.0	24.2	26.5	34 40.6	24.7	26.8	68
69	32 22.5	22.7	24.8	33 16.9	23.2	25.1	34 11.2	23.6	25.4	35 05.3	24.1	25.7	69
70	32 45.2	+22.1	23.7	33 40.1	+22.5	24.0	34 34.8	+23.0	24.3	35 29.4	+23.5	24.6	70
71	33 07.3	21.5	22.6	34 02.6	21.9	22.9	34 57.8	22.4	23.2	35 52.9	22.9	23.4	71
72	33 28.8	20.9	21.5	34 24.5	21.3	21.8	35 20.2	21.8	22.0	36 15.8	22.2	22.3	72
73	33 49.7	20.2	20.4	34 45.8	20.7	20.6	35 42.0	21.0	20.9	36 38.0	21.5	21.1	73
74	34 09.9	19.7	19.3	35 06.5	20.0	19.5	36 03.0	20.5	19.7	36 59.5	20.8	20.0	74
75	34 29.6	+18.9	18.1	35 26.5	+19.4	18.3	36 23.5	+19.7	18.6	37 20.3	+20.1	18.8	75
76	34 48.5	18.4	17.0	35 45.9	18.7	17.2	36 43.2	19.0	17.4	37 40.4	19.4	17.6	76
77	35 06.9	17.6	15.8	36 04.6	18.0	16.0	37 02.2	18.3	16.2	37 59.8	18.7	16.4	77
78	35 24.5	17.0	14.6	36 22.6	17.2	14.8	37 20.5	17.6	15.0	38 18.5	17.9	15.2	78
79	35 41.5	16.3	13.5	36 39.8	16.6	13.6	37 38.1	16.9	13.8	38 36.4	17.1	14.0	79
80	35 57.8	+15.6	12.3	36 56.4	+15.8	12.4	37 55.0	+16.1	12.6	38 53.5	+16.4	12.8	80
81	36 13.4	14.8	11.1	37 12.2	15.1	11.2	38 11.1	15.3	11.4	39 09.9	15.5	11.5	81
82	36 28.2	14.2	9.9	37 27.3	14.4	10.0	38 26.4	14.5	10.1	39 25.4	14.8	10.3	82
83	36 42.4	13.3	8.7	37 41.7	13.5	8.8	38 40.9	13.8	8.9	39 40.2	14.0	9.0	83
84	36 55.7	12.7	7.4	37 55.2	12.8	7.5	38 54.7	13.0	7.6	39 54.2	13.1	7.8	84
85	37 08.4	+11.9	6.2	38 08.0	+12.0	6.3	39 07.7	+12.1	6.4	40 07.3	+12.3	6.5	85
86	37 20.3	11.1	5.0	38 20.0	11.2	5.1	39 19.8	11.3	5.1	40 19.6	11.4	5.2	86
87	37 31.4	10.3	3.7	38 31.2	10.4	3.8	39 31.1	10.5	3.9	40 31.0	10.5	3.9	87
88	37 41.7	9.5	2.5	38 41.6	9.6	2.5	39 41.6	9.6	2.6	40 41.5	9.7	2.6	88
89	37 51.2	8.8	1.3	38 51.2	8.8	1.3	39 51.2	8.8	1.3	40 51.2	8.8	1.3	89
90	38 00.0	+7.9	0.0	39 00.0	+7.9	0.0	40 00.0	+7.9	0.0	41 00.0	+7.9	0.0	90
	38°			39°			40°			41°			

Dec.	42° Hc	d	Z	43° Hc	d	Z	44° Hc	d	Z	45° Hc	d	Z	Dec.
°	° ′	′	°	° ′	′	°	° ′	′	°	° ′	′	°	°
0	5 56.2	−40.4	95.4	5 50.5	−41.1	95.5	5 44.7	−41.9	95.6	5 38.9	−42.7	95.7	0
1	5 15.8	40.5	96.1	5 09.4	41.3	96.2	5 02.8	41.9	96.3	4 56.2	42.7	96.4	1
2	4 35.3	40.4	96.9	4 28.1	41.2	96.9	4 20.9	42.0	97.0	4 13.5	42.7	97.1	2
3	3 54.9	40.6	97.6	3 46.9	41.3	97.7	3 38.9	42.1	97.7	3 30.8	42.8	97.8	3
4	3 14.3	40.5	98.3	3 05.6	41.3	98.4	2 56.8	42.0	98.4	2 48.0	42.8	98.5	4
5	2 33.8	−40.6	99.1	2 24.3	−41.4	99.1	2 14.8	−42.1	99.2	2 05.2	−42.8	99.2	5
6	1 53.2	40.6	99.8	1 42.9	41.3	99.8	1 32.7	42.1	99.9	1 22.4	42.9	99.9	6
7	1 12.6	40.6	100.5	1 01.6	41.4	100.6	0 50.6	42.1	100.6	0 39.5	−42.8	100.6	7
8	0 32.0	−40.7	101.3	0 20.2	−41.4	101.3	0 08.5	−42.2	101.3	0 03.3	+42.8	78.7	8
9	0 08.7	+40.6	78.0	0 21.2	+41.3	78.0	0 33.7	+42.1	78.0	0 46.1	42.9	78.0	9
10	0 49.3	+40.6	77.2	1 02.5	+41.4	77.3	1 15.8	+42.0	77.3	1 29.0	+42.8	77.3	10
11	1 29.9	40.6	76.5	1 43.9	41.3	76.5	1 57.8	42.1	76.6	2 11.8	42.8	76.6	11
12	2 10.5	40.6	75.8	2 25.2	41.4	75.8	2 39.9	42.1	75.9	2 54.6	42.7	75.9	12
13	2 51.1	40.5	75.0	3 06.6	41.3	75.1	3 22.0	42.0	75.1	3 37.3	42.8	75.2	13
14	3 31.6	40.6	74.3	3 47.8	41.3	74.4	4 04.0	42.0	74.4	4 20.1	42.7	74.5	14
15	4 12.2	+40.4	73.6	4 29.1	+41.2	73.6	4 46.0	+41.9	73.7	5 02.8	+42.6	73.8	15
16	4 52.6	40.4	72.8	5 10.3	41.2	72.9	5 27.9	41.9	73.0	5 45.4	42.6	73.1	16
17	5 33.0	40.4	72.1	5 51.5	41.1	72.2	6 09.8	41.8	72.3	6 28.0	42.5	72.4	17
18	6 13.4	40.3	71.3	6 32.6	41.0	71.4	6 51.6	41.8	71.5	7 10.5	42.5	71.7	18
19	6 53.7	40.3	70.6	7 13.6	41.0	70.7	7 33.4	41.7	70.8	7 53.0	42.4	71.0	19
20	7 34.0	+40.1	69.8	7 54.6	+40.9	70.0	8 15.1	+41.6	70.1	8 35.4	+42.3	70.2	20
21	8 14.1	40.1	69.1	8 35.5	40.8	69.2	8 56.7	41.5	69.4	9 17.7	42.3	69.5	21
22	8 54.2	40.0	68.3	9 16.3	40.7	68.5	9 38.2	41.4	68.6	10 00.0	42.1	68.8	22
23	9 34.2	39.9	67.6	9 57.0	40.6	67.7	10 19.6	41.4	67.9	10 42.1	42.1	68.1	23
24	10 14.1	39.7	66.8	10 37.6	40.5	67.0	11 01.0	41.2	67.2	11 24.2	41.9	67.3	24
25	10 53.8	+39.7	66.1	11 18.1	+40.4	66.2	11 42.2	+41.1	66.4	12 06.1	+41.8	66.6	25
26	11 33.5	39.6	65.3	11 58.5	40.3	65.5	12 23.3	41.0	65.7	12 47.9	41.7	65.9	26
27	12 13.1	39.4	64.5	12 38.8	40.1	64.7	13 04.3	40.8	64.9	13 29.6	41.6	65.1	27
28	12 52.5	39.3	63.8	13 18.9	40.0	64.0	13 45.1	40.8	64.2	14 11.2	41.4	64.4	28
29	13 31.8	39.1	63.0	13 58.9	39.9	63.2	14 25.9	40.5	63.4	14 52.6	41.3	63.7	29
30	14 10.9	+39.0	62.2	14 38.8	+39.7	62.4	15 06.4	+40.5	62.7	15 33.9	+41.1	62.9	30
31	14 49.9	38.8	61.4	15 18.5	39.5	61.6	15 46.9	40.2	61.9	16 15.0	41.0	62.1	31
32	15 28.7	38.7	60.6	15 58.0	39.4	60.9	16 27.1	40.1	61.1	16 56.0	40.8	61.4	32
33	16 07.4	38.4	59.8	16 37.4	39.2	60.1	17 07.2	39.9	60.3	17 36.8	40.6	60.6	33
34	16 45.8	38.3	59.0	17 16.6	39.0	59.3	17 47.1	39.7	59.6	18 17.4	40.4	59.8	34
35	17 24.1	+38.1	58.2	17 55.6	+38.8	58.5	18 26.8	+39.6	58.8	18 57.8	+40.2	59.1	35
36	18 02.2	37.9	57.4	18 34.4	38.6	57.7	19 06.4	39.3	58.0	19 38.0	40.1	58.3	36
37	18 40.1	37.7	56.6	19 13.0	38.4	56.9	19 45.7	39.1	57.2	20 18.1	39.8	57.5	37
38	19 17.8	37.4	55.8	19 51.4	38.2	56.1	20 24.8	38.9	56.4	20 57.9	39.6	56.7	38
39	19 55.2	37.3	54.9	20 29.6	37.9	55.2	21 03.7	38.6	55.6	21 37.5	39.3	55.9	39
40	20 32.5	+36.9	54.1	21 07.5	+37.7	54.4	21 42.3	+38.4	54.7	22 16.8	+39.1	55.1	40
41	21 09.4	36.8	53.3	21 45.2	37.4	53.6	22 20.7	38.1	53.9	22 55.9	38.8	54.2	41
42	21 46.2	36.4	52.4	22 22.6	37.2	52.7	22 58.8	37.9	53.1	23 34.7	38.6	53.4	42
43	22 22.6	36.2	51.6	22 59.8	36.9	51.9	23 36.7	37.6	52.2	24 13.3	38.3	52.6	43
44	22 58.8	35.9	50.7	23 36.7	36.6	51.0	24 14.3	37.3	51.4	24 51.6	38.0	51.7	44
45	23 34.7	+35.7	49.8	24 13.3	+36.3	50.2	24 51.6	+37.0	50.5	25 29.6	+37.7	50.9	45
46	24 10.4	35.3	48.9	24 49.6	36.0	49.3	25 28.6	36.7	49.6	26 07.3	37.4	50.0	46
47	24 45.7	35.0	48.1	25 25.6	35.7	48.4	26 05.3	36.4	48.8	26 44.7	37.1	49.1	47
48	25 20.7	34.6	47.2	26 01.3	35.4	47.5	26 41.7	36.1	47.9	27 21.8	36.7	48.3	48
49	25 55.3	34.3	46.2	26 36.7	35.0	46.6	27 17.8	35.6	47.0	27 58.5	36.4	47.4	49
50	26 29.6	+34.0	45.3	27 11.7	+34.6	45.7	27 53.4	+35.4	46.1	28 34.9	+36.1	46.5	50
51	27 03.6	33.6	44.4	27 46.3	34.3	44.8	28 28.8	34.9	45.2	29 11.0	35.6	45.5	51
52	27 37.2	33.2	43.5	28 20.6	33.9	43.8	29 03.7	34.6	44.2	29 46.6	35.3	44.6	52
53	28 10.4	32.9	42.5	28 54.5	33.5	42.9	29 38.3	34.2	43.3	30 21.9	34.8	43.7	53
54	28 43.3	32.4	41.6	29 28.0	33.1	42.0	30 12.5	33.8	42.3	30 56.7	34.4	42.7	54
55	29 15.7	+32.0	40.6	30 01.1	+32.7	41.0	30 46.3	+33.3	41.4	31 31.1	+34.0	41.8	55
56	29 47.7	31.6	39.7	30 33.8	32.2	40.0	31 19.6	32.9	40.4	32 05.1	33.6	40.8	56
57	30 19.3	31.1	38.7	31 06.0	31.8	39.0	31 52.5	32.4	39.4	32 38.7	33.1	39.8	57
58	30 50.4	30.7	37.7	31 37.8	31.3	38.0	32 24.9	32.0	38.4	33 11.8	32.6	38.8	58
59	31 21.1	30.2	36.7	32 09.1	30.8	37.0	32 56.9	31.4	37.4	33 44.4	32.1	37.8	59
60	31 51.3	+29.7	35.7	32 39.9	+30.4	36.0	33 28.3	+31.0	36.4	34 16.5	+31.6	36.8	60
61	32 21.0	29.2	34.6	33 10.3	29.8	35.0	33 59.3	30.5	35.4	34 48.1	31.1	35.8	61
62	32 50.2	28.7	33.6	33 40.1	29.3	34.0	34 29.8	29.9	34.3	35 19.2	30.5	34.7	62
63	33 18.9	28.2	32.5	34 09.4	28.7	32.9	34 59.7	29.3	33.3	35 49.7	30.0	33.7	63
64	33 47.1	27.6	31.5	34 38.1	28.2	31.8	35 29.0	28.8	32.2	36 19.7	29.3	32.6	64
65	34 14.7	+27.0	30.4	35 06.3	+27.6	30.8	35 57.8	+28.2	31.1	36 49.0	+28.8	31.5	65
66	34 41.7	26.5	29.3	35 33.9	27.1	29.7	36 26.0	27.6	30.0	37 17.8	28.2	30.4	66
67	35 08.2	25.9	28.2	36 01.0	26.4	28.6	36 53.6	26.9	28.9	37 46.0	27.5	29.3	67
68	35 34.1	25.2	27.1	36 27.4	25.8	27.5	37 20.5	26.3	27.8	38 13.5	26.9	28.2	68
69	35 59.3	24.6	26.0	36 53.2	25.1	26.3	37 46.8	25.7	26.7	38 40.4	26.2	27.0	69
70	36 23.9	+24.0	24.9	37 18.3	+24.5	25.2	38 12.5	+25.0	25.5	39 06.6	+25.5	25.9	70
71	36 47.9	23.3	23.7	37 42.8	23.8	24.1	38 37.5	24.3	24.4	39 32.1	24.8	24.7	71
72	37 11.2	22.7	22.6	38 06.6	23.1	22.9	39 01.8	23.6	23.2	39 56.9	24.0	23.5	72
73	37 33.9	21.9	21.4	38 29.7	22.4	21.7	39 25.4	22.8	22.0	40 20.9	23.3	22.3	73
74	37 55.8	21.2	20.2	38 52.1	21.6	20.5	39 48.2	22.1	20.8	40 44.2	22.6	21.1	74
75	38 17.0	+20.6	19.1	39 13.7	+20.9	19.3	40 10.3	+21.3	19.6	41 06.8	+21.7	19.9	75
76	38 37.6	19.7	17.9	39 34.6	20.2	18.1	40 31.6	20.5	18.4	41 28.5	20.9	18.6	76
77	38 57.3	19.0	16.6	39 54.8	19.3	16.9	40 52.1	19.8	17.1	41 49.4	20.2	17.4	77
78	39 16.3	18.3	15.4	40 14.1	18.6	15.6	41 11.9	18.9	15.9	42 09.6	19.2	16.1	78
79	39 34.6	17.4	14.2	40 32.7	17.8	14.4	41 30.8	18.1	14.6	42 28.8	18.4	14.8	79
80	39 52.0	+16.7	12.9	40 50.5	+16.9	13.1	41 48.9	+17.2	13.3	42 47.2	+17.5	13.6	80
81	40 08.7	15.8	11.7	41 07.4	16.1	11.9	42 06.1	16.3	12.1	43 04.7	16.7	12.2	81
82	40 24.5	15.0	10.4	41 23.5	15.2	10.6	42 22.4	15.5	10.8	43 21.4	15.7	10.9	82
83	40 39.5	14.1	9.2	41 38.7	14.3	9.3	42 37.9	14.5	9.4	43 37.1	14.7	9.6	83
84	40 53.6	13.3	7.9	41 53.0	13.5	8.0	42 52.4	13.7	8.1	43 51.8	13.8	8.3	84
85	41 06.9	+12.4	6.6	42 06.5	+12.5	6.7	43 06.1	+12.7	6.8	44 05.6	+12.9	6.9	85
86	41 19.3	11.5	5.3	42 19.0	11.7	5.4	43 18.8	11.7	5.4	44 18.5	11.9	5.5	86
87	41 30.8	10.7	4.0	42 30.7	10.7	4.0	43 30.5	10.8	4.1	44 30.4	10.9	4.2	87
88	41 41.5	9.7	2.7	42 41.4	9.8	2.7	43 41.3	9.9	2.7	44 41.3	9.8	2.8	88
89	41 51.2	8.8	1.3	42 51.2	8.8	1.4	43 51.2	8.8	1.4	44 51.1	8.9	1.4	89
90	42 00.0	+7.9	0.0	43 00.0	+7.9	0.0	44 00.0	+7.9	0.0	45 00.0	+7.8	0.0	90
	42°			43°			44°			45°			

S. Lat. { L.H.A. greater than 180°......Zn=180°−Z; L.H.A. less than 180°...........Zn=180°+Z

83°, 277° L.H.A. LATITUDE SAME NAME AS DECLINATION

N. Lat. {L.H.A. greater than 180°......Zn=Z; L.H.A. less than 180°............Zn=360°−Z}

Dec.	38°			39°			40°			41°		
	Hc	d	Z	Hc	d	Z	Hc	d	Z	Hc	d	Z
°	° ′	′	°	° ′	′	°	° ′	′	°	° ′	′	°
0	5 30.7	+37.0	94.3	5 26.1	+37.9	94.4	5 21.4	+38.7	94.5	5 16.6	+39.5	94.6
1	6 07.7	37.0	93.5	6 04.0	37.8	93.6	6 00.1	38.7	93.7	5 56.1	39.5	93.8
2	6 44.7	37.0	92.7	6 41.8	37.8	92.9	6 38.8	38.5	93.0	6 35.6	39.4	93.1
3	7 21.7	36.8	91.9	7 19.6	37.6	92.1	7 17.3	38.5	92.2	7 15.0	39.2	92.3
4	7 58.5	36.8	91.2	7 57.2	37.6	91.3	7 55.8	38.4	91.4	7 54.2	39.3	91.6
5	8 35.3	+36.6	90.4	8 34.8	+37.5	90.5	8 34.2	+38.3	90.7	8 33.5	+39.1	90.8
6	9 11.9	36.6	89.6	9 12.3	37.4	89.7	9 12.5	38.2	89.9	9 12.6	39.0	90.0
7	9 48.5	36.4	88.7	9 49.7	37.3	88.9	9 50.7	38.2	89.1	9 51.6	38.9	89.3
8	10 24.9	36.3	87.9	10 27.0	37.1	88.1	10 28.9	37.9	88.3	10 30.5	38.8	88.5
9	11 01.2	36.2	87.1	11 04.1	37.1	87.3	11 06.8	37.9	87.5	11 09.3	38.7	87.7
10	11 37.4	+36.1	86.3	11 41.2	+36.9	86.5	11 44.7	+37.7	86.7	11 48.0	+38.6	86.9
11	12 13.5	35.9	85.5	12 18.1	36.7	85.7	12 22.4	37.6	85.9	12 26.6	38.4	86.2
12	12 49.4	35.7	84.7	12 54.8	36.6	84.9	13 00.0	37.5	85.1	13 05.0	38.3	85.4
13	13 25.1	35.6	83.9	13 31.4	36.5	84.1	13 37.5	37.3	84.3	13 43.3	38.1	84.6
14	14 00.7	35.4	83.0	14 07.9	36.3	83.3	14 14.8	37.1	83.5	14 21.4	38.0	83.8
15	14 36.1	+35.3	82.2	14 44.2	+36.1	82.5	14 51.9	+37.0	82.7	14 59.4	+37.8	83.0
16	15 11.4	35.0	81.4	15 20.3	35.9	81.6	15 28.9	36.7	81.9	15 37.2	37.6	82.2
17	15 46.4	34.9	80.5	15 56.2	35.7	80.8	16 05.6	36.6	81.1	16 14.8	37.4	81.4
18	16 21.3	34.6	79.7	16 31.9	35.5	80.0	16 42.2	36.4	80.2	16 52.2	37.3	80.5
19	16 55.9	34.5	78.8	17 07.4	35.3	79.1	17 18.6	36.2	79.4	17 29.5	37.0	79.7
20	17 30.4	+34.2	78.0	17 42.7	+35.1	78.3	17 54.8	+35.9	78.6	18 06.5	+36.8	78.9
21	18 04.6	34.0	77.1	18 17.8	34.9	77.4	18 30.7	35.8	77.7	18 43.3	36.6	78.1
22	18 38.6	33.7	76.2	18 52.7	34.6	76.6	19 06.5	35.5	76.9	19 19.9	36.4	77.2
23	19 12.3	33.5	75.4	19 27.3	34.4	75.7	19 42.0	35.3	76.0	19 56.3	36.1	76.4
24	19 45.8	33.3	74.5	20 01.7	34.1	74.8	20 17.3	35.0	75.2	20 32.4	35.9	75.5
25	20 19.1	+32.9	73.6	20 35.8	+33.9	73.9	20 52.3	+34.7	74.3	21 08.3	+35.6	74.7
26	20 52.0	32.7	72.7	21 09.7	33.6	73.1	21 27.0	34.5	73.4	21 43.9	35.4	73.8
27	21 24.7	32.4	71.8	21 43.3	33.3	72.2	22 01.5	34.1	72.6	22 19.3	35.0	72.9
28	21 57.1	32.1	70.9	22 16.6	33.0	71.3	22 35.6	33.9	71.7	22 54.3	34.8	72.1
29	22 29.2	31.8	70.0	22 49.6	32.7	70.4	23 09.5	33.6	70.8	23 29.1	34.5	71.2
30	23 01.0	+31.5	69.1	23 22.3	+32.3	69.5	23 43.1	+33.3	69.9	24 03.6	+34.1	70.3
31	23 32.5	31.1	68.1	23 54.6	32.1	68.5	24 16.4	32.9	69.0	24 37.7	33.8	69.4
32	24 03.6	30.8	67.2	24 26.7	31.6	67.6	24 49.3	32.6	68.0	25 11.5	33.5	68.5
33	24 34.4	30.4	66.3	24 58.3	31.4	66.7	25 21.9	32.2	67.1	25 45.0	33.2	67.5
34	25 04.8	30.1	65.3	25 29.7	31.0	65.7	25 54.1	31.9	66.2	26 18.2	32.7	66.6
35	25 34.9	+29.7	64.3	26 00.7	+30.6	64.8	26 26.0	+31.5	65.2	26 50.9	+32.5	65.7
36	26 04.6	29.3	63.4	26 31.3	30.2	63.8	26 57.5	31.1	64.3	27 23.4	32.0	64.7
37	26 33.9	28.9	62.4	27 01.5	29.8	62.9	27 28.6	30.8	63.3	27 55.4	31.6	63.8
38	27 02.8	28.5	61.4	27 31.3	29.4	61.9	27 59.4	30.3	62.3	28 27.0	31.2	62.8
39	27 31.3	28.1	60.4	28 00.7	29.0	60.9	28 29.7	29.8	61.4	28 58.2	30.8	61.8
40	27 59.4	+27.6	59.4	28 29.7	+28.5	59.9	28 59.5	+29.5	60.4	29 29.0	+30.3	60.9
41	28 27.0	27.2	58.4	28 58.2	28.1	58.9	29 29.0	29.0	59.4	29 59.3	29.9	59.9
42	28 54.2	26.7	57.4	29 26.3	27.6	57.9	29 58.0	28.5	58.4	30 29.2	29.4	58.9
43	29 20.9	26.2	56.4	29 53.9	27.1	56.9	30 26.5	28.0	57.3	30 58.6	29.0	57.9
44	29 47.1	25.8	55.4	30 21.0	26.7	55.8	30 54.5	27.6	56.3	31 27.6	28.4	56.8
45	30 12.9	+25.3	54.3	30 47.7	+26.1	54.8	31 22.1	+27.0	55.3	31 56.0	+28.0	55.8
46	30 38.2	24.7	53.3	31 13.8	25.7	53.7	31 49.1	26.6	54.2	32 24.0	27.4	54.7
47	31 02.9	24.2	52.2	31 39.5	25.1	52.7	32 15.7	25.9	53.2	32 51.4	26.9	53.7
48	31 27.1	23.7	51.1	32 04.6	24.5	51.6	32 41.6	25.5	52.1	33 18.3	26.3	52.6
49	31 50.8	23.1	50.0	32 29.1	24.0	50.5	33 07.1	24.9	51.0	33 44.6	25.8	51.5
50	32 13.9	+22.6	49.0	32 53.1	+23.5	49.4	33 32.0	+24.3	49.9	34 10.4	+25.1	50.5
51	32 36.5	22.0	47.9	33 16.6	22.8	48.3	33 56.3	23.7	48.8	34 35.5	24.6	49.4
52	32 58.5	21.4	46.8	33 39.4	22.3	47.2	34 20.0	23.1	47.7	35 00.1	24.0	48.2
53	33 19.9	20.8	45.6	34 01.7	21.6	46.1	34 43.1	22.5	46.6	35 24.1	23.3	47.1
54	33 40.7	20.2	44.5	34 23.3	21.0	45.0	35 05.6	21.8	45.5	35 47.4	22.7	46.0
55	34 00.9	+19.5	43.4	34 44.3	+20.4	43.9	35 27.4	+21.2	44.3	36 10.1	+22.1	44.8
56	34 20.4	18.9	42.2	35 04.7	19.7	42.7	35 48.6	20.5	43.2	36 32.2	21.3	43.7
57	34 39.3	18.3	41.1	35 24.4	19.0	41.5	36 09.1	19.9	42.0	36 53.5	20.7	42.5
58	34 57.6	17.6	39.9	35 43.4	18.4	40.4	36 29.0	19.2	40.9	37 14.2	20.0	41.3
59	35 15.2	16.9	38.8	36 01.8	17.7	39.2	36 48.2	18.4	39.7	37 34.2	19.2	40.2
60	35 32.1	+16.2	37.6	36 19.5	+17.0	38.0	37 06.6	+17.7	38.5	37 53.4	+18.5	39.0
61	35 48.3	15.5	36.4	36 36.5	16.2	36.8	37 24.3	17.0	37.3	38 11.9	17.8	37.8
62	36 03.8	14.8	35.2	36 52.7	15.5	35.6	37 41.3	16.3	36.1	38 29.7	17.0	36.5
63	36 18.6	14.1	34.0	37 08.2	14.8	34.4	37 57.6	15.5	34.9	38 46.7	16.2	35.3
64	36 32.7	13.3	32.8	37 23.0	14.0	33.2	38 13.1	14.7	33.6	39 02.9	15.5	34.1
65	36 46.0	+12.6	31.6	37 37.0	+13.3	32.0	38 27.8	+14.0	32.4	39 18.4	+14.6	32.8
66	36 58.6	11.9	30.4	37 50.3	12.5	30.7	38 41.8	13.1	31.1	39 33.0	13.8	31.6
67	37 10.5	11.0	29.1	38 02.8	11.7	29.5	38 54.9	12.3	29.9	39 46.8	13.0	30.3
68	37 21.5	10.3	27.9	38 14.5	10.9	28.3	39 07.2	11.6	28.6	39 59.8	12.1	29.0
69	37 31.8	9.6	26.6	38 25.4	10.1	27.0	39 18.8	10.6	27.4	40 11.9	11.3	27.8
70	37 41.4	+8.7	25.4	38 35.5	+9.3	25.7	39 29.4	+9.9	26.1	40 23.2	+10.5	26.5
71	37 50.1	7.9	24.2	38 44.8	8.4	24.5	39 39.3	9.0	24.8	40 33.7	9.5	25.2
72	37 58.0	7.1	22.9	38 53.2	7.7	23.2	39 48.3	8.1	23.5	40 43.2	8.7	23.9
73	38 05.1	6.3	21.6	39 00.9	6.7	21.9	39 56.4	7.3	22.2	40 51.9	7.8	22.6
74	38 11.4	5.5	20.4	39 07.6	6.0	20.7	40 03.7	6.5	20.9	40 59.7	6.9	21.3
75	38 16.9	+4.7	19.1	39 13.6	+5.1	19.4	40 10.2	+5.5	19.6	41 06.6	+6.0	19.9
76	38 21.6	3.9	17.8	39 18.7	4.3	18.1	40 15.7	4.7	18.3	41 12.6	5.1	18.6
77	38 25.5	3.0	16.6	39 23.0	3.4	16.8	40 20.4	3.7	17.0	41 17.7	4.2	17.3
78	38 28.5	2.2	15.3	39 26.4	2.5	15.5	40 24.1	2.9	15.7	41 21.9	3.2	16.0
79	38 30.7	1.4	14.0	39 28.9	1.7	14.2	40 27.0	2.0	14.4	41 25.1	2.3	14.6
80	38 32.1	+0.5	12.7	39 30.6	+0.8	12.9	40 29.0	+1.1	13.1	41 27.4	+1.5	13.3
81	38 32.6	-0.3	11.5	39 31.4	-0.1	11.6	40 30.1	+0.2	11.8	41 28.9	+0.4	12.0
82	38 32.3	1.2	10.2	39 31.3	0.9	10.3	40 30.3	-0.6	10.5	41 29.3	-0.4	10.6
83	38 31.1	1.9	8.9	39 30.4	1.8	9.0	40 29.7	1.6	9.2	41 28.9	1.4	9.3
84	38 29.2	2.8	7.6	39 28.6	2.6	7.7	40 28.1	2.5	7.8	41 27.5	2.3	8.0
85	38 26.4	-3.7	6.3	39 26.0	3.5	6.4	40 25.6	-3.3	6.5	41 25.2	-3.2	6.6
86	38 22.7	4.4	5.1	39 22.5	4.3	5.1	40 22.3	4.3	5.2	41 22.0	4.1	5.3
87	38 18.3	5.3	3.8	39 18.2	5.3	3.8	40 18.0	5.1	3.9	41 17.9	5.1	4.0
88	38 13.0	6.1	2.5	39 12.9	6.0	2.6	40 12.9	6.0	2.6	41 12.8	5.9	2.6
89	38 06.9	6.9	1.3	39 06.9	6.9	1.3	40 06.9	6.9	1.3	41 06.9	6.9	1.3
90	38 00.0	-7.7	0.0	39 00.0	-7.7	0.0	40 00.0	-7.7	0.0	41 00.0	-7.8	0.0
	38°			39°			40°			41°		

42°			43°			44°			45°			Dec.
Hc	d	Z	Hc	d	Z	Hc	d	Z	Hc	d	Z	
° ′	′	°	° ′	′	°	° ′	′	°	° ′	′	°	°
5 11.8	+40.3	94.7	5 06.8	+41.1	94.8	5 01.8	+41.8	94.9	4 56.6	+42.6	95.0	0
5 52.1	40.2	94.0	5 47.9	41.0	94.1	5 43.6	41.7	94.2	5 39.2	42.5	94.3	1
6 32.3	40.1	93.2	6 28.9	40.9	93.3	6 25.3	41.7	93.4	6 21.7	42.4	93.5	2
7 12.4	40.1	92.5	7 09.8	40.9	92.6	7 07.0	41.7	92.7	7 04.1	42.4	92.8	3
7 52.5	40.0	91.7	7 50.7	40.8	91.8	7 48.7	41.5	92.0	7 46.5	42.3	92.1	4
8 32.5	+40.0	91.0	8 31.5	+40.7	91.1	8 30.2	+41.5	91.3	8 28.8	+42.3	91.4	5
9 12.5	39.8	90.2	9 12.2	40.6	90.4	9 11.7	41.4	90.5	9 11.1	42.1	90.7	6
9 52.3	39.7	89.4	9 52.8	40.5	89.6	9 53.1	41.3	89.8	9 53.2	42.1	90.0	7
10 32.0	39.6	88.7	10 33.3	40.4	88.9	10 34.4	41.2	89.1	10 35.3	41.9	89.2	8
11 11.6	39.5	87.9	11 13.7	40.3	88.1	11 15.6	41.1	88.3	11 17.2	41.9	88.5	9
11 51.1	+39.4	87.1	11 54.0	+40.2	87.4	11 56.7	+40.9	87.6	11 59.1	+41.7	87.8	10
12 30.5	39.2	86.4	12 34.2	40.0	86.6	12 37.6	40.9	86.8	12 40.8	41.6	87.0	11
13 09.7	39.1	85.6	13 14.2	39.9	85.8	13 18.5	40.7	86.1	13 22.4	41.5	86.3	12
13 48.8	39.0	84.8	13 54.1	39.8	85.1	13 59.2	40.5	85.3	14 03.9	41.4	85.6	13
14 27.8	38.8	84.0	14 33.9	39.6	84.3	14 39.7	40.4	84.6	14 45.3	41.2	84.8	14
15 06.6	+38.6	83.2	15 13.5	+39.4	83.5	15 20.1	+40.3	83.8	15 26.5	+41.0	84.1	15
15 45.2	38.5	82.5	15 52.9	39.3	82.7	16 00.4	40.1	83.0	16 07.5	40.9	83.3	16
16 23.7	38.2	81.7	16 32.2	39.1	81.9	16 40.5	39.9	82.2	16 48.4	40.7	82.5	17
17 01.9	38.1	80.8	17 11.3	38.9	81.2	17 20.4	39.7	81.5	17 29.1	40.6	81.8	18
17 40.0	37.9	80.0	17 50.2	38.7	80.4	18 00.1	39.6	80.7	18 09.7	40.3	81.0	19
18 17.9	+37.7	79.2	18 28.9	+38.5	79.5	18 39.7	+39.3	79.9	18 50.0	+40.2	80.2	20
18 55.6	37.4	78.4	19 07.4	38.3	78.7	19 19.0	39.1	79.1	19 30.2	39.9	79.4	21
19 33.0	37.2	77.6	19 45.7	38.1	77.9	19 58.1	38.9	78.3	20 10.1	39.8	78.6	22
20 10.2	37.0	76.7	20 23.8	37.9	77.1	20 37.0	38.7	77.5	20 49.9	39.5	77.8	23
20 47.2	36.8	75.9	21 01.7	37.6	76.3	21 15.7	38.4	76.6	21 29.4	39.2	77.0	24
21 24.0	+36.5	75.1	21 39.3	+37.3	75.4	21 54.1	+38.2	75.8	22 08.6	+39.1	76.2	25
22 00.5	36.2	74.2	22 16.6	37.1	74.6	22 32.3	38.0	75.0	22 47.7	38.8	75.4	26
22 36.7	35.9	73.3	22 53.7	36.8	73.7	23 10.3	37.6	74.1	23 26.5	38.5	74.6	27
23 12.6	35.7	72.5	23 30.5	36.5	72.9	23 47.9	37.4	73.3	24 05.0	38.2	73.7	28
23 48.3	35.3	71.6	24 07.0	36.2	72.0	24 25.3	37.1	72.4	24 43.2	37.9	72.9	29
24 23.6	+35.0	70.7	24 43.2	+35.9	71.1	25 02.4	+36.8	71.6	25 21.1	+37.7	72.0	30
24 58.6	34.7	69.8	25 19.1	35.6	70.3	25 39.2	36.4	70.7	25 58.8	37.3	71.2	31
25 33.3	34.4	68.9	25 54.7	35.3	69.4	26 15.6	36.2	69.8	26 36.1	37.0	70.3	32
26 07.7	34.1	68.0	26 30.0	34.9	68.5	26 51.8	35.8	68.9	27 13.1	36.7	69.4	33
26 41.8	33.6	67.1	27 04.9	34.6	67.5	27 27.6	35.4	68.0	27 49.8	36.3	68.5	34
27 15.4	+33.3	66.1	27 39.5	+34.2	66.6	28 03.0	+35.1	67.1	28 26.1	+36.0	67.6	35
27 48.7	32.9	65.2	28 13.7	33.8	65.7	28 38.1	34.7	66.2	29 02.1	35.6	66.7	36
28 21.6	32.6	64.3	28 47.5	33.4	64.8	29 12.8	34.3	65.3	29 37.7	35.2	65.8	37
28 54.2	32.1	63.3	29 20.9	33.0	63.8	29 47.1	33.9	64.3	30 12.9	34.8	64.8	38
29 26.3	31.7	62.3	29 53.9	32.6	62.8	30 21.0	33.5	63.4	30 47.7	34.4	63.9	39
29 58.0	+31.2	61.4	30 26.5	+32.1	61.9	30 54.5	+33.1	62.4	31 22.1	+33.9	62.9	40
30 29.2	30.8	60.4	30 58.6	31.7	60.9	31 27.6	32.6	61.4	31 56.0	33.5	62.0	41
31 00.0	30.3	59.4	31 30.3	31.3	59.9	32 00.2	32.1	60.4	32 29.5	33.1	61.0	42
31 30.3	29.9	58.4	32 01.6	30.7	58.9	32 32.3	31.7	59.4	33 02.6	32.6	60.0	43
32 00.2	29.3	57.3	32 32.3	30.3	57.9	33 04.0	31.2	58.4	33 35.2	32.0	59.0	44
32 29.5	+28.9	56.3	33 02.6	+29.7	56.9	33 35.2	+30.6	57.4	34 07.2	+31.6	58.0	45
32 58.4	28.3	55.3	33 32.3	29.3	55.8	34 05.8	30.1	56.4	34 38.8	31.0	56.9	46
33 26.7	27.8	54.2	34 01.6	28.6	54.8	34 35.9	29.6	55.3	35 09.8	30.5	55.9	47
33 54.5	27.2	53.2	34 30.2	28.2	53.7	35 05.5	29.0	54.3	35 40.3	30.0	54.8	48
34 21.7	26.7	52.1	34 58.4	27.5	52.6	35 34.5	28.5	53.2	36 10.3	29.3	53.8	49
34 48.4	+26.0	51.0	35 25.9	+27.0	51.5	36 03.0	+27.8	52.1	36 39.6	+28.8	52.7	50
35 14.4	25.5	49.9	35 52.9	26.3	50.4	36 30.8	27.3	51.0	37 08.4	28.1	51.6	51
35 39.9	24.8	48.8	36 19.2	25.7	49.3	36 58.1	26.6	49.9	37 36.5	27.5	50.5	52
36 04.7	24.2	47.7	36 44.9	25.1	48.2	37 24.7	26.0	48.8	38 04.0	26.9	49.4	53
36 28.9	23.6	46.5	37 10.0	24.4	47.1	37 50.7	25.3	47.6	38 30.9	26.2	48.2	54
36 52.5	+22.9	45.4	37 34.4	+23.8	45.9	38 16.0	+24.6	46.5	38 57.1	+25.5	47.1	55
37 15.4	22.2	44.2	37 58.2	23.0	44.8	38 40.6	23.9	45.3	39 22.6	24.7	45.9	56
37 37.6	21.5	43.0	38 21.2	22.4	43.6	39 04.5	23.2	44.1	39 47.3	24.1	44.7	57
37 59.1	20.8	41.9	38 43.6	21.6	42.4	39 27.7	22.4	42.9	40 11.4	23.3	43.5	58
38 19.9	20.0	40.7	39 05.2	20.9	41.2	39 50.1	21.8	41.7	40 34.7	22.6	42.3	59
38 39.9	+19.3	39.5	39 26.1	+20.1	40.0	40 11.9	+20.9	40.5	40 57.3	+21.7	41.1	60
38 59.2	18.6	38.2	39 46.2	19.3	38.8	40 32.8	20.1	39.3	41 19.0	21.0	39.8	61
39 17.8	17.7	37.0	40 05.5	18.5	37.5	40 52.9	19.4	38.0	41 40.0	20.1	38.6	62
39 35.5	17.0	35.8	40 24.0	17.8	36.3	41 12.3	18.5	36.8	42 00.1	19.3	37.3	63
39 52.5	16.2	34.5	40 41.8	16.9	35.0	41 30.8	17.6	35.5	42 19.4	18.5	36.1	64
40 08.7	+15.3	33.3	40 58.7	+16.0	33.8	41 48.4	+16.8	34.2	42 37.9	+17.5	34.8	65
40 24.0	14.5	32.0	41 14.7	15.2	32.5	42 05.2	16.0	33.0	42 55.4	16.7	33.5	66
40 38.5	13.6	30.7	41 29.9	14.4	31.2	42 21.2	15.0	31.7	43 12.1	15.7	32.1	67
40 52.1	12.8	29.5	41 44.3	13.4	29.9	42 36.2	14.1	30.3	43 27.8	14.9	30.8	68
41 04.9	12.0	28.2	41 57.7	12.6	28.6	42 50.3	13.2	29.0	43 42.7	13.9	29.5	69
41 16.9	+11.0	26.9	42 10.3	+11.6	27.3	43 03.5	+12.3	27.7	43 56.6	+12.9	28.1	70
41 27.9	10.1	25.5	42 21.9	10.8	25.9	43 15.8	11.3	26.3	44 09.5	11.9	26.8	71
41 38.0	9.3	24.2	42 32.7	9.8	24.6	43 27.1	10.4	25.0	44 21.4	11.0	25.4	72
41 47.3	8.3	22.9	42 42.5	8.8	23.3	43 37.5	9.4	23.6	44 32.4	10.0	24.0	73
41 55.6	7.4	21.6	42 51.3	7.9	21.9	43 46.9	8.4	22.3	44 42.4	8.9	22.6	74
42 03.0	+6.4	20.2	42 59.2	+6.9	20.6	43 55.3	+7.4	20.9	44 51.3	+7.9	21.2	75
42 09.4	5.5	18.9	43 06.1	6.0	19.2	44 02.7	6.5	19.5	44 59.2	6.9	19.8	76
42 14.9	4.6	17.6	43 12.1	5.0	17.8	44 09.2	5.4	18.1	45 06.1	5.9	18.4	77
42 19.5	3.6	16.2	43 17.1	4.0	16.5	44 14.6	4.4	16.7	45 12.0	4.8	17.0	78
42 23.1	2.7	14.9	43 21.1	3.0	15.1	44 19.0	3.4	15.3	45 16.8	3.8	15.6	79
42 25.8	+1.7	13.5	43 24.1	+2.1	13.7	44 22.4	+2.4	14.0	45 20.6	+2.7	14.2	80
42 27.5	+0.8	12.1	43 26.2	1.0	12.3	44 24.8	1.3	12.6	45 23.3	1.6	12.8	81
42 28.3	-0.2	10.8	43 27.2	+0.1	11.0	44 26.1	+0.3	11.2	45 24.9	+0.6	11.3	82
42 28.1	1.2	9.4	43 27.3	-1.0	9.6	44 26.4	-0.7	9.8	45 25.5	-0.4	9.9	83
42 26.9	2.1	8.1	43 26.3	1.9	8.2	44 25.7	1.7	8.4	45 25.1	1.6	8.5	84
42 24.8	-3.1	6.7	43 24.4	-2.9	6.8	44 24.0	-2.8	7.0	45 23.5	-2.6	7.1	85
42 21.7	4.0	5.4	43 21.5	3.9	5.5	44 21.2	3.8	5.6	45 20.9	3.6	5.7	86
42 17.7	4.9	4.0	43 17.6	4.9	4.1	44 17.4	4.8	4.2	45 17.3	4.7	4.2	87
42 12.8	6.0	2.7	43 12.7	5.9	2.7	44 12.6	5.8	2.8	45 12.6	5.8	2.8	88
42 06.8	6.8	1.3	43 06.8	6.8	1.4	44 06.8	6.8	1.4	45 06.8	6.8	1.4	89
42 00.0	-7.8	0.0	43 00.0	-7.8	0.0	44 00.0	-7.8	0.0	45 00.0	-7.8	0.0	90
42°			43°			44°			45°			

83°, 277° L.H.A. LATITUDE SAME NAME AS DECLINATION

LAT 42°N LAT 42°N

LHA ♈	Hc	Zn	Hc	Zn	Hc	Zn	Hc	Zn	Hc	Zn	Hc	Zn	Hc	Zn
	Kochab		♦VEGA		ARCTURUS		♦SPICA		REGULUS		♦POLLUX		CAPELLA	
180	52 24	018	19 09	055	53 38	118	33 35	155	51 17	228	37 00	277	22 20	313
181	52 37	017	19 45	055	54 17	119	33 53	156	50 44	229	36 16	277	21 47	313
182	52 50	017	20 22	056	54 56	121	34 11	157	50 10	230	35 32	278	21 15	313
183	53 03	017	20 59	056	55 34	122	34 27	158	49 36	231	34 48	278	20 43	314
184	53 16	016	21 36	057	56 12	123	34 43	160	49 00	233	34 04	279	20 11	314
185	53 28	016	22 14	057	56 49	124	34 59	161	48 25	234	33 20	280	19 39	315
186	53 41	016	22 51	058	57 25	126	35 13	162	47 48	235	32 36	280	19 07	315
187	53 53	016	23 29	058	58 01	127	35 26	163	47 12	236	31 52	281	18 36	316
188	54 05	015	24 07	059	58 36	128	35 39	164	46 34	237	31 08	281	18 05	316
189	54 16	015	24 45	059	59 11	130	35 50	165	45 57	238	30 24	282	17 35	317
190	54 28	015	25 23	060	59 45	131	36 01	167	45 18	239	29 41	282	17 04	317
191	54 39	014	26 02	060	60 18	133	36 11	168	44 40	240	28 57	283	16 34	318
192	54 50	014	26 41	061	60 50	134	36 20	169	44 01	241	28 14	284	16 05	318
193	55 00	014	27 20	061	61 22	136	36 28	170	43 22	242	27 31	284	15 35	319
194	55 11	013	27 59	062	61 52	138	36 35	171	42 42	243	26 48	285	15 06	319
	♦VEGA		Rasalhague		ARCTURUS		♦SPICA		REGULUS		♦POLLUX		Dubhe	
195	28 38	062	24 21	095	62 22	139	36 41	173	42 02	244	26 04	285	63 31	329
196	29 18	063	25 05	096	62 50	141	36 46	174	41 21	245	25 22	286	63 08	328
197	29 57	063	25 49	096	63 17	143	36 51	175	40 41	246	24 39	286	62 44	328
198	30 37	064	26 34	097	63 44	145	36 54	176	40 00	247	23 56	287	62 20	327
199	31 17	064	27 18	098	64 09	147	36 56	178	39 19	248	23 13	288	61 56	326
200	31 57	064	28 02	098	64 32	149	36 58	179	38 37	249	22 31	288	61 31	326
201	32 38	065	28 46	099	64 55	151	36 58	180	37 55	250	21 49	289	61 06	326
202	33 18	065	29 30	100	65 16	153	36 58	181	37 13	251	21 07	289	60 41	325
203	33 59	066	30 14	101	65 35	155	36 56	182	36 31	252	20 25	290	60 15	325
204	34 39	066	30 58	101	65 53	157	36 54	184	35 49	252	19 43	291	59 49	324
205	35 20	067	31 41	102	66 10	159	36 50	185	35 06	253	19 01	291	59 23	324
206	36 01	067	32 25	103	66 24	162	36 46	186	34 23	254	18 20	292	58 57	324
207	36 43	068	33 08	104	66 38	164	36 41	187	33 40	255	17 38	292	58 30	323
208	37 24	068	33 51	105	66 49	166	36 35	189	32 57	256	16 57	293	58 03	323
209	38 05	069	34 34	105	66 58	169	36 27	190	32 14	256	16 16	293	57 37	323
	♦DENEB		VEGA		Rasalhague		ANTARES		♦ARCTURUS		REGULUS		♦Dubhe	
210	22 29	049	38 47	069	35 17	106	13 34	146	67 06	171	31 31	257	57 09	323
211	23 03	049	39 29	070	36 00	107	13 59	147	67 12	174	30 47	258	56 42	322
212	23 37	050	40 11	070	36 43	108	14 23	148	67 16	176	30 03	259	56 15	322
213	24 11	050	40 52	070	37 25	109	14 46	149	67 18	178	29 20	259	55 47	322
214	24 45	050	41 35	071	38 07	110	15 09	150	67 19	181	28 36	260	55 20	322
215	25 20	051	42 17	071	38 49	110	15 31	151	67 17	183	27 52	261	54 52	322
216	25 54	051	42 59	072	39 31	111	15 53	151	67 13	186	27 08	262	54 24	321
217	26 29	052	43 41	072	40 12	112	16 14	152	67 08	188	26 23	262	53 56	321
218	27 04	052	44 24	073	40 53	113	16 34	153	67 01	191	25 39	263	53 29	321
219	27 40	053	45 07	073	41 34	114	16 54	154	66 52	193	24 55	264	53 01	321
220	28 15	053	45 49	074	42 15	115	17 13	155	66 41	195	24 11	265	52 32	321
221	28 51	054	46 32	074	42 55	116	17 32	156	66 28	198	23 26	265	52 04	321
222	29 27	054	47 15	075	43 35	117	17 50	157	66 14	200	22 42	266	51 36	321
223	30 03	054	47 58	075	44 15	118	18 07	157	65 58	202	21 57	267	51 08	321
224	30 40	055	48 41	075	44 54	119	18 24	158	65 40	204	21 13	267	50 40	321
	DENEB		♦ALTAIR		Rasalhague		ANTARES		♦ARCTURUS		Denebola		♦Dubhe	
225	31 16	055	18 56	095	45 33	120	18 40	159	65 21	206	40 34	251	50 11	321
226	31 53	056	19 41	096	46 11	121	18 56	160	65 00	209	39 52	252	49 43	321
227	32 30	056	20 25	097	46 49	122	19 11	161	64 38	211	39 09	253	49 15	321
228	33 07	056	21 09	097	47 27	123	19 25	162	64 15	213	38 27	254	48 47	321
229	33 44	057	21 53	098	48 04	124	19 38	163	63 50	215	37 44	255	48 18	321
230	34 21	057	22 38	099	48 40	125	19 51	164	63 24	216	37 01	255	47 50	321
231	34 59	058	23 22	099	49 16	127	20 03	165	62 57	218	36 17	256	47 22	321
232	35 37	058	24 06	100	49 52	128	20 14	166	62 29	220	35 34	257	46 54	321
233	36 15	058	24 49	101	50 27	129	20 25	167	62 00	222	34 50	258	46 25	321
234	36 53	059	25 33	102	51 01	130	20 35	168	61 30	223	34 07	259	45 57	321
235	37 31	059	26 17	102	51 35	132	20 44	169	60 58	225	33 23	259	45 29	321
236	38 09	060	27 00	103	52 08	133	20 52	169	60 26	227	32 39	260	45 01	321
237	38 48	060	27 44	104	52 40	134	21 00	170	59 54	228	31 55	261	44 33	321
238	39 27	060	28 27	105	53 12	136	21 07	171	59 20	230	31 11	262	44 05	321
239	40 05	061	29 10	105	53 42	137	21 14	172	58 45	231	30 27	262	43 37	321
	♦DENEB		ALTAIR		Rasalhague		♦ANTARES		ARCTURUS		Denebola		♦Dubhe	
240	40 44	061	29 53	106	54 12	138	21 19	173	58 10	233	29 43	263	43 10	322
241	41 23	061	30 35	107	54 42	140	21 24	174	57 35	234	28 58	264	42 42	322
242	42 03	062	31 18	108	55 10	141	21 28	175	56 58	235	28 14	265	42 14	322
243	42 42	062	32 00	109	55 37	143	21 31	176	56 21	237	27 30	265	41 47	322
244	43 21	062	32 42	109	56 04	144	21 34	177	55 44	238	26 45	266	41 19	322
245	44 01	063	33 24	110	56 29	146	21 36	178	55 06	239	26 01	267	40 52	322
246	44 41	063	34 06	111	56 54	148	21 37	179	54 27	240	25 16	267	40 25	322
247	45 20	063	34 48	112	57 17	149	21 37	180	53 48	242	24 32	268	39 58	323
248	46 00	064	35 29	113	57 39	151	21 37	181	53 09	243	23 47	269	39 30	323
249	46 40	064	36 10	114	58 00	153	21 36	182	52 29	244	23 03	269	39 04	323
250	47 21	064	36 50	115	58 20	154	21 34	183	51 49	245	22 18	270	38 37	323
251	48 01	065	37 31	116	58 39	156	21 31	184	51 08	246	21 33	271	38 10	323
252	48 41	065	38 11	116	58 56	158	21 28	185	50 27	247	20 49	271	37 43	324
253	49 22	065	38 51	117	59 12	160	21 24	186	49 46	248	20 04	272	37 17	324
254	50 02	066	39 30	118	59 27	162	21 19	187	49 05	249	19 20	273	36 51	324
	♦DENEB		ALTAIR		Nunki		♦ANTARES		ARCTURUS		♦Alkaid		Kochab	
255	50 43	066	40 09	119	16 48	154	21 13	188	48 23	250	56 02	300	54 32	346
256	51 24	066	40 48	120	17 07	154	21 07	189	47 41	251	55 24	300	54 21	345
257	52 05	067	41 26	121	17 26	155	21 00	190	46 59	252	54 45	300	54 09	345
258	52 46	067	42 04	122	17 45	156	20 52	191	46 16	253	54 06	300	53 57	345
259	53 27	067	42 41	123	18 02	157	20 43	192	45 34	254	53 28	300	53 45	344
260	54 08	067	43 18	124	18 19	158	20 34	192	44 51	254	52 49	300	53 33	344
261	54 49	068	43 55	126	18 36	159	20 24	193	44 08	255	52 11	300	53 21	344
262	55 30	068	44 31	127	18 52	160	20 13	194	43 25	256	51 32	301	53 08	343
263	56 12	068	45 06	128	19 07	161	20 02	195	42 41	257	50 54	301	52 55	343
264	56 53	068	45 41	129	19 21	162	19 50	196	41 58	258	50 16	301	52 42	343
265	57 35	069	46 16	130	19 35	162	19 37	197	41 14	259	49 38	301	52 29	343
266	58 16	069	46 50	131	19 48	163	19 24	198	40 30	259	48 59	301	52 15	342
267	58 58	069	47 23	132	20 00	164	19 10	199	39 46	260	48 22	302	52 02	342
268	59 40	069	47 55	134	20 12	165	18 55	200	39 02	261	47 44	302	51 48	342
269	60 21	070	48 27	135	20 23	166	18 39	201	38 18	262	47 06	302	51 34	342

LHA ♈	Hc	Zn	Hc	Zn	Hc	Zn	Hc	Zn	Hc	Zn	Hc	Zn	Hc	Zn
	♦Alpheratz		ALTAIR		Nunki		♦ANTARES		ARCTURUS		♦Alkaid		Kochab	
270	17 41	067	48 59	136	20 33	167	18 23	202	37 34	262	46 28	302	51 20	341
271	18 22	067	49 29	137	20 43	168	18 06	203	36 50	263	45 51	303	51 05	341
272	19 03	068	49 59	139	20 52	169	17 49	203	36 06	264	45 13	303	50 51	341
273	19 45	068	50 28	140	21 00	170	17 31	204	35 21	265	44 36	303	50 36	341
274	20 26	069	50 56	141	21 07	171	17 12	205	34 37	265	43 59	303	50 22	341
275	21 08	069	51 23	143	21 14	172	16 53	206	33 52	266	43 21	304	50 07	340
276	21 50	070	51 50	144	21 20	173	16 33	207	33 08	267	42 44	304	49 52	340
277	22 32	071	52 15	146	21 25	174	16 12	208	32 23	267	42 08	304	49 37	340
278	23 14	071	52 40	147	21 29	175	15 51	209	31 39	268	41 31	305	49 21	340
279	23 56	072	53 04	149	21 33	176	15 30	210	30 54	269	40 54	305	49 06	340
280	24 39	072	53 26	150	21 36	177	15 07	210	30 10	270	40 18	305	48 51	340
281	25 21	073	53 48	152	21 38	178	14 44	211	29 25	270	39 41	306	48 35	340
282	26 04	073	54 08	153	21 39	179	14 21	212	28 40	271	39 05	306	48 20	339
283	26 47	074	54 28	155	21 40	180	13 57	213	27 56	272	38 29	306	48 04	339
284	27 30	075	54 46	157	21 40	181	13 33	214	27 11	272	37 53	306	47 48	339
	♦Mirfak		Alpheratz		♦ALTAIR		Rasalhague		♦ARCTURUS		Alkaid		Kochab	
285	13 22	033	28 13	075	55 03	158	55 07	219	26 27	273	37 17	307	47 32	339
286	13 47	033	28 56	076	55 19	160	54 38	220	25 42	273	36 42	307	47 16	339
287	14 11	034	29 39	076	55 34	162	54 09	222	24 58	274	36 06	307	47 00	339
288	14 36	034	30 22	077	55 47	163	53 39	223	24 13	275	35 31	308	46 44	339
289	15 01	035	31 06	077	55 59	165	53 08	225	23 29	275	34 56	308	46 28	339
290	15 27	035	31 49	078	56 10	167	52 36	226	22 44	276	34 21	309	46 12	339
291	15 53	036	32 33	079	56 20	169	52 04	227	22 00	277	33 46	309	45 56	339
292	16 19	036	33 17	079	56 28	170	51 31	229	21 16	277	33 11	309	45 40	339
293	16 45	037	34 01	080	56 35	172	50 57	230	20 32	278	32 37	310	45 24	339
294	17 12	037	34 45	080	56 40	174	50 23	231	19 48	279	32 03	310	45 07	339
295	17 39	038	35 29	081	56 44	176	49 48	232	19 03	279	31 29	310	44 51	339
296	18 07	038	36 13	081	56 47	177	49 12	234	18 20	280	30 55	311	44 35	339
297	18 34	039	36 57	082	56 48	179	48 36	235	17 36	280	30 21	311	44 19	339
298	19 02	039	37 41	083	56 48	181	47 59	236	16 52	281	29 48	311	44 02	339
299	19 31	040	38 25	083	56 46	183	47 22	237	16 08	282	29 14	312	43 46	339
	Mirfak		♦Alpheratz		Enif		♦ALTAIR		Rasalhague		Alphecca		♦Kochab	
300	19 59	040	39 10	084	50 38	138	56 43	185	46 45	238	34 25	277	43 30	339
301	20 28	040	39 54	084	51 08	139	56 39	186	46 07	239	33 41	277	43 14	339
302	20 57	041	40 38	085	51 37	140	56 33	188	45 28	240	32 56	278	42 57	339
303	21 26	041	41 23	086	52 05	142	56 26	190	44 49	241	32 12	279	42 41	339
304	21 56	042	42 07	086	52 32	143	56 18	192	44 10	242	31 28	279	42 25	339
305	22 26	042	42 52	087	52 58	145	56 08	194	43 30	243	30 44	280	42 09	339
306	22 56	043	43 36	088	53 24	146	55 57	195	42 50	244	30 00	280	41 53	339
307	23 26	043	44 21	088	53 48	148	55 44	197	42 10	245	29 17	281	41 36	339
308	23 57	044	45 05	089	54 12	149	55 31	199	41 30	246	28 33	282	41 20	339
309	24 28	044	45 50	090	54 34	151	55 16	200	40 49	247	27 49	282	41 04	339
310	24 59	044	46 35	090	54 55	152	54 59	202	40 07	248	27 06	283	40 48	339
311	25 30	045	47 19	091	55 15	154	54 42	204	39 26	249	26 22	283	40 32	339
312	26 02	045	48 04	092	55 34	156	54 24	205	38 44	250	25 39	284	40 17	339
313	26 34	046	48 48	092	55 52	157	54 04	207	38 02	251	24 56	285	40 01	339
314	27 06	046	49 33	093	56 09	159	53 43	209	37 20	251	24 13	285	39 45	339
	CAPELLA		♦Alpheratz		FOMALHAUT		♦ALTAIR		Rasalhague		VEGA		♦Kochab	
315	11 13	036	50 17	094	13 24	154	53 21	210	36 38	252	62 36	275	39 29	339
316	11 39	037	51 02	094	13 43	155	52 59	212	35 55	253	61 52	276	39 14	340
317	12 06	037	51 46	095	14 02	156	52 35	213	35 13	254	61 08	276	38 58	340
318	12 33	038	52 31	096	14 20	157	52 10	215	34 30	255	60 23	277	38 43	340
319	13 01	038	53 15	097	14 37	158	51 44	216	33 46	256	59 39	277	38 27	340
320	13 29	039	53 59	098	14 53	159	51 17	217	33 03	256	58 55	278	38 12	340
321	13 57	039	54 43	098	15 10	159	50 50	219	32 20	257	58 11	278	37 57	340
322	14 25	040	55 27	099	15 25	160	50 22	220	31 36	258	57 27	279	37 42	340
323	14 54	040	56 11	100	15 40	161	49 52	222	30 53	259	56 43	279	37 26	340
324	15 23	041	56 55	101	15 54	162	49 23	223	30 09	259	55 59	280	37 12	340
325	15 52	041	57 39	102	16 07	163	48 52	224	29 25	260	55 15	280	36 57	341
326	16 22	042	58 23	103	16 20	164	48 20	225	28 41	261	54 31	281	36 42	341
327	16 52	042	59 06	104	16 32	165	47 48	227	27 57	262	53 47	281	36 27	341
328	17 22	043	59 49	105	16 44	165	47 16	228	27 13	262	53 04	282	36 13	341
329	17 52	043	60 32	106	16 55	166	46 42	229	26 29	263	52 20	282	35 58	341
	♦CAPELLA		Hamal		Diphda		♦FOMALHAUT		ALTAIR		♦VEGA		Kochab	
330	18 23	044	36 15	090	19 10	139	17 05	167	46 08	230	51 36	283	35 44	341
331	18 54	044	37 00	091	19 39	140	17 14	168	45 34	231	50 53	283	35 30	342
332	19 26	045	37 44	091	20 07	141	17 23	169	44 59	233	50 10	284	35 16	342
333	19 57	045	38 29	092	20 35	142	17 31	170	44 23	234	49 26	284	35 02	342
334	20 29	046	39 13	093	21 02	143	17 39	171	43 47	235	48 43	285	34 48	342
335	21 01	046	39 58	093	21 29	144	17 46	172	43 10	236	48 00	285	34 35	342
336	21 34	047	40 42	094	21 55	144	17 52	173	42 33	237	47 17	285	34 21	342
337	22 06	047	41 27	095	22 21	145	17 57	174	41 56	238	46 34	286	34 08	343
338	22 39	048	42 11	096	22 46	146	18 02	174	41 18	239	45 51	286	33 54	343
339	23 12	048	42 56	096	23 10	147	18 06	175	40 39	240	45 09	287	33 41	343
340	23 46	049	43 40	097	23 34	148	18 09	176	40 00	241	44 26	287	33 28	343
341	24 19	049	44 24	098	23 57	149	18 11	177	39 21	242	43 43	288	33 15	343
342	24 53	050	45 08	099	24 20	150	18 13	178	38 42	243	43 01	288	33 03	344
343	25 27	050	45 52	099	24 42	151	18 14	179	38 02	244	42 19	289	32 50	344
344	26 01	050	46 36	100	25 03	152	18 15	180	37 22	245	41 36	289	32 38	344
	♦CAPELLA		ALDEBARAN		Diphda		♦FOMALHAUT		ALTAIR		♦VEGA		Kochab	
345	26 36	051	15 36	082	25 24	153	18 14	181	36 41	246	40 54	290	32 26	344
346	27 10	051	16 20	082	25 44	154	18 13	182	36 01	246	40 12	290	32 14	344
347	27 45	052	17 04	083	26 03	155	18 12	183	35 20	247	39 31	290	32 02	345
348	28 20	052	17 48	084	26 21	156	18 09	184	34 38	248	38 49	291	31 50	345
349	28 56	053	18 33	084	26 39	157	18 06	185	33 57	249	38 07	291	31 39	345
350	29 31	053	19 17	085	26 56	158	18 02	185	33 15	250	37 26	292	31 27	345
351	30 07	053	20 01	086	27 13	159	17 58	186	32 33	251	36 44	292	31 16	346
352	30 43	054	20 46	086	27 28	160	17 52	187	31 51	252	36 03	293	31 05	346
353	31 19	054	21 30	087	27 43	161	17 46	188	31 09	252	35 22	293	30 54	346
354	31 55	055	22 15	087	27 57	162	17 40	189	30 26	253	34 41	294	30 44	346
355	32 32	055	22 59	088	28 11	163	17 32	190	29 43	254	34 01	294	30 33	347
356	33 08	055	23 44	089	28 23	164	17 24	191	29 00	255	33 20	295	30 23	347
357	33 45	056	24 29	089	28 35	165	17 16	192	28 17	255	32 39	295	30 13	347
358	34 22	056	25 13	090	28 46	166	17 06	193	27 34	256	31 59	296	30 03	347
359	34 59	057	25 58	091	28 56	167	16 56	194	26 51	257	31 19	296	29 53	348

TABLE 5.—Precession and Nutation Correction

Each entry is given as mi. and °.

1976

L.H.A. ♈	N. 89°	N. 80°	N. 70°	N. 60°	N. 50°	N. 40°	N. 20°	0°	S. 20°	S. 40°	S. 50°	S. 60°	S. 70°	S. 80°	S. 89°	L.H.A. ♈
0	1 020	1 030	1 050	1 050	1 060	1 060	1 070	1 070	1 060	1 060	1 050	1 040	1 030	1 010	1 350	0
30	1 040	1 060	1 060	1 070	1 070	1 070	1 070	1 070	1 070	1 060	1 050	1 040	0 —	0 —	1 320	30
60	1 070	1 080	1 080	1 080	1 080	1 080	1 080	1 080	1 080	1 080	0 —	0 —	0 —	0 —	1 290	60
90	1 100	1 100	1 100	1 100	1 100	1 100	1 100	1 100	1 100	1 100	0 —	0 —	0 —	0 —	1 260	90
120	1 130	1 120	1 120	1 110	1 110	1 110	1 110	1 110	1 110	1 120	1 130	0 —	0 —	0 —	1 230	120
150	1 160	1 140	1 130	1 120	1 120	1 120	1 110	1 110	1 120	1 120	1 130	1 140	1 150	1 170	1 200	150
180	1 190	1 170	1 150	1 140	1 130	1 120	1 120	1 110	1 110	1 120	1 120	1 130	1 140	1 150	1 170	180
210	1 220	0 —	0 —	1 140	1 130	1 120	1 110	1 110	1 110	1 110	1 110	1 110	1 120	1 130	1 140	210
240	1 250	0 —	0 —	0 —	1 —	1 110	1 100	1 100	1 100	1 100	1 100	1 100	1 100	1 100	1 110	240
270	1 280	0 —	0 —	0 —	1 —	1 080	1 080	1 090	1 090	1 090	1 080	1 080	1 080	1 080	1 080	270
300	1 310	0 —	0 —	0 —	1 050	1 060	1 070	1 070	1 070	1 070	1 070	1 070	1 070	1 060	1 050	300
330	1 350	1 010	1 030	1 040	1 050	1 060	1 070	1 070	1 070	1 060	1 060	1 060	1 050	1 040	1 020	330
360	1 020	1 030	1 050	1 050	1 060	1 060	1 070	1 070	1 060	1 060	1 050	1 040	1 030	1 010	1 350	360

1977

L.H.A. ♈	N. 89°	N. 80°	N. 70°	N. 60°	N. 50°	N. 40°	N. 20°	0°	S. 20°	S. 40°	S. 50°	S. 60°	S. 70°	S. 80°	S. 89°	L.H.A. ♈
0	1 010	1 030	1 040	1 050	2 060	2 060	2 070	2 070	2 070	2 060	1 050	1 050	1 030	1 010	1 350	0
30	1 040	1 050	1 060	2 070	2 070	2 070	2 070	2 070	2 070	1 060	1 050	1 040	1 010	1 340	1 320	30
60	1 070	1 080	2 080	2 080	2 080	2 080	2 080	2 080	2 080	1 070	1 070	0 —	0 —	1 300	1 290	60
90	1 100	1 100	2 100	2 100	2 090	2 090	2 090	2 090	2 100	1 100	1 100	0 —	0 —	1 250	1 260	90
120	1 130	1 120	1 110	2 110	2 110	2 110	2 110	2 110	2 110	1 120	1 130	1 140	1 180	1 210	1 230	120
150	1 160	1 140	1 130	2 120	2 120	2 120	2 110	2 110	2 120	2 120	1 130	1 140	1 150	1 180	1 200	150
180	1 190	1 170	1 150	1 140	1 130	2 120	2 120	2 110	2 110	2 120	2 120	2 120	1 140	1 150	1 170	180
210	1 220	1 200	1 170	1 140	1 130	1 120	2 110	2 110	2 110	2 110	2 110	2 110	1 130	1 130	1 140	210
240	1 250	1 240	0 —	0 —	1 120	1 110	2 100	2 100	2 100	2 100	2 100	2 100	2 100	1 110	1 110	240
270	1 280	1 290	0 —	0 —	1 080	1 080	2 080	2 090	2 090	2 090	2 090	2 090	2 080	1 080	1 080	270
300	1 310	1 330	1 010	1 040	1 050	1 060	2 070	2 070	2 080	2 070	2 070	2 070	1 070	1 060	1 050	300
330	1 340	1 000	1 030	1 040	1 050	2 060	2 070	2 070	2 070	2 060	2 060	2 060	1 050	1 040	1 020	330
360	1 010	1 030	1 040	1 050	2 060	2 060	2 070	2 070	2 070	2 060	1 050	1 050	1 030	1 010	1 350	360

1978

L.H.A. ♈	N. 89°	N. 80°	N. 70°	N. 60°	N. 50°	N. 40°	N. 20°	0°	S. 20°	S. 40°	S. 50°	S. 60°	S. 70°	S. 80°	S. 89°	L.H.A. ♈
0	1 010	1 030	2 040	2 050	2 060	2 060	3 070	3 070	3 070	2 060	2 050	2 050	1 030	1 020	1 350	0
30	1 040	2 050	2 060	2 070	2 070	3 070	3 070	3 070	2 070	2 060	2 050	1 040	1 010	1 350	1 320	30
60	1 070	2 070	2 080	2 080	3 080	3 080	3 080	3 080	2 080	1 070	1 060	1 040	0 —	1 310	1 290	60
90	1 100	2 100	2 100	2 090	3 090	3 090	3 090	3 090	2 090	1 100	1 100	0 —	0 —	1 260	1 260	90
120	1 130	2 120	2 110	2 110	3 110	3 110	3 100	3 110	2 110	2 120	1 130	1 140	1 180	1 210	1 230	120
150	1 160	1 140	2 130	2 120	2 120	3 120	3 110	3 110	3 120	2 120	1 130	1 140	1 160	1 180	1 200	150
180	1 190	1 170	1 150	2 130	2 130	2 120	3 120	3 110	3 110	2 120	2 120	2 130	2 140	1 150	1 170	180
210	1 220	1 200	1 170	1 140	2 130	2 120	2 110	3 110	3 110	3 110	2 110	2 120	2 120	2 130	1 140	210
240	1 250	1 230	0 —	1 140	1 120	1 110	2 100	3 100	3 100	3 100	3 100	2 100	2 100	2 110	1 110	240
270	1 280	1 280	0 —	0 —	1 080	1 080	2 090	3 090	3 090	3 090	3 090	2 090	2 090	2 080	1 080	270
300	1 310	1 330	1 000	1 040	1 060	2 060	2 070	3 080	3 080	3 080	3 070	2 070	2 070	2 060	1 050	300
330	1 340	1 000	1 030	1 040	2 050	2 060	3 070	3 070	3 070	2 060	2 060	2 060	1 050	1 040	1 020	330
360	1 010	1 030	2 040	2 050	2 060	2 060	3 070	3 070	3 070	2 060	2 050	2 050	1 030	1 020	1 350	360

1979

L.H.A. ♈	N. 89°	N. 80°	N. 70°	N. 60°	N. 50°	N. 40°	N. 20°	0°	S. 20°	S. 40°	S. 50°	S. 60°	S. 70°	S. 80°	S. 89°	L.H.A. ♈
0	1 010	2 030	2 040	2 050	3 060	3 060	4 070	4 070	3 070	3 060	3 050	2 050	2 040	2 020	1 000	0
30	2 040	2 050	2 060	3 060	3 070	3 070	4 070	4 070	3 070	2 060	2 050	2 040	1 020	1 350	1 330	30
60	2 070	2 070	2 080	3 080	3 080	4 080	4 080	3 080	3 080	2 070	1 060	1 040	1 350	1 310	1 300	60
90	2 100	2 090	3 090	3 090	3 090	4 090	4 090	3 090	3 090	2 100	1 100	0 —	0 —	1 260	1 260	90
120	2 130	2 120	2 110	3 110	3 110	3 100	4 100	3 100	3 110	2 120	2 130	1 140	1 180	1 210	1 230	120
150	2 150	2 140	2 130	3 120	3 120	3 110	4 110	4 110	3 110	3 120	2 130	2 140	1 160	1 180	1 200	150
180	1 180	2 160	2 150	2 130	3 130	3 120	3 120	4 110	4 110	3 120	3 120	2 130	2 140	2 150	1 170	180
210	1 210	1 190	1 160	2 140	2 130	2 120	3 110	4 110	4 110	3 110	3 110	3 120	2 120	2 130	2 140	210
240	1 250	1 230	1 190	1 140	1 120	2 110	3 100	3 100	4 100	4 100	3 100	3 100	2 100	2 110	2 110	240
270	1 280	1 280	0 —	0 —	1 080	2 090	3 090	3 090	4 090	4 090	3 090	3 090	3 090	2 090	2 080	270
300	1 310	1 330	1 000	1 040	2 060	2 070	3 070	3 080	4 080	3 080	3 070	3 070	2 070	2 060	2 060	300
330	1 340	1 000	1 020	2 040	2 050	3 060	3 070	4 070	4 070	3 070	3 060	3 060	2 050	2 040	2 030	330
360	1 010	2 030	2 040	2 050	3 060	3 060	4 070	4 070	3 070	3 060	3 050	2 050	2 040	2 020	1 000	360

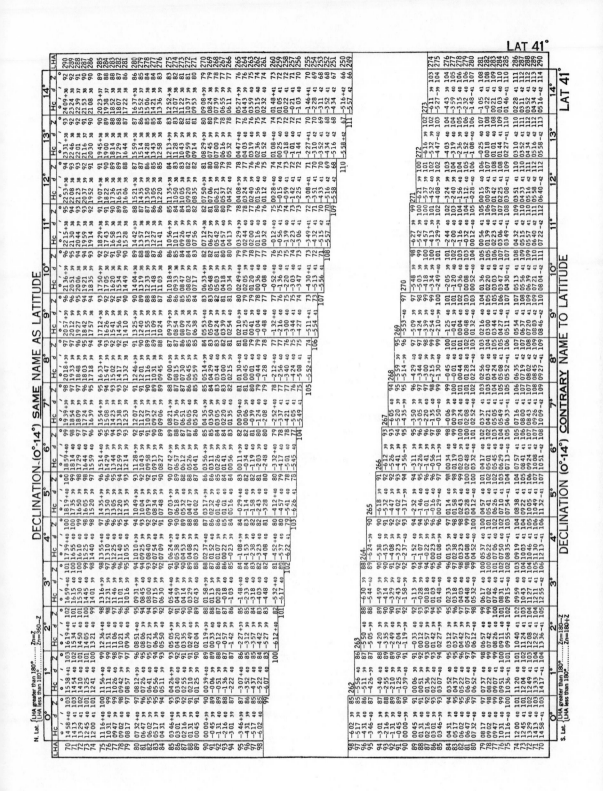

DECLINATION (0°–14°) SAME NAME AS LATITUDE

N. Lat. {LHA greater than 180° ...... Zn=Z / LHA less than 180° ...... Zn=360−Z}

DECLINATION (0°–14°) CONTRARY NAME TO LATITUDE

S. Lat. {LHA greater than 180° ...... Zn=180−Z / LHA less than 180° ...... Zn=180+Z}

N. Lat. {LHA greater than 180°........ Zn=Z / LHA less than 180°........... Zn=360−Z}

DECLINATION (0°-14°) CONTRARY NAME TO LATITUDE

LHA	0° Hc	0° d	0° Z	1° Hc	1° d	1° Z	2° Hc	2° d	2° Z	3° Hc	3° d	3° Z	4° Hc	4° d	4° Z
	° ′	′	°	° ′	′	°	° ′	′	°	° ′	′	°	° ′	′	°
69	15 42	41	104	15 01	42	105	14 19	41	106	13 38	41	106	12 57	42	107
68	16 25	41	105	15 44	41	106	15 03	41	106	14 22	42	107	13 40	42	108
67	17 09	41	106	16 28	42	106	15 46	41	107	15 05	42	108	14 23	42	109
66	17 53	42	106	17 11	41	107	16 30	42	108	15 48	42	109	15 06	42	109
65	18 36	−42	107	17 54	−41	108	17 13	−42	109	16 31	−42	109	15 49	−43	110
64	19 19	42	108	18 37	42	109	17 55	42	109	17 13	42	110	16 31	43	111
63	20 02	42	109	19 20	42	109	18 38	42	110	17 56	43	111	17 13	42	112
62	20 45	42	109	20 03	42	110	19 21	43	111	18 38	43	112	17 55	43	112
61	21 28	43	110	20 45	42	111	20 03	43	112	19 20	43	112	18 37	43	113
60	22 10	−42	111	21 28	−43	112	20 45	−43	112	20 02	−43	113	19 19	−44	114
59	22 52	42	112	22 10	43	112	21 27	44	113	20 43	43	114	20 00	44	115
58	23 34	43	112	22 51	43	113	22 08	43	114	21 25	44	115	20 41	44	115
57	24 16	43	113	23 33	44	114	22 49	43	115	22 06	44	115	21 22	44	116
56	24 58	44	114	24 14	43	115	23 31	44	115	22 47	45	116	22 02	44	117
55	25 39	−44	115	24 55	−44	115	24 11	−44	116	23 27	−44	117	22 43	−45	118
54	26 20	44	116	25 36	44	116	24 52	45	117	24 07	44	118	23 23	45	119
53	27 01	44	116	26 17	45	117	25 32	45	118	24 47	45	119	24 02	45	119
52	27 41	44	117	26 57	45	118	26 12	45	119	25 27	45	119	24 42	46	120
51	28 21	44	118	27 37	46	119	26 51	45	120	26 06	45	120	25 21	46	121
50	29 01	−45	119	28 16	−45	120	27 31	−46	120	26 45	−46	121	25 59	−46	122
49	29 41	46	120	28 55	45	120	28 10	46	121	27 24	46	122	26 38	47	123
48	30 20	46	121	29 34	46	121	28 48	46	122	28 02	46	123	27 16	47	124
47	30 59	46	122	30 13	47	122	29 26	46	123	28 40	47	124	27 53	47	124
46	31 37	46	122	30 51	47	123	30 04	47	124	29 17	47	125	28 30	47	125
45	32 15	−46	123	31 29	−47	124	30 42	−48	125	29 54	−47	126	29 07	−48	126
44	32 53	47	124	32 06	47	125	31 19	48	126	30 31	48	126	29 43	48	127
43	33 30	47	125	32 43	48	126	31 55	48	127	31 07	48	127	30 19	48	128
42	34 07	48	126	33 19	48	127	32 31	48	128	31 43	48	128	30 55	49	129
41	34 43	48	127	33 55	48	128	33 07	48	129	32 19	49	129	31 30	49	130
40	35 19	−48	128	34 31	−49	129	33 42	−49	129	32 53	−49	130	32 04	−49	131
39	35 55	49	129	35 06	49	130	34 17	49	130	33 28	50	131	32 38	49	132
38	36 30	49	130	35 41	50	131	34 51	49	131	34 02	50	132	33 12	50	133
37	37 04	49	131	36 15	50	132	35 25	50	132	34 35	50	133	33 45	51	134
36	37 38	50	132	36 48	50	133	35 58	50	134	35 08	51	134	34 17	51	135
35	38 11	−50	133	37 21	−50	134	36 31	−51	135	35 40	−51	135	34 49	−51	136
34	38 44	51	134	37 53	50	135	37 03	51	136	36 12	52	136	35 20	51	137
33	39 16	51	135	38 25	51	136	37 34	51	137	36 43	52	137	35 51	52	138
32	39 48	52	136	38 56	51	137	38 05	52	138	37 13	52	138	36 21	52	139
31	40 19	52	138	39 27	52	138	38 35	52	139	37 43	53	139	36 50	52	140
30	40 49	−52	139	39 57	−53	139	39 04	−52	140	38 12	−53	141	37 19	−53	141
29	41 18	52	140	40 26	53	140	39 33	53	141	38 40	53	142	37 47	53	142
28	41 47	53	141	40 54	53	142	40 01	53	142	39 08	53	143	38 15	54	143
27	42 15	53	142	41 22	53	143	40 29	54	143	39 35	54	144	38 41	54	145
26	42 43	54	143	41 49	54	144	40 55	54	145	40 01	54	145	39 07	54	146
25	43 09	−54	145	42 15	−54	145	41 21	−54	146	40 27	−55	146	39 32	−54	147
24	43 35	54	146	42 41	55	146	41 46	54	147	40 52	55	148	39 57	55	148
23	44 00	54	147	43 06	55	148	42 11	56	148	41 15	55	149	40 20	55	149
22	44 24	55	148	43 29	55	149	42 34	55	149	41 39	56	150	40 43	56	151
21	44 48	56	150	43 52	55	150	42 57	56	151	42 01	56	151	41 05	56	152
20	45 10	−56	151	44 14	−56	152	43 18	−56	152	42 22	−56	153	41 26	−57	153
19	45 32	57	152	44 35	56	153	43 39	56	153	42 43	57	154	41 46	57	154
18	45 52	56	154	44 56	57	154	43 59	57	155	43 02	57	155	42 05	57	156
17	46 12	57	155	45 15	57	156	44 18	57	156	43 21	57	156	42 24	58	157
16	46 31	58	156	45 33	57	157	44 36	57	157	43 39	58	158	42 41	58	158
15	46 48	−57	158	45 51	−58	158	44 53	−58	159	43 55	−58	159	42 57	−57	159
14	47 05	58	159	46 07	58	160	45 09	58	160	44 11	58	160	43 13	58	161
13	47 20	58	161	46 22	58	161	45 24	58	161	44 26	59	162	43 27	58	162
12	47 35	59	162	46 36	58	162	45 38	58	163	44 40	59	163	43 41	59	163
11	47 48	58	164	46 50	59	164	45 51	59	164	44 52	59	164	43 53	58	165
10	48 01	−59	165	47 02	−59	165	46 03	−59	166	45 04	−59	166	44 05	−59	166
9	48 12	59	166	47 13	59	167	46 14	60	167	45 14	59	167	44 15	59	167
8	48 22	59	168	47 23	60	168	46 23	59	168	45 24	59	169	44 25	60	169
7	48 31	60	169	47 31	59	170	46 32	60	170	45 32	59	170	44 33	60	170
6	48 38	59	171	47 39	60	171	46 39	59	171	45 40	60	171	44 40	60	172
5	48 45	−60	172	47 45	−59	173	46 46	−60	173	45 46	−60	173	44 46	−60	173
4	48 50	59	174	47 51	60	174	46 51	60	174	45 51	60	174	44 51	60	174
3	48 55	60	175	47 55	60	176	46 55	60	176	45 55	60	176	44 55	60	176
2	48 58	60	177	47 58	60	177	46 58	60	177	45 58	60	177	44 58	60	177
1	48 59	60	179	47 59	60	179	46 59	60	179	45 59	60	179	44 59	59	179
0	49 00	−60	180	48 00	−60	180	47 00	−60	180	46 00	−60	180	45 00	−60	180

LHA	5° Hc	5° d	5° Z	6° Hc	6° d	6° Z	7° Hc	7° d	7° Z	8° Hc	8° d	8° Z	9° Hc	9° d	9° Z
	° ′	′	°	° ′	′	°	° ′	′	°	° ′	′	°	° ′	′	°
69	12 15	41	108	11 34	42	109	10 52	42	109	10 10	42	110	09 28	42	111
68	12 58	41	109	12 17	42	109	11 35	42	110	10 53	43	111	10 10	42	112
67	13 41	42	109	12 59	42	110	12 17	42	111	11 35	43	112	10 52	42	112
66	14 24	42	110	13 42	43	111	12 59	42	112	12 17	43	112	11 34	42	113
65	15 06	−42	111	14 24	−43	112	13 41	−42	112	12 59	−43	113	12 16	−43	114
64	15 48	42	112	15 06	43	112	14 23	43	113	13 40	43	114	12 57	43	114
63	16 31	43	112	15 48	43	113	15 05	43	114	14 22	44	114	13 38	43	115
62	17 12	43	113	16 29	43	114	15 46	43	114	15 03	44	115	14 19	43	116
61	17 54	43	114	17 11	44	114	16 27	43	115	15 44	44	116	15 00	44	117
60	18 35	−43	115	17 52	−44	115	17 08	−44	116	16 24	−44	117	15 40	−44	117
59	19 16	43	115	18 33	44	116	17 49	44	117	17 05	45	117	16 20	44	118
58	19 57	44	116	19 13	44	117	18 29	44	117	17 45	45	118	17 00	45	119
57	20 38	45	117	19 53	44	118	19 09	45	118	18 24	44	119	17 40	45	120
56	21 18	45	118	20 33	44	118	19 49	45	119	19 04	45	120	18 19	45	120
55	21 58	−45	118	21 13	−45	119	20 28	−45	120	19 43	−45	121	18 58	−46	121
54	22 38	45	119	21 53	46	120	21 07	45	121	20 22	46	121	19 36	45	122
53	23 17	45	120	22 32	46	121	21 46	46	121	21 00	45	122	20 15	47	123
52	23 56	46	121	23 10	45	122	22 25	46	122	21 39	47	123	20 52	46	124
51	24 35	46	122	23 49	46	122	23 03	47	123	22 16	46	124	21 30	47	124
50	25 13	−46	123	24 27	−46	123	23 41	−47	124	22 54	−47	125	22 07	−47	125
49	25 51	46	123	25 05	47	124	24 18	47	125	23 31	47	125	22 44	47	126
48	26 29	47	124	25 42	47	125	24 55	47	126	24 08	48	126	23 20	47	127
47	27 06	47	125	26 19	47	126	25 32	48	126	24 44	48	127	23 56	48	128
46	27 43	47	126	26 56	48	127	26 08	48	127	25 20	48	128	24 32	48	129
45	28 19	−47	127	27 32	−48	128	26 44	−49	128	25 55	−48	129	25 07	−49	130
44	28 55	48	128	28 07	48	128	27 19	49	129	26 30	48	130	25 42	49	130
43	29 31	48	129	28 43	49	129	27 54	49	130	27 05	49	131	26 16	49	131
42	30 06	49	130	29 17	49	130	28 28	49	131	27 39	49	132	26 50	50	132
41	30 41	49	131	29 52	50	131	29 02	49	132	28 13	50	133	27 23	50	133
40	31 15	−50	132	30 25	−49	132	29 36	−50	133	28 46	−50	133	27 56	−50	134
39	31 49	50	133	30 59	50	133	30 09	50	134	29 19	51	134	28 28	50	135
38	32 22	50	133	31 32	51	134	30 41	50	135	29 51	51	135	29 00	51	136
37	32 54	50	134	32 04	51	135	31 13	51	136	30 22	51	136	29 31	51	137
36	33 26	50	135	32 36	52	136	31 44	51	137	30 53	51	137	30 02	52	138
35	33 58	−51	137	33 07	−52	137	32 15	−51	138	31 24	−52	138	30 32	−52	139
34	34 29	52	138	33 37	52	138	32 45	52	139	31 53	52	139	31 01	52	140
33	34 59	52	139	34 07	52	139	33 15	52	140	32 23	53	140	31 30	52	141
32	35 29	53	140	34 36	52	140	33 44	53	141	32 51	53	141	31 58	53	142
31	35 58	53	141	35 05	53	141	34 12	53	142	33 19	53	142	32 26	53	143
30	36 26	−53	142	35 33	−53	142	34 40	−53	143	33 47	−54	143	32 53	−54	144
29	36 54	54	143	36 00	53	143	35 07	54	144	34 13	54	145	33 19	54	145
28	37 21	54	144	36 27	54	145	35 33	54	145	34 39	54	146	33 45	54	146
27	37 47	54	145	36 53	54	146	35 59	55	146	35 04	54	147	34 10	55	147
26	38 13	55	146	37 18	54	147	36 24	55	147	35 29	55	148	34 34	55	148
25	38 38	−55	147	37 43	−55	148	36 48	−55	148	35 53	−56	149	34 57	−55	149
24	39 02	56	149	38 06	55	149	37 11	55	150	36 16	56	150	35 20	56	151
23	39 25	56	150	38 29	55	150	37 34	56	151	36 38	56	151	35 42	56	152
22	39 47	56	151	38 51	56	151	37 55	56	152	36 59	56	152	36 03	56	153
21	40 09	56	152	39 13	57	153	38 16	56	153	37 20	57	154	36 23	56	154
20	40 29	−56	153	39 33	−57	154	38 36	−56	154	37 40	−57	155	36 43	−57	155
19	40 49	56	155	39 53	57	155	38 56	57	156	37 59	57	156	37 02	58	156
18	41 08	57	156	40 11	57	156	39 14	57	157	38 17	58	157	37 19	57	157
17	41 26	57	157	40 29	58	158	39 31	57	158	38 34	58	158	37 36	57	159
16	41 43	57	158	40 46	58	159	39 48	58	159	38 50	58	160	37 52	57	160
15	42 00	−58	160	41 02	−58	160	40 04	−58	160	39 06	−58	161	38 08	−59	161
14	42 15	58	161	41 17	59	161	40 18	58	162	39 20	58	162	38 22	59	162
13	42 29	58	162	41 31	59	163	40 32	58	163	39 34	59	163	38 35	58	164
12	42 42	58	164	41 44	59	164	40 45	59	164	39 46	58	165	38 48	59	165
11	42 55	59	165	41 56	59	165	40 57	59	166	39 58	59	166	38 59	59	166
10	43 06	−59	166	42 07	−59	167	41 08	−59	167	40 09	−59	167	39 10	−60	167
9	43 16	59	168	42 17	59	168	41 18	60	168	40 18	59	168	39 19	59	169
8	43 25	59	169	42 26	60	169	41 26	59	169	40 27	59	170	39 28	60	170
7	43 33	59	170	42 34	60	171	41 34	59	171	40 35	60	171	39 35	59	171
6	43 40	59	172	42 41	60	172	41 41	60	172	40 41	59	172	39 42	60	172
5	43 46	−59	173	42 47	−60	173	41 47	−60	173	40 47	−60	174	39 47	−59	174
4	43 51	60	175	42 51	59	175	41 52	60	175	40 52	60	175	39 52	60	175
3	43 55	60	176	42 55	60	176	41 55	60	176	40 55	60	176	39 55	59	176
2	43 58	60	177	42 58	60	177	41 58	60	177	40 58	60	177	39 58	60	177
1	44 00	60	179	43 00	60	179	42 00	60	179	41 00	60	179	40 00	60	179
0	44 00	−60	180	43 00	−60	180	42 00	−60	180	41 00	−60	180	40 00	−60	180

LHA	10° Hc	10° d	10° Z	11° Hc	11° d	11° Z	12° Hc	12° d	12° Z	13° Hc	13° d	13° Z	14° Hc	14° d	14° Z	LHA
	° ′	′	°	° ′	′	°	° ′	′	°	° ′	′	°	° ′	′	°	
69	08 46	42	112	08 04	42	112	07 22	42	113	06 40	43	114	05 57	42	114	291
68	09 28	42	112	08 46	43	113	08 03	42	114	07 21	43	114	06 38	42	115	292
67	10 10	43	113	09 27	42	114	08 45	43	114	08 02	43	115	07 19	43	116	293
66	10 52	43	114	10 09	43	114	09 26	43	115	08 43	43	116	08 00	43	117	294
65	11 33	−43	114	10 50	−43	115	10 07	−43	116	09 24	−44	117	08 40	−43	117	295
64	12 14	43	115	11 31	44	116	10 47	43	117	10 04	44	117	09 20	43	118	296
63	12 55	44	116	12 11	43	117	11 28	44	117	10 44	44	118	10 00	44	119	297
62	13 36	44	117	12 52	44	117	12 08	44	118	11 24	44	119	10 40	44	119	298
61	14 16	44	117	13 32	44	118	12 48	44	119	12 04	45	119	11 19	44	120	299
60	14 56	−44	118	14 12	−45	119	13 27	−44	119	12 43	−45	120	11 58	−44	121	300
59	15 36	45	119	14 51	44	120	14 07	45	120	13 22	45	121	12 37	45	122	301
58	16 15	44	120	15 31	45	120	14 46	45	121	14 01	45	122	13 16	46	122	302
57	16 55	45	120	16 10	46	121	15 24	45	122	14 39	45	122	13 54	46	123	303
56	17 34	46	121	16 48	45	122	16 03	46	123	15 17	46	123	14 31	45	124	304
55	18 12	−45	122	17 27	−46	123	16 41	−46	123	15 55	−46	124	15 09	−46	125	305
54	18 51	46	123	18 05	46	123	17 19	47	124	16 32	46	125	15 46	46	125	306
53	19 28	46	124	18 42	46	124	17 56	47	125	17 09	46	126	16 23	47	126	307
52	20 06	46	124	19 20	47	125	18 33	47	126	17 46	47	126	16 59	47	127	308
51	20 43	47	125	19 56	46	126	19 10	48	126	18 22	47	127	17 35	47	128	309
50	21 20	−47	126	20 33	−47	127	19 46	−48	127	18 58	−47	128	18 11	−48	129	310
49	21 57	48	127	21 09	47	127	20 22	48	128	19 34	48	129	18 46	48	129	311
48	22 33	48	128	21 45	48	128	20 57	48	129	20 09	48	130	19 21	48	130	312
47	23 08	48	128	22 20	48	129	21 32	48	130	20 44	49	130	19 55	48	131	313
46	23 44	49	129	22 55	48	130	22 07	49	131	21 18	49	131	20 29	49	132	314
45	24 18	−48	130	23 30	−49	131	22 41	−49	131	21 52	−49	132	21 03	−50	133	315
44	24 53	49	131	24 04	49	132	23 15	50	132	22 25	49	133	21 36	50	134	316
43	25 27	50	132	24 37	49	133	23 48	50	133	22 58	50	134	22 08	50	134	317
42	26 00	49	133	25 11	50	134	24 21	50	134	23 31	51	135	22 40	50	135	318
41	26 33	50	134	25 43	50	134	24 53	50	135	24 03	51	136	23 12	51	136	319
40	27 06	−51	135	26 15	−50	135	25 25	−51	136	24 34	−51	137	23 43	−51	137	320
39	27 38	51	136	26 47	51	136	25 56	51	137	25 05	51	137	24 14	52	138	321
38	28 09	51	137	27 18	51	137	26 27	52	138	25 35	51	138	24 44	52	139	322
37	28 40	52	138	27 48	51	138	26 57	52	139	26 05	52	139	25 13	52	140	323
36	29 10	52	139	28 18	52	139	27 26	52	140	26 34	52	140	25 42	52	141	324
35	29 40	−52	140	28 48	−52	140	27 56	−53	141	27 03	−52	141	26 11	−53	142	325
34	30 09	52	140	29 17	53	141	28 24	53	142	27 31	53	142	26 38	53	143	326
33	30 38	53	141	29 45	53	142	28 52	53	143	27 59	53	143	27 06	54	144	327
32	31 05	53	143	30 12	53	143	29 19	53	144	28 26	54	144	27 32	53	145	328
31	31 33	54	144	30 39	53	144	29 46	54	145	28 52	54	145	27 58	54	146	329
30	31 59	−53	145	31 06	−54	145	30 12	−54	146	29 18	−55	146	28 23	−54	147	330
29	32 25	54	146	31 31	54	146	30 37	54	147	29 43	55	147	28 48	54	148	331
28	32 51	55	147	31 56	54	147	31 02	55	148	30 07	55	148	29 12	55	149	332
27	33 15	55	148	32 20	55	148	31 25	55	149	30 30	55	149	29 35	55	150	333
26	33 39	55	149	32 44	55	149	31 49	56	150	30 53	55	150	29 58	56	151	334
25	34 02	−55	150	33 07	−56	150	32 11	−55	151	31 16	−56	151	30 20	−56	152	335
24	34 24	55	151	33 29	56	151	32 33	56	152	31 37	56	152	30 41	56	153	336
23	34 46	56	152	33 50	56	153	32 54	56	153	31 58	57	153	31 01	56	154	337
22	35 07	56	153	34 11	57	154	33 14	56	154	32 18	57	154	31 21	57	155	338
21	35 27	57	154	34 30	56	155	33 34	57	155	32 37	57	156	31 40	57	156	339
20	35 46	−57	156	34 49	−57	156	33 52	−57	156	32 55	−57	157	31 58	−57	157	340
19	36 04	57	157	35 07	57	157	34 10	57	157	33 13	58	158	32 15	57	158	341
18	36 22	57	158	35 25	58	158	34 27	58	159	33 29	57	159	32 32	58	159	342
17	36 39	58	159	35 41	58	159	34 43	58	160	33 45	57	160	32 48	58	160	343
16	36 55	58	160	35 57	58	161	34 59	59	161	34 00	58	161	33 02	58	161	344
15	37 09	−58	161	36 11	−58	162	35 13	−58	162	34 15	−59	162	33 16	−58	163	345
14	37 23	58	163	36 25	58	163	35 27	59	163	34 28	58	163	33 30	59	164	346
13	37 37	59	164	36 38	59	164	35 39	58	164	34 41	59	165	33 42	59	165	347
12	37 49	59	165	36 50	59	165	35 51	59	166	34 52	59	166	33 53	59	166	348
11	38 00	59	166	37 01	59	166	36 02	59	167	35 03	59	167	34 04	59	167	349
10	38 10	−59	167	37 11	−59	168	36 12	−59	168	35 13	−59	168	34 14	−60	168	350
9	38 20	60	169	37 20	59	169	36 21	59	169	35 22	60	169	34 22	59	169	351
8	38 28	59	170	37 29	60	170	36 29	59	170	35 30	60	170	34 30	59	171	352
7	38 36	60	171	37 36	60	171	36 36	59	172	35 37	60	172	34 37	59	172	353
6	38 42	60	172	37 42	59	173	36 43	60	173	35 43	60	173	34 43	59	173	354
5	38 48	−60	174	37 48	−60	174	36 48	−60	174	35 48	−60	174	34 48	−59	174	355
4	38 52	60	175	37 52	60	175	36 52	60	175	35 52	59	175	34 53	60	175	356
3	38 56	60	176	37 56	60	176	36 56	60	176	35 56	60	176	34 56	60	176	357
2	38 58	60	178	37 58	60	178	36 58	60	178	35 58	60	178	34 58	60	178	358
1	39 00	60	179	38 00	60	179	37 00	60	179	36 00	60	179	35 00	60	179	359
0	39 00	−60	180	38 00	−60	180	37 00	−60	180	36 00	−60	180	35 00	−60	180	360

S. Lat. {LHA greater than 180°........ Zn=180−Z / LHA less than 180°........... Zn=180+Z}

DECLINATION (0°-14°) CONTRARY NAME TO LATITUDE

LAT 41°

DECLINATION (15°–29°) SAME NAME AS LATITUDE

N. Lat. { LHA greater than 180° ..... Zn=Z / LHA less than 180° ..... Zn=360−Z }

LHA	15° Hc / d / Z	16°	17°	18°	19°	20°	21°	22°	23°	24°	25°	26°	27°	28°	29°	LHA
0	64 00 +60 180	…	…	…	…	…	…	…	…	…	…	…	…	…	78 00 +60 180	360
1	63 59 60 178														77 58 60 176	359
2	63 57 60 176														77 54 60 172	358
…	…														…	…
69	25 32 37 79														33 41 32 79	291

(Full interior sight-reduction data table: 70 LHA rows × declination columns 15° through 29°, each column giving Hc, d, and Z.)

S. Lat. { LHA greater than 180° ..... Zn=180−Z / LHA less than 180° ..... Zn=180+Z }

DECLINATION (15°–29°) SAME NAME AS LATITUDE

TABLE III.—Correction to Tabulated Altitude for Minutes of Declination

d / ′	1	2	3	4	5	6	7	8	9	10	11	12	13	14	15	16	17	18	19	20	21
0	0	0	0	0	0	0	0	0	0	0	0	0	0	0	0	0	0	0	0	0	0
1	0	0	0	0	0	0	0	0	0	0	0	0	0	0	0	0	0	0	0	0	0
2	0	0	0	0	0	0	0	0	0	0	0	0	0	0	0	1	1	1	1	1	1
3	0	0	0	0	0	0	0	0	0	0	1	1	1	1	1	1	1	1	1	1	1
4	0	0	0	0	0	0	0	1	1	1	1	1	1	1	1	1	1	1	1	1	1
5	0	0	0	0	0	0	1	1	1	1	1	1	1	1	1	1	1	2	2	2	2
6	0	0	0	0	0	1	1	1	1	1	1	1	1	1	2	2	2	2	2	2	2
7	0	0	0	0	1	1	1	1	1	1	1	1	2	2	2	2	2	2	2	2	2
8	0	0	0	1	1	1	1	1	1	1	1	2	2	2	2	2	2	2	3	3	3
9	0	0	0	1	1	1	1	1	1	2	2	2	2	2	2	2	3	3	3	3	3
10	0	0	0	1	1	1	1	1	2	2	2	2	2	2	2	3	3	3	3	3	4
11	0	0	1	1	1	1	1	1	2	2	2	2	2	3	3	3	3	3	3	4	4
12	0	0	1	1	1	1	1	2	2	2	2	2	3	3	3	3	3	4	4	4	4
13	0	0	1	1	1	1	2	2	2	2	2	3	3	3	3	3	4	4	4	4	5
14	0	0	1	1	1	1	2	2	2	2	3	3	3	3	4	4	4	4	4	5	5
15	0	0	1	1	1	2	2	2	2	2	3	3	3	4	4	4	4	4	5	5	5
16	0	1	1	1	1	2	2	2	2	3	3	3	3	4	4	4	5	5	5	5	6
17	0	1	1	1	1	2	2	2	3	3	3	3	4	4	4	5	5	5	5	6	6
18	0	1	1	1	2	2	2	2	3	3	3	4	4	4	4	5	5	5	6	6	6
19	0	1	1	1	2	2	2	3	3	3	3	4	4	4	5	5	5	6	6	6	7
20	0	1	1	1	2	2	2	3	3	3	4	4	4	5	5	5	6	6	6	7	7
21	0	1	1	1	2	2	2	3	3	4	4	4	5	5	5	6	6	6	7	7	7
22	0	1	1	1	2	2	3	3	3	4	4	4	5	5	6	6	6	7	7	7	8
23	0	1	1	2	2	2	3	3	3	4	4	5	5	5	6	6	7	7	7	8	8
24	0	1	1	2	2	2	3	3	4	4	4	5	5	6	6	6	7	7	8	8	8
25	0	1	1	2	2	2	3	3	4	4	5	5	5	6	6	7	7	8	8	8	9
26	0	1	1	2	2	3	3	3	4	4	5	5	6	6	6	7	7	8	8	9	9
27	0	1	1	2	2	3	3	4	4	4	5	5	6	6	7	7	8	8	9	9	9
28	0	1	1	2	2	3	3	4	4	5	5	6	6	7	7	7	8	8	9	9	10
29	0	1	1	2	2	3	3	4	4	5	5	6	6	7	7	8	8	9	9	10	10
30	0	1	2	2	2	3	4	4	4	5	6	6	6	7	8	8	8	9	10	10	10
31	1	1	2	2	3	3	4	4	5	5	6	6	7	7	8	8	9	9	10	10	11
32	1	1	2	2	3	3	4	4	5	5	6	6	7	7	8	9	9	10	10	11	11
33	1	1	2	2	3	3	4	4	5	6	6	7	7	8	8	9	9	10	10	11	12
34	1	1	2	2	3	3	4	5	5	6	6	7	7	8	8	9	10	10	11	11	12
35	1	1	2	2	3	4	4	5	5	6	6	7	8	8	9	9	10	10	11	12	12
36	1	1	2	2	3	4	4	5	5	6	7	7	8	8	9	10	10	11	11	12	13
37	1	1	2	2	3	4	4	5	6	6	7	7	8	9	9	10	10	11	12	12	13
38	1	1	2	3	3	4	4	5	6	6	7	8	8	9	10	10	11	11	12	13	13
39	1	1	2	3	3	4	5	5	6	6	7	8	8	9	10	10	11	12	12	13	14
40	1	1	2	3	3	4	5	5	6	7	7	8	9	9	10	11	11	12	13	13	14
41	1	1	2	3	3	4	5	5	6	7	8	8	9	10	10	11	12	12	13	14	14
42	1	1	2	3	4	4	5	6	6	7	8	8	9	10	10	11	12	13	13	14	15
43	1	1	2	3	4	4	5	6	6	7	8	9	9	10	11	11	12	13	14	14	15
44	1	1	2	3	4	4	5	6	7	7	8	9	10	10	11	12	12	13	14	15	15
45	1	2	2	3	4	4	5	6	7	8	8	9	10	10	11	12	13	14	14	15	16
46	1	2	2	3	4	5	5	6	7	8	8	9	10	11	12	12	13	14	15	15	16
47	1	2	2	3	4	5	5	6	7	8	9	9	10	11	12	13	13	14	15	16	16
48	1	2	2	3	4	5	6	6	7	8	9	10	10	11	12	13	14	14	15	16	17
49	1	2	2	3	4	5	6	7	7	8	9	10	11	11	12	13	14	15	16	16	17
50	1	2	2	3	4	5	6	7	8	8	9	10	11	12	12	13	14	15	16	17	18
51	1	2	3	3	4	5	6	7	8	8	9	10	11	12	13	14	14	15	16	17	18
52	1	2	3	3	4	5	6	7	8	9	10	10	11	12	13	14	15	16	16	17	18
53	1	2	3	4	4	5	6	7	8	9	10	11	11	12	13	14	15	16	17	18	19
54	1	2	3	4	4	5	6	7	8	9	10	11	12	13	14	14	15	16	17	18	19
55	1	2	3	4	5	6	6	7	8	9	10	11	12	13	14	15	16	16	17	18	19
56	1	2	3	4	5	6	7	7	8	9	10	11	12	13	14	15	16	17	18	19	20
57	1	2	3	4	5	6	7	8	9	10	10	11	12	13	14	15	16	17	18	19	20
58	1	2	3	4	5	6	7	8	9	10	11	12	13	14	14	15	16	17	18	19	20
59	1	2	3	4	5	6	7	8	9	10	11	12	13	14	15	16	17	18	19	20	21

d / ′	22	23	24	25	26	27	28	29	30	31	32	33	34	35	36	37	38	39	40	41	42
0	0	0	0	0	0	0	0	0	0	0	0	0	0	0	0	0	0	0	0	0	0
1	0	0	0	0	0	0	0	0	0	1	1	1	1	1	1	1	1	1	1	1	1
2	1	1	1	1	1	1	1	1	1	1	1	1	1	1	1	1	1	1	1	1	1
3	1	1	1	1	1	1	1	1	2	2	2	2	2	2	2	2	2	2	2	2	2
4	1	2	2	2	2	2	2	2	2	2	2	2	2	2	2	2	3	3	3	3	3
5	2	2	2	2	2	2	2	2	2	3	3	3	3	3	3	3	3	3	3	3	4
6	2	2	2	2	3	3	3	3	3	3	3	3	3	4	4	4	4	4	4	4	4
7	3	3	3	3	3	3	3	3	4	4	4	4	4	4	4	4	4	5	5	5	5
8	3	3	3	3	3	4	4	4	4	4	4	4	5	5	5	5	5	5	5	5	6
9	3	3	4	4	4	4	4	4	4	5	5	5	5	5	5	6	6	6	6	6	6
10	4	4	4	4	4	4	5	5	5	5	5	6	6	6	6	6	6	6	7	7	7
11	4	4	4	5	5	5	5	5	6	6	6	6	6	6	7	7	7	7	7	8	8
12	4	5	5	5	5	5	6	6	6	6	6	7	7	7	7	7	8	8	8	8	8
13	5	5	5	5	6	6	6	6	6	7	7	7	7	8	8	8	8	8	9	9	9
14	5	5	6	6	6	6	7	7	7	7	7	8	8	8	8	9	9	9	9	10	10
15	6	6	6	6	6	7	7	7	8	8	8	8	8	9	9	9	10	10	10	10	10
16	6	6	6	7	7	7	7	8	8	8	9	9	9	9	10	10	10	10	11	11	11
17	6	7	7	7	7	8	8	8	8	9	9	9	10	10	10	10	11	11	11	12	12
18	7	7	7	8	8	8	8	9	9	9	10	10	10	10	11	11	11	12	12	12	13
19	7	7	8	8	8	9	9	9	10	10	10	10	11	11	11	12	12	12	13	13	13
20	7	8	8	8	9	9	9	10	10	10	11	11	11	12	12	12	13	13	13	14	14
21	8	8	8	9	9	9	10	10	10	11	11	12	12	12	13	13	13	14	14	14	15
22	8	8	9	9	10	10	10	11	11	11	12	12	12	13	13	14	14	14	15	15	15
23	8	9	9	10	10	10	11	11	12	12	12	13	13	13	14	14	15	15	15	16	16
24	9	9	10	10	10	11	11	12	12	12	13	13	14	14	14	15	15	16	16	16	17
25	9	10	10	10	11	11	12	12	12	13	13	14	14	15	15	15	16	16	17	17	18
26	10	10	10	11	11	12	12	13	13	13	14	14	15	15	16	16	16	17	17	18	18
27	10	10	11	11	12	12	13	13	14	14	14	15	15	16	16	17	17	18	18	18	19
28	10	11	11	12	12	13	13	14	14	14	15	15	16	16	17	17	18	18	19	19	20
29	11	11	12	12	13	13	14	14	14	15	15	16	16	17	17	18	18	19	19	20	20
30	11	12	12	12	13	14	14	14	15	16	16	16	17	18	18	18	19	20	20	20	21
31	11	12	12	13	13	14	14	15	16	16	17	17	18	18	19	19	20	20	21	21	22
32	11	12	13	13	14	14	15	15	16	17	17	18	18	19	19	20	20	21	21	22	22
33	12	13	13	14	14	15	15	16	16	17	18	18	19	19	20	20	21	21	22	23	23
34	12	13	14	14	15	15	16	16	17	18	18	19	19	20	20	21	22	22	23	23	24
35	13	13	14	15	15	16	16	17	18	18	19	19	20	20	21	22	22	23	23	24	24
36	13	14	14	15	16	16	17	17	18	19	19	20	20	21	22	22	23	23	24	25	25
37	14	14	15	15	16	17	17	18	18	19	20	20	21	22	22	23	23	24	25	25	26
38	14	15	15	16	16	17	18	18	19	19	20	20	21	22	23	23	24	25	25	26	27
39	14	15	16	16	17	18	18	19	20	20	21	21	22	23	23	24	25	25	26	27	27
40	15	15	16	17	17	18	19	19	20	21	21	22	23	23	24	25	25	26	27	27	28
41	15	16	16	17	18	18	19	20	20	21	22	23	23	24	25	25	26	27	27	28	29
42	15	16	17	18	18	19	20	20	21	22	22	23	24	24	25	26	27	27	28	29	29
43	16	16	17	18	19	19	20	21	22	22	23	24	24	25	26	27	27	28	29	29	30
44	16	17	18	18	19	20	21	21	22	23	23	24	25	26	26	27	28	29	29	30	31
45	16	17	18	19	20	20	21	22	22	23	24	25	26	26	27	28	28	29	30	31	32
46	17	18	18	19	20	21	21	22	23	24	25	25	26	27	28	28	29	30	31	31	32
47	17	18	19	20	20	21	22	23	24	24	25	26	27	27	28	29	30	31	31	32	33
48	18	18	19	20	21	22	22	23	24	25	26	26	27	28	29	30	30	31	31	32	33
49	18	19	20	20	21	22	23	24	24	25	26	27	28	29	29	30	31	32	33	33	34
50	18	19	20	21	22	22	23	24	25	26	27	28	28	29	30	31	32	32	33	34	35
51	19	20	20	21	22	23	24	25	26	26	27	28	29	30	31	31	32	33	34	35	36
52	19	20	21	22	23	23	24	25	26	27	28	29	29	30	31	32	33	34	35	36	36
53	19	20	21	22	23	24	25	26	26	27	28	29	30	31	32	33	34	34	35	36	37
54	20	21	22	22	23	24	25	26	27	28	29	30	31	32	32	33	34	35	36	37	38
55	20	21	22	23	24	25	26	27	28	28	29	30	31	32	33	34	35	36	37	38	38
56	21	21	22	23	24	25	26	27	28	29	30	31	32	33	34	35	35	36	37	38	39
57	21	22	23	24	25	26	27	28	28	29	30	31	32	33	34	35	36	37	38	39	40
58	21	22	23	24	25	26	27	28	29	30	31	32	33	34	35	36	37	38	39	40	41
59	22	23	24	25	26	27	28	29	30	30	31	32	33	34	35	36	37	38	39	40	41

d / ′	43	44	45	46	47	48	49	50	51	52	53	54	55	56	57	58	59	60	d / ′
0	0	0	0	0	0	0	0	0	0	0	0	0	0	0	0	0	0	0	0
1	1	1	1	1	1	1	1	1	1	1	1	1	1	1	1	1	1	1	1
2	1	1	2	2	2	2	2	2	2	2	2	2	2	2	2	2	2	2	2
3	2	2	2	2	2	2	2	2	3	3	3	3	3	3	3	3	3	3	3
4	3	3	3	3	3	3	3	3	3	3	4	4	4	4	4	4	4	4	4
5	4	4	4	4	4	4	4	4	4	4	4	4	5	5	5	5	5	5	5
6	4	4	4	5	5	5	5	5	5	5	5	5	6	6	6	6	6	6	6
7	5	5	5	5	5	6	6	6	6	6	6	6	6	7	7	7	7	7	7
8	6	6	6	6	6	6	7	7	7	7	7	7	7	7	8	8	8	8	8
9	6	7	7	7	7	7	7	8	8	8	8	8	8	8	9	9	9	9	9
10	7	7	8	8	8	8	8	8	8	9	9	9	9	9	10	10	10	10	10
11	8	8	8	8	9	9	9	9	9	10	10	10	10	10	10	11	11	11	11
12	9	9	9	9	9	10	10	10	10	10	11	11	11	11	11	12	12	12	12
13	9	10	10	10	10	10	11	11	11	11	11	12	12	12	12	13	13	13	13
14	10	10	10	11	11	11	11	12	12	12	12	13	13	13	13	14	14	14	14
15	11	11	11	12	12	12	12	12	13	13	13	14	14	14	15	14	15	15	15
16	11	12	12	12	13	13	13	13	14	14	14	14	15	15	15	15	16	16	16
17	12	12	13	13	13	14	14	14	14	15	15	15	16	16	16	16	17	17	17
18	13	13	14	14	14	14	15	15	15	16	16	16	16	17	17	17	18	18	18
19	14	14	14	15	15	15	16	16	16	16	17	17	17	18	18	18	19	19	19
20	14	15	15	15	16	16	16	17	17	17	18	18	18	19	19	19	20	20	20
21	15	15	16	16	16	17	17	18	18	18	19	19	19	20	20	20	21	21	21
22	16	16	16	17	17	18	18	18	19	19	19	20	20	21	21	21	22	22	22
23	16	17	17	18	18	18	19	19	20	20	20	21	21	21	22	22	23	23	23
24	17	18	18	18	19	19	20	20	20	21	21	22	22	22	23	23	24	24	24
25	18	18	19	19	20	20	20	21	21	22	22	22	23	23	24	24	25	25	25
26	19	19	20	20	20	21	21	22	22	23	23	23	24	24	25	25	26	26	26
27	19	20	20	21	21	22	22	22	23	23	24	24	25	25	26	26	27	27	27
28	20	21	21	21	22	22	23	23	24	24	25	25	26	26	27	27	28	28	28
29	21	21	22	22	23	23	24	24	25	25	26	26	27	27	28	28	29	29	29
30	22	22	22	23	24	24	24	25	26	26	26	27	28	28	28	29	30	30	30
31	22	23	23	24	24	25	25	26	26	27	27	28	28	29	29	30	30	31	31
32	23	23	24	25	25	26	26	27	27	28	28	29	29	30	30	31	31	32	32
33	24	24	25	25	26	26	27	28	28	29	29	30	30	31	31	32	32	33	33
34	24	25	26	26	27	27	28	28	29	29	30	31	31	32	32	33	33	34	34
35	25	26	26	27	27	28	29	29	30	30	31	32	32	33	33	34	34	35	35
36	26	26	27	28	28	29	29	30	31	31	32	32	33	34	34	35	35	36	36
37	27	27	28	28	29	30	30	31	31	32	33	33	34	35	35	36	36	37	37
38	27	28	28	29	30	30	31	32	32	33	34	34	35	35	36	37	37	38	38
39	28	29	29	30	31	31	32	32	33	34	34	35	36	36	37	38	38	39	39
40	29	29	30	31	31	32	33	33	34	35	35	36	37	37	38	39	39	40	40
41	29	30	31	31	32	33	33	34	35	36	36	37	38	38	39	40	40	41	41
42	30	31	32	32	33	34	34	35	36	36	37	38	38	39	40	41	41	42	42
43	31	32	32	33	34	34	35	36	37	37	38	39	39	40	41	42	42	43	43
44	32	32	33	34	34	35	36	37	37	38	39	40	40	41	42	43	43	44	44
45	32	33	34	34	35	36	37	38	38	39	40	40	41	42	43	44	44	45	45
46	33	34	34	35	36	37	38	38	39	40	41	41	42	43	44	44	45	46	46
47	34	34	35	36	37	38	38	39	40	41	42	42	43	44	45	45	46	47	47
48	34	35	36	37	38	38	39	40	41	42	42	43	44	45	46	46	47	48	48
49	35	36	37	38	38	39	40	41	42	42	43	44	45	46	47	47	48	49	49
50	36	37	38	38	39	40	41	42	42	43	44	45	46	47	48	48	49	50	50
51	37	37	38	38	39	40	41	42	43	44	45	46	47	48	48	49	50	51	51
52	37	38	39	40	41	42	42	43	44	45	46	47	48	49	49	50	51	52	52
53	38	39	40	41	42	42	43	44	45	46	47	48	49	49	50	51	52	53	53
54	39	40	40	41	42	43	44	45	46	47	48	49	50	50	51	52	53	54	54
55	39	40	41	42	43	44	45	46	47	48	49	50	50	51	52	53	54	55	55
56	40	41	42	43	44	45	46	47	48	49	49	50	51	52	53	54	55	56	56
57	41	42	43	44	45	46	47	48	48	49	50	51	52	53	54	55	56	57	57
58	42	43	43	44	45	46	47	48	49	50	51	52	53	54	55	56	57	58	58
59	42	43	44	45	46	47	48	49	50	51	52	53	54	55	56	57	58	59	59

Course				l	p
°	°	°	°		
000	180	180	360	1.00	0.00
005	175	185	355	1.00	0.09
010	170	190	350	0.98	0.17
015	165	195	345	0.97	0.26
020	160	200	340	0.94	0.34
025	155	205	335	0.91	0.42
030	150	210	330	0.87	0.50
035	145	215	325	0.82	0.57
040	140	220	320	0.77	0.64
045	135	225	315	0.71	0.71
050	130	230	310	0.64	0.77
055	125	235	305	0.57	0.82
060	120	240	300	0.50	0.87
065	115	245	295	0.42	0.91
070	110	250	290	0.34	0.94
075	105	255	285	0.26	0.97
080	100	260	280	0.17	0.98
085	095	265	275	0.09	1.00
090	090	270	270	0.00	1.00

Lm	p to DLo	Lm	p to DLo	Lm	p to DLo
°		°		°	
0	1.00	30	1.15	60	2.00
5	1.00	35	1.22	65	2.37
10	1.02	40	1.30	70	2.92
15	1.04	45	1.41	75	3.86
20	1.06	50	1.56	80	5.76
25	1.10	55	1.74	85	11.47

Alt.	L/H	Alt.	L/H	Alt.	L/H
°		°		°	
5	11.430	35	1.428	65	0.466
10	5.671	40	1.192	70	0.364
15	3.732	45	1.000	75	0.268
20	2.747	50	0.839	80	0.176
25	2.145	55	0.700	85	0.087
30	1.732	60	0.577	90	0.000

Useful Equations & Rules

Distance - Speed - Time

$$D = S \times T \qquad S = \frac{D}{T} \qquad T = \frac{D}{S}$$

> Where D is distance in nautical miles (statute miles)
> S is speed in knots (miles per hour)
> T is time in hours and decimal fractions

$$60\,D = S \times T' \quad S = \frac{60D}{T'} \quad T' = \frac{60D}{S}$$

> T' is time in minutes and decimal fractions

Distance to visible horizon

$$D = 1.144\sqrt{h}$$

> Where D is distance, in n mi
> h is height, in feet

$$D = 2.072\sqrt{h'}$$

> Where h' is height, in meters

Distance to radar horizon (approximate)

$$D = 1.22\sqrt{h}$$
$$D = 2.21\sqrt{h'}$$

Nautical miles - statute miles

$$N\ mi = 1.15\ st\ mi \qquad St\ mi = 0.869\ n\ mi$$

Basic metric conversion factors

1 inch = 2.54 centimeters	1 pound = 0.4536 kilograms
1 foot = 0.3048 meters	1 gallon (U.S.) = 3.785 liters
1 n mi = 1.852 kilometers	

Deviation - Variation

```
        T
+W  |   |  +E
    |   V  |
-E  |   M  |  -W
    |   D  |
    ▼   C
```

True - Relative Bearings

> True Bearings = Relative Bearing + True Heading
> Relative Bearing = True Bearing - True Heading

Height of tide

$$H_D = H_L + (H_H - H_L)\left[\frac{1 - \cos\left(\frac{T_D \sim T_L}{T_H \sim T_L} \times 180°\right)}{2}\right]$$

Where H_D is height at desired time

H_H is height at high water

H_L is height at low water

T_D is desired time

T_H is time of high water

T_L is time of low water

~ indicates absolute difference, smaller quantity subtracted from larger

$$T_D = T_L + (T_H \sim T_L)\left[\frac{\cos^{-1}\left\{1 - 2\left(\dfrac{H_D - H_L}{H_H - H_L}\right)\right\}}{180°}\right]$$

Strength of tidal current

$$S_D = S_M\left[\cos\left\{90° - \left(\frac{T_D}{T_M} \quad \frac{T_S}{T_S} \quad \underline{x}\ 90°\right)\right\}\right]$$

Where S_D is strength at desired time

S_M is strength of maximum current

T_D is desired time

T_M is time of maximum current

T_S is time of slack

$$T_D = T_S + \left[\left(\frac{90° - \cos^{-1}\dfrac{S_D}{S_M}}{90°}\right)\left(T_M \sim T_S\right)\right]$$

Time zone conversion

$GMT = ZT + ZD$

Where GMT is Greenwich Mean Time

ZT is zone time

ZD is zone description (+ or -)

Time - Arc conversion

1 second (time) = 0.25'	1' = 4 seconds (time)
4 seconds = 1'	1° = 4 minutes
1 minute = 15' = 0.25°	15° = 1 hour
4 minutes = 1°	
1 hour = 15°	

Zone time - local mean time

    LMT = ZT + DLo East
          ZT - DLo West
          Where LMT is time on local meridian
                DLo is difference in longitude between local
                    meridian and central meridian of zone

Hour angle conversion

    LHA (Aries or body) = GHA - longitude West
                          GHA + longitude East

Course (Azimuth) angle - true course (azimuth)

    C N D° E = Cn D°
    C S D° E = Cn 180° - D°
    C N D° W = Cn 360° - D°
    C S D° W = Cn 180° + D°

            Where C is course angle (Z for azimuth angle)
                  Cn is true course (Zn for true azimuth)
                  D is any value of degrees to maximum of 90° or 180°

Sight reduction

    $Hc = \sin^{-1}(\sin L \sin d \overset{+}{\sim} \cos L \cos d \cos t)$
            Where Hc is computed altitude of body
                  L is latitude
                  d is declination
                  t is meridian angle
                  $\overset{+}{\sim}$ is + when L and d are of same name; ~ when L
                      and d are of contrary names

    $Z = \sin^{-1}\left(\dfrac{\cos d \sin t}{\cos Hc}\right)$
            Where Z is azimuth angle of body

Plane sailing

    $D = \dfrac{\ell}{\cos C}$
            Where D is distance, in n mi
                  ℓ is difference in latitude, in minutes
                  C is course angle

    $D = \dfrac{p}{\sin C}$
            Where p is departure, in n mi

    $C = \tan^{-1} \dfrac{p}{\ell}$

Mid-latitude sailing

$$DLo = \frac{p}{\cos L_m}$$

Where L_m is mid(mean) latitude

$$C = \tan^{-1}\left(\frac{DLo \cos L_m}{\ell}\right)$$

Where DLo is difference in longitude, in minutes

$$D = \frac{\ell}{\cos C}$$

Mercator sailing

$$m = M_1 \sim M_2$$

Where m is difference in meridional parts

M_1 and M_2 are meridional parts of departure point and destination

$$C = \frac{DLo}{m}$$

$$D = \frac{\ell}{\cos C}$$

Great-circle sailing

$$D = 60 \cos^{-1}(\sin L_1 \sin L_2) + (\cos L_1 \cos L_2 \cos DLo)$$

$$C = \sin^{-1}\left(\frac{\cos L_2 \sin DLo}{\sin (D \div 60)}\right)$$

Where C is initial course angle (or bearing)

$$L_V = \cos^{-1}(\cos L_1 \sin C)$$

Where L_V is latitude of vertex

$$DLo_V = \sin^{-1}\left(\frac{\cos C}{\sin L_V}\right)$$

Where DLo_V is difference in longitude, in degrees, between point of departure and vertex

$$\lambda_V = \lambda_1 + DLo_V$$

Where λ_V is longitude of vertex

$$D_V = \sin^{-1}(\cos L_1 \sin DLo_V)$$

Where D is distance from point of departure to vertex, in degrees

$$L_X = \tan^{-1}(\cos DLo_{VX} \tan L_V)$$

Where DLo_{VX} is interval of longitude on either side of vertex
L_X is latitude of a point on great-circle track

Worksheets

COMPLETE TIDE TABLE

Date:_____

Substation   _____

Reference Station   _____

HW Time Difference   _____

LW Time Difference   _____

Difference in height of HW   _____

Difference in height of LW   _____

<u>Reference Station</u>   <u>Substation</u>

HW _____ _____   _____ _____

LW _____ _____   _____ _____

HW _____ _____   _____ _____

LW _____ _____   _____ _____

HW _____ _____   _____ _____

LW _____ _____   _____ _____

HEIGHT OF TIDE AT ANY TIME

Locality:_____ Time:_____ Date:_____

Duration of Rise or Fall: _____

Time from Nearest Tide: _____

Range of Tide: _____

Height of Nearest Tide: _____

Corr. from Table 3:   _____

Height of Tide at: _____   _____

COMPLETE CURRENT TABLE

Locality: _____   Date: _____

Reference Station: _____

Time Difference: Slack Water: _____
                     Maximum Current: _____
Velocity Ratio: Maximum Flood: _____
                     Maximum Ebb: _____

Flood Direction: _____
Ebb Direction: _____

Reference Station: _____ Locality: _____

_____ _____   _____ _____
_____ _____   _____ _____
_____ _____   _____ _____
_____ _____   _____ _____
_____ _____   _____ _____
_____ _____   _____ _____
_____ _____   _____ _____
_____ _____   _____ _____
_____ _____   _____ _____

VELOCITY OF CURRENT AT ANY TIME

Int. between slack and desired time: _____
Int. between slack and maximum current: _____   (Ebb) (Flood)
Maximum current: _____
Factor, Table 3:   _____
Velocity: _____
Direction: _____

DURATION OF SLACK

Times of maximum current: _____ _____
Maximum current: _____ _____
Desired maximum: _____ _____
Period – Table 4:   _____ _____
Sum of periods: _____
Average period: _____
Time of slack: _____
Duration of slack: From: _____ To: _____

Sight Reduction
using Pub. 229

C_____

S_____

Body								
IC		+	–	+	–	+	–	+	–
Dip (Ht ')								
Sum								
hs								
ha								
Alt. Corr								
Add'l.								
H.P. ( )								
Corr. to ha								
Ho (Obs Alt)								
Date								
DR Lat								
DR Long								
Obs. Time								
WE (S+, F–)								
ZT								
ZD (W+, E–)								
GMT								
Date (GMT)								
Tab GHA	v							
GHA incr'mt.								
SHA or v Corr.								
GHA								
±360 if needed								
aλ (–W, +E)								
LHA								
Tab Dec	d							
d Corr (+ or –)								
True Dec								
a Lat (N or S)		Same Cont.		Same Cont.		Same Cont.		Same Cont.
Dec Inc	(±)d							
Hc (Tab. Alt.)								
tens	DS Diff.							
units	DS Corr.		+		+		+		+
Tot. Corr. (+ or –)								
Hc (Comp. Alt.)								
Ho (Obs. Alt.)								
a (Intercept)			A T		A T		A T		A T
Z								
Zn (°T)								

Fix L: _____ N/S   Fix λ: _____ E/W

Body				
IC				
Dip				
Sum				
Hs				
Ha				
Alt Corr.				
Ho (obs alt.)				
Date				
DR Lat				
DR Long				
Obs Time				
WE (S+, F-)				
ZT				
ZD (W+, E-)				
GMT				
Date (GMT)				
Tab GHA γ				
GHA incr'mt.				
GHA γ				
Aλ (-W, +E)				
LHA γ				
A Lat				
Hc				
Ho				
a T A	T A	T A	T A	T A
Zn				
P&N Corr.				

FIX LAT _____   LONG _____

Body		
IC		
Dip (Ht. ͵)		
Ro		
S.D.		
Sum		
hs		
P in A (Moon)		
Ho		
Date		
DR Lat		
DR Long		
Obs Time		
WE		
ZT		
ZD		
GMT		
Date (GMT)		
Tab GHA		
GHA incrmt		
SHA		
GHA		
± 360		
a λ (− W, + E)		
LHA		
Tab Dec		
a Lat	s c	s c
Dec Inc		
Tab Hc		
Dec corr		
Hc		
Ho		
a	ᴬ/ᵀ	ᴬ/ᵀ
Z		
Zn		

IC	
Dip (Ht. ͵)	
Sum	
hs	
ha	
Alt. Corr	
TB (hs < 10°)	
Ho	
Date	
DR Lat.	
DR Long	
Obs time	
WE (S +, F −)	
ZT	
ZD (W +, E −)	
GMT	
Date (GMT)	
Tab GHA ♈	
GHA Incrmt	
GHA ♈	
DR Long	
LHA ♈	
a₀	
a₁	
a₂	
Add'n'1	
Sub total	
Corr to Ho	
Ho	
Lat	
True Az	
Gyro Brg	
Gyro Error	

LATITUDE AT L.A.N.	Z (N S)	Z (N S)	Z (N S)	Z (N S)
FIRST ESTIMATE				
Date				
DR Latitude				
DR λ				
Central Meridian				
dλ (arc)				
dλ (time)				
Mer. Pass. (LMT)				
ZT (est) 1st				
SECOND ESTIMATE	/////	/////	/////	/////
DR λ				
Central Meridian				
dλ (arc)				
dλ (time)				
Mer. Pass. (LMT)				
ZT (est) 2nd				
ZT (actual)				
ZD (W+, E−)				
GMT				
Date (GMT)				
Tab. Dec. d(+ or −)				
d Corr. (+ or −)				
True Dec.				
IC				
Dip (Ht ')				
Sum				
hs (at LAN)				
ha				
Alt. Corr.				
89-60.0	89-60.0	89-60.0	89-60.0	89-60.0
Ho	−	−	−	−
Zenith Dist.				
True Dec.				
Latitude				

NOTES:

83

L_1 _____ λ_1 _____

L_2 _____ λ_2 _____

_____ DLO _____ E/W

| | EXACT | | DISTANCE | | INITIAL CSE | |
	DEG	MIN	Hc DIFF (+or−)	CORR (+or−)	Z DIFF (+or−)	CORR (+or−)
L_1(LAT)						
L_2(DEC)						
DLo(LHA)						

TOTAL (+or−)

TAB Hc   TAB Z

89−60.0   EXACT Z N/S   E/W

EXACT Hc _____   CSE _____

COALT _____

DIST _____

NOTE

DLo WEST _____   LHA = DLo

DLo EAST _____   LHA = 360 − DLo

Z LABELED N/S FOR L_1
E/W FOR DLo

IF GREAT CIRCLE DIST EXCEEDS 5400 MILES:

LHA = 180 − DLo
Z   = 180 − EXACT Z
DIST = Hc + 5400 mi

Answers

1. 15.9 n mi; 164.6 st mi

2. 1110; 0356; 1414; 1234; 0018

3. 5.0 km; 55 m; 6.1 m; 12.8 m

4. 12.4 n mi; 62 ft; 3 fathoms, 4 ft

5. 14°12'; 35°36'

6. 42°44' or 2,564'; 37°52' or 2,272'

7. 54°57'S; 1°23'S

8. 357 n mi (661 km)

9. 003°; 092°; 123°; 318°; 197°

10. 247°; 000° or 360°; 033°; 165°

11. 193 n mi (357 km)

12. 3.8 n mi (7.1 km); 13.0 in (33.1 cm)

13. a - V; b - Y; c - X; d - U; e - Z; f - S; g - R; h - M;
    i - P; j - T; k - W; l - N

14. (a) True (b) True (c) False (d) False (e) True (f) True (g) False

15. 045°; 112°30' or 112.5°; 202.5°; 348°45' or 348.8°

16. SE, SSE, NNW

17. 2°W

18. 3°E; 8°W

19. 16°W; 9°W

20.

T	V	M	D	C	CE
114	6W	120	3W	123	9W
040	7W	047	2E	045	5W
225	6E	219	3E	216	9E
303	2W	305	2E	303	0
002	4E	358	6W	004	2W
278	5E	273	5E	268	10E
234	3W	237	10E	227	7E

21. 1.5°W

22. 2.5°E

23. 317°

24. 069.5°

25. 6.6 mi; 8.3 mi

26. 18.3 mi

27. 21 mi for standard "clear" visibility

28. 86 yards

29. 24°C; 57°F; -23°C; 21°F; -8°F

30. 4h 05m; 24m; 6h 53m

31. 9.4 mi; 39.6 mi

32. 3.4 minutes; 4h 56m

33. 7.7 kn; 10.5 kn

34. 18 minutes; 1 hour 45 minutes

35. 0517 PDT, 0.0 ft; 0817 PDT, -0.8 ft

36. 1545 PDT, 5.4 ft; 1443 PDT, 4.7 ft

37. 1143 PDT, 5.5 ft; 1714 PDT, 1.3 ft

38. 0848 PDT, -1.3 ft; 1456 PDT, 5.0 ft

39. 2.4 ft

40. 2.0 m

41. 1154 PDT

42. 20.2 m

43. (a) 0624 LMT; (b) 1844 ZT

44. (a) Last quarter; (b) 25 November, 1731 GMT; (c) 21 June, 1214 GMT

45. Set 265°, drift 0.7 knots

46. 1140 EDT

47. 0801 EDT, 2.2 kn

48. 1138; 1519, 3.0 kn, ebbing (060°)

49. 0.5 kn, ebbing (100°)

50. 1620 EDT

51. 0.8 kn, flooding (115°); 0346 EDT, 17 May

52. 1748 EDT

53. 23 minutes

54. 1 hour, 18 minutes

55. 1610 DR: L33°12.0'N, λ78°41.3'W.   1610 fix: L33°14.4'N, λ78°44.3W.
(Individual solutions of problems involving plotting may have
differences of a few tenths of a minute of latitude and/or
longitude; such variances from the stated answer are acceptable.)

56. 1720 fix: L33°10.0'N, λ79°00.0'W

57. 1815 fix: L33°07.9'N, λ79°13.0'W

58. 1830 fix: L33°21.4'N, λ79°05.3'W

59. 144°, 292°, 039°

60. 067°, 216°, 026°

61. 1430 fix: L36°01.2'N, λ9°58.1'E

62. 1120 RFix: L17°47.8'S, λ121°42.8'W

63. 1620 RFix: L17°46.2'S, λ121°42.8'W

64. 1130 RFix: L17°52.6'S, λ11°18.0'E

65. 1745 RFix: L41°00.8'N, λ54°42.9'W

66. 1542 DR: L35°11.2'N, λ20°15.3'E.   1542 RFix: L35°09.3'N, λ20°10.0'E

67. 5.6 miles; 5.0 miles

68. 8.0 miles

69. 4.0 miles; 2.8 miles

70. 2.8 miles; 2.5 miles

71. 3.9 miles

72. NMT 033°

73. 0552 DR: L29°01.9'S, λ4°41.6'E.   0552 EP: L29°04.6'S, λ4°40.7'E

74. 1545 DR: L32°01.1'N, λ127°04.6'W.   1545 EP: L32°02.6'E, λ127°04.9'W

75. No

76. Nearer

77. TR 045°; SOA 12.3 knots

78. C 131°; S 12.1 knots

79. C 167°; S 9.4 knots

80. TR 272°; SOA 8.8 knots

81. C 276°; SOA 16.0 knots

82. C 47°; SOA 15.6 knots

83. Set 110°; drift 1.8 knots

84. Set 017°; drift 1.5 knots

85. 1115 RFix: L21°51.4'S, λ141°01.7'W

86. DR: L26°07.9'S, λ47°18.1'E EP: L26°10.5'S, λ47°14.7'E

87. EP: L22°07.7'N, λ172°19.2'W

88. 301°

89. 1.1 miles

90. 1.4 miles

91. (a) 085° on Light A; (b) 070°; (c) 164° on Light A

92. C 017°, S 15.0 knots; CPA 4.7 miles at 0917

93. C 330°, S 11.1 knots; CPA 1.5 miles at 1648, bearing 124°

94. DRM 034°; SRM 11.6 knots

95. C 330°, S 11.1 knots

96. C 102.5°, 0350

97. (a) At 2240, 319.5° at 11.4 miles; (b) 9.6 miles, bearing 277°

98. (a) C 240 S18.4 knots
     (b) Course changed to 265°, speed reduced to 12.2 knots
     (c) Course changed to 240°, speed increased to 14.9 knots
     (d) CPA 2.9 miles at 0904, bearing 019.5°

99. (a) C 095°, S 18.0 knots
     (b) C 107°, S 18.0 knots
     (c) 2.2 miles at 2316

100. (a) C312°
     (b) 5 hours, 33 minutes
     (c) 1936

101. (a) C336°
     (b) 1 hour, 13 minutes

102. 038°, 14 knots

103. (a) LHA 95°57'; t 95°57'W
     (b) LHA 344°45'; t 15°15'E

104. (a) LHA 34°04'; t 34°04'W
     (b) LHA 128°59'; t 128°59'W

105. GHA 339°51.0'

106. (a) 73°42.0'
     (b) 29°46.8'
     (c) 68°12.8'

107. (a) 48°18.7'
     (b) 60°12.7'
     (c) 118°14.9'

108. (a) 064° (b) 121° (c) 122° (d) 302° (e) 272°

109. (a) 14.9 mi Toward (b) 3.9 mi Away

110. 216°08.7'

111. 22°36.0'

112. SHA 328°, dec 23°N; the star is Hamal (#6)

113. IC = -0.8'

114. IC = +1.7'

115. ha = 39°12.6'

116. Ho = 43°05.8'

117. Ho = 23°05.7'

118. Ho = 64°14.2'

119. Ho = 47°03.0'

120. Ho = 22°22.5'

121. -0.6'

122. $+1^m 47^s$

123. (a) 1°04.5' (b) $26^m 50^s$

124. (a) $3^h 42^m 19^s$ (b) $4^h 59^m 48^s$

125. (a) 22-47-56, preceding day (b) 7-30-03, same day

126. (a) +8 (b) -5

127. (a) 16-22-33, 9 February (b) 17-23-34, 15 March (c) 00-04-05, 19 July (d) 06-30-40, 1 November

128. (a) 0536 (b) 0554 (c) 12-06-17 (d) 1910

129. $8^m 52^s$ slow

130. WE $2^m 31^s$ fast; CE $1^m 12^s$ fast

131. 3.4^s per day losing for the ten-day period

132. $18^m 46^s$ fast

133. (a) 98°41.5' (b) 297°51.1'

134. GHA 118°32.5'; Dec N22°22.3'; SD 15.8'

135. GHA 101°30.5'; Dec S16°58.4'; SD 16.4'; HP 1°00.2'

136. GHA 344°02.7'; Dec N9°01.4'

137. GHA 4°51.2'; Dec N17°58.7'

138. GHA 31°14.0; Dec N28°57.8'

139. GHA 243°18'; Dec S12°57'; SD 16'; HP 59'

140. GHA 231°53'; Dec N22°31.3'; SD 15.8'

141. GHA 166°18'; Dec N9°09'

142. GHA 127°31'; Dec S16°41'

143. Hc 66°34.0'; Zn 036.2°

144. Hc 13°12.4'; Zn 317.8°

145. Hc 13°45.7'; Zn 110.3°

146. Hc 76°01.4'; Zn 065.0°

147. Capella, Alpheratz, Fomalhaut, Altair, Rasalhague, Vega, Kochab

148. Hc 42°59'; Zn 072°

149. Hc 18°49'; Zn 091°

150. Hc 12°03'; Zn 256°

151. Hc 59°02'; Zn 123.2°

152. 2°01.8'; or 121.8 miles

153. (a) 18.1' Away; (b) 12.6' Toward

154. 1842 fix: L34°24.1'N, λ156°57.1'E

155. 1928 fix: L29°03.4'S, λ94°19.0'E

156. 1204 fix: L33°56.1'S, λ121°58.8'W

157. 1200 RFix: L40°54.2'N, λ168°09.9'E

158. 1200 RFix: L27°53.8'N, λ42°23.1'W

159. DR: L43°53.1'S, λ133°44.1'E; AP: L44°00.0'S, λ133°36.7'E;
a: 6.0A; Zn: 254.7°

160. DR: L43°53.4'S, λ133°46.0'E; AP: L44°00.0'S, λ134°14.5'E;
a: 15.2T; Zn: 319.9°

161. 0524 fix: L43°57.2'S, λ133°46.1'E

162. aL 44°00.0'S, aλ 135°02.1'E; a 9.2A; Zn 042.7°

163. aL 35°00.0'S; aλ 48°34.4'E; a 16.9T: Zn 031.3°

164. aL 39°00.0'N; aλ 160°02.9'E; a 10.3T; Zn 227.5°

165. aL 38°00.0'S; aλ 159°19.8'W; a 2.7T; Zn 261.4°

166. aL 38°00.0'S; aλ 131°39.2'W; a 4.5T; Zn 299.0°

167. aL 35°00.0'N; aλ 59°46.9'W; a 3.0T; Zn 209.6°

168. aL 42°00.'S; aλ 19°00'W; a 15T; Zn 064°; P&N correction 1 mile, 120°

169. 2002 fix: L41°58'N, λ34°45'W

170. aL 41°00'S; aλ 161°17'E; a: 5A; Zn: 042°

171. aL 41°00'S; aλ 36°53'W; a: 8T; Zn: 264°

172. aL 41°00'N; aλ 152°30'E; a: 13T; Zn: 262°

173. a: 5.0T; Zn: 106.3°

174. 12-11-24 ZT

175. 11-49-39 ZT

176. 1149 ZT

177. 42°00.4'N

178. 40°07.7'N

179. 8°53.3'N

180. 37°06.4'N

181. 39°18.4'N

182. 19°18'N

183. (a) 0629 (b) 1910

184. (a) 0528 (b) 1550

185. (a) 0435 (b) 1705

186. (a) 2141 (b) 0938

187. 0625 ZT

188. 1702 ZT

189. 0701 ZT

190. (a) 0428 ZT (b) 1727 ZT

191. (a) 0645 ZT (b) 1835 ZT

192. 2338 ZT

193. 0.4°W (rounded to 0.5°W)

194. 1.3°W (rounded to 1.5°W)

195. 0.8°W (rounded to 1.0°W)

196. L47°37.5'S, λ23°28.9'W

197. C 101.4°; Dist 2,224.9 mi

198. C 122.0°; Dist 4,949.6 mi

199. (a) 1,979.8 mi (b) 221.9°

200. (a) 7,635.8 mi (b) 233.9° (c) L37°02'S, λ178°23'E
     (d) 20°   34°28'S   157°08'W
          40°   27°29'S   135°12'W
          60°   17°32'S   116°22'W
          80°   6°01'S   99°39'W
         100°   5°59'N   83°37'W

201. (a) 3,600.8 mi (b) 112.5° (c) L40°43.4'S, λ20°15.1'W
     (d) 10°   L39°58.7'S, λ33°21.1'W
               L39°58.7'S, λ 7°09.1'W
         20°   L37°48.7'S, λ45°54.3'W
               L37°48.7'S, λ 5°24.1'E

202. (a) 4,424.9 mi (b) 303.1°

203. (a) 3.82 MHz (b) 4,210 kHz (c) 9.35 GHz

204. (a) 1.91 m; 3.2 cm (b) 5,639 MHz or 5.639 GHz

205. 238°

206. L47°19'N, λ3°56'W

207. 51°

208. 19°10'N ($\pm$ 30')

209. 21°20'N

210. (a) GHA 37°54.5'; Dec 23°04.4'S
     (b) GHA 135°07.9'
     (c) SHA 264°07.8'; Dec 52°41.0'S

211. (a) 63 mi (b) 24 mi

212. 6 mi

213. (a) 208°G (b) 266°G (c) 042°G (d) 248°T (e) 282°T

214. Sunrise: 0853 LMT, 0536 GMT. Sunset: 1533 LMT, 1216 GMT

215. Morning twilight: 0708 LMT, 0351 GMT. Evening twilight: 1718 LMT, 1401 GMT

216. Moonrise: 0800 LMT, 1210 GMT. Moonset: 0200 LMT, 0610 GMT, 27 January. The moon is gibbous, just before the first quarter.